Praise for *Hands-On Salesforce Data Cloud*

This is a most impressive book. It combines a comprehensive view of the topic with specific information on the details of using Salesforce Data Cloud. It will be a huge help to Data Cloud deployment teams and business users.

—David Raab, founder and CEO, Customer Data Platform Institute

This book is the first, and already definitive, practical guide to setting up, managing, using, and optimizing Salesforce Data Cloud.

— Martin Kihn, SVP Strategy, Salesforce Marketing Cloud

A must-have reference and guide for any team implementing Salesforce Data Cloud. Joyce Avila doesn't miss a step in how to get up and running with Data Cloud fast.

— Erika McGrath, global vice president, Salesforce Data Cloud and MarTech Practice, Astound Digital

This book has supercharged my knowledge and understanding of the Salesforce Data Cloud offering. This book is a must for anyone planning to implement Salesforce Data Cloud.

—Michael Hopkins, PMP

Just as Data Cloud unifies and activates your organization's data at scale, this book brilliantly unifies the resources, concepts, and actionable guide you need to understand the once-in-a-career opportunity Data Cloud provides. Joyce elegantly simplifies the platform's history and technical components, weaving them together into practical walkthroughs. One of the best career investments one can make.

—Alex Romano, Salesforce technical architect

In *Hands-On Salesforce Data Cloud,* Joyce goes through the evolution of Salesforce Data Cloud. She gives novices and advanced data scientists alike the building blocks that allow them to become acquainted and get up close and personal with the platform that has set a cooling Salesforce market afire.

—*Anh Phuong Ta, technical product owner and Salesforce evangelist, Nissan North America, Inc.*

History is littered with great technology that never took off. Success is not determined by functionality but is based on the ability of teams to understand how to apply that technology to business problems, which is why this book is so valuable. It provides a comprehensive understanding of the Data Cloud capabilities and how they should be implemented. It should be the go-to reference for every Data Cloud consultant and project.

—*Ian Gotts, CEO/CMO, Elements.cloud*

This book is intended for Salesforce architects, administrators, and developers who have prior experience with Salesforce technology and are interested in learning about Data Cloud, including its features and terminology. It provides guidance on how to improve your skills in designing, configuring, building, and deploying Data Cloud solutions. Throughout the book, you will acquire the skills needed to communicate effectively with both internal and external stakeholders about Salesforce Data Cloud and customer data platforms (CDPs). Additionally, you will gain insights into identifying scenarios where the Data Cloud platform is a viable implementation solution and leveraging artificial intelligence capabilities within the platform.

—*Jai Balani, senior data engineer, Netflix, Inc.*

Hands-On Salesforce Data Cloud

Implementing and Managing a
Real-Time Customer Data Platform

Joyce Kay Avila
Foreword by Martin Kihn

Beijing · Boston · Farnham · Sebastopol · Tokyo

Hands-On Salesforce Data Cloud

by Joyce Kay Avila

Copyright © 2024 Joyce Kay Avila. All rights reserved.

Published by O'Reilly Media, Inc., 1005 Gravenstein Highway North, Sebastopol, CA 95472.

O'Reilly books may be purchased for educational, business, or sales promotional use. Online editions are also available for most titles (*http://oreilly.com*). For more information, contact our corporate/institutional sales department: 800-998-9938 or *corporate@oreilly.com*.

Acquisitions Editor: Andy Kwan
Development Editor: Michele Cronin
Production Editor: Clare Laylock
Copyeditor: Doug McNair
Proofreader: Sonia Saruba

Indexer: nSight, Inc.
Interior Designer: David Futato
Cover Designer: Karen Montgomery
Illustrator: Kate Dullea and nSight, Inc.

August 2024:   First Edition

Revision History for the First Edition
2024-08-09:   First Release

See *http://oreilly.com/catalog/errata.csp?isbn=9781098147860* for release details.

978-1-098-14786-0

[LSI]

Table of Contents

Foreword

Back in 2016–17, I was a research VP at Gartner covering a new technology category called customer data platforms (CDPs), and the most common question my team and I got was "What is this thing called a CDP?" That is not a rhetorical question: we counted how many times people asked the question, and they really wanted to know.

At the time, CDPs were power-walking up the Gartner Hype Cycle, and the man who first named them—the marketing technology consultant David Raab—delivered a keynote address at the 2018 MarTech Conference in Boston called "CDP Cures Baldness!"

Raab was kidding about baldness (I think)—but it's true that as CDPs reached the peak of inflated expectations in the late 2010s, a majority of larger enterprises with complex customer data diasporas at least considered adding a CDP into their stack. Most of them now have at least one.

The CDP category grew from almost nothing in the mid-2010s to an estimated $10 billion market in 2025, according to the International Data Corporation (IDC). As a tech-historical phenomenon, the CDP is unusual. It's also enjoyed an ongoing carto-graphic evolution as different users have drawn different boundaries around it and customer relationship management (CRM), master data management, data ware-houses, lakes, marts, and more.

In fact, the CDP arose to solve a very specific problem in enterprise technology: trapped data. Its first proponents were marketers, particularly retailers, who had inherited (or built) dozens of fairly disconnected applications and customer data stores. All these different apps and databases could contain information about the very same customer, isolated on their own desert island, trapped in a single channel, table, or queue.

The CDP's purpose was to free that data and connect it to a single profile; apply iden-tity management; and organize the profile so that it could be analyzed, modeled, seg-mented, sent to other systems, and finally put to use. To say that CDPs create "just another silo"—something I heard far too often in the early days—is to me like saying that Google's search engine creates "just another website." CDPs make other things make sense.

Salesforce joined the CDP movement in 2020, and its solution ultimately evolved into Salesforce Data Cloud, the subject of this masterful hands-on book by Joyce Kay Avila. From the beginning, Salesforce approached the "trapped data" problem from a special perspective, driven by its position as the leading CRM and service platform. Ultimately, Data Cloud became the fastest-growing organic product Salesforce ever launched and among the fastest-growing software products ever.

There is a family resemblance between CRM and CDP. After all, the *C* in both has the same meaning. Salesforce had the advantage of already running a widely used platform as a service (PaaS), built on a metadata framework, with no-code UI (Lightning), a partner application marketplace (AppExchange), advanced analytics capabilities (Einstein), and a learning platform (Trailhead).

All it needed was a business to consumer (B2C)-scale data lakehouse, supporting both batch and real-time processing. So, in addition to its single-platform vision, Data Cloud was built to support the new architectural data patterns present in the modern enterprise (see Chapter 2). Other considerations were openness and extensibility—no "locked" data—and support for real-time queries, machine learning (ML), and AI.

I first encountered Joyce Kay Avila at Salesforce Connections, the annual marketing and commerce event in Chicago. I'd known her by reputation as a YouTube influencer and evangelist for Salesforce and Snowflake, and later through her excellent *Snowflake: The Definitive Guide* (O'Reilly, 2022). She is a born explainer, deeply knowledgeable about the use of these technologies as both a practitioner and a synthesist.

We are delighted that Joyce has decided to build on her years of experience in the Salesforce ecosystem to write *Hands-On Salesforce Data Cloud*. It's the first, and already definitive, practical guide to setting up, managing, using, and optimizing this popular solution. She puts all the elements in context and has a clarity of voice I wish other technology writers could copy and paste.

Particularly pointed are the sections on identity resolution (Chapter 10) and on segmentation and activation (Chapter 12). Identity management is a complicated topic, central to the idea of a unified profile. Some form of segmentation or analytics based on more complete and timely user profiles is still the primary use case for Data Cloud, and both themes are unraveled very clearly here.

Where is Data Cloud—and even the CDP category—going? Some of the newer capabilities outlined in Chapter 2 point the way. Widespread adoption of cloud-native warehouses like Snowflake drove a lot of interest in zero-extract, transform, load (zero ETL) data sharing with Data Cloud, and this capability was introduced as Bring

Your Own Lake (BYOL) in 2024, starting with Snowflake and Google's BigQuery. Similarly, data graphs and vector databases were introduced to support unstructured data access.

Unstructured data is at the heart of the newer Generative AI (GenAI) applications. These are already making enterprise software easier to use (via copilots) and more powerful. The use of AI and GenAI extends well beyond generating text and images into analytics, prediction, automation, and decisions—but nothing happens without trusted data. The AI revolution is in fact a data revolution.

All of this makes untrapping data essential for the AI-ready enterprise, and we're lucky to have a guide like Joyce Kay Avila to help us understand how to do this with Salesforce Data Cloud.

— Martin Kihn
New York, NY
April 2024

Preface

The Year of Data Cloud

It's a milestone year for Salesforce as they celebrate their 25th anniversary in 2024. Never one to rest on past successes, Salesforce continues with grand plans for the future. Marc Benioff, cofounder and CEO of Salesforce, has said this is the "Year of Data Cloud." I believe he hit the mark. I started writing this book at the end of 2022 and I've been doing hands-on work with the new Data Cloud platform since February 2023. Ever since then, I've experienced the platform evolve in ways I didn't expect and at a pace I couldn't have imagined. Given what I've observed in these last 21 months, it certainly does feel like this is the Year of Data Cloud.

But what exactly is Salesforce Data Cloud? Salesforce has long been known as the global leader in CRM software, and its products are used by more than 150,000 customers worldwide. Data Cloud is a near real-time CDP at the heart of the Salesforce modern data tech stack. It is a powerful and complex platform that yields value for the entire organization, not just for those few who have direct access to the Data Cloud app within Salesforce.

Salesforce's Data Cloud platform is built from the ground up, with a completely new architecture. First, Salesforce built a data lake house as a way to store large volumes of data and leverage Salesforce's canonical data model for data harmonization. Then the automated identity resolution process made it possible to unify data from disparate sources to achieve a single source of truth. That was just the beginning. Powerful segmentation and activation functionality were added next. Data action features were enabled so that users could automatically send instructions to both internal and external targets. This year, many new native connectors were added. Recently, near real-time capabilities were made possible with features like data graphs. Index configuration and vector databases were just added so users could leverage Data Cloud to unlock the power of unstructured data.

The addition of functionality like data graphs and vector databases were the final pieces Data Cloud needed to empower all business users with the tools to easily access, use, and act on all their data. Data Cloud is at the very heart of an organization's first-party data strategy. It's open and extensible, too. Marketers, salespeople, service engineers, strategists, and analysts can take advantage of Data Cloud's many value activities in a variety of different ways. One way users can unlock the power of Data Cloud value activities is by using Einstein Copilot as their conversational AI assistant. It's now possible to do so because of data graphs and vector databases built on top of a solid Data Cloud foundation.

Technological development is happening globally at a rapid and accelerating pace—it's a challenge for anyone to know all the changes. For Salesforce to keep up, they've had to innovate quickly on Data Cloud, and there's been nothing like it in the 25 years of the company. Salesforce Trailblazers are leaders and innovators who've successfully built their careers or companies in the Salesforce ecosystem. They are committed life-long learners, but it's been a struggle for many Trailblazers to keep informed about important new and frequently released Data Cloud features and functionality. Most Salesforce core new features are released three times a year. In contrast, new Data Cloud features are released up to twice a month. Also, it's necessary to understand how the various parts of this new platform are related to each other, to the existing Salesforce core platform, and to external platforms.

There's an overwhelming amount of information about Salesforce Data Cloud to learn and understand. It's challenging, too, because getting hands-on access is difficult due to Data Cloud being a usage-based platform where credits are consumed. The new Data Cloud architecture also requires learning a new vocabulary. That's where this book can help.

My goal in writing this book was to bring together all the information in one central place and to simplify the Data Cloud complexity in ways that Salesforce Trailblazers understand. To tell the complete Data Cloud story, it was necessary to go beyond just describing where to point and click in the user interface. It was important to explain the underlying reasons why Data Cloud is needed as part of an organization's first-party data strategy. Sharing best practices learned from the trenches, describing how to take advantage of Data Cloud's open and extensible platform, and providing an implementation guide and glossary are valuable pieces of information included in the book. Most importantly, I wanted to convey how Salesforce Data Cloud is a transformative platform built to empower users to unlock the value of their structured and unstructured data.

Who Is This Book For?

This book is essential reading for technology and data professionals who use customer data to make critical business decisions and for anyone who wants to set themselves apart as a Salesforce professional. Whether you're an experienced Salesforce professional or someone who is just beginning their Salesforce journey, there is plenty of information in this book for you to get started with Salesforce's new customer data platform features. Those who will get the most from this book will typically find themselves in one of the following roles:

- Salesforce solution architects and consultants
- Salesforce technical architects
- Salesforce administrators
- Salesforce Marketing Cloud developers
- Enterprise architects and data engineers
- Data scientists and business analysts

With this book, Salesforce solution architects and consultants can focus on learning about customer data platforms in general to be prepared to identify when Data Cloud is a good choice for a particular use case. They'll also want to take a deep dive into how to implement Salesforce Data Cloud and how to make choices from the specific Salesforce AppExchange partners who can help to extend Data Cloud functionality. Solution architects and consultants are tasked with recommending the right products to internal and external customers, and they can use this book as a guide when they need to research alternatives for new or different use cases that arise.

Salesforce technical architects are experts in the functional, platform, and integration architecture of Salesforce and will be most interested to discover the details of Data Cloud's hyperscale platform architecture. They'll want to learn how to take advantage of open data access by leveraging Salesforce's strategic partners like Amazon, Databricks, Google, Microsoft, and Snowflake. Salesforce technical architects are expected to be the Salesforce domain experts. Thus, they'll likely rely on this Salesforce Data Cloud book as a reference when having those high-level Data Cloud conversations.

Salesforce administrators will need to understand the basics and beyond in order to troubleshoot and maintain a Salesforce Data Cloud platform. Administrators will also benefit from learning about Data Cloud best practices to which they can refer. Salesforce Marketing Cloud developers will gain an understanding of how Data Cloud can be used to build a Customer 360 unified profile and thus can be leveraged to deliver a customized personal experience for customers.

In addition to Salesforce-specific roles, some more general roles will also find this book to be a valuable resource, including enterprise architects, data engineers, data scientists, and business analysts. Enterprise architects will gain an appreciation of how Salesforce Data Cloud and a data platform such as Snowflake or Amazon can be part of an overall cloud strategy solution that involves a near real-time customer data platform. Business analysts and data scientists, especially those who have experience using Salesforce, can quickly learn how to extract valuable insights from Data Cloud. They'll also discover the benefits of a Bring Your Own AI approach to the data that exists in Salesforce and external platforms.

While it's not necessary to have in-depth knowledge about Salesforce, you should at least be familiar with customer relationship management (CRM) concepts in general. You'll get the most out of this book if you have at least one to two years of experience in any of the following topical areas:

- Data warehouse or data lake workload management
- Database administration
- Data privacy and security management
- Sales and opportunity management and forecasting
- Digital marketing campaign development
- Ecommerce task automation
- Nonprofit fundraising
- Health care patient information management
- Salesforce-specific roles

There is also a lot of value in this book for data stakeholders, such as IT team leads, technical managers, directors of technical teams, or those who want to keep current with modern data technologies and trends.

Goals of the Book

This book is written with detailed explanations, instructions, and best practices to help build a solid foundational knowledge of Data Cloud vocabulary and processes. In addition, screenshots of the user interface are provided along the way for those who have little or no access to their own Data Cloud environment.

By the end of the book, you will understand:

- The importance of managing first-party data as an asset
- The foundations of any customer data platform

- The origins of Salesforce Data Cloud and why it's a good choice for many use cases
- The significance of having open data access
- The advantages of a customer data platform that can operate in near real time
- The need to unlock the power of unstructured data

And you will be able to:

- Use a proper Data Cloud vocabulary to engage in meaningful conversations with stakeholders
- Develop a plan to execute a Data cloud project
- Set up Salesforce Data Cloud with user roles and permissions
- Complete the foundational steps needed to build a unified customer profile
- Connect Salesforce Data Cloud to external data sources
- Develop a Customer 360 Data Model and Data Cloud mapping strategy
- Implement identity resolution and segmentation in Data Cloud
- Design constituent components upon which to extract value from Data Cloud
- Build calculated, streaming, and real-time insights using Data Cloud
- Use a variety of techniques to build and publish segments to activation platforms
- Create data graphs and vector databases to augment large language model (LLM) capabilities
- Administer Data Cloud by following best practices
- Leverage Salesforce's strategic partners to extend your Data Cloud project

Navigating the Book

Data Cloud is a Salesforce platform built from the ground up. As such, there are many new terms you'll be introduced to as you work your way through the chapters. You can feel confident you're expanding your Data Cloud vocabulary with each new topic and, when in doubt, there is a glossary provided for you at the end of the book.

The book begins with a history of customer data platforms, an explanation of the customer data problem, and why organizations need a customer data platform for their first-party data strategy. Chapter 2 provides an in-depth look at the Data Cloud architecture for those who are interested in the more technical details of how Data Cloud works under the hood.

Chapters 1 and 2 give context about Salesforce's new Data Cloud. The remaining chapters provide the details needed to unlock value from your structured and unstructured data using the Data Cloud platform. Chapter 3 introduces you to Data Cloud's key business value activities, each of which you'll learn more about in subsequent chapters. You'll get glimpses of the art-of-the-possible while also understanding the importance of building a solid foundation upon which you can extract value. You'll discover there are six key steps you'll need to complete for any first-time Data Cloud implementation.

At this point in the book, you may want to start getting hands-on with Data Cloud. It's OK to get hands-on in a training environment, but before you do so in a production environment, I strongly recommend you finish reading the remaining chapters in the book first. There are many things about a Data Cloud implementation that can't be undone easily or at all. And because Data Cloud is a consumption-based pricing model, you should understand the implications of your actions before beginning to implement anything in your own production environment.

When you are ready to provision your Data Cloud org for the first time, Chapter 4 will guide you through the process. You'll only need to provision your org once, but there is information in Chapter 4 that Salesforce administrators may want to bookmark. It's a good reference chapter for Data Cloud maintenance and user admin tasks.

Chapter 5 is devoted to describing Data Cloud menu options that will appear in the Data Cloud app once you provision your org. The menu tabs are presented in alphabetical order, each with a screenshot and a brief description. This information will be especially helpful for readers who don't have Data Cloud access or who have access to some, but not all, of the features available in the Data Cloud platform. It's important to know that certain menu tabs exist so you can ask your administrator for access or obtain the necessary add-on licenses from your Salesforce account executive.

Chapters 6 through 10, along with Chapter 4, describe six required Data Cloud foundational steps. These steps create data connections, establish data ingestion, perform data modeling, build data transforms, implement data mapping, and complete the identity resolution process. The last foundational step, identity resolution, results in a unified profile that goes to the very heart of the Data Cloud's purpose. A lot of content is devoted to these foundational steps because they are critical to the success of a Data Cloud implementation project.

Chapter 11 delves into the topic of consuming and actioning Data Cloud data. In that chapter, you'll learn how to build constituent components like calculated, streaming, and real-time insights. You'll also learn about key value activities like copy field enhancements, related list enhancements, data actions, and Data Cloud–triggered flows. These key value activities make it possible for individuals to receive direct value while in the normal flow of work.

Chapter 12 focuses on segmentation and activation. Segments are groupings of customers that can be published as an audience to multiple activation platforms. Data Cloud has many powerful ways to create segments. It's even possible to use Einstein AI capabilities to build your segments in Data Cloud.

There are many reasons to implement Salesforce Data Cloud but none more compelling than what is described in Chapter 13. The combination of AI and Data Cloud is what allows organizations to unlock the power of unstructured data with vector databases and to use data graphs to support real-time actionable insights.

After you've finished navigating the last chapter, you'll find a glossary and two appendices that provide some guidance for Data Cloud implementation. There's no one right way to approach a Data Cloud implementation project. This guide will provide a starting point you can use to construct your own Data Cloud project implementation plan.

For even more content, including a list of Salesforce Data Cloud standard DMOs in support of the Customer 360 canonical data model, visit the supplemental repository (*https://oreil.ly/SuppRep_HandsOn-Salesforce*).

Code Examples

Salesforce is a pioneer in the data democratization trend and is well-known for empowering business people with their low-code/no-code platform. Low-code/no-code platforms reduce the need for manual coding. Within the Salesforce Data Cloud platform, SQL code is only required to create streaming data transforms, and not every Data Cloud implementation needs streaming data transforms. In all other instances, Data Cloud does the heavy lifting for the user who only needs to navigate the clicks, not code user interface. Thus, there are few code examples provided in the book. Instead, the book includes many screenshots of the Data Cloud user interface along with step-by-step instructions and recommended best practices.

Conventions Used in This Book

The following typographical conventions are used in this book:

Italic
: Indicates new terms, URLs, email addresses, filenames, and file extensions.

`Constant width`
: Used for program listings, as well as within paragraphs to refer to program elements such as variable or function names, databases, data types, environment variables, statements, and keywords.

Constant width bold

> Shows commands or other text that should be typed literally by the user.

Constant width italic

> Shows text that should be replaced with user-supplied values or by values determined by context.

 This element signifies a tip or suggestion.

 This element signifies a general note.

 This element indicates a warning or caution.

O'Reilly Online Learning

 For more than 40 years, *O'Reilly Media* has provided technology and business training, knowledge, and insight to help companies succeed.

Our unique network of experts and innovators share their knowledge and expertise through books, articles, and our online learning platform. O'Reilly's online learning platform gives you on-demand access to live training courses, in-depth learning paths, interactive coding environments, and a vast collection of text and video from O'Reilly and 200+ other publishers. For more information, visit *https://oreilly.com*.

How to Contact Us

Please address comments and questions concerning this book to the publisher:

O'Reilly Media, Inc.
1005 Gravenstein Highway North
Sebastopol, CA 95472
800-889-8969 (in the United States or Canada)
707-827-7019 (international or local)
707-829-0104 (fax)
support@oreilly.com
https://www.oreilly.com/about/contact.html

We have a web page for this book, where we list errata, examples, and any additional information. You can access this page at *https://oreil.ly/hands-on-salesforce*.

For news and information about our books and courses, visit *https://oreilly.com*.

Find us on LinkedIn: *https://linkedin.com/company/oreilly-media*.

Watch us on YouTube: *https://youtube.com/oreillymedia*.

Acknowledgments

The content in this book was written out of order for a variety of reasons. There was also a flurry of writing activity in every chapter as we approached the deadline. I've tried to inject as much new content as possible so that nothing was left out of the book. But there is a point where I have to stop, and that time has come. Composing the acknowledgements is the last thing for me to do.

I've enjoyed meeting biweekly with Michele Cronin, the development editor for this book. She's an amazing editor and a really great human. We always talk about the book, of course, but I never know where the conversation is going to take us. This is the second O'Reilly book I've worked on with Michele, and while I'm excited for the Salesforce Data Cloud book to be published, I'm not looking forward to the meeting invites with Michele disappearing off my calendar. I know Michele has many other projects on her plate, and I look forward to reading the new O'Reilly books Michele currently has in the works.

Speaking of really great humans, there are so many incredibly positive things to be said about Clare Laylock, the production editor for this book. I'm in awe at the way she keeps track of all the requirements and how she incorporates the many requested changes that never seem to stop coming her way. And she handles it all with such grace under pressure. This is the second O'Reilly book I've worked on with Clare, and I can't imagine trusting my book to anyone else.

In addition to Michele and Clare, there's an entire O'Reilly team who make this book possible. Doug McNair (copyeditor), Sonia Saruba (proofreader), and Tom Dinse (indexer) have spent hours pouring over the contents of the book so the quality of the final product is what you'd expect from an O'Reilly book. David Futato (interior designer), Karen Montgomery (cover designer), and Kate Dullea (illustrator) have made the book wonderfully appealing. I appreciate all their contributions.

As I'm nearing the end and looking forward to the book being published, I think back to how it all started. The origins of the book began in 2022 when Andy Kwan, the acquisitions editor, and I brainstormed ideas for a new project, and we decided on Salesforce Data Cloud as the topic for a new book. I really wanted to write a Salesforce book and am glad I've had the opportunity. For one thing, it led me to the world's foremost experts in this area, Martin Kihn and David Raab.

A big part of my journey has been courtesy of the Salesforce Partner Enablement Success team headed by Tracy Novotny. I first met members of the team when I attended an in-person Data Cloud training session at the 2023 Salesforce Connections event in Chicago. Since then, I've had a lot of interactions with this incredible team that includes Aravind Raman, Christopher Long, Matt Wash, and Vlad Silak. I'm especially indebted to Matt Wash who responded to numerous last-minute questions I needed answered before the book went into production.

The exciting part of the journey for me has been taking the knowledge I've amassed about Data Cloud and finding the best way to synthesize it and share it with others. That has involved writing and rewriting chapters multiple times. Making the chapters better can only be done with feedback from others. I've been fortunate to have received constructive feedback and nuggets of information from several experts, including Chandra Nayak, Ian Gotts, Jai Balani, James Weakley, Jared Thilenius, Jeremy HayDraude, Joel Hutchison, Mark Cane, Martin Kihn, Muralidhar Krishnaprasad, Peter Burns, Rahul Auradkar, Robert Saenz, and Ryan Goodman. I'm especially thankful to Danielle Larregui and Michael Hopkins, two of the technical book reviewers who provided feedback for all chapters.

There's an amazing number of people who've cheered me on day in and day out. My fellow Snowflake Data Superheroes provided an incredible support network, as did many Snowflake employees like Aran Sakzenian, Dash Desai, Elsa Mayer, Monique Lupu, Sanjay Kattimani, Scott Redding, and Shelby Haurin-Collier. Aysha Marie Zouain, Brandon Davis, Ed Sandoval, Monhamed Bentriou, and Ryan Hill are wonderful people who motivated me to keep going. A special shout out to fellow authors Jodi Hrbek, Maja Ferle, and Sarah Thanawalla who understand what it means to spend weekends and evenings writing and rewriting until you get it just right. I'm thankful for everyone's encouragement.

Authors, editors, publishers—they really know the level of commitment and effort it takes to get a book across the finish line to the printer. Seeing your book in print and holding it in your hands for the first time is such a rewarding feeling. I like paper books. There's just something about the tactile experience of turning the pages of a book that makes me feel like I'm progressing in my learning journey. There's another benefit of authoring a printed book about a technical topic—your family has something tangible they can use to explain what it is that you do for a living.

My mom, Carolyn Kay Hare, wasn't born a digital native, but she's very tech savvy. And she takes every opportunity to pull my O'Reilly books from her shelf to show everyone who comes to visit. It's a great feeling to know my mom is so proud of me, just like I'm really proud of my own daughter.

My daughter, Alanna Kay Avila, currently lives 6,761 miles from home in a village in the Ozurgeti municipality of Guria in western Georgia (the country). Kveda Bakhvi is Alanna's temporary home for the next 23 months while she serves as a volunteer in the Peace Corps. I miss her very much. Fortunately, we communicate every day and we never run out of things to talk about. For one thing, Alanna is Salesforce certified and always asks how the book is progressing. I never tire of hearing about her Peace Corps adventures, and I'm always excited for her when a care package arrives from home. The first copy of the book I get my hands on will immediately go express mail to Alanna.

My husband and best friend, Robert, deserves a medal for everything he's done while I've authored a second book. Writing the first O'Reilly book was a journey during which Robert did more than his fair share of taking care of things at home. This second O'Reilly book has turned out to be an epic adventure with a lot more effort required than I could have imagined when I signed up for the task many months ago. There's always a lot of give and take in a good relationship, but our world has revolved around me and this book for several months now, and Robert hasn't complained. I'm incredibly grateful that I have a partner who supports me unconditionally. I'm looking forward to evenings and weekends together where I won't ask Robert to review and edit my chapters, and I'll not ask him to talk with me at length about Salesforce Data Cloud anymore.

I'm thankful all the stars aligned, making it possible to get this book published in time to contribute to the Salesforce 25th anniversary celebration in such a meaningful way.

CHAPTER 1

Salesforce Data Cloud Origins

Salesforce Data Cloud (Data Cloud for short) is a near real-time customer data platform that can provide value to several different functional teams within an organization. A *customer data platform* (CDP) is primarily a *data store*—a repository for persistently storing and managing collections of data that support marketing and customer experience use cases.

A CDP gathers all available first-party customer data from an organization's customer relationship management (CRM) software, websites, automation platforms, email marketing software, and point-of-sale (POS) systems into a single repository. Next, it ingests third-party and sometimes second-party data to augment the first-party data. The CDP then aggregates all the information to build unified customer profiles that can be used to create business value across the entire organization in a variety of ways.

In 2013, the term *customer data platform* (CDP) was coined by David Raab, who is often referred to as "the father of CDP." CDPs first appeared in the Gartner Hype Cycle in 2016, and that same year, the Customer Data Platform Institute (*https://www.cdpinstitute.org*) was founded by David Raab.

In 2019, Salesforce launched *Customer 360 Audiences*, its first CDP product. In 2021, Martin Kihn coauthored with Chris O'Hara the book *Customer Data Platforms: Use People Data to Transform the Future of Marketing Engagement* (Wiley, 2020). Among other things, Martin is the SVP of Strategy for Salesforce Marketing Cloud. In 2024, Gartner released its inaugural Gartner Magic Quadrant for Customer Data Platforms, in which Salesforce was named a leader in the CDP category.

Salesforce has long been known as the global leader in CRM software. Its products are used by more than 150,000 customers worldwide to harness the power of automation and AI. When leveraging real-time data, its products are further used to make customer experiences more personal, valuable, and memorable.

Salesforce has a rich and interesting history (*https://oreil.ly/nGf0M*) that began in 1999. It was the first software as a service (SaaS) company built from scratch and is today one of the most valuable cloud computing companies in the world. Salesforce's early approach of building solutions in the cloud, considered revolutionary at the time, is now common practice. Salesforce's longevity and continued success can be attributed to its vibrant user community as well as its ability to innovate quickly.

Salesforce has introduced many product solutions created exclusively for the non-technical business user community. The Salesforce Lightning component-based framework, Flow Builder, Dynamic Forms, and Dynamic Actions, as well as the Force.com platform as a service (PaaS) offering, are some of the low-code/no-code Salesforce offerings. These types of solutions are designed to make it relatively easy for *citizen developers* (business users with little to no professional coding experience) to quickly design, build, and launch applications without the need to understand or manage the underlying systems. Many benefits accrue to using low-code/no-code solutions, including faster time to value, decreased costs, and enhanced innovation.

Salesforce innovates in many ways by improving existing products, creating new products, and acquiring successful companies that fit naturally with existing Salesforce product offerings. Recent Salesforce acquisitions include Slack, Tableau, and MuleSoft. Like most enterprises offering a full suite of products, Salesforce often rebrands its existing products to better align with the overall portfolio of products and simplify its terminology. The rebranding of the Salesforce Data Cloud is no exception.

Evolution of the Salesforce Data Cloud Platform

The current-day Salesforce Data Cloud platform began as *Customer 360 Audiences*—a Salesforce Marketing Cloud product launched on November 19, 2019. Marketers used this early Salesforce CDP version to more effectively create and manage audience segmentation.

Customer 360 Audiences (C360A) was frequently used with *Interaction Studio* powered by *Thunderhead*—another Salesforce Marketing Cloud product that gave marketers the ability to pull in external sources and model the data. A few months later, Salesforce announced it had acquired *Evergage*, a CDP platform and real-time personalization platform. Interaction Studio then became powered by Evergage instead of Thunderhead.

In May 2021, C360A was rebranded to *Salesforce CDP*. This rebranding occurred at the same time as identity resolution capabilities were added to the product. *Identity resolution* is what makes it possible to build a single source of truth for a complete 360-degree view of the customer. Later, Salesforce rebranded Salesforce CDP to *Salesforce Customer Data Platform*, which was a change in name only.

In September 2022, the product was rebranded again to *Salesforce Genie Data Cloud*. This rebranding coincided with Salesforce unveiling *Genie* as its new hyperscale real-time data platform. This was a major announcement, and it represented a fork in the road where the Salesforce CDP stock-keeping unit (SKU) still existed but a new Genie Data Cloud SKU was also created. The CDP SKU retained the pricing model based primarily on number of licenses, whereas the Genie SKU was the first-ever Salesforce consumption-based pricing model. Importantly, full feature parity didn't exist between the two SKUs.

The main reason for the difference in feature parity was the difference in architecture. The CDP SKU gave access to features built on a transactional database, which was Salesforce's traditional architecture. However, the new Data Cloud SKU offered access to a near real-time hyperscale data platform that had been built from the ground up to support new architecture that would solve many of the existing challenges with the current architecture (Figure 1-1). Chapter 2 explains in detail the new Data Cloud architecture.

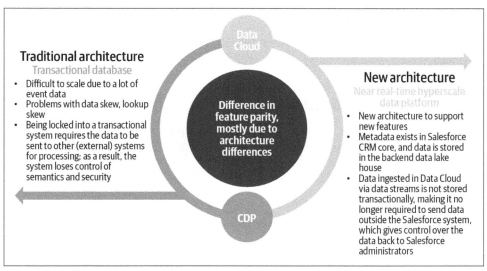

Figure 1-1. New Data Cloud architecture makes more features possible

A few months later, around February 2023, Salesforce rebranded the product to *Salesforce Customer Data Cloud* (Figure 1-2). This time, the rebranding removed *Genie* from the name. Not long afterward, the word "Customer" was removed from the product name. However, the "Customer Data Cloud" naming convention was used for licenses and permission sets in Data Cloud production orgs several months after the word "Customer" was removed from the product name.

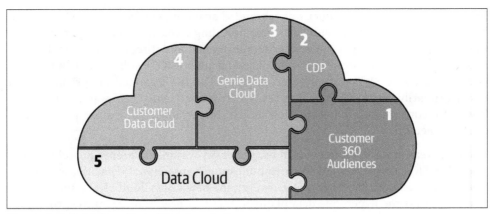

Figure 1-2. Salesforce Data Cloud evolution

At the time of the last rebranding, which removed the *Genie* name, Salesforce initially developed separate Data Cloud product SKUs, mostly for marketing purposes. Specifically, Salesforce advertised the availability of Data Cloud for Marketing, Data Cloud for Tableau, Data Cloud for Health, and Bring Your Own Lake (BYOL) Data Cloud. However, there were no platform differences among the Data Cloud offerings for the different SKUs.

Frequent and Rapid Changes

It's exciting, but also challenging, to keep up with the numerous and rapid changes that are happening with the Salesforce Data Cloud platform. Throughout this book, I've referred to additional resources available for supporting your Data Cloud journey over the long term.

Two important modifications happened at the same time as the rebranding from a CDP SKU to the Data Cloud SKU. First, the Data Cloud SKU didn't require an organization to purchase Salesforce Marketing Cloud, whereas the CDP SKU was an offering that was available only to those who had purchased Salesforce Marketing Cloud. Second, Salesforce's pricing model shifted to a usage-based consumption model for the first time.

Importantly, because of the pricing structure difference between the old customer data platform SKU and the new Data Cloud SKU, some of the newer Salesforce Data Cloud features and functionalities will not be available on the old customer data platform SKU. To access the newer functionality in full, upgrading to the newer Data Cloud SKU is required.

There are some Data Cloud features that will be limited or not available on the old SKU. Throughout this book, the features and functionalities of Salesforce Data Cloud will be described for the most current SKU. When known and wherever possible, any limitations of the old SKU will be called out.

Where Salesforce Data Cloud Fits in the Salesforce Tech Stack

As we'll see in later chapters, the Salesforce Data Cloud application is accessible as an application in the Salesforce core platform. Even though users access the Data Cloud application after logging in to the Salesforce core platform, the data ingested by Data Cloud is actually stored within an off-core data lake managed by Salesforce (Figure 1-3). The Salesforce off-core data lake storage is discussed in detail in Chapter 2.

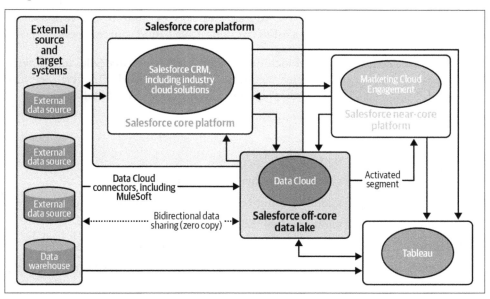

Figure 1-3. Salesforce Data Cloud high-level blueprint example

Salesforce Data Cloud is most often used in conjunction with Salesforce CRM core applications, including the Sales Cloud and Service Cloud objects. There also exist industry cloud use cases where the more traditional Sales Cloud and Service Cloud are replaced with specialized industry clouds with metadata and workflows more relevant to specific industries. Examples include Salesforce Health Cloud and Financial Services Cloud.

Data Cloud is billed separately from Salesforce CRM and industry cloud licenses. Tableau, Marketing Cloud Engagement, Marketing Cloud Account Engagement, Marketing Cloud Personalization, B2C Commerce Cloud, Loyalty Management Cloud, and Marketing Cloud Growth licenses are additional licenses that need to be obtained if your organization plans to make use of those platforms and tools.

If your organization doesn't plan on using platforms like Tableau or Marketing Cloud, then you'll not need to purchase those licenses to access Salesforce Data Cloud. Reach out to your Salesforce account representative or your Salesforce implementation partner for more in-depth discussion of which Salesforce licenses would be needed for your specific use cases.

Figure 1-3 highlights some of the basic components of a typical Data Cloud implementation. Marketing Cloud Engagement and Tableau are included in the high-level blueprint example, but they're not required. We'll see in later chapters how Salesforce Data Cloud actually works as we take deep dives into more of the possible inputs and outputs of the platform. Just to give you an idea now of some of the various data inputs we'll be discussing, here is a list of common Data Cloud source inputs:

- Salesforce CRM, which could include the traditional Salesforce Sales and Service Cloud, or it could include Health Cloud, Education Cloud, Financial Services Cloud, Nonprofit Cloud, or other Salesforce industry-specific clouds
- Salesforce Loyalty Management Cloud
- Salesforce B2C Commerce Cloud
- Omnichannel Inventory Cloud
- Salesforce Marketing Cloud Engagement (previously ExactTarget)
- Salesforce Marketing Cloud Account Engagement (previously Pardot)
- Salesforce Marketing Cloud Growth Edition
- Salesforce Marketing Cloud Personalization (previously Interaction Studio)
- External cloud storage such as Amazon S3, Microsoft Azure Storage, Google Cloud Storage (GCS), or PostgreSQL
- Bidirectional data sharing with data platforms like Snowflake, Google BigQuery, and Amazon Redshift
- External original sources such as Adobe Campaign, Attentive, Emarsys, Epsilon, Oracle Responsys, Vibes, Google Ads, Meta Ads, and more

Over the last nearly 25 years, Salesforce has built a mature product with many different types of solution offerings, some of which are quite complex. This book will go into Salesforce Data Cloud. If you find that you have gaps in your Salesforce knowledge or you need to round out your knowledge in other areas, you can leverage free training at Salesforce Trailhead (*https://trailhead.salesforce.com*), engage with the

Trailblazer Community (*https://oreil.ly/7u9fe*), or read the *Practical Salesforce Architecture* book by Paul McCollum (O'Reilly, 2023). If you are employed by a Salesforce partner, you can access the Partner Learning Camp training materials. If you are a military member, veteran, or spouse, you can also access Salesforce Military (*https://oreil.ly/8AHw8*) for free training opportunities and support.

Today's Salesforce Data Cloud can be a part of the solution for many different use cases, not just for Marketing Cloud. However, given the origin of Data Cloud, it's not surprising that many Data Cloud implementations thus far have addressed use cases aimed at solving marketers' problems. Throughout this book, we'll highlight the different use cases that can be addressed by using this Salesforce Data Cloud while acknowledging that today's use cases are still heavily focused on solving some important marketing problems.

Where the Customer Data Platform Fits in the Martech Stack

A *marketing technology stack* (Martech stack) is a collection of specialized software solutions that are used by marketers exclusively for marketing. It also includes many multipurpose software systems or platforms supporting critical business objectives. One such example is an organization's CRM software.

An organization's CRM solution is frequently used by teams outside of marketing, including customer service, sales, operations, and finance. Each of these teams may retain unique information about a customer, and if the organization's teams share some components of the tech stack, like the CRM, they can centralize customer information. This allows for a more complete view of the customer by the organization.

This is important because every interaction with a customer or potential customer impacts an organization's marketing efforts. Because of this, the modern definition of who uses the Martech stack has expanded beyond marketing alone and now includes customer service agents, billing specialists, and data scientists. We'll see this is especially true of CDPs, which were developed to solve marketing-specific problems but now support many other types of use cases like fraud detection and health care patient outcomes.

Today's Modern Martech Stack

The Martech stack humbly began as a simple customer list entered into a digital database. It then blossomed with the advent and advancement of the internet as a global marketing tool. Technology continues to evolve, and new tools and systems are being added to the stack in an effort to keep pace with the changes. Figure 1-4 includes eight of the most common components of a modern Martech stack. One of the most recent additions to the Martech stack is the CDP.

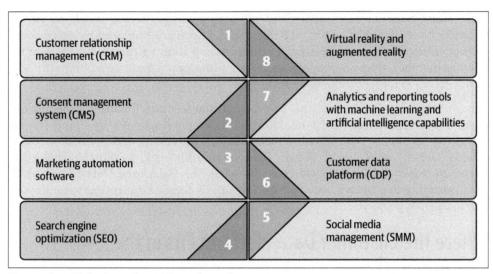

Figure 1-4. Today's modern Martech stack

CDPs have been around for a little more than a decade and have been embraced by enterprises that need to centrally manage their customer data to remain in compliance with emerging privacy regulations. Some CDPs include modern features like customer journey orchestration, look-alike modeling, and marketing automation functionality. Many CDPs even come standard with or support Generative and Predictive AI capabilities. CDPs will likely not solve all your use cases, but they can serve as a centralized source of your unified customer data to inform the rest of your technology stack.

The Future of the Martech Stack

Marketers have many powerful new technologies at their disposal to leverage for the future. Virtual reality and augmented reality are exciting new ways to market to customers, and near real-time data capabilities now allow marketers to observe customer activity without having to wait hours or days to assemble reports.

Low-code/no-code ML and AI capabilities are options from a variety of SaaS companies. These advanced analytics capabilities can help in many ways. For one thing, they can provide more insights into omnichannel marketing efforts and the impact of those multichannels on the overall customer journey. Even traditional marketing channels have gotten a technology makeover. A quick response (QR) code can be added to traditional print marketing collateral, and fully digitized billboards are no longer a rarity.

Your initial thoughts might be that these technologically advanced tools surely have allowed marketers to convey more relevant, effective, and timely messaging to customers. In reality, that's the exception rather than the rule. The primary reasons why are the customer data problem and the excessive exploitation of technology, which together have obstructed the marketing industry from achieving the nirvana of right customer, right message, right time. We'll cover this in detail later on.

Establishing a complete 360-degree view of a customer hasn't been a priority for most organizations because they've had cheaper alternatives that are effective. Television ads, radio advertising, and print advertising are relatively expensive when compared to digital marketing alternatives such as social media, email marketing, and search engine optimization (SEO). As technology becomes less expensive, the cost of digital marketing gets even cheaper. Thus, marketers have more of an incentive to overload target audiences with messages within every possible channel rather than to spend money building a 360-degree view of each customer.

As we'll see, marketers' excessive exploitation of technology has caused an uproar. Consumers have felt abused and that their rights to privacy have been violated. They have begun reporting spam more frequently, unsubscribing to email lists, blocking digital cookies and tracking, and disabling notifications. They have also responded by using secondary email addresses and/or temporary disposable addresses, which further exacerbates the customer data problem. As a result, governments have intervened with regulations enforcing rights to privacy.

The good news is that we have options available to solve these two problems. Before we discuss them, let's dive just a little deeper into the problems so we can understand and better appreciate the urgency with which we need to act.

The Customer Data Problem

Organizations delight customers when they are able to solve their problems quickly and make their customers' experiences more personal, valuable, and memorable. However, it's difficult, if not impossible, for an organization to accomplish these things when it doesn't have a coherent, complete view of its customer.

Customer data problems are what make it impossible to get a complete view of the customer. They mainly occur because of separate data silos and the proliferation of several cross-devices per individual. Thus, marketers either fail to recognize an individual as someone known or don't have a complete picture of the customer because they can't match up the existing data pieces about the customer. In clarification, let's consider the two main customer data types: known and unknown.

Known Customer Data

Known customer data is often composed of personally identifiable information (PII), such as an email address the customer willingly provided when they completed a purchase or signed up for newsletters and loyalty programs. This first-party known data is incredibly valuable; it's real information about a real person received with consent.

Problems arise, though, when these data points exist in separate silos. Sales and service departments, commerce websites, and marketing web forms will likely store known customer data in different formats and in different locations. In an effort to stitch together PII and other known customer data for each of these different business units, brands, or regions, the original data from each source may be replicated many times, across the organization.

Then, when the source data gets updated in one place, the copies existing elsewhere rarely get updated. Imagine a scenario where one customer recently moved and updated their phone number and mailing address with the sales department and those details do not get updated with the customer service department. Thus, when the customer calls a different department and provides their new phone number to an agent, they do not appear as a known customer, and all the rich history about the customer is not available to the agent.

This is further complicated because a single customer can have different name variations like "Robert" and "Bob," along with multiple email addresses and phone numbers. These types of variations can occur within one platform within an organization, such as a CRM shared by different internal departments, and they can also occur within third-party platforms connected to the organization.

The consequences of having separate data silos often get in the way of providing a delightful experience across touch points and time. Yet it's important to have an accurate and complete view of a known customer because marketing efforts to delight an established customer are considerably less costly than acquiring a new customer.

That is one reason why existing data about known customers forms the backbone of any first-party data strategy. A CDP excels at stitching together known customer data from separate data silos, and we discuss using a CDP to build a first-party data strategy in the next section.

Unknown Audience Data

Unknown audiences are established customers or potential customers who are engaging with the organization in some way but whose current engagement activity doesn't result in unique identifiers that can be assigned specifically to individuals in the organization's system. Each customer may have visited a website or clicked on an ad, for example, but not made a purchase at that moment on that particular device.

Perhaps they took up their research later in the day on a different device that created another unique identifier that can't be matched to an individual. All these unique identifiers exist in isolation unless and until the individual becomes known to us on that device. At that point, identity resolution for unknown audiences can occur by associating pseudonymous unknown identifiers with known data.

Putting the Pieces Together

Solving the customer data problem that results from having separate data silos requires a single, unifying strategy involving identity resolution, which can be provided by a CDP. A CDP is a relatively new addition to the Martech stack and should not be confused with a data management platform (DMP). A DMP collects and organizes audience data from various sources, including online, offline, and mobile sources; the organized data in a DMP can then be used for segmentation and activation.

Both CDPs and DMPs allow organizations to examine aggregated data to better understand how customers as a whole move through the sales funnel. Both collect similar types of anonymous web and digital data, but a CDP connects an anonymous visitor with an established consumer's unified profile once that visitor becomes known. CDPs primarily use first-party data and some second-party data, whereas DMPs mostly use third-party data with some second-party data.

DMPs rely heavily on cookie technology to identify behaviors and have frequently been used when marketers need third-party data for short-term customer leads and conversion. CDPs, on the other hand, are used to bring together siloed sets of individual data (Figure 1-5). For that reason, you'll want to work with a CDP if you need long-term customer engagement that requires first-party data.

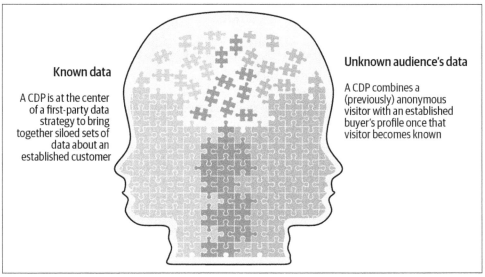

Known data

A CDP is at the center of a first-party data strategy to bring together siloed sets of data about an established customer

Unknown audience's data

A CDP combines a (previously) anonymous visitor with an established buyer's profile once that visitor becomes known

Figure 1-5. Piecing together a known unified profile and unknown audience data

Marketers have continued to rely on DMPs, rather than developing a first-party data strategy, because of the continued reliance on relatively inexpensive cookie technology. Many marketers still rely on digital marketing cookies as a major part of their customer data strategy. As we'll learn in the next section, there have been a lot of arguments against using third-party cookies. As a result, the consensus is against their use, so there's no better time than now for your organization to review the use of digital marketing cookies. So, what exactly are digital marketing cookies?

Digital Marketing Cookies

Websites create *digital marketing cookies*, which are small JavaScript text files that collect and store user activity, to track a user's behavior. Cookies contain a unique identifier that allows a website to identify the individual when they return to the website. Cookies can include information like usernames and passwords, making it easier to log in to various sites. Cookies can also contain information such as shopping activity and which items were left in a digital shopping cart.

There are different types of cookies. Most are either *first-party cookies*, which work only on a single domain, or *third-party cookies*, which track users across multiple domains.

First-, Second-, and Third-Party Cookies

First-party cookies aren't shared with other websites or advertising partners. Instead, they are created and used only in a single domain. First-party cookie data is important because it contains information such as language settings and personal identifiers that can improve the user experience and provide a more personalized service. It's possible to delete first-party cookies at any time, but if you do so, you'll need to log back in to any websites you visit.

Sometimes, the website a customer visits will ask them to accept a cookie to proceed, and in some cases, the website visitor might not be able to use key features of the website if they don't accept. When prompted to accept cookies, visitors are given options on which cookies to accept if more than one type of cookie is being captured. Because first-party cookies are designed to improve the user experience of a website and are limited to only a single domain, most people generally trust and accept first-party cookies.

Third-party cookies, on the other hand, are created in one domain but shared across all the third-party domains that use the same tracking code. The primary function of a third-party cookie is to display advertisements as a result of the information gathered by tracking a user's activity.

Most web browsers automatically accept first-party cookies, but third-party cookies, which can also be cleared from a web browser at any time, are already being blocked by some browsers such as Safari and Mozilla Firefox. Google, the leading internet browser worldwide, plans to completely deprecate all third-party cookies in the latter half of 2024 as described in the Privacy Sandbox for the Web initiative (*https://oreil.ly/RVUaF*). This initiative, led by Google but placed on hold by British regulators (see the following subsection), will, when implemented, phase out third-party cookies and help limit other forms of tracking by restricting the amount of information sites can access.

Privacy concerns and related regulatory requirements caused by the excessive exploitation of technology are at the root of why many web browsers are beginning to block third-party cookies. As you would expect, this presents challenges for advertisers.

Second-party cookies are less prevalent, but it's expected they'll become more popular as third-party cookies cease to exist. *Second-party cookies* are created in one domain and only used in that domain, but the first-party data collected is then shared by the website owner with its trusted partners.

The Future of Cookies

We've already seen changes in how cookies are being used. In early 2020, most websites began asking visitors to accept cookies. This change was prompted, in part, by user privacy concerns that resulted in the California Consumer Privacy Act (CCPA) and the European Union's (EU's) General Data Protection Regulation Act (GDPR).

Google planned to fully deprecate third-party cookies by the end of 2024. However, in April 2024, the United Kingdom's Competition and Markets Authority (CMA) ordered Google to halt its deprecation of third-party cookies temporarily amid anti-competitive concerns. In July 2024, Google announced a new path for Privacy Sandbox on the web that may delay the deprecation of third-party cookies indefinitely. Instead of completely deprecating third-party cookies, Google has proposed a different way of achieving a more private web experience. Discussions are ongoing with regulators on what the path forward will be.

In addition to Google's efforts to create a more private web experience for individuals Apple has introduced Intelligent Tracking Prevention (ITP) 2.0, which makes it impossible for third-party cookies to be used for cross-site tracking. Apple iOS recent updates have also given users the ability to manage their own data sharing on their apps. Both of these changes make better protections possible and are a win for consumer privacy, but they represent a new challenge for marketers.

The good news here is that the death of third-party cookies as we've known them will likely force marketers to develop a sound first-party data strategy and be more intentional in building and engaging with audiences. Instead of focusing primarily on cheap digital advertising to drive sales, marketers will need to focus more on conversion rate optimization and creating better customer experiences. Building long-term relationships with customers and providing more personalized marketing could also help organizations build more customer loyalty and increase customer lifetime value.

Driven by data privacy concerns and regulation changes, cheap and easy access to third-party data is on its way out. It's time for organizations to consider alternative marketing strategies such as adopting a first-party data strategy.

Building a First-Party Data Strategy

A *first-party data strategy* involves collecting customer data and using it to improve marketing efforts to build stronger customer relationships through personalization and creating more customer value. Building a first-party data strategy has always been important to marketers but is even more so now. There's a new sense of urgency because of the deprecation of third-party cookies and stricter data privacy regulations and compliance requirements. As a result, marketers are exploring new and better ways to provide the best digital experiences by building more personalized relationships with customers and potential customers.

A CDP is at the center of building a first-party data strategy, and the focus of this book will be to explore the Salesforce Data Cloud in much detail. You may never need more than the Salesforce Data Cloud to build your first-party data strategy, but if you do need more, there are ways to go beyond your successful implementation of Salesforce Data Cloud to extend your first-party data strategy.

Extending the First-Party Data Strategy

First-party data that arises from a consumer's direct interaction with the organization certainly helps marketers understand quite a bit about their customers, but more information is often needed to get a complete picture of each customer. Second- and third-party data help fill in the gaps.

A CDP is at the heart of your first-party data strategy and brings together first-, second-, and third-party customer data to build a single customer view. A data clean room can be an extension of an organization's first-party data strategy by providing access to the very third-party data being taken away by privacy laws and the end of cookies. When used together, a CDP and a data clean room provide opportunities for organizations to process and analyze data more efficiently while still managing data in a compliant way.

Data clean room defined

The purpose of a *data clean room* is to assist organizations in processing and analyzing aggregated data that comes from trusted partners. In essence, a data clean room is built to create a secure and anonymous private data exchange for the parties involved. None of the parties have direct access to the other's data, but the results of data matches allow all the partners to enrich their own data.

Marketers can use data clean rooms for a variety of reasons. Using aggregated data, they can better determine customer lifetime value and understand how customers interact with certain brands, and they can potentially identify look-alike audiences and build new segments. Data clean rooms can also be useful for finding wasted ad spending and avoiding duplicated effort across channels.

Types of data clean rooms

The most common data clean rooms are *walled gardens* from ad media publishers like Google Ads Data Hub and Amazon Marketing Cloud. With these types of data clean rooms, you're able to analyze your ads' performance from the individual publisher's platform. However, analyzing performance from a cross-platform perspective is not possible, and there may also be restrictions on how you can use the data.

Some custom-built data clean rooms are offered by advertising technology (Adtech) vendors. It's recommended that you perform your due diligence before engaging with a custom-made data clean room to make sure it has the requisite security you expect and that the data will be appropriately pseudonymized to safeguard the privacy of your customer.

Private data clean rooms are commonly built by brands and content owners, and several partners' datasets can be shared to create an omnichannel view of the customer. Walmart Connect, NBCUniversal One Platform, and Disney data clean rooms are examples of private data clean rooms built on the Snowflake platform. Because these data clean rooms are cloud agnostic, they can connect to and function with any cloud environment an advertiser brand might use.

Data Clean Rooms and Customer Data Platforms Working Together

It's possible for an organization to connect its CDP to a data clean room to allow its first-party data to be anonymized and analyzed alongside third-party sources. Depending on the type of data clean room used, marketers could create segments and build targeted audiences to be shared with the organization's CDP where it can be sent to connected marketing platforms for activation.

Extending the first-party data strategy with data clean rooms is only made possible once you've unified and harmonized your individual customer data. For that, you'll need to acquire a CDP.

Customer Data Platform Acquisition Approaches

Choosing a CDP acquisition approach for your organization is an important decision because CDP implementations can be very costly in terms of both time and money. *If your organization has already selected Salesforce Data Cloud, then you're ready for Chapter 2.*

However, if your organization is still evaluating CDP products, you're most likely deciding between a composable CDP and a CDP suite. If so, this section will provide you with some general guidelines and helpful suggestions for selecting the right CDP approach.

Build, Buy, or Compose?

There are three main approaches to acquiring a CDP. At one extreme, a CDP can be built completely from scratch, generally at considerable cost in terms of both time and money. At the other end of the spectrum, buying a CDP suite is most often the quickest way to get up and running on a CDP. Somewhere in the middle is the third option: constructing a composable CDP solution using Lego-style pieces of technology.

A number of factors will likely be considered when evaluating the approaches to acquiring a CDP, and each organization has a unique process for making these types of decisions. That said, there are a few general guidelines for selecting the right CDP that are applicable to most organizations.

Narrowing the Focus

It may be possible to quickly rule out at least one and perhaps more of the CDP acquisition types by navigating the decision-making flowchart provided in Figure 1-6. You can start by asking if your organization has the resources with the appropriate experience and expertise to build enterprise-level applications from scratch.

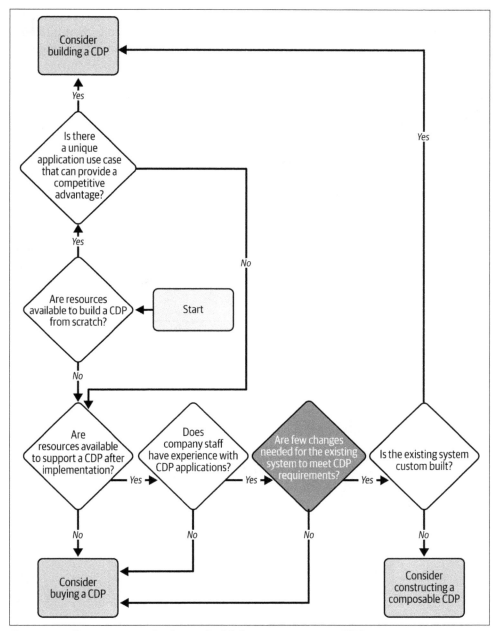

Figure 1-6. Determining whether to build, buy, or compose a CDP

Building a CDP from scratch takes a lot of time and money, so you won't find it to be a cost-saving approach. There are few reasons you'd want to ever consider building a CDP from scratch; it really is an intensive process. One reason to consider it might be if you need a unique CDP application that will give you a competitive advantage.

Composable Customer Data Platforms versus a Customer Data Platform Suite

It's much more likely that your organization would either buy or compose a CDP. To realistically consider the composable approach, your organization needs to have resources with sufficient technical skill sets to maintain the CDP after implementation. The more individual CDP components your organization uses to build out the CDP solution, the more varied skill sets will be required.

Each organization will likely have a unique set of requirements for its CDP, but there are five common components of most CDPs. Figure 1-7 defines the common components of the CDP system, but it's also important to consider where your data sources exist and whether the data will have to leave your secure system as part of fulfilling the CDP requirements.

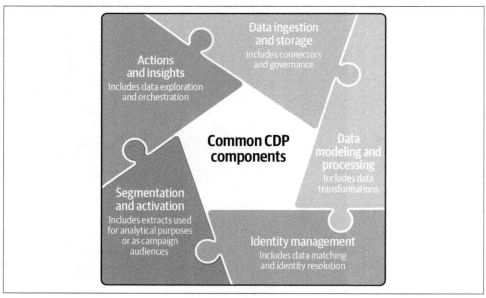

Figure 1-7. Common CDP components

Your development team will also need to possess the necessary CDP domain expertise to know what components to select and how to build a composable CDP. Otherwise, you'll want to consider buying a CDP solution.

For many organizations, the situation is usually not so clear-cut that they can quickly know whether the preferred acquisition path is to build or to buy. Most often, a more detailed analysis will need to be undertaken to determine just how much, if any, of the existing systems and platforms can be used to meet an organization's CDP requirements. In the flowchart (Figure 1-6), the central question is "Are few changes needed for the existing system to meet CDP requirements?" If the current system meets most of the CDP requirements and is not a custom-built solution, then a composable approach may be worth exploring.

Other Cost and Performance Considerations

In addition to evaluating requirement gaps, you'll likely want to consider cost, efficiency, maintainability, and scalability. The various pieces needed to complete a composable CDP solution might be less costly than buying a full CDP suite, but the cost could end up being excessive if there are too many components to add, they are costly to integrate with the current system, or overhead costs increase significantly. Overhead increases because more skill set dependencies arise when you add several new components, and increased maintenance is needed when more connectors exist. There are also more vendors to manage and interact with. Scalability is more challenging with composable CDPs because all the pieces need to scale individually as well as together.

Buying a CDP solution means you'll always have to pay for licensing. However, buying a CDP often results in a lower total cost of ownership and accelerated time to value. Fewer unique skill sets are needed because a CDP suite frequently includes prebuilt, low-code/no-code options and because platform system maintenance is handled by the vendor. Acquiring a CDP system by buying it generally incurs a much lower risk than building or composing one because the vendor can demonstrate the capabilities of a platform that is built and ready to be used. Buying a CDP suite means, though, that you are reliant on the vendor to prioritize new feature requests and maintenance needs. Figure 1-8 summarizes some of the main differences among the approaches.

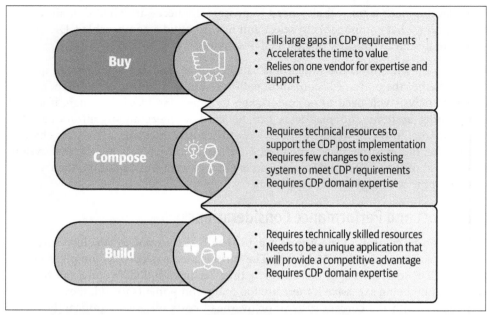

Figure 1-8. CDP acquisition approaches

Buying a CDP is often a great approach, but doing so means you'll be relying on the vendor to provide all the expertise and support. Thus, a very important consideration when deciding from which specific vendor to buy a CDP solution is evaluating how likely it is that the vendor will continue to invest in its CDP platform in the future.

Because this is a hands-on book about Salesforce Data Cloud, we'll assume that your organization has already decided to implement Salesforce Data Cloud or that it is seriously considering Data Cloud as its CDP of choice. Therefore, going forward, we'll be diving only into Salesforce Data Cloud as the CDP solution.

Summary

In this chapter, we discovered why now is the time marketers should be implementing a CDP to solve the customer data problem. Of the three CDP acquisition approaches, the "Buy" approach is often selected to help shorten the time to value.

One of the best known CDPs available to purchase is Salesforce Data Cloud, which is the focus of this book. In this chapter, we learned about the evolution of Salesforce Data Cloud, and in the next chapter, we'll take a deep dive into the foundations of the Salesforce Data Cloud platform.

CHAPTER 2

Foundations of Salesforce Data Cloud

As we saw in Chapter 1, there are lots of problems that can be solved with Salesforce Data Cloud. It requires some initial setup, but on a day-to-day basis, Data Cloud will be managed by an administrator. In addition to an administrator, there will likely be a number of different end users who will need access to the unified data within Data Cloud.

Many of those Salesforce end users might be working within the Sales Cloud or Service Cloud applications on a daily basis, and those users may never need direct access to the Data Cloud application. Instead, Data Cloud data might be surfaced within their Sales Cloud or Service Cloud applications as data enhancements, like related lists.

In addition to surfacing data in Sales and Service cloud applications, Salesforce Data Cloud is often used for marketing purposes. In those scenarios, there will likely be more end users working within the Data Cloud application. It is to be expected that data aware specialists, marketing specialists, and marketing managers will be directly or indirectly responsible for creating and activating segments within Data Cloud.

The Data Cloud platform will need to be provisioned and made ready for the end users before they can get access to the Data Cloud application and data. Data Cloud setup and first-time implementation can be challenging for several reasons. For one thing, bringing together large amounts of disparate data from many different internal and external sources often requires a considerable amount of effort, a variety of skill sets, and much coordination between various departments and data owners.

Data Cloud implementation team roles will likely consist of a project manager, business analyst, quality assurance (QA) specialist, Salesforce admin, and Salesforce developer, plus one or more architects. There are some clearly defined and specialized roles needed for a Data Cloud implementation, but it's not unusual for individuals on the team to take on more than one role. It's important to understand the various roles of the team members because these builders will need access to the Data Cloud application to set up the platform for end users.

We'll learn much more about Salesforce Data Cloud implementations in future chapters, but it's important to realize that, because the Data Cloud platform is still relatively new, there is not an abundance of experienced Salesforce Data Cloud experts. That's great news if you're an individual looking to enhance your current skill set or seek a new career role.

There are many different Salesforce-specific roles that can benefit from learning about Salesforce Data Cloud (Figure 2-1). There are also opportunities for app developers to create new applications to support these Salesforce-specific end users and to offer those Data Cloud applications on the Salesforce AppExchange.

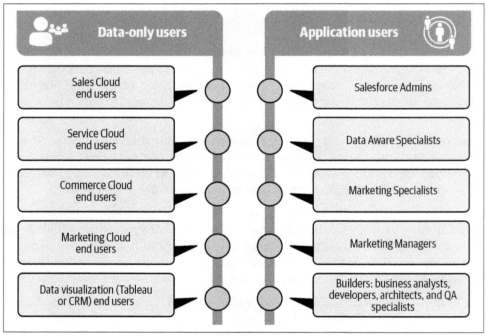

Figure 2-1. Salesforce Data Cloud data-only users and application users

Having a background in Salesforce core or Salesforce Marketing Cloud is certainly helpful for many of the Data Cloud roles, but there are also great opportunities for data architects and data engineers who have experience with public cloud technologies and platforms from technology partners like Amazon, Databricks, Google, Microsoft, and Snowflake. Cloud data architects typically have a better understanding of how to architect solutions for consumption-based pricing platforms, and that is important for Salesforce Data Cloud, which is Salesforce's first offering to be billed based on usage.

Transitioning to a consumption-based platform like Salesforce Data Cloud makes sense for an organization from both a cost perspective and an architecture perspective. Let's consider both.

From a cost perspective, some licensed users may use a traditional licensed-based platform very often, whereas other users may rarely log in. Yet, you're paying the same cost for both people who have the same license. However, with a consumption-based platform, you're charged for actual usage of the resources, like storage and computing. We also just discussed how there could be many Salesforce users who receive downstream value from Data Cloud without ever logging in to the Data Cloud platform.

From an architecture perspective, there are also benefits of transitioning to a consumption-based platform. The more you optimize your architecture and build it in a scalable way on a consumption-based platform, the more money you can save. You're actually rewarded, with cost savings, for building more efficient and effective architecture.

Architects play a key role in Data Cloud implementation projects, and this chapter will be of special interest to those who have a desire to become Data Cloud architects. The entirety of this book focuses on the concepts and details you can use to become knowledgeable about the Salesforce Data Cloud platform, but if your desire is to become a Salesforce Data Cloud architect, you'll want to make sure you have a good understanding of Salesforce architecture constraints. You can find a good explanation of general Salesforce data and architecture constraints in *Practical Salesforce Architecture* by Paul McCollum (O'Reilly, 2023).

In this chapter, we'll focus on some foundational Data Cloud concepts. We'll start by focusing on some special considerations for architects, and we'll then cover both the functional aspects and technical details of Salesforce Data Cloud. Lastly, we'll take a look at some of Data Cloud's unique datastore features.

Special Considerations for Architects

Sometime between 2012 and 2016, our world entered an age of digital data growth called the Zettabyte Era (*https://oreil.ly/CSAF2*), which is a period of human and computer science history marked by the massive growth of all forms of global IP traffic. These forms of digital data come from many sources; they include stored data from security cameras, voice data from cell phone calls, public internet data, and data from online streaming services.

Today, the volume of data created, captured, copied, stored, and consumed exceeds two zettabytes per week. One *zettabyte* is the equivalent of one trillion gigabytes, so it's no surprise that companies find it difficult to provide end users access to all this data, which needs to be refined, analyzed, and made available in actionable ways.

Many organizations therefore have begun a transformation process to implement a new data strategy to better gain insights from data and learn how to build data-driven products at scale.

In 2020, Salesforce began building its Data Cloud platform from the ground up to give organizations a platform where they can collect large volumes of customer data into a single source of truth (SSOT) for harmonizing, unifying, and nurturing information. Salesforce built its Data Cloud data lake storage on top of Amazon Web Services (AWS). In addition, Salesforce began a new effort to modernize the data infrastructure of its Salesforce core platform, which is now migrating from Oracle databases to Salesforce Hyperforce hosted on AWS.

This is an exciting time for architects working in the Salesforce ecosystem as Salesforce continues to innovate and rearchitect its platform for the modern era. Once fully implemented, Salesforce's *single platform approach* will streamline Salesforce functionality and better support new AI possibilities, including new Einstein capabilities. It's important for architects to understand the driving factors behind these changes as well as the challenges of building a data-driven platform.

Data-Driven Pattern Use Cases

Building a modern data system is complicated by the fact that there are many new architectural data patterns emerging to address many different kinds of modern-day, data-driven use cases. For example, event processing requires storage patterns needed for streaming data ingestion and transformations (which we call *ingests* and *transforms* for short). Analytics needs to be supported by batch ingests and batch transforms along with columnar stores. Salesforce has identified six major data-driven pattern use cases that are supported by Data Cloud (Figure 2-2).

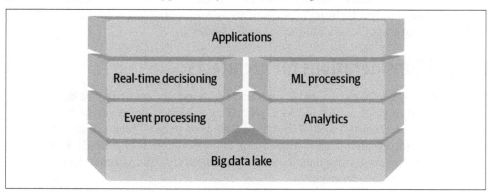

Figure 2-2. Data patterns supported by Salesforce Data Cloud

The underlying technical details of how these data paradigms are supported by the Salesforce Data Cloud storage layers are described in "Storage Layering" on page 43. For now, let's take a look at the main architectural considerations Salesforce needed to address as it was building the Salesforce data-driven platform.

Considerations for Building a Data-Driven Platform

Salesforce defined some data principles it used as foundational concepts for building Data Cloud:

- Cold, warm, and hot data storage layers for data access
- Interchangeable events and tables
- Multimodal access
- Support for machine learning (ML) and analytics
- High-performance query layer for analytics
- All data is typed with Salesforce metadata

Storing large amounts of petabyte-sized data is expensive, so Salesforce was challenged to build a platform that could take advantage of cost savings for cold storage while still making the most relevant data quickly available to users. Most importantly, the movement between the different layers of cold, warm, and hot storage needed to be seamless to the end user.

Creating interchangeable events and tables, the second principle, is a revolutionary concept that Salesforce implemented. Transactional and analytical data are typically stored separately, but to have a meaningful customer 360-degree view, you need a way to view all the data. To help make this happen, Salesforce generates a row in a table for every event, including Data Cloud operations such as insights and segments.

Data Cloud is an *open and extensible platform*—a system built on open source technologies, which means the data is not locked. The data storage formats are not proprietary; you can access the data with different modes such as a structured query language (SQL), Salesforce Object Query Language (SOQL), Salesforce REST API, webhooks, platform events, journey events, lightning components, and more.

Making sure Data Cloud could support ML and high-performing queries for analytics was top of mind for Salesforce when building the new platform. As part of the design, snapshots and partitions were built to provide features like *time travel*, which allows you to go back to a previous version of the data without needing to do anything special.

One of the most important data principles specific to Salesforce Data Cloud is that everything on the platform needs to support the Salesforce business user experience. All Data Cloud data is typed with Salesforce metadata, so there is a consistent experience for users of the Salesforce system. Designing this consistent user experience in Data Cloud as part of the overall Salesforce system design is the responsibility of the Data Cloud architect, and Salesforce provides a number of resources to assist architects in their role. The *Salesforce Well-Architected* series (*https://oreil.ly/z2QqZ*) began in early 2023, and already there is a large body of knowledge put forth.

Salesforce Well-Architected Resources

The concept of a *well-architected* framework was established in 2015 by AWS, and other cloud providers followed suit. These well-architected frameworks provide best practices and guidance on how to design and deploy workloads on their respective platforms.

Similar to other well-architected frameworks, Salesforce Well-Architected provides guidance in the form of whitepapers. However, Salesforce is a little different from the other platforms, so its version of the well-architected framework is also different. For one thing, at the end of each Salesforce Well-Architected whitepaper, you'll find a section for relevant tools and a section for relevant resources.

Salesforce Well-Architected (*http://architect.salesforce.com*) is the result of collaborations between Salesforce internal product experts, people on the engineering team, and thought leaders in the Salesforce ecosystem. The framework is built around the three main concepts of being trusted, easy, and adaptable.

You'll want to familiarize yourself with the Salesforce Well-Architected resources if your goal is to become a Salesforce Data Cloud architect. The Relevant Tools section will give you the details about the actual features you can leverage within Salesforce to help improve your solution, and everything in this section maps back to the key topics. Within the Relevant Resources section, you'll find a list of documentation you can use to better understand core concepts and implement what you've learned. Salesforce created these Well-Architected whitepapers and resources to make sure everyone who is building architecture with Salesforce products knows what a healthy solution looks like.

Data Cloud Technical Capability Map

Salesforce architects also have access to the Salesforce Template Gallery (*https://oreil.ly/N-O1s*), which includes Salesforce data models and prebuilt artifacts. One of these artifacts is the Salesforce Data Cloud Technical Capability Map (*https://oreil.ly/NDHtW*) level-1 documentation and implementation diagram. It shows the technical capabilities of the platform and the product mix involved in supporting those technical capabilities. According to the Salesforce capability map, there are five major Salesforce Data Cloud technical capabilities. Two are managed by Salesforce, and three are accessible to end users (Figure 2-3).

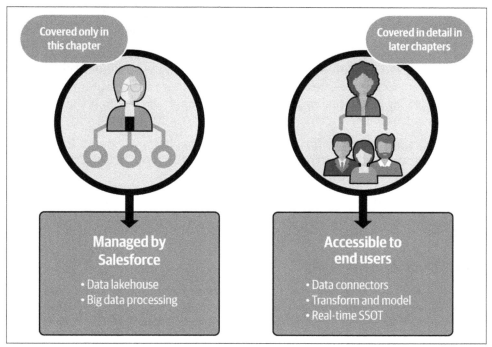

Figure 2-3. Capabilities of Salesforce Data Cloud

The data lakehouse and big data processing are described in "Under the Hood: Data Cloud Technical Details" on page 41. Many of the features within each of the other three technical capabilities are directly accessible by Data Cloud end users, and that is where we will focus most of our attention in this book.

Data Cloud Key Functional Aspects

Salesforce Data Cloud makes it possible for you to connect and harmonize large volumes of data that lead to value. How exactly do end users tap into the Data Cloud key functional aspects to make that happen? The Salesforce Data Cloud capabilities accessible to end users include the ability to build connectors and ingress, transform and model the data, and create a real-time SSOT (Figure 2-3). This real-time SSOT can personalize experiences such as real-time recommendations, real-time service bots, and real-time sales engagements.

To better understand how Salesforce Data Cloud actually works its magic, let's first review some general key data concepts that we will then associate with the five major steps of the Data Cloud lifecycle. We'll briefly discuss those five activities, which are the stepping stones to creating value in the Data Cloud platform. We'll also touch on a few important points about connecting multiple Salesforce Clouds and then wrap up with a brief overview of Salesforce AppExchange for Data Cloud.

Overall, this section is a brief introduction to Data Cloud's key functional aspects. As we'll discover in later chapters, a variety of data connectors are made available to Data Cloud users to set up data streams. These connectors ingest data from within Salesforce and also ingest external sources into Data Cloud. Data ingestion and storage is the subject of Chapter 6.

Data modeling, data transformations, and data mapping are covered in detail in Chapters 7, 8, and 9, respectively. Additionally, the real-time SSOT features supported by CDP processing are the subject of Chapter 10.

Chapters 11, 12, and 13 describe in detail how to extract value from Data Cloud. They describe functionality such as Data Cloud enrichments, data actions, segmentation and activation, and Einstein capabilities that make use of Data Cloud data.

General Key Data Concepts

The more than two zettabytes per week of data being generated and stored today include a combination of unstructured, semistructured, and structured data types. *Structured data* is typically quantifiable data that can be captured in a row-column relational database. Examples include first-party data like address details and other demographic information.

Semistructured data is more fluid than structured data, but it does have some properties like tags or metadata to make it easier to organize, whereas *unstructured data* doesn't have an associated data structure or model. Comma-separated values (CSV), extensible markup language (XML), and JavaScript Object Notation (JSON) are common semistructured formats. Examples of unstructured data include PDFs, text files, social media content, sensor data, photographs, and audio files. The majority of data by volume is unstructured data.

Finding ways to harness the power of this vast data requires different architectural patterns due to the sheer amount of data, the speed at which the data is being generated and ingested, and the varied types of data formats.

Earlier, we looked at the six data pattern use cases supported by Salesforce Data Cloud and the considerations the Salesforce team worked with while building out Data Cloud. Now, let's look at Data Cloud from the perspective of describing the data itself that will be ingested, processed, and made available for end users of Data Cloud to extract value. It's important to understand how the data creates value because creating is at the center of how Data Cloud works its magic (Figure 2-4).

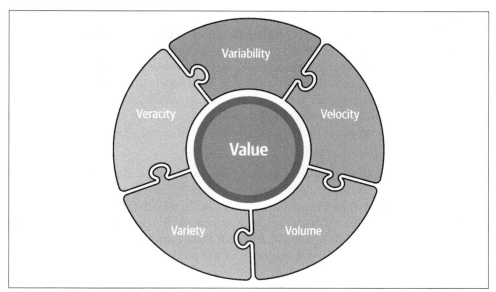

Figure 2-4. Creating value is at the center of Data Cloud data

Six dimensional factors generally describe all data, and together, they are known as the *six Vs* of data. Here are detailed explanations of all of them:

Variability

This is the consistency of the data; it includes the quality, format, and meaning of the data. In other words, variability is how far apart the data points are from each other and from the center of a distribution. Some data, like thermometer readings, might be recorded every hour, at very regular intervals. Other data might only be recorded when a triggered event, like the activation of a motion detector, occurs. It isn't likely you can affect variability at the source, but understanding the expected variability of the data is often a factor in the other characteristics. An example would be making a decision about the velocity at which you want to set up ingestion (i.e., batch or streaming) based on the known variability of that data source.

Velocity

This is the speed at which data is generated, ingested, and processed. At one end of the spectrum, there's low velocity, for which batch processing for ingesting and processing data at intervals is used. At the other end is real-time or near real-time processing for higher-velocity data, such as data used with Internet of Things (IoT) devices and mobile applications. There isn't necessarily more value for higher-velocity data than for lower-velocity data, especially because there is an increased cost to ingest data at a higher velocity. Consider whether your use case requires higher velocity or whether a lower-velocity batch ingestion is sufficient to meet your needs.

Volume

This is the amount of data that's generated, ingested, and stored. Different data sources could easily have different volumes. For example, IoT devices are likely to stream millions of events per minute, whereas an ecommerce platform might have hundreds or thousands of orders a minute. We know that insights benefit from having higher data volumes, but not all data points may be needed for your particular use case(s). Consider which data sources are needed for your use case(s). For example, there's no requirement to ingest all fields in all data source files or objects.

Variety

This is the variety of data sources and formats, which include structured data (like relational databases), semistructured data (like CSV, JSON, and XML), unstructured data (like PDFs and emails), and binary data (like images, audio, and video). With Data Cloud, you're not limited to accessing only structured data. The new vector database in Salesforce Data Cloud will provide you with a way to include unstructured data as part of the process to ground your large language models (LLMs).

Veracity

This is the accuracy and reliability of the data. Incomplete source data and data from unreliable sources affect the quality of the data. It's doubtful you'll have control over the veracity of all data you'll ingest in Data Cloud, which is why you need to consider whether transformations are needed, either before ingesting or after ingesting the data.

Value

This is to the relevance and usefulness of the data. All of the other five factors have an impact on the value that can be derived from the data. Most organizations seeking to create more value for themselves include some aspect of *data and AI democratization*, which provides the foundation for team members to access and understand the data they need to make informed decisions, irrespective of their technical knowledge.

Architects understand that building a solid foundation and scalable solutions requires evaluating these six characteristics for the data that will be ingested into Data Cloud, processed, and made available to end users. Business value is achieved when the processed data can be used to analyze and predict, or when users can set up automation actions or activate personalized segments.

A Salesforce CRM is often the platform where first-party data exists for many organizations, but these same organizations frequently have external event- or engagement-related data that exists outside of the Salesforce CRM platform. Stitching together all these different data sources to create a unified profile unlocks the possibility that value can be extracted and data and AI democratization achieved. That's where the real magic happens.

How Data Cloud Works Its Magic

There are many different ways Data Cloud can provide business value. We define *business value* in terms of requirements that are documented as use cases. *Use cases* link an organizational goal to an outcome by defining the requirements needed to accomplish that goal. In Data Cloud, those goals are accomplished by undertaking key business value activities achieved by leveraging data and AI democratization (Figure 2-5). Chapter 3 is devoted to explaining Data Cloud value activities and describing in detail how Data Cloud works its magic.

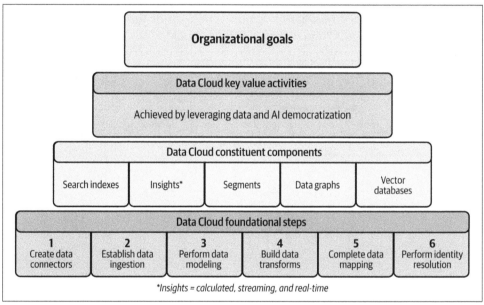

Figure 2-5. How Data Cloud works its magic

You'll notice that reaching the value activities level requires some foundational steps and constituent components. Stitching together many different data sources and creating a unified individual profile or unified account profile are necessary foundational steps.

Building constituent components is also an important precursor to achieving value from Data Cloud investment (Figure 2-5). Building these constituent components includes creating insights and building segments. We'll talk more about these steps and components in Chapter 3 and beyond. Understanding both of these will assist you in developing an effective solution blueprint and an achievable implementation strategy for your Data Cloud implementation.

An important consideration, as you're designing the roadmap for your Data Cloud use case implementations, is determining where you'll be provisioning your new Data Cloud organization (org). You can provision Data Cloud in an existing org, or you can stand up a new Salesforce org for your Data Cloud instance. It's possible to connect multiple Salesforce Clouds to the Data Cloud platform, but there are some caveats.

Connecting Multiclouds

It's possible to connect multiple external sources and multiple Commerce Clouds to Data Cloud, but it's only possible to connect one each of the Salesforce Marketing Cloud and the Marketing Cloud Personalization dataset to Data Cloud (Figure 2-6).

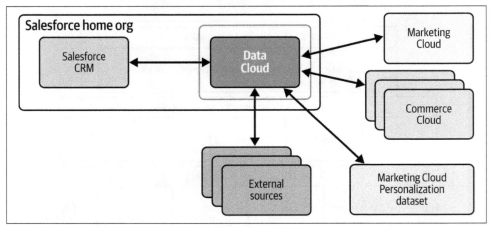

Figure 2-6. Using Data Cloud in a single existing CRM org

It's not unusual for an organization to have multiple Salesforce CRM instances, especially if it is an enterprise that has made lots of company acquisitions and each of those acquired companies has its own Salesforce instance. It's also possible to connect one or more Salesforce CRM orgs to Salesforce Data Cloud.

Establishing Remote Org Connections for Data Cloud Remote Orgs

What will be described in this section and throughout the book is how Data Cloud currently supports connections between multiple Salesforce CRM orgs. Connections to Salesforce data source orgs allow data to be ingested from these connected orgs into the home org and then allow data action targets to be set up for the connected orgs. In the near future, remote org connections will be made available that will allow for a bidirectional connection between a Salesforce source org and the Data Cloud home org, making the source org a Data Cloud remote org. Establishing the Salesforce CRM org as a Data Cloud remote org will make it possible for the Data Cloud remote org to access the same platform features that exist in the Data Cloud home org today. For example, it will be possible in the remote org to use Flow, SOQL, enrichments, Lightning Web Components (LWCs), reports, and more.

The Salesforce CRM org where your Data Cloud instance is provisioned is considered to be your home org or your primary org. You can use the Salesforce CRM Connector to ingest CRM data from within the home org into Data Cloud, assuming you're using the home org for Sales Cloud, Service Cloud, an industry cloud such as Health Cloud or Financial Services Cloud, or Loyalty Management Cloud.

If you plan to ingest data from the Salesforce Loyalty Management Cloud, it must be located in the home Salesforce org (Figure 2-7). Additionally, your home Salesforce org is the location where you'll want to install any Salesforce AppExchange applications you plan to use for Data Cloud.

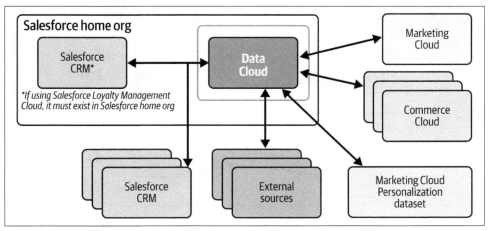

Figure 2-7. Connecting multiple CRM orgs with an existing CRM org

Sometimes, it may be necessary to set up Salesforce Data Cloud in a standalone org (Figure 2-8). This is often true when the existing org is heavily regulated or when the Data Cloud Admin users are different from the Salesforce CRM Admin users.

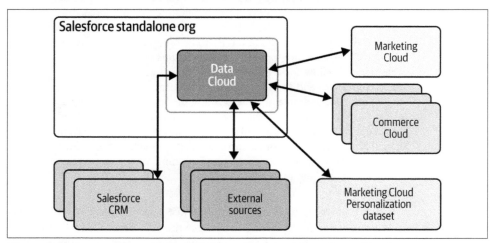

Figure 2-8. Connecting multiple CRM orgs to a standalone Data Cloud org

The multiple CRM external orgs can be production orgs or sandbox orgs. The relationship between Salesforce CRM orgs and Data Cloud orgs can be one to one, one to many, or many to one (Figure 2-9).

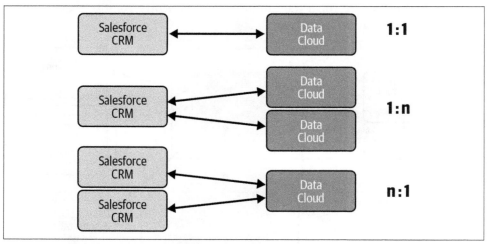

Figure 2-9. Salesforce CRM: Data Cloud topology

The Commerce Cloud topology can be one to one, one to many, or many to many (Figure 2-10). A single Commerce Cloud can be connected to more than one Data Cloud org, and a Data Cloud org can be connected to more than one Commerce Cloud.

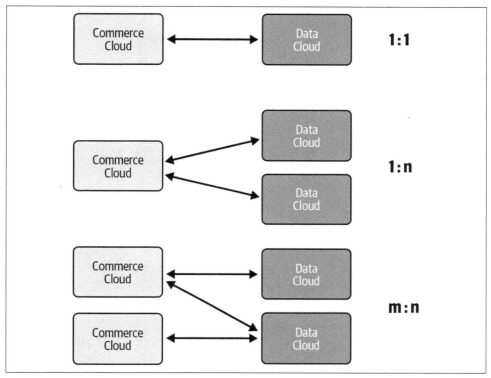

Figure 2-10. Salesforce Commerce Cloud: Data Cloud topology

There is a one-to-one and a one-to-many relationship between a Salesforce Marketing Cloud account, as indicated by the Marketing Cloud Enterprise ID (EID), which is also equivalent to the parent business unit member ID (MID). One Marketing Cloud account can be connected to one or more Data Cloud orgs, but a single Data Cloud org can only be connected to one Marketing Cloud account (Figure 2-11). Data Cloud connects to Marketing Cloud at the account level, but it's possible to select a specific business unit within the account when activating segments from Data Cloud.

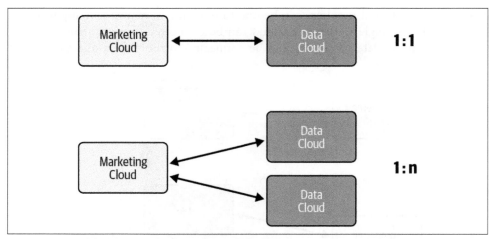

Figure 2-11. Salesforce Marketing Cloud: Data Cloud topology

The possibilities for the topology of the Salesforce Marketing Cloud Personalization accounts and Data Cloud orgs are a bit different from those of the other topologies. This topology focuses on the datasets within a Marketing Cloud Personalization account. Any specific dataset can be connected to only one Data Cloud org, but a Data Cloud org can be connected to one or more datasets, even if those datasets are located within different Marketing Cloud Personalization accounts (Figure 2-12).

It's important to remember that when making these architectural decisions, your Salesforce account executive and implementation partner can help guide you if you're not sure what Data Cloud architecture best supports your use cases. Topology options should be evaluated for your specific use cases, and the decision on whether to provision Data Cloud in an existing CRM org or as a standalone org is an important one. These decisions might be influenced by considerations about workflows, data governance, security models, existing integrations, and more. Also, closely related to these main architectural considerations is the concept of data spaces, which we'll discuss next.

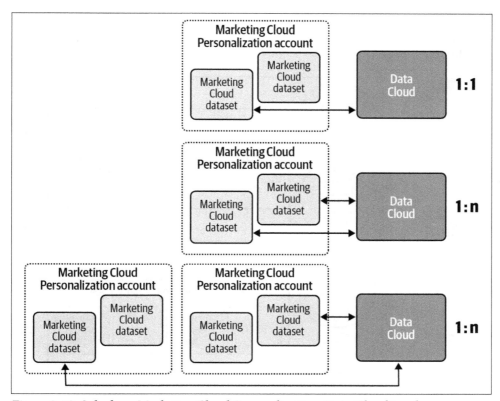

Figure 2-12. Salesforce Marketing Cloud Personalization: Data Cloud topology

Data Spaces

Data spaces are logical partitions to organize your Data Cloud data for profile unification, insights, and marketing. Data spaces can be used to segregate your data within a single Data Cloud instance, alleviating most organizations' needs to otherwise have multiple Data Cloud instances.

Data spaces make it possible to segregate data, metadata, and processes into different categories. Common data space categories include brand, region, and department. End users are given the ability to see and work on data only in the context of their particular category.

Not a Data Residency Solution

Data spaces are not intended for supporting data residency solutions. *Data residency solutions* are meant to resolve issues concerning the physical geographical location and movement of data and metadata. In contrast, data spaces are logical partitions of data.

Data streams and data lake objects (DLOs) are accessible across data spaces. It's possible to associate a DLO with a data space with or without filters, and you can add a DLO to more than one data space (Figure 2-13).

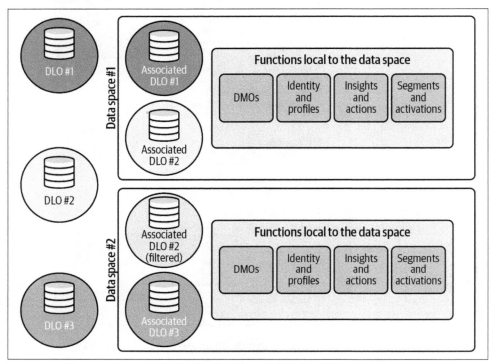

Figure 2-13. Data spaces within Salesforce Data Cloud

Data model objects (DMOs) and other platform features like identity resolution, insights and actions, and segmentation are specific to users of a particular data space (Figure 2-13). Security access within that data space is still controlled through permission sets. Not all data space features are data space aware, but the following features are data space aware:

- Data shares from BYOL
- Data graphs
- Identity resolution
- Calculated insights (CIs)
- Data actions
- Segmentation
- Activation

Every Data Cloud org is created with a default data space, and all Data Cloud objects are mapped to the default data space unless and until you create other data spaces. For all examples throughout this book, we'll be using only the default data space.

Application Lifecycle Management with Sandboxes

Data Cloud in sandbox environments was introduced in June 2024, and the ability to deploy changes from a sandbox to production with the Salesforce DevOps Center was introduced in July 2024. With the addition of Data Cloud in sandbox environments, it's possible to build, test, and deploy Data Cloud in a secure, trusted environment.

Sandboxes make it easier to solve for key development use cases and to address common change management needs quickly and securely. They let you develop, train, and test with a copy of the production environment to mitigate the risk of disrupting live production data and workflows.

Data Cloud metadata and configurations are automatically replicated as part of sandbox provisioning. This is done within the same sandboxes that are used today, not a separate sandbox, because Data Cloud is part of the Salesforce platform. The first two steps to provision a sandbox environment with Data Cloud are the same ones you'd perform to provision a Salesforce sandbox for any other purpose (Figure 2-14).

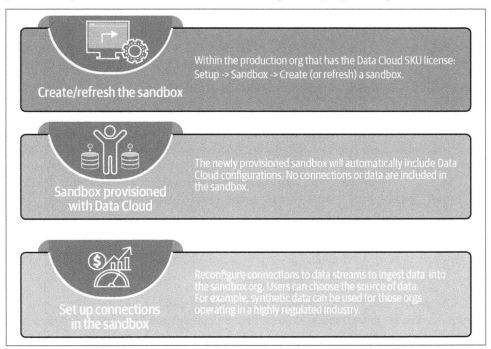

Figure 2-14. Steps to provision a sandbox environment with Data Cloud

The last step, setting up connections in the sandbox, is what you'll need to do so that data appears in your sandbox environment for Data Cloud purposes. It's possible to establish connections to synthetic data sources so you can use test data rather than production data. This is especially important for organizations operating in a highly regulated industry. It can also be useful to connect to synthetic sources so you can limit the amount of data ingested. This is an important consideration because Data Cloud consumption charges apply to usage within a sandbox as well as usage within your production environment.

Salesforce AppExchange and Data Kits

Salesforce AppExchange is an enterprise cloud computing marketplace launched by Salesforce in 2005. AppExchange has had more than 11 million installs and includes a number of solutions, free and paid. The Salesforce AppExchange Data Cloud product collection (*https://oreil.ly/zf_EM*) includes data activation apps, data enrichment apps, and a data strategy experts section.

The Salesforce independent software vendor (ISV) packaging strategy for Data Cloud is unique. ISV partners create data kits to simplify deployment of Data Cloud data streams in a customer org through a managed package installation. A *data kit* is a portable and customizable bundle of independently packageable metadata in the form of templates, and because data kits store templates instead of actual metadata, they can be materialized and deployed multiple times. For example, a data kit can be deployed into a subscriber's Data Cloud org many times for different whitespaces.

Data kits can be created easily from within the user interface without writing any code. In a developer org, an ISV partner creates a managed package by performing the following steps:

1. Configure Data Cloud metadata in the namespaced Salesforce Developer Edition org, including data streams, DLOs and transforms, DMOs and mappings, and CIs. You can visit the Data Cloud Extensibility Readiness Matrix (*https://oreil.ly/HqsbK*) to access the latest information on what is packageable.

2. Create a new data kit and add the newly created CRM data streams and data model to the new data kit. The package kit will suggest related feature metadata.

3. Add the data kit to the managed package and make the managed package available on Salesforce AppExchange.

Data kits are always created from the default data space, but they can be deployed to any data space. It's best practice to use a data kit rather than Salesforce Metadata API for metadata movement.

Data Cloud apps contain only Data Cloud metadata, and that metadata is added to a data kit that is then added to a package. Metadata components included in a managed package must adhere to certain rules that determine its behavior in a subscriber org. Those rules define whether you and/or the subscriber can change or delete components after the managed package is installed. More information about second-generation managed packages (*https://oreil.ly/qZg3L*) (managed 2GPs) can be reviewed in the Salesforce developer documentation online.

As of April 2024, managed 2GPs are available to Salesforce Partners for use in building Data Cloud apps. There are significant advantages to using managed 2GPs (Table 2-1).

Table 2-1. Comparison of second- and first-generation managed packaging

	Managed 2GP	Managed 1GP
Collaboration level	Easy	Becomes challenging at scale
Development environments	Partner Business Org (PBO) and namespace org	Partner Business Org (PBO), many packaging orgs, many patch orgs
Packages per namespace	Many	One
Source of truth	Version control system	Metadata in packaging org
User expertise level	More experience needed	Less experience needed
Versioning	Flexible	Linear and more prone to errors

Second-generation packaging is developed with the Developer Experience command-line interface, making it source driven. This allows ISV partners to manage their version control with tools of their choosing, rather than being required to keep their development metadata in an org.

Under the Hood: Data Cloud Technical Details

Salesforce Data Cloud is at the heart of the Salesforce modern data tech stack. Salesforce Einstein AI and Flow automation services harness the power of the hyperscale near real-time data of Data Cloud.

You'll notice that it's possible to use only the Salesforce CRM transactional database to power some of your Einstein AI strategy. However, you'd benefit greatly from the near real-time hyperscale capabilities of Salesforce Data Cloud to get a complete 360-degree view upon which to build your AI and data strategy (Figure 2-15).

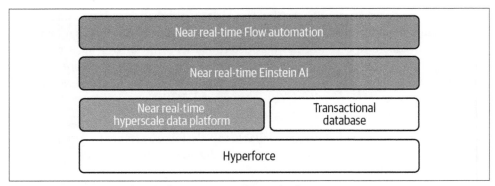

Figure 2-15. Integrated Salesforce Customer 360 platform

Data Cloud is built on *Hyperforce*, the next-generation Salesforce infrastructure architecture. Salesforce chose AWS as the cloud provider upon which to build Hyperforce, and each Hyperforce region is configured and deployed in at least three separate locations called availability zones (AZs). Salesforce maintains an FAQ page (*https://oreil.ly/AXoHu*) with up-to-date information about Hyperforce.

Salesforce Data Cloud has been built from the ground up as an open and extensible data platform that allows organizations to seamlessly integrate their Salesforce Data Cloud org with other platforms in a trusted manner. However, Data Cloud still uses the core Salesforce org capabilities for things like reports and dashboards, Flow, and authentication.

Sharing Rules and Data Access

Sharing rules and data access restrictions works differently in Data Cloud than in Salesforce CRM. More information about sharing rules and data access can be found in Chapter 4.

Data Cloud data can be enriched using applications from Salesforce AppExchange and with first-party advertising platforms such as Meta, Google, and Amazon Ads. Data Cloud can also be extended with the BYOL capabilities. Using BYOL, data access can be extended bidirectionally with Snowflake, Google BigQuery, and Amazon Redshift.

Using Bring Your Own Model (BYOM) capabilities, it's possible to use Data Cloud data in externally created predictive models from Amazon SageMaker, Databricks, and Google Vertex AI. LLM capabilities within the trusted Salesforce platform can be extended with the Bring Your Own LLM (BYOLLM) technologies of Azure OpenAI and IBM watsonx. More information about BYOL and BYOLLM can be found in Chapter 13.

How Data Cloud Is Architected on Amazon Web Services

Building Salesforce Data Cloud from the ground up began in 2020 with the start of the data lakehouse project. A newly formed Data Cloud big data processing compute layer team in India undertook the complex task of migrating data from Marketing Cloud Intelligence (MCI) to a new data lakehouse.

This team was responsible for overseeing the building of the Salesforce data lakehouse on top of Apache Iceberg and then migrating the existing MCI customer data to the data lakehouse. The team used Airflow, an open source tool, to create, schedule, and track workflows needed to migrate the data. This set the stage for large amounts of data to be ingested directly into the data lakehouse, where it could be processed by Spark and Presto. After the ingested data is processed and unified, it can be segmented using Trino, a tool that divides queries into multiple chunks and collates the data, all within fractions of a second. All of these pieces of technology, combined with ultra-performance query services like Amazon Athena and Amazon EMR, support the management of record-level updates and SQL queries in the Salesforce Data Cloud lakehouse.

The result of combining these best-in-class pieces of technology is that Data Cloud can easily handle petabyte-scale data because Salesforce stores all Data Cloud data in a data lakehouse, rather than in a relational database. Within the data lakehouse, the data is stored in an Apache Parquet file format in Amazon Simple Storage Service (Amazon S3) buckets. *Parquet* is an open source format that leverages a columnar-style file format rather than a row-oriented CSV data format. The Salesforce profile data lives in Amazon DynamoDB, a hot store. All of these were designed as part of the unique Salesforce storage layering system.

Storage Layering

Storage layering, which supports metadata at the storage level, is a new concept. Salesforce Data Cloud data is stored in a Parquet file format, which gives you columnar warehouse file storage access. Parquet is an industry standard columnar format that helps with queries at scale, but users understand tables, so there is a dependency on Iceberg as a table format. The metadata sitting on top of Parquet data is Apache Iceberg, which is also an open source solution.

On top of Iceberg is Salesforce core metadata and all of the robust data model relationships expertly crafted by Salesforce. That layer is called the *cloud table*, which is a concept unique to Salesforce. This is the layer where Salesforce can share data with third-party platforms like Snowflake. The integration between Salesforce and these third-party platforms is at the file level.

On top of that is the *lake library*, an abstraction of the cloud table layer (Figure 2-16). The lake library supports Spark Dataframes and tuples, which are frequently used for handling streaming data at scale for data-intensive purposes like data science and machine learning. The lake library layer will be important when Salesforce opens up this layer to developers, like Spark developers, who want to access the Data Cloud data and have access to the library to work with. On top of the storage layer are big data services like Spark and Trino.

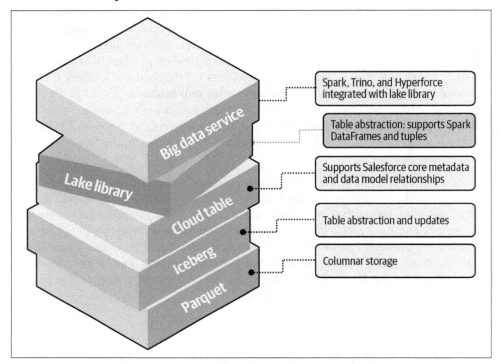

Figure 2-16. Storage layering supports metadata at the storage level

Storage layering supports metadata at the storage level and makes capabilities like BYOL possible. The way Data Cloud is architected on AWS, including storage layering, is how Salesforce supports the six data-driven pattern use cases described previously: big data lake, event processing, analytics, real-time decisioning, ML processing, and applications.

As you would expect, you can only have real-time decision-making capabilities if information is available in near real time. To make information available in near real time, the architecture must support near real-time ingestion and near real-time data processing.

Near Real-Time Ingestion and Data Processing

From a data flow architecture perspective, data ingestion into Data Cloud is accomplished via real-time, streaming, or batch ingestion methods (Figure 2-17). Ingested data is stored in the Salesforce data lakehouse, where it can be processed in near real time. Data Cloud value activities leverage the lakehouse data for insights and exploration capabilities that provide the basis for decision making and actions.

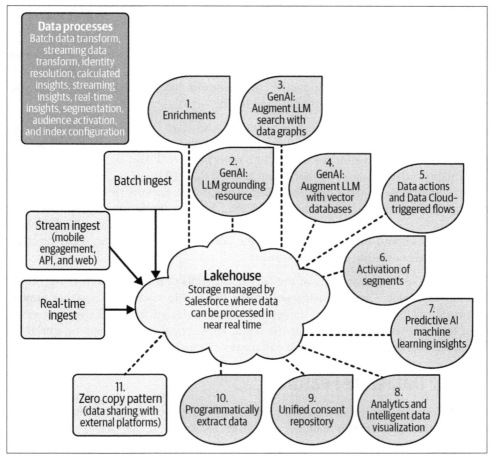

Figure 2-17. Data Cloud supports batch and near real-time ingestion and processing

I've included 10 of those Data Cloud value activities in Figure 2-17, indicated by the numbered teardrops. An 11th use case shown is the zero copy pattern that provides bidirectional data-sharing capabilities with external platforms. One more Data Cloud value activity, in addition to these 11 use cases, will be discussed further in Chapter 3.

Real-Time Decision Making and Action Require Real-Time Ingestion

Whether any particular data outflow value activity can truly be acted upon in near real time will depend in part on whether the source data used for the value category is ingested in a stream or batch fashion.

From an implementation perspective, you'll want to think through the velocity of the data coming in and the velocity of the data you need as an output. Is it all streaming end to end, is it a batch, or is it a combination?

From a best-practices perspective, understanding the sensitivity of the end-to-end path is important because it comes with an associated cost. Data Cloud has a consumption-based pricing model, which means you pay for what you use, and you pay more for near real-time activities than batch.

For example, the Salesforce Customer Data Cloud Rate Card (*https://oreil.ly/hktt8*) currently has a streaming data pipeline usage multiplier that is two and half times the rate of a batch data pipeline for one million rows processed. You'll also notice that the multiplier for data share rows shared out is more than 10 times the multiplier for the data federation or sharing rows accessed. Thus, it's important to understand these consumption multipliers and the Data Cloud billable usage types (*https://oreil.ly/bdq4B*) before you create the architect blueprint for your Data Cloud implementation. That way, you can carefully weigh the cost versus the benefits of the options, with the goal of creating a scalable solution.

Thus far, we've looked at some of the technical details of the built-from-the-ground-up Salesforce Data Cloud constructed on the hyperscale platform. These are important concepts for architects, but the typical Salesforce Data Cloud end user may never need to know what goes on under the hood. However, there are some unique Data Cloud datastore features with which end users will need to be familiar.

Unique Datastore Features

Many Salesforce applications are built on a common *core* platform and thus share the same datastore. Examples include Salesforce Sales Cloud, Service Cloud, Health Cloud, Education Cloud, and several industry clouds like Loyalty Management Cloud and Net Zero Cloud. There are a few exceptions today, but Salesforce plans for almost all applications to eventually exist within the common core platform. The Salesforce roadmap also includes the continuation of transitioning away from the traditional Oracle relational database datastores to Hyperforce, the next-generation Salesforce infrastructure architecture.

While Salesforce has been transitioning its core platform to Hyperforce, it's also been busy building the Data Cloud platform from the ground up. Earlier in the chapter, we took a look under the hood at the technical details of Salesforce Data Cloud to better understand how Data Cloud has been built to handle a variety of data-driven architectural patterns. Fortunately, Salesforce abstracted away for the end user the complexities of managing the Salesforce data lakehouse upon which the Data Cloud storage and processing relies.

Salesforce designed new datastore features for end users to take advantage of the powerful new features of Data Cloud without having to understand or manage the underlying architecture. Let's take an introductory look now at new data entities that are unique to Data Cloud, the BYOL capabilities, and data spaces.

Data Cloud Data Entities

A *data entity* is an abstraction of a physical implementation of database tables. Within Salesforce Data Cloud, there exist data stream entities and data model entities (Figure 2-18).

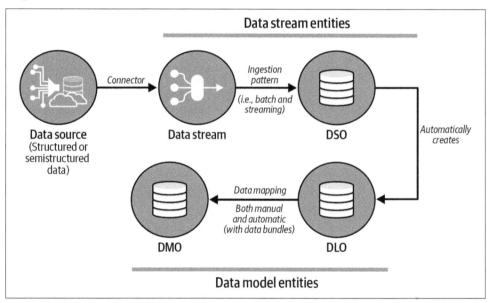

Figure 2-18. Data Cloud data entities for structured and semistructured data

The purpose of data stream entities is to make it easy to connect to and ingest data from a source object with a scheduled refresh. Data stream entities include data source objects (DSOs) and data lake objects (DLOs). A *DSO* can include any internal Salesforce system data from Sales Cloud, Service Cloud, Loyalty Management Cloud, Marketing Cloud, or any other Salesforce Cloud. DSOs can also include data from external sources like Amazon S3. *DLOs* are automatically created from DSOs.

Data model entities are built by mapping data from one or more data streams. Data model entities include DLOs and data model objects (DMOs). *DMOs* are sets of entities and their relationships that are used to describe the data in the DLOs with consistent semantics. Standard Data Cloud DMOs follow the Salesforce Customer 360 Data Model, and just like the 360 model, standard Data Cloud DMOs can be extended by adding custom fields.

Along with standard and custom DMO types, there are new object types in Data Cloud for DMOs created automatically from processes. Some examples include ADG (for data graphs), Bridge (for link objects), Derived (for unification objects), Insights, Semantic, Segment Membership, and Activation Audience. Each Data Cloud DMO also has an associated category like Profile, Engagement, Other, Segment Membership, Activation Membership, Chunk, and Index. We'll learn more about DMO types and categories in later chapters. For now, it's important to know that DMOs have both a type, which describes the DMO structure, and a category, which describes the data stored in the DMO.

Data streams are a familiar concept for those who have worked with the Salesforce MCI platform, previously known as Datorama. Data Cloud data streams are built with the flexibility needed to support data ingestion at a much more granular level.

DSOs, DLOs, and DMOs are unique to the Salesforce Data Cloud platform. These are the six main objects accessible in the Salesforce Data Cloud UI, where users can ingest, store, transform, unify, and take action with customer data. Here's a quick summary of those objects and their characteristics:

- A DSO is the transient staging cloud storage object that temporarily holds the original source data in the original file format.
- A DLO is a persistent cloud storage object where transformed data is permanently stored in a Parquet format in the data lake.
- A DMO is the logical view of the harmonized data created from the data mapping process to the Salesforce metadata structure represented by the Customer 360 Data Model.
- An unstructured DLO (UDLO) is the cloud storage container for unstructured data details.
- An unstructured DMO (UDMO) is a logical grouping of unstructured data details.
- An external DLO is the cloud storage object containing metadata for the data federated from an external data source, which acts as a reference pointing to the data persistently stored in an external data source.

Data is ingested into DSOs, which are used for temporary staging, and transformed DSO data is stored in persistent DLO storage. The way the data is stored in the Data

Cloud data lake, as described in "Storage Layering" on page 43, is different from how other Salesforce objects are stored, as structured *Objects* in a transactional database.

DLO data is harmonized and presented to the user as a logical or materialized view known as a DMO (Figure 2-19). DMOs also include post-unification data that has undergone the identity resolution process. Thus, DMOs include materialized views like Unified Individual along with the Customer 360 DMOs, which are the logical views of the mapped DLO data.

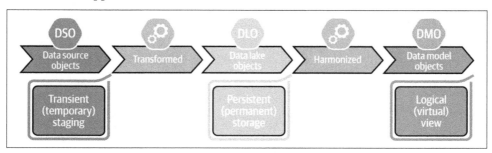

Figure 2-19. Data Cloud storage for ingested structured and semistructured data

DMOs are organized into different primary subject areas, including Party, Engagement, Privacy, Loyalty, and Case. The subject areas organize Salesforce standard data models into related groupings. They also help Data Cloud architects and data modelers more easily leverage the existing Salesforce metadata developed for the Salesforce core platform.

Data stored in Salesforce DMOs can also be joined with external data. The data can also be made usable with predictive and AI models created outside of Salesforce. This is accomplished in collaboration with other partners through the Zero Copy Partner Network. More information about the Partner Network can be found in Chapter 13, and leveraging the network is but one way you can realize value faster from your Data Cloud implementation. Earlier in the chapter, we discussed how data kits can be used to simplify deployment of Data Cloud data streams, and using starter data bundles is another option to help you achieve Data Cloud value realization faster.

Starter Data Bundles

A *starter data bundle* imports into Data Cloud predefined Salesforce objects from various Salesforce Clouds. Starter data bundles are available for use with Salesforce native connectors, and some of those Salesforce connectors offer multiple data bundle options. Starter data bundles reduce implementation time because bundles include data stream definitions that incorporate mapping from a Salesforce data source to the Data Cloud DMO structure.

For example, the Marketing Cloud starter data bundles include bundle options for Email, MobileConnect, and MobilePush datasets. The *Email* dataset includes email engagement events such as sends, opens, clicks, bounces, complaints, unsubscribes, and Einstein Engagement Scoring.

Here are some of the Salesforce data objects and datasets for which starter data bundles are available:

- Salesforce Sales Cloud
- Salesforce Service Cloud
- Salesforce Loyalty Management Cloud
- Salesforce Unified Health Scoring
- Salesforce B2C Commerce
- Salesforce Omnichannel Inventory
- Salesforce Marketing Cloud
- Salesforce Marketing Cloud Account Engagement
- Salesforce Marketing Cloud Personalization

Some data bundle datasets are available in more than one starter data bundle. An example is the Salesforce CRM Contact Mappings dataset, which is available in both the Sales and Service Cloud starter data bundles. It's expected that more starter data bundles will be added in the future. The Salesforce developers' Data Cloud Reference Guide (*https://oreil.ly/RXBxi*) includes an up-to-date list of all the starter data bundles and data bundle datasets. If you click on any of the starter data bundle names in the reference guide, you'll get access to the specific DLO to DMO mapping for that bundle.

Summary

We began the chapter by considering some of the special Data Cloud considerations for architects, and we then looked at the Data Cloud key functional aspects, including the various topologies for connecting multiclouds. Afterward, we took a deep dive into the more technical details of Data Cloud, including how Data Cloud makes use of storage layering and how near real-time ingestion and data processing are made possible.

We closed out the chapter with an important discussion of the unique datastore features, including Data Cloud data entities, the bidirectional data-sharing capabilities of Data Cloud, and starter data bundles. In the next chapter, we'll turn our attention to the business value realization that can be obtained with Salesforce Data Cloud and discuss how the platform can be used to achieve data and AI democratization.

CHAPTER 3

Business Value Activities

In Chapter 2, we learned how the Data Cloud architecture was built from the ground up to make the Salesforce customer data platform (CDP) unique. Unlike traditional CDPs that only utilize batch processing, Data Cloud can operate in a near real-time manner to deliver the most up-to-date information for immediate action. This opens up many new possibilities for organizations implementing Salesforce Data Cloud as part of their first-party data strategy.

The last chapter described the technology that powers Data Cloud. In this chapter, we'll learn about the many ways Salesforce Data Cloud provides benefits to the entire organization. You'll be introduced to the value creation process that empowers functional teams with key value activities they can use to transform their enterprise into a future-ready organization. We'll discuss different ways an organization can leverage those key value activities by providing a brief explanation of 12 different key business value activities made possible by Data Cloud.

Later chapters will give in-depth details about the 12 key business value activities and how you can achieve them. The purpose of this chapter is to make you aware of them so you can begin planning with the end goal in mind. Implementing Data Cloud is similar to planning a vacation where you first have to decide on the destination so you can map your route. Knowing the final destination also informs whether to bring winter coats and thick socks for snow skiing in the mountains or sandals and bathing suits for snorkeling if you're headed to a tropical climate. Of course, you could purchase airline tickets last-minute, arrange a hotel room on-site, and buy clothing and suitcases after you arrive. You'll be limited to only readily available items, and you'll end up paying significantly more in total for your vacation than if you had simply planned ahead. In much the same way, starting your Data Cloud journey with the end goals in mind actually makes it possible to accelerate the time to value and do so in a much more cost-effective way.

Achieving Goals with Data and AI Democratization

Salesforce is a pioneer in the data democratization trend and is well-known for empowering business people with their low-code/no-code platform. Low-code/no-code platforms reduce the need for manual coding. Instead, end users leverage pre-built components and use visual, drag-and-drop elements for application development and automating workflows. Salesforce Data Cloud is the ultimate low-code/no-code customer data platform and was built in such a way that it's not unusual for Data Cloud users to never use SQL while working in the Data Cloud platform.

Within the Data Cloud platform, SQL code is only required to create Streaming Data Transforms, and not every Data Cloud implementation needs Streaming Data Transforms. In all other instances, Data Cloud does the heavy lifting for the user who only needs to navigate the clicks-no-code user interface. Data democratization makes valuable company data easily accessible and understandable to employees whose roles are typically outside of the traditional IT function. Salesforce Data Cloud leverages this data democratization achievement to help prepare employees for an AI era.

To better leverage Predictive and Generative AI capabilities, Salesforce Data Cloud is integrated with the Salesforce Einstein 1 platform. Data Cloud brings together all data, from first-party to third-party data, and all data types, including unstructured data. The Einstein 1 platform then leverages this rich Data Cloud data, Salesforce CRM data, low-code/no-code development activities, and AI functionality within a single comprehensive platform surrounded by the Einstein Trust Layer. The Einstein Trust Layer includes a set of agreements, security technology, and the data and privacy controls that support AI democratization for employees whose roles are typically outside of the traditional IT function.

Data Cloud provides the building blocks to power the tools that will shift employees' work toward a more conversational and intuitive AI-focused way of uncovering new opportunities and achieving goals faster. The value extracted from Data Cloud helps organizations achieve these important goals, also referred to sometimes as organizational themes. Although not all organizations have the same end goals, here are five strategic ways organizations may benefit from a Data Cloud implementation:

- Increasing operational efficiency
- Strengthening customer relationships
- Unlocking hidden opportunities
- Mitigating risk and enhancement of compliance
- Achieving sustainable growth

To better explain how Data Cloud provides business value that can help organizations achieve these goals, I've created a classification system that describes the steps, components, and activities (Figure 3-1) involved in achieving an organization's goals using Salesforce Data Cloud.

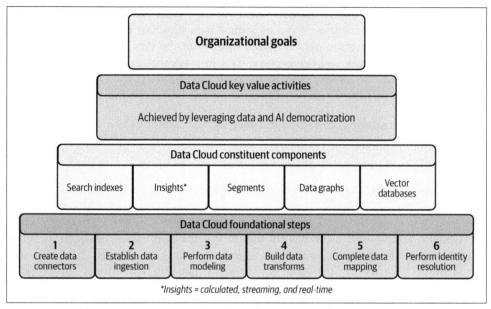

Figure 3-1. Achieving organizational goals with Data Cloud

To begin with, there are six foundational steps required before value can be extracted from Data Cloud. These steps create data connections, establish data ingestion, perform data modeling, build data transforms, complete data mapping, and produce unified profiles with the identity resolution process.

We'll learn more about each of these six required Data Cloud foundational steps in subsequent chapters:

- Step 1: Create data connectors (in Chapters 4 and 6)
- Step 2: Establish data ingestion (in Chapter 6)
- Step 3: Perform data modeling (in Chapter 7)
- Step 4: Build data transforms (in Chapter 8)
- Step 5: Complete data mapping (in Chapter 9)
- Step 6: Perform identity resolution (in Chapter 10)

The last foundational step, identity resolution, results in a Unified Individual profile that goes to the very heart of Data Cloud's purpose. As we learned in Chapter 1, customer data problems often make it impossible to get a complete view of the customer.

That's where a CDP like Salesforce Data Cloud comes in handy. Data Cloud can build the SSOT view that gives us the complete view of the customer.

As part of an organization's first-party data strategy, Data Cloud stitches together a 360-degree view of the customer from individual data silos. But it isn't enough to have that SSOT view of the customer. We need to explore the data, extract insights, and package up the customer 360-degree view data in ways that can be acted on in real time, when needed. We achieve these by building Data Cloud constituent components. We'll explore several Data Cloud constituent components in later chapters:

- Calculated, streaming, and real-time insights (in Chapter 11)
- Segments (in Chapter 12)
- Data graphs (in Chapter 13)
- Vector databases (in Chapter 13)
- Search indexes (in Chapter 13)

Constituent components are certainly useful, but the real value comes from being able to leverage those streaming insights, segments, data graphs, vector databases, and search indexes for use in key value activities. In that way, constituent components lead to value creation.

This chapter's main focus is to give a brief overview of the various value activities that we'll explore in detail in later chapters. As noted in Chapter 2, whether any particular value activity can truly be acted upon in near real time will depend in part on whether the source data used for the value category is ingested in a stream or batch fashion.

Some of the new key value activities have been built by Salesforce to support the Data Cloud platform as an open and extensible platform that can be connected to and integrated with trusted partners within the Salesforce Zero Copy Partner Network. The Zero Copy Partner Network makes it possible to connect and act on any data within the Partner Network without duplicating sources. Zero copy technology partners include Amazon, Databricks, Google, Microsoft, and Snowflake. We'll learn more about the Partner Network in Chapter 13.

The following list includes 12 Data Cloud key value activities and the chapters in which we discuss them:

- Data Cloud enrichments (in Chapter 11)
- GenAI: LLM grounding resource with structured data (in Chapter 13)
- GenAI: augment LLM search with data graphs for near real-time searches (in Chapter 13)
- GenAI: augment LLM search with vector databases for unstructured data (in Chapter 13)

- Data actions and Data Cloud–triggered flows (in Chapter 11)
- Activation of segments (in Chapter 12)
- Predictive AI ML insights (in Chapter 13)
- Analytics and intelligent data visualization (in Appendix B)
- Unified consent repository (in Chapter 7)
- Programmatic extraction of data (in Chapter 11)
- External platform data sharing (in Chapter 13)
- GenAI: linking and using custom LLMs (in Chapter 13)

You'll notice that 4 of the 12 activities are related to GenAI, and one makes use of bidirectional data sharing capabilities with external data platforms. These are brand-new Salesforce capabilities, and, of course, they're built to work with Data Cloud. It is possible to use Salesforce CRM data as an LLM grounding resource, but the other three GenAI capabilities and the bidirectional data sharing require access to Data Cloud functionality and/or Data Cloud data.

As mentioned, you'll notice in Figure 3-1 that before reaching the Data Cloud key value activity level, there are foundational steps to be taken and constituent components that must be built. These steps are detailed in later chapters, but their introduction here speaks to their importance. Extracting value from Salesforce Data Cloud depends on the completion of these foundational steps and the building of constituent components.

Building Your Data Cloud Vocabulary

As with any new technology platform, especially one as comprehensive as Salesforce Data Cloud, you'll need to understand some key terminology to speak the language. It's important we use the same common terms when referring to the way Salesforce Data Cloud operates and generates value.

If you're an engineer, developer, administrator, or architect, you may be part of a team responsible for Data Cloud implementation. If so, you'll need to communicate with your team as well as with stakeholders outside of your team. You could be a business analyst responsible for gathering requirements that need to be communicated to the implementation team, or you might be responsible for preparing an evaluation of the return on investment (ROI) for a Data Cloud project where it's necessary to communicate with several others to understand the art of the possible for Data Cloud for your organization. Communicating among teams requires a common vocabulary.

You were introduced to some new Data Cloud terms in Chapter 2, and here are more key terms that we use in this chapter to help you build your Data Cloud vocabulary.

Key Terms Used in This Chapter

- Activation
- Bring Your Own Lake (BYOL)
- Bring Your Own Large Language Model (BYOLLM)
- Bring Your Own Model (BYOM)
- Calculated insight (CI)
- Calculated Insights object (CI object)
- Data action
- Data graph
- Data lake object (DLO)
- Data model object (DMO)
- Data source object (DSO)

- Einstein 1 platform
- Einstein Copilot
- Harmonization
- Identity resolution
- Model Builder
- Predictive Insight
- Prompt Builder
- Segmentation
- Streaming insight
- Unified profile
- Visualization insight

It's OK if you don't fully understand what each of these terms means as you go through this chapter; the intent is to introduce you to new terms that you'll come across in more detail in subsequent chapters. Becoming familiar with some key terms now will help you gain a better appreciation of what Data Cloud can do. You can find a comprehensive list of key terms and their definitions in the Glossary.

Value Creation Process

Data Cloud offers a rich set of features businesses can use to extract value for their organization. Data Cloud uses out-of-the-box (OOTB) connectors to ingest data from disparate sources that can be used to unify customer data at scale. This harmonized and unified data can enrich CRM data and can be used to create segments and predictive insights, all while providing the ability to trace back to original sources. Data Cloud also allows you to create more automated and connected experiences for your internal team as well as for your customers.

There are a variety of Data Cloud capabilities you can use and many different ways to build out these capabilities in your Salesforce Data Cloud instance. How your organization will specifically use Data Cloud to extract value is dependent on how many disparate sources you have, the volume of your data, where you are now in your data democratization journey, and many other factors.

Organizations implementing Data Cloud most often do so because their data exists in multiple systems of record, including in external data sources and within various Salesforce platforms. As a result, it's likely that data dependencies exist, making it difficult and time-consuming to implement complex Data Cloud use cases quickly or implement multiple use cases at once. Therefore, it's important that we evaluate these Data Cloud value categories separately as well as holistically. For one thing, we need to consider that some of the categories have the potential to bring more value to certain functional roles than others. You'll want to make sure the people in those roles have an opportunity to weigh in on which use cases are their top priorities.

For first-time Data Cloud implementations, it's best practice for your team to focus on key use cases with a quick path to value that can be accomplished with the data you have today. Thus, your organization will need to prioritize use cases by selecting from the various value categories. Understanding the value a particular use case can bring to the various teams will help you more easily identify high-impact, low-implementation effort use cases.

Realize that Data Cloud has the potential to have a big impact on the entire organization and that therefore it's important to take a holistic view of the Data Cloud value creation process. Understanding that holistic view of how Data Cloud operates and what it has to offer has effects on how it's introduced into your organization.

It's also crucial that stakeholders understand that there are six required foundational steps they must take before constituent components (Figure 3-2) can be developed and value can be extracted from Data Cloud—they can't just "plug and play."

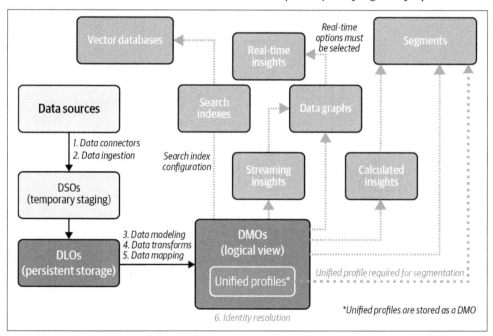

Figure 3-2. Data Cloud foundational steps and constituent components

As we review this diagram, more things become very apparent. For one, you'll notice that DMOs are the source of all constituent components and thus the source of all downstream value activities. *Unified profiles* are a special type of DMO that results from the identity resolution process, and DMOs are some of the basic data storage objects within Data Cloud.

In Chapter 2, we discussed these DSOs and learned that Salesforce manages the underlying architecture for all Data Cloud storage. Within the Data Cloud user interface, DLO and DMO metadata can be managed by Salesforce users. DLOs, created from DSOs, are mapped to standard and custom DMOs automatically as well as manually in the UI. With the appropriate access, Data Cloud users can add any new custom fields and create new custom DMOs needed to complete the data modeling, data transformation, and data mapping processes.

Note that you'll first need to complete these foundational steps (Figure 3-3) to use DMOs. The first five foundational steps are absolutely required before any constituent components can be created and value can be extracted from Salesforce Data Cloud; these five steps are not optional. A sixth foundational step, identity resolution, is required for both segmentation and related list enrichments, and it is also important for many of the other value activities.

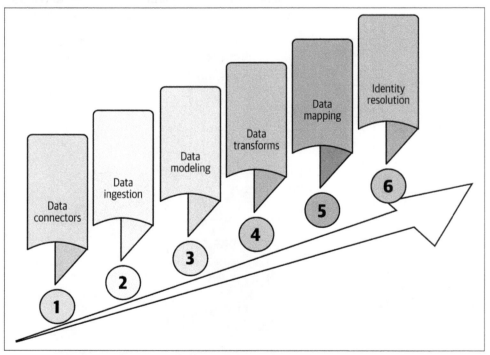

Figure 3-3. Foundational steps required to create Data Cloud value

The importance of DMOs cannot be overstated. They are the building blocks for all constituent components and ultimately all downstream value activities. The value extracted from Data Cloud will only be as good as the data in your DMOs, so the time spent planning for the data modeling, data transformations, and data mapping processes will be time well spent because it's difficult to modify or reverse these processes once implemented.

Data modeling, data transforms, and data mapping are covered in detail in Chapters 7 and 9, respectively. Chapters 4 and 6 will help guide you through setting up data connectors and data ingestion processes. After completing the initial five required foundational steps to create relevant DMOs, you'll want to create unified profiles through the identity resolution process, which is detailed in Chapter 10.

Creating unified profiles is important because identity resolution, resulting in unified profiles, is required for segmentation and related list enrichments. To accomplish segmentation in Data Cloud, the identity resolution process is required because segments can be created only on profile objects. In addition, unified profiles are often the inputs into other constituent components and ultimately into downstream value activities.

DMOs are used for constituent components, including those we use to create calculated and streaming insights, build segments, and create data graphs and vector databases. Ultimately, these constituent components will provide inputs needed to extract value in the form of Data Cloud enrichments, data actions, ML predictions, and more. We'll learn about creating insights, building segments, and creating data graphs and vector databases in later chapters.

Data Cloud Key Value Activities

As we learned in Chapter 1, many companies are in need of a first-party data strategy solution that can benefit from a CDP. Salesforce Data Cloud is an obvious choice for many organizations, and not surprisingly, Salesforce was named a leader (*https:// oreil.ly/q4xdP*) in the inaugural 2024 Gartner Magic Quadrant for Customer Data Platforms in recognition of its Data Cloud platform.

For many reasons, Data Cloud inherently enables organizations (especially those that already use Salesforce CRM) to shorten time to value. Data Cloud incorporates Salesforce prebuilt connectors to make data ingestion quick and easy, while Salesforce standard metadata, encompassing data modeling best practices, is native to the platform and ready to go immediately. Salesforce has a built-in trust layer for security, and the Data Cloud user interface is already familiar to Salesforce end users.

Among Salesforce's strengths are its multicloud capabilities. Thus, current Salesforce CRM customers can often take advantage of their existing Salesforce investment by leveraging Data Cloud as their CDP of choice. Once implemented, Data Cloud can provide business value in many ways (Figure 3-4).

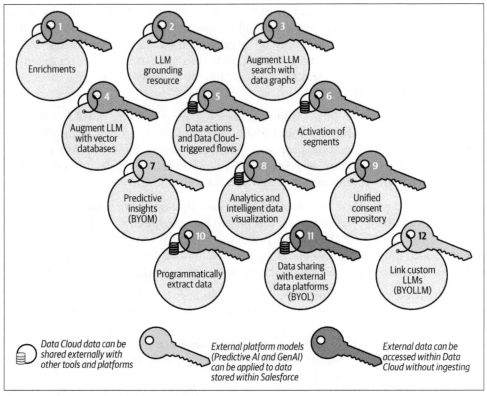

Figure 3-4. Data Cloud key value activities

Throughout this book, we'll dive deep into learning how to set up Data Cloud connectors and data streams to ingest external data sources and Salesforce Data Cloud source data into Data Cloud. We'll learn how to leverage AI capabilities within the Salesforce platform, in the flow of work, using Einstein Studio-invoked prompts and Einstein Copilot. We'll also discover ways to use Data Cloud data externally through data actions, activation of segments, analytics business intelligence tools and platforms, programmatic extracts of Data Cloud data, and bidirectional data sharing.

As we discuss Data Cloud key value activities, some things will become more obvious. Notably, we'll get a much deeper understanding of how Data Cloud is an open and extensible platform. Data Cloud uses BYOL bidirectional data sharing capabilities and leverages the Einstein Studio BYOM and BYOLLM to take advantage of other platforms and tools in which some organizations have already made investments.

Let's start by looking at Data Cloud enrichments, a key value activity type that should be familiar to most Salesforce users.

Data Cloud Enrichments

Much first-party Salesforce CRM data is stored in the Sales and Service clouds, which include Person Account, Contact, Lead, Opportunity, and Case objects. Data Cloud can enrich this CRM information by surfacing selected CIs or other fields from DMOs. The purpose of CIs is to aggregate DMO data or derive scores from the data.

At this time, Data Cloud enrichments are available to place on Account, Contact, and Lead objects using the Object Manager. However, it will soon be possible to enrich the following Salesforce objects within Setup: Account, Asset, Case, Contact, Financial Account, Fleet, Individual, Lead, Location, Opportunity, Vehicle, Work Order, and Work Order Line Item.

There are two different ways you can use Data Cloud to enrich CRM Person Account, Contact, and Lead data. The first way is by surfacing customer engagement data as a *related list*, in which you're able to show the information and interactions from several different source systems or business units from supported DMOs. For example, the related list enrichment could display Marketing Cloud email engagement for a contact via a Data Cloud related list.

The other way is by using a copy field enrichment to surface a specific field value from either a DMO or CI object. For example, you could surface a CI object that provides an individual customer's lifetime value score calculated using aggregated data from multiple source systems.

 ### Cost Impact

Data Cloud copy field enrichments use a batch job to sync data between Data Cloud and your CRM org records. Data Cloud related list enrichments also incur querying costs when accessed in Salesforce CRM, and this is different from other related lists in Salesforce CRM, most of which do not incur querying costs.

As we'll see in Chapter 11, Data Cloud enrichments are created easily from within the Salesforce Setup Object Manager using the DMOs and CI objects created in Data Cloud. For data to be available in DMOs and to be used in CIs, the foundational steps need to be completed.

Using Data Cloud DMOs and CI objects to create Data Cloud enrichments is a way to get a quick win from your Data Cloud implementation early in the process. Other Data Cloud value categories may have a much greater impact on the ROI of your Data Cloud implementation, but they will likely require more planning and effort. One such example is building the necessary Data Cloud framework to support the increased productivity and improved accuracy that can be achieved with GenAI functionality.

Large Language Model Grounding Resource for Structured Data

GenAI brings to organizations the possibility of automating human work and improving the customer and employee experience. Implementing AI isn't easy, though. It often takes a great deal of time, money, and specialized expertise. Fortunately for Salesforce users, there are AI tools built right into Salesforce so that users can leverage AI capabilities in the normal flow of work. Salesforce makes AI democratization possible through its Einstein 1 platform.

Salesforce makes it easy to give generative tools automatic access to Salesforce CRM and Data Cloud data by giving users the option of selecting that data as a resource in a prompt. Using Prompt Builder's "clicks, not code" UI, it's easy to incorporate field values from Data Cloud when building a prompt to draft personalized emails, for example. The concept of hydrating the prompt with an organization's specific business context and customer data is also known as *grounding*. Don't worry if you're not quite sure how Salesforce Prompt Builder and GenAI capabilities work. We'll cover the Einstein 1 platform in detail in Chapter 13.

Augmenting Large Language Model Search with Data Graphs and Vector Databases

One of the things we'll learn in Chapter 13 is just how critical business data is for an organization's AI strategy. Within Data Cloud, vector databases and data graphs are powerful constituent components full of rich business data. They are used to provide context to an Einstein Studio prompt.

Vector databases in Data Cloud allow you to harness the combined power of unstructured and structured data. *Unstructured data* includes PDFs, text files, social media content, sensor data, photographs, and audio files. The majority of data by volume is unstructured data, and so its importance cannot be overstated. We'll learn about vector databases in Chapter 13.

We'll also learn about *data graphs*, which are precalculated or materialized views of your Data Cloud data that make it possible to use your Data Cloud data in near real time. Using data graphs and vector databases to augment your Einstein Studio prompts can be achieved with Einstein Copilot GenAI assistant. There are also other ways to invoke prebuilt Einstein Studio prompts (Figure 3-5) and Einstein Copilot standard and custom actions, which we'll explore in more detail in Chapter 13.

We previously stated that business data is critical to an AI strategy. Data matters. It matters a lot. It's good to remember that a successful Data Cloud implementation is dependent on completing the foundational steps well so that the right amount of quality data is available to power the Einstein 1 platform GenAI capabilities. Those same foundational steps needed to build data graphs and vector databases are also needed for other Data Cloud key value activities, like data actions.

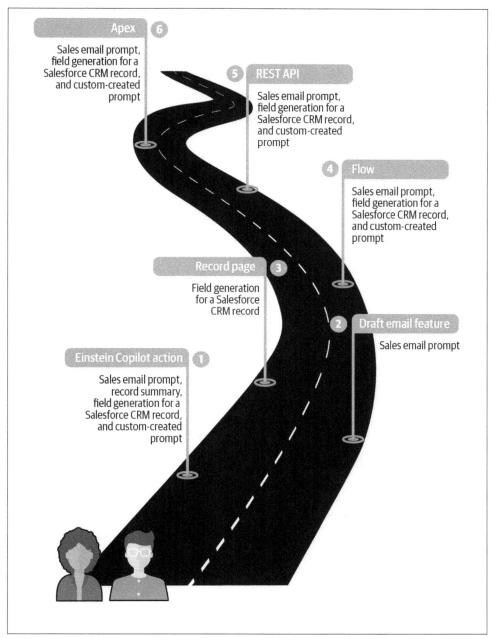

Apex 6

Sales email prompt,
field generation for a
Salesforce CRM record,
and custom-created
prompt

REST API 5

Sales email prompt,
field generation for a
Salesforce CRM record,
and custom-created
prompt

Flow 4

Sales email prompt,
field generation for a
Salesforce CRM record,
and custom-created
prompt

Record page 3

Field generation
for a Salesforce
CRM record

Draft email feature 2

Sales email prompt

Einstein Copilot action 1

Sales email prompt,
record summary,
field generation for a
Salesforce CRM record,
and custom-created
prompt

Figure 3-5. Multiple ways to invoke an Einstein Studio prompt within the flow of work

Data Actions and Data Cloud–Triggered Flows

Data actions are events sent by Data Cloud to predefined targets whenever certain conditions are met. Data action targets include platform events, webhooks, and Salesforce Marketing Cloud. The data action targets then use the events to trigger their own downstream business processes.

Both calculated and streaming insights can be used as inputs to a data action (Figure 3-6). When data actions are powered by streaming insights, it's possible to have near real-time results. For example, a customer service representative can receive a data action alerting them to a customer who viewed troubleshooting pages on a company's website before contacting the service department.

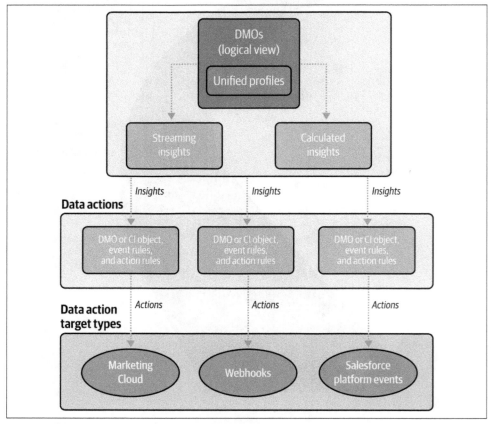

Figure 3-6. Data actions are powered by insights

Data actions will be described in more detail in Chapter 11. An important thing to know now is that data actions are very powerful. For example, a data action can send one individual at a time into a marketing journey, based on a change in a DMO or CI object value. That is the ultimate in 1:1 segmentation and personalization. Of course, groups of customers can still be sent into a marketing journey by activation of segments.

Activation of Segments

Activation of segments is one of the most common and powerful use cases for Data Cloud. Data Cloud can leverage a great deal of data to create segments that offer a personalized customer experience. You'll remember that identity resolution must be undertaken to create unified profiles because unified profiles are required for Data Cloud segmentation. Another interesting aspect of Data Cloud segmentation is that it's possible to accept ML inputs and receive segments from Tableau into Data Cloud (Figure 3-7).

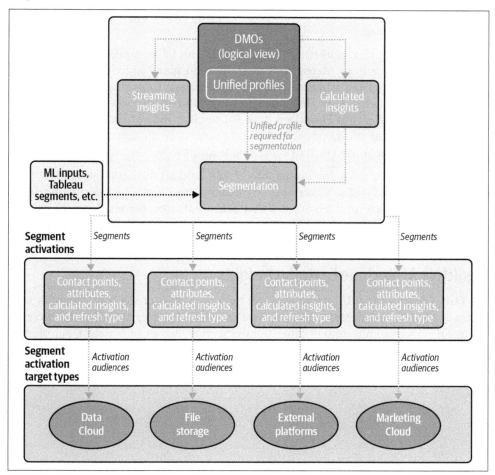

Figure 3-7. Activation of segments

We explore segmentation and activation in Chapter 12, where we'll cover advanced segmentation options like Einstein lookalike segments, nested segments, and waterfall segments. The Data Cloud segmentation capabilities are powerful today and are expected to become even more robust and refined in future releases.

Segments created in Data Cloud are frequently activated to Salesforce Marketing Cloud. Activated Data Cloud segments automatically create Marketing Cloud data extensions, which are then used to send customers into Marketing Cloud journeys. A *marketing journey* manages all the stages of the customer lifecycle and thus can be connected to many different marketing campaigns and promotions.

Other possible activation targets include external platforms like LinkedIn and Google Ads, and file storage targets like Amazon S3, Secure File Transfer Protocol (SFTP), Microsoft Azure Blob, and GCS. In addition, Data Cloud itself can be an activation target used for publishing to other Salesforce apps, like Loyalty Management Cloud and Commerce Cloud.

Sending someone into a Marketing Cloud journey can be accomplished using either activations or data actions. *Activations* typically send many individuals at one time into a marketing journey, whereas *data actions* send one individual at a time into a journey, based on a change in DMO or CI object value. As we saw in "Data Actions and Data Cloud–Triggered Flows" on page 64, sending individuals into a journey is only one of the many things possible with data actions. In contrast, activation's main purpose is to send segments to activation targets for inclusion in marketing journeys.

As mentioned, there are many inputs into Data Cloud segmentation, including unified profiles, other DMOs, CIs, streaming insights, and segment information from Tableau. You'll notice from Figure 3-7 that ML predictions are also used to help in Data Cloud segmentation. In addition to being useful for segmentation, ML predictions have a great many uses and benefits.

Predictive AI Machine Learning Insights

For Data Cloud users, ML predictions can help marketers create more relevant segments to help increase conversion, improve cross-selling opportunities, and increase the impact of discounts, among other things. Service teams can benefit from predictive insights by using the information to reduce the likelihood of escalation, increase net promoter scores, and reduce the risk of customer churn.

Within the Data Cloud application, you can leverage Model Builder capabilities. *Model Builder* is part of the Salesforce Einstein 1 platform, which gives you the option to build your own ML model from scratch. Alternatively, you can take advantage of connected models already built by data science teams using Amazon SageMaker, Databricks, or Google Vertex AI. These are often referred to as the Data Cloud Bring Your Own Model (BYOM) capabilities. Whether the predictive model is built within Salesforce or an external model like Amazon SageMaker is used, the model makes use of data stored in Data Cloud.

ML predictions created using Salesforce Model Builder can be used as inputs into segmentation. Predictions from Model Builder can also be useful to other teams within your organization. One example is the finance team, which can benefit from predictive insights that include Data Cloud data and other enterprise data. Some of those use cases include the ability to better forecast revenue, reduce costs, maximize margins, and reduce compliance risk.

The various teams within an organization often undertake efforts to understand ML predictions and their downstream implications by using business intelligence (BI) tools and analytics platforms to create visually appealing charts and dashboards.

Analytics and Intelligent Data Visualization

Analytics tools and platforms provide visualization insights and other ways to discover and interpret patterns in data. Specifically, there exists a Salesforce CRM Analytics application, accessible within the Salesforce core platform. It's also possible to use external BI platforms like Tableau and Microsoft Power BI, and there are also Salesforce native intelligent apps that can be used to surface certain insights quickly, using OOTB capabilities.

For example, Salesforce Segment Intelligence offers a way for marketers to measure and increase the impact of their marketing activity (Figure 3-8). Segment Intelligence combines Data Cloud and CRM Analytics capabilities to provide insights into segments across multiple channels, engagement types, and conversion sources. Once set up, Segment Intelligence can help improve an organization's ROI with actionable performance insights to leverage more relevant audiences and campaigns.

Figure 3-8. Segment Intelligence dashboard

There are a variety of strategic reasons why an organization might choose to use a particular CRM Analytics tool or more than one platform for visualization insights. We'll not be providing comparisons of or justification for specific BI tools in this book. Our discussions will be limited primarily to the CRM Analytics app, Tableau, and Segment Intelligence platforms because those are Salesforce's analytics and visualization products.

In addition to the specialized intelligent apps like Segment Intelligence and Amazon Insights, organizations frequently use analytics tools to aggregate and analyze segmentation effectiveness. It can be especially helpful to utilize Tableau to combine customer data with external data, like product or sales data for analytical purposes. It's also possible to analyze Data Cloud data spaces in Tableau to gain insights into brands or channels.

In addition to segment information, CRM Analytics and Tableau are both excellent tools for visualizing CIs and Data Cloud DMO information. Strategists frequently use analytics at the aggregate level, whereas some of the other teams make greater use of more granular, individual customer data and insights. In summary, analytics and intelligent data visualizations give organizations the information they need to make better strategic decisions and increase the efficiency and effectiveness of their marketing, sales, and service teams.

Unified Consent Repository

Marketing, sales, and service teams should be in touch with customers in all the right ways because sending unwanted communications to customers and prospects isn't just poor business practice—it's also against the law. It's easy to violate privacy and anti-spam laws when you don't have a complete view of the customer, and disparate customer opt-out preferences are not shared among data silos.

Data Cloud can help by aggregating consent from many disconnected sources into a *unified consent repository* to help create a more cohesive customer preference data strategy. This is made possible by leveraging the Salesforce Consent Data Model. More information about the Consent Data Model is included in Chapter 7.

In addition to the standard data model that supports aggregating consent, it's also possible to use Salesforce Flow actions to bring consent data into Data Cloud with *ingestion on demand* capabilities. This ensures you have the most up-to-date consent preferences within Data Cloud. More information about ingestion on demand using Flow actions can be found in "Ingestion API Connector" on page 174.

Programmatic Extraction of Data

Sometimes, it's necessary to programmatically extract data or metadata from a source so that it can be used in another tool or within another platform. Extracting this information programmatically gives you much greater control over how and what you extract. For example, you can use a Profile API to specifically look up and search customer profile-related information in Data Cloud that can be included in your external web or mobile apps. It's also possible to use a Python connector to fetch data from Data Cloud in pandas DataFrames. Chapter 11 discusses how to programmatically extract data and metadata from Salesforce Data Cloud.

Bidirectional Data Sharing with External Data Platforms

We've just discussed how DMOs, CIs, segmentations, and other Data Cloud data can be used for creating insights and other purposes. We've also mentioned that the data can be programmatically extracted for use outside of Data Cloud. In addition, that same data can be shared externally without needing to transmit a copy of the data. Sharing Data Cloud data with external platforms is also known as *using data-out capabilities.*

Certain external data platforms like Snowflake, Google BigQuery, and Amazon Redshift can receive DMO data, insights, segmentation data, data graphs, and more from Salesforce Data Cloud via data shares. These data shares can be used outside of Salesforce in trusted ways, including leveraging Data Cloud data to create more personalized user experiences on a customized application.

Data from external platforms can also be shared to Data Cloud using *data-in* capabilities. This externally shared data can be joined with Salesforce Data Cloud data without you ever needing to move the data.

This bidirectional sharing is sometimes referred to as the BYOL capabilities in Data Cloud. It's made possible because of the unique Salesforce Data Cloud architecture and the collaboration with trusted technology partners like Google and Snowflake. This is welcome news to organizations that have already made investments in these other platforms.

The data sharing approach means that organizations can access real-time data in a secure and governed way across various platforms, thus minimizing risks, costs, and challenges from traditional extract, transform, and load (ETL) methods. Data stored in external platforms is made accessible in Salesforce Data Cloud through federated access, and data stored in Data Cloud is made accessible in external platforms via data shares. We'll discuss more details about bidirectional data sharing in Chapter 13.

Linking Custom Large Language Models

Using Salesforce Model Builder within Salesforce Data Cloud, it's possible to link your own custom LLMs from an external platform. Examples include Microsoft Azure OpenAI and IBM watsonx.

This new BYOLLM approach gives you the ability to configure new LLM models and test prompts in a playground environment before deploying a model to production. More information about BYOLLM can be found in Chapter 13.

Other Key Value Activities

We've described 12 key value activities briefly in this chapter, and we'll dive deeper into each of those activities in future chapters. Business value achievable with Salesforce Data Cloud isn't limited to these 12 value activities, though. For example, you can access Data Cloud objects when using SOQL in your Apex coding after you create the necessary relationships. It's even possible to manage field- and record-level access when using Apex with Data Cloud objects.

Data Cloud is an open and extensible platform that brings with it many options to leverage constituent components to build new and innovative value activities. As the Salesforce Data Cloud platform continues to evolve, we can expect more constituent components upon which to build more value. Salesforce Data Cloud continues to be an innovative and quickly evolving platform.

What Data Cloud Is Not

We've reviewed 12 different ways to extract value from Cloud, but it's also important to call out a few things from previous sections and explain what Data Cloud is not.

Previously, we described how we could analyze Data Cloud data using BI platforms and tools to create visualization insights. It's important to note that these BI tools are external to Salesforce Data Cloud. CRM Analytics is accessible as an app within the Salesforce CRM core platform, but it's a distinctly separate platform. Data Cloud is not a BI platform, although it's possible to use Data Cloud data within BI platforms and tools like CRM Analytics, Tableau, and Power BI.

Data Cloud includes several prebuilt connectors, making it possible to ingest data from many sources, and it offers some data transformation capabilities within the Data Cloud UI. However, Data Cloud is neither an ETL tool nor a data cleansing tool. It's also not a backup and disaster recovery platform.

Data Cloud is not a consent management platform, but it can aggregate consent from disparate sources. Data Cloud can also handle data deletion requests. Data deletion requests submitted using the Consent API delete the specified Individual entity and any entities for which a relationship has been defined between that entity's identifying attribute and the Individual ID attribute.

Importantly, Data Cloud creates a unified profile rather than a golden record typically found in a master data management (MDM) platform. Data Cloud is not an MDM platform, although it can work alongside one.

Data Cloud is a near real-time CDP that can provide value to several different functional teams within an organization. In the next section, we'll explore how various functional roles can extract value from Data Cloud.

Value by Functional Roles

Most organizations create internal teams based on functional roles like marketing, sales, service, support, operations, data science, strategy, and R&D. Individuals who perform these roles may realize value from within the Data Cloud application, if they've been granted access. Alternatively, they might not have direct access to Data Cloud but instead could be the downstream recipients of Data Cloud value. Examples of some downstream value categories include Data Cloud enrichments, predictive insights, and analytics visualization insights. Thus, direct access to the Salesforce Data Cloud application in the Salesforce user interface is not a requirement for receiving value from the Data Cloud platform.

Here, we're not focused on access to the Data Cloud app or the specifics of how to set up the Salesforce Data Cloud architecture. That will come later. As we'll learn in later chapters, access to Data Cloud is granted based on personas rather than decided by functional role. For example, Data Cloud personas include Data Cloud Administrators, Data Cloud users, marketing administrators, marketing managers, marketing specialists, and data aware specialists. As an example, the various members of the marketing team might be mapped to different personas and thus have different Data Cloud accesses granted.

Within Salesforce, personas are based on the general tasks users perform in their roles. An important consideration in describing these tasks is to define the granular level of data needed for that persona to accomplish its tasks. The *granular level* is the level of detail at which data is collected, analyzed, and used. Data with a low granular level would have fewer pieces of information, whereas data with a high granular level would have more.

Summary or aggregated data, like total sales by region, is an example of data with a low granular level. Total annual sales for the entire organization would have an even lower granular level. Individual customer sales records are examples of data with a very high granular level.

Members of various functional teams might require different levels of granular data to accomplish their tasks. Therefore, there are certain value categories that may be more useful than others for certain roles because some of the value categories offer value at a more granular level.

Value at the Highest Granular Level

Data Cloud enrichments, GenAI capabilities, data actions, activation of segments, and Predictive AI ML insights surface the necessary data for tasks requiring high granular level data access. For example, in previous sections, we learned that Data Cloud enrichments are displayed on individual Person Account, Contact, or Lead records. Data actions trigger actions based on an individual record change, and activations of segments are used to create more personalized experiences and journeys for many individual customers at the same time. Finally, ML insights can be used to help predict individual customer behavior.

Data Cloud enrichments, data actions, activation of segments, and Predictive AI ML insights provide granular level data access. In addition to those four key value activities, both of the GenAI key value activities described earlier provide granular level data access. This granular level data access allows employees to efficiently create more effective interactions with individual customers, and the GenAI key value activities are powered by AI democratization tools like Einstein Prompt Builder and Einstein Copilot, which we'll learn more about in Chapter 13.

Within an organization, various roles are the recipients of Data Cloud value that is accessible to them right in the flow of their work. However, the marketing, sales, and service teams (Figure 3-9) likely benefit most from key value activities powered by Data Cloud, especially for value created at a granular level. This makes sense since these teams are the ones that interact most with individual customers on a regular basis.

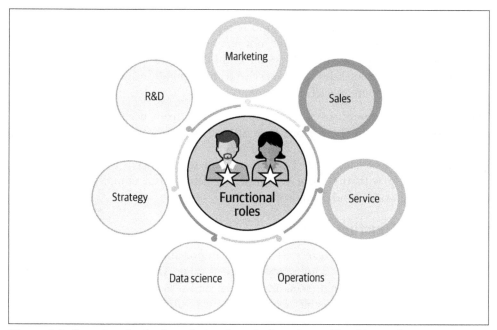

Figure 3-9. Functional roles benefitting directly from Data Cloud key value activities

ML predictions are a unique category. The outputs of the ML predictions, such as propensity to churn, are used by marketing, sales, and service teams, but complex ML prediction models are frequently created by data scientists. Interestingly, there are many Salesforce Einstein models built natively into the platform that can be accessed by marketing, sales, and service teams, and with the Model Builder drag-and-drop functionality, it's very possible for these teams to build their own predictive models.

In general, marketing, sales, and service teams make the most use of granular level data, but some members of those teams may use aggregate level data in addition to, or instead of, highly granular data. Aggregate level data is at a lower granular level, but often, there's the ability to access more detailed data when needed. For example, many analytics and visualization tools allow users to easily drill down to more detailed data.

Value at the Aggregate Level

Strategists and the research and development (R&D) team benefit greatly from the visualization insights created with analytics tools like Tableau and CRM Analytics. The marketing, sales, and service teams frequently make use of visualization insights at the aggregate level but also benefit from being able to drill down to reach higher levels of granularity when desired.

We've learned that Salesforce Data Cloud is a powerful and complex platform that yields value for the entire organization, not just for those few who have direct access to the Data Cloud app within Salesforce. Employees who benefit most from Data Cloud include marketers, sales teams, service teams, operations teams, data scientists, strategists, and members of R&D departments.

There are many different ways in which employees from across the organization access customer data in the performance of their job, at both the granular and the aggregate level. In addition to the critical jobs those teams do, there are two other important roles to be discussed. The information technology (IT) and data governance teams help with the more technical, regulatory, and compliance aspects of building out the Data Cloud framework.

Other Critical Functional Roles

The IT and data governance teams are two very important functional roles that play a critical part in getting Data Cloud ready to extract value. The IT team usually consists of developers, architects, engineers, and testers, and it is common to have IT team members who are knowledgeable about a variety of different technology tools and platforms.

Data Cloud implementations will likely need to include several people from the IT team, especially because many of the data sources ingested by Data Cloud come from sources external to Salesforce. The IT team will probably have the most knowledge about those external sources, and its members will also possess the skill sets needed to help with data ingestion, data transformations, and data modeling.

The data governance team manages data-related risks for the entire enterprise and on all platforms used by the organization. Governance professionals ensure the right information flows securely to the right people. As part of its role, the data governance team is responsible for ensuring compliance with data-related standards and regulations.

The data governance team often includes data stewards who manage enterprise data assets, enforce naming convention standards, and maintain definitions of business terms. Effective data governance processes result in better data quality, which ultimately makes compliance easier to achieve. The data governance team is usually separate from the data security team, which is responsible for protecting organizational data against threats.

It's recommended that you involve the IT and data governance teams early in the planning process for Data Cloud implementation because of the critical roles they'll play. Soliciting their feedback and getting their buy-in is as important as getting buy-in from those teams that'll be utilizing value extracted from Data Cloud.

Change Management Process: A Necessary Ingredient

The marketing, sales, service, operations, data science, strategy, and R&D teams will be recipients of value created as a result of Data Cloud implementation. While this is an exciting opportunity for an organization, it's important to remember that change is often disconcerting to people, even when the change is expected to bring about positive results. Getting ready for a first-time Data Cloud implementation project often means you'll need to leverage a change management process to guide and support affected individuals.

As part of the change management process, you'll want to get internal alignment with product owners and decision makers. Make sure you have the right team in place for discussions to ensure clarity and agreement on the priorities and objectives. Data Cloud implementation discussions should involve administrators of existing Salesforce Clouds and external platforms to ensure that the proper domain expertise is represented. This is especially important if your organization uses several Salesforce Clouds or stores data on external platforms.

A primary benefit of change management is ensuring the success of new initiatives, like Data Cloud implementations. That's because a successful digital transformation implementation takes time and it isn't without risk. Identifying potential roadblocks early and mitigating risk can help reduce the amount of time required for implementation and will minimize the impact on people, so gaining buy-in from those who will be affected should be an important goal.

Data Cloud users will need to be trained on how to use Data Cloud functionality. You'll also want to consider the post-implementation tasks needed to support new Data Cloud users. This might include updating process documentation and user guides, and it might also mean adjusting metrics and changing reward structures.

Value of a Salesforce Implementation Partner

A first-time Data Cloud implementation will probably involve and affect many different teams and individuals within your organization. Although your organization likely has Salesforce experts on staff at this time, it's unlikely they've been through a Data Cloud implementation. First-time Data Cloud implementations include distinct stages, each of which needs to be planned in detail and builds on the previous stage.

First-Time Data Cloud Implementations Require Much Expertise

The completion of foundational steps and the building of constituent components needed for a first-time Data Cloud implementation are complicated and require a great deal of expertise. It's especially difficult to undo or redo the foundational steps. Therefore, when it comes to Data Cloud implementation planning, you should carefully consider everything before deciding whether to go it alone or bring on an implementation partner to help you navigate the process.

Organizations frequently struggle to figure out how to best approach a Data Cloud implementation, given the many different ways to extract value using Data Cloud. Discovery sessions can help identify relevant use cases, but you'll also want to prioritize the Data Cloud use cases and start with a high-impact, low-effort use case.

Salesforce implementation partners have experience with well-architected frameworks for Data Cloud, to help architect solutions with future costs in mind. This is especially important for a Data Cloud implementation because Data Cloud fees are calculated differently from traditional Salesforce costs. Salesforce Data Cloud has consumption-based pricing, rather than the usual license fees per user model.

Hiring an implementation partner incurs a cost, but there are many benefits that can help to offset those costs. Importantly, the Salesforce consultants working for implementation partners can help shorten your time to value by identifying and prioritizing your Data Cloud use cases. In addition, Salesforce consultants can train your end users on how to effectively use Data Cloud features to extract the most value from the platform. A Salesforce implementation partner can also help guide your technical teams in learning how to expand on a first-time Data Cloud implementation to support additional use cases.

User Stories and Project Management

Most Salesforce implementations are undertaken using the *Agile methodology*, which is an iterative approach to delivering a project. Agile project management focuses on continuous releases that incorporate users' feedback. Using the Agile methodology, user stories are created, and the purpose of user stories is to explain how a software feature will provide value to a group of people. A user story is normally written in the following manner: "As a [persona], I want to [action] so that [benefit]." Here are some examples:

- As a *service agent*, I want to provide *proactive, personalized customer service* to my customers based on a 360-degree view of my customer so that I can decrease case resolution time and increase customer satisfaction (CSAT) scores.

- As a *marketer*, I want to build an actionable unified profile for *segmentation and activation* so that I can achieve faster segmentation and increase conversions.

- As a *sales professional*, I want to be able to *cross-sell and identify whitespace opportunities across my lines of business* so that I can increase cross-selling and upselling opportunities, improve forecasting, and increase customer lifetime value.

- As a *data governance specialist*, I want to build a unified profile of customers for *aggregating consent preferences* so that I can ensure our organization is in compliance with laws and regulations.

- As a *strategist*, I want to build a unified profile of my customers and *deliver instant, actionable insights* so that faster insights are available to the teams.

Creating user stories is important, no matter which project management approach you take for an implementation project. Most Data Cloud implementations are best approached using more of a waterfall approach than an Agile approach, however. The foundational steps need to be completed in a certain order, and all steps must be completed before constituent components can be created. It's difficult and time-consuming to undo and redo steps, and it also consumes consumption credits to do so.

A waterfall approach can help to define more clearly any dependencies and also places more emphasis on design and planning. It's even more important to focus on design and planning for a first-time Data Cloud implementation. With a well-thought-out design, the actual time spent in hands-on keyboard implementing isn't long because of Data Cloud's low-code/no-code functionality. After the first implementation, all subsequent enhancements will likely take less planning and less time because the foundation is already in place.

Our previous examples include user stories for service agents, marketers, sales professionals, data governance specialists, and strategists. We've discussed how Data Cloud has the potential to bring value to roles across the entire organization, but given the unique value proposition, who in the organization usually decides Data Cloud is the right path forward?

Who Decides?

Salesforce provides many specialized solutions for marketers, sales professionals, service agents and more. For example, there is the Salesforce Marketing Cloud suite, Salesforce Sales Cloud, and Salesforce Service Cloud. The decision to purchase licenses for each of these Salesforce Clouds usually falls to the leaders in those functional areas, but Data Cloud is different.

It's not unusual for a senior executive to weigh in on the decision to purchase a CDP like Data Cloud because of the unique value proposition to the entire organization.

It's possible for a Data Cloud initiative to create unified customer profiles that are critical for functional teams and support many organizational themes (Figure 3-10).

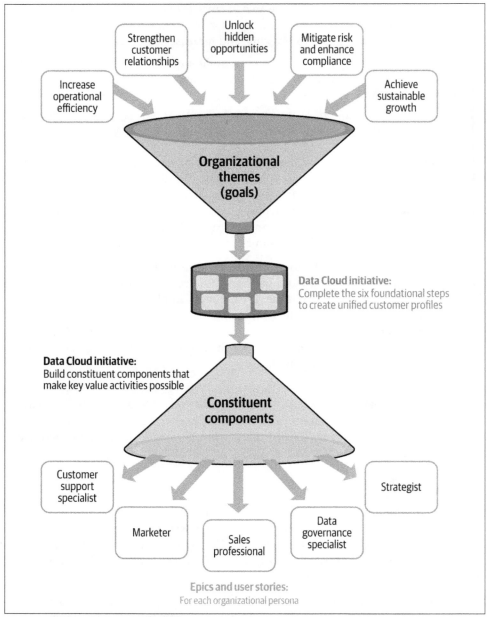

Figure 3-10. Data Cloud initiative supports many organizational themes

Often, it's the Chief Information Officer (CI object) or another senior executive who makes the decision on whether a CDP is the right solution for an organization, based on input from the marketing, sales, and service teams and others. If you're providing input to the decision maker or you are the decision maker, it could be helpful to learn more about other companies that have successfully implemented Data Cloud. As we take a look at those companies, you'll notice that the Data Cloud solution has been implemented by organizations in a wide variety of industries.

Value in Action: Industry Focus

We started the chapter by exploring the various value categories that provide an overview of some Salesforce Data Cloud use cases from a technical perspective. We then took a look at different functional roles in an organization and how they could make use of aggregated Data Cloud data, as well as highly granular-level data. Now, let's take a look at some ways different industries might want to implement Data Cloud. We'll turn our attention first to the travel, transportation, and hospitality industry.

Travel, Transportation, and Hospitality Industry

People travel for many reasons, including for family vacations, to attend concerts or youth and professional sports events, and for business trips to build client relationships or to attend conferences. Not surprisingly, demand for travel plunged at the onset of the pandemic in early 2020 and picked back up again in late 2021. Over the last few years, airlines and hospitality providers have ridden a wave of pent-up demand and experienced a boom that has led to a continuing recovery of cross-border and international travel.

A lasting effect of the pandemic is a shift to remote and hybrid working arrangements that offer workers more flexibility in planning their leisure travel activities. It also means longer trips where leisure travelers spend some of their vacation time working remotely or extending a work trip to enjoy a few days of personal time at their destination. The increase in *bleisure travel*, the blending of business and leisure travel, offers new opportunities for the hospitality industry. This shift in the way we work has resulted in more trips, longer stays, and increased revenue for those involved in the hospitality industry.

The travel, transportation, and hospitality industry is a vast and varied one. It includes organizations that directly or indirectly participate in economic activities that contribute to or depend on the travel, tourism, and hospitality sectors. This includes hotels, resorts, restaurants, caterers, bars, casinos, nightclubs, museums, theme parks, sports arenas, concert venues, airlines, car rental companies, passenger trains and buses, and airports.

Recovery and growth in the travel, transportation, and hospitality industry is expected to continue, but there are challenges. For one, the industry faces a widespread labor shortage, partly because of the exodus of industry workers during the pandemic and partly due to the nature of the work in this industry. Front desk agents, housekeepers, and maintenance staff laid off at hotels during COVID found jobs in retail, food service, and construction.

One possibility for resolving these labor issues, especially in the hotel industry, is to empower industry workers with the digital tools needed to keep up with travelers' high expectations and to offer customers an improved, digitally enhanced experience they can navigate themselves. That is exactly what Salesforce Data Cloud and the Einstein 1 platform aim to do.

As a first step to creating a more seamless customer experience, Data Cloud matches anonymous first-party and engagement data with known unified profiles to provide a more complete view of the customer. Data Cloud powers Einstein 1 platform ML and GenAI capabilities to provide many benefits to the travel and tourism industry, including hyperpersonalized customer experiences and call center efficiencies.

For example, a customer's hotel stay can be instantly and automatically customized based on known preferences like favorite pillow type and personal habits such as previous lighting and room temperature settings. Call center workers can quickly resolve any questions or complaints that arise because they'll have the most up-to-date and complete information about the customer at their fingertips, along with help and recommendations from the Einstein 1 platform.

Vendors in the travel, transportation, and hospitality industry frequently take advantage of data sharing capabilities to form an even more complete view of the customer. Airlines, car rental agencies, and hotels often join together to offer combined loyalty programs and rewards for their shared customers to build brand loyalty and offer an even more personalized customer experience.

Some notable Salesforce Data Cloud customers in this industry include Air India, Heathrow Airport, and Turtle Bay Resort. Let's take a quick look at some of the challenges these organizations were facing before their Data Cloud implementation.

Air India

Air India is the premier airline of India. Like all airlines, Air India operates in a fiercely competitive sector where mergers and acquisitions are quite common. Data challenges emerge in these industries because of the decentralized data that accumulates over time, and these data silos exist in a variety of different tech stacks as a result of airlines acquiring and merging with other airlines that have their own technology platforms and tools.

For Air India, the prevalence of siloed data meant it was difficult for customer service agents to get a complete view of passengers. Using Data Cloud, Air India connected to a single customer view of all of its siloed customer data from call centers, passenger service systems, and enterprise data lakehouses.

Heathrow Airport

Heathrow Airport was an early adopter of Salesforce Data Cloud. As one of the largest airports in the world, Heathrow set a goal to create a more seamless and consistently personalized customer experience for the millions of people who travel through it every year.

Before its Data Cloud implementation, Heathrow Airport had 14 front-end websites and 45 back-end systems, which they replaced with the Salesforce platform. Using advanced location technology and Data Cloud's powerful identity resolution features, Heathrow Airport was able to recognize anonymous travelers and use near real-time capabilities to deliver personalized customer journeys. In addition, Heathrow empowered its employees and partners with Salesforce's Einstein 1 platform, making it possible for passengers to gain access to the right airport services at just the right time. The result, according to the customer success story details (*https://oreil.ly/HZ2e-*), was a 30% increase of its digital revenue.

Turtle Bay Resort

An even more compelling Data Cloud success story can be found in Turtle Bay Resort's digital transformation, which leverages Data Cloud data to power Turtle Bay's AI-driven personalization. Turtle Bay's solution incorporates Salesforce Service Cloud, Marketing Cloud, Marketing Cloud Personalization, Data Cloud, and Einstein AI.

Using Salesforce multicloud solutions with Data Cloud at the center, Turtle Bay stitched together a consolidated view of the customer, allowing it to create more targeted segments for marketing. Using Einstein AI capabilities, Turtle Bay is also better able to personalize prearrival communications, make more relevant recommendations for adventures that appeal to each guest, and more efficiently handle a wide range of questions using AI-generated replies.

Data Cloud use cases for the travel, transportation, and hospitality industry are numerous and varied, partly because this industry is large and diverse. Continued expected growth in this industry means that companies are investing more in technology platforms like Data Cloud that will help them provide a consistently personalized customer experience. This is especially important in the post-cookie world, where third-party cookies are phased out and marketers shift toward relying more on first-party data.

Other Industries

It's not just the travel, transportation, and hospitality industry that is implementing Salesforce Data Cloud, though. There are many other industries where Data Cloud also makes sense.

Consumer goods and retail industries

As you'd imagine, the consumer goods and retail industries can leverage Salesforce Data Cloud to deepen customer engagement. Companies like General Mills, Williams-Sonoma, and Casey's are examples.

In a recent customer success video (*https://oreil.ly/CDWW9*) created by Salesforce, General Mills describes how it uses Data Cloud to better understand the interconnectivity of its different brands, which also helps it uncover customer trends in ways that were previously not possible. Before Data Cloud, it was challenging for General Mills to get that complete view of the customer, primarily because it doesn't own the transactional data that exists at the retail store level. However, Salesforce Data Cloud combines General Mills' first-party data with second-party data about its customers, and with that, General Mills is now able to define its customer segments in a more relevant way to provide a more personal experience.

Financial services, automotive, health care, life sciences, and manufacturing industries

Other industries benefitting from Salesforce Data Cloud include companies in the financial services, automotive, health care, life sciences, and manufacturing industries. A few notable companies from these industries that have implemented Data Cloud include Baptist Health, Mascoma Bank, Formula 1, and Ford Motor Company.

Financial services companies endeavoring to grow deposits and generate more revenue from existing customers can use Data Cloud to activate segments based on major life events like graduation, marriage, childbirth, retirement, and inheritance. Health care and life sciences companies can combine data from multiple health telematics systems to calculate a Unified Health Score or identify critical points for intervention in care.

It's important to remember that financial services and health care companies are required by regulatory bodies to take extra care to protect individuals' health and financial information. It's possible for organizations using Data Cloud to fulfill these requirements. As proof, Salesforce maintains a comprehensive set of compliance certifications (*https://oreil.ly/IbrSG*) for Data Cloud that include Health Insurance Portability and Accountability Act (HIPAA), General Data Protection Regulation (GDPR), and System and Organization Controls (SOC) 1, 2, and 3 compliance, among others.

Nonprofit industry

There are many other companies and industries that have successfully implemented Salesforce Data Cloud, and not all of them are for-profit enterprises. The nonprofit industry is one where there's often lots of historical first-party donor and engagement data that exists from a variety of external sources. For example, a nonprofit could have separate platforms for donation administration, fundraising efforts, advocacy support, and volunteer management. This makes the nonprofit industry a good candidate for a CDP like Salesforce Data Cloud.

My direct experience is that Data Cloud can bring a great deal of value to nonprofits. Data Cloud can unify engagement data across multiple emails and IDs to help nonprofits identify high net worth individuals and highly engaged donors. It also helps them identify lapsed donors with whom they've had recent engagement.

Similarities among implementations

Data Cloud implementation plans may look quite different among the various industries, but there are many things that most of these implementations have in common. A quick look at the details of those companies highlighted on the Salesforce customer success site (*https://oreil.ly/s9PRq*) confirms some things for us.

First, the featured organizations use more than one Salesforce platform or service as part of their multicloud strategy. Most of them utilize Salesforce Marketing Cloud and leverage Salesforce Einstein AI products and tools in addition to Salesforce Data Cloud. Second, all of the organizations that implemented Data Cloud did so with the help of a Salesforce partner or Salesforce Professional Services. Third, the vast majority of customer success stories profiled enterprise customers, the largest type of companies. There are some exceptions. One example is BACA Systems, a midsize fabrication company utilizing state-of-the-art robotic and computer numerical control (CNC)-based machinery.

Now that we've looked at various industries and specific companies making use of Data Cloud, what are some takeaways? One of the most important takeaways is that Salesforce Data Cloud can handle large volumes of data, as evidenced by some of the big enterprise customers that are successfully using Data Cloud. If you've been in the Salesforce ecosystem for a few years, you'll recognize what a significant achievement this is for Salesforce. The Data Cloud platform can easily ingest and process trillions of records because of the new Data Cloud architecture described in Chapter 2.

Enterprise customers are more likely to be using Data Cloud, but they aren't the only ones who can leverage Data Cloud functionality. Midmarket and small to midsize businesses can also extract value from Data Cloud, especially when Data Cloud data is used as the input for a multicloud data architecture. Examples include activating segments created in Data Cloud to the Marketing Cloud and leveraging unified profile and engagement data for Einstein ML and AI purposes.

The Data Cloud near real-time capabilities can provide customers with a magical experience. Airport customers can get near real-time information about parking availability, near real-time alerts of the expected wait time for the security lines, and an immediate coupon for certain shops within the terminal that are relevant to the person's interests and preferences.

Financial services companies can use near real-time information to detect potential fraudulent activity. Educational institutions can intervene quickly whenever a student visits their web pages for information about dropping a class. The student can be immediately put into a specific journey aimed at informing the student of options, and an alert can be sent right away to the student's advisor.

Organizations and companies in different industries have successfully implemented Data Cloud. In doing so, they've increased operational efficiency and strengthened customer relationships. They've also unlocked hidden opportunities. For example, nonprofits are better able to identify areas where they can increase recurring donations once they have a more complete and accurate view of their high-value donors.

Certain industries, like the financial services and health care industries, are able to better mitigate risk and enhance compliance after Data Cloud implementation. Data Cloud provides a scalable solution for achieving AI democratization and, as such, sets the stage for organizations to more likely achieve a sustainable growth rate.

We've just described some of the goals organizations hope to achieve by implementing Salesforce Data Cloud. As shown back in Figure 3-1, Data Cloud can provide a foundation for data and AI democratization that can help companies ultimately achieve their goals.

Summary

The list of value categories presented in this chapter covers common categories in basic ways, but there are additional methods with which to amplify the value categories presented. The use of data spaces, which we mentioned in Chapter 2, is one such example. Using data spaces makes it possible to segregate data, metadata, and processes among many brands, departments, or regions.

Additionally, other Salesforce applications like Loyalty Management Cloud, Marketing Cloud Intelligence (formerly Datorama), Marketing Cloud Personalization (formerly Interaction Studio), and Marketing Cloud Growth (new for 2024) can be used in conjunction with Data Cloud. This is possible because Data Cloud is tightly integrated with other Salesforce tools and platforms.

There are a myriad of ways to put together a modern data tech stack with the Salesforce Data Cloud as the centerpiece. A best practice is to carefully consider your particular organization's Data Cloud use cases and then prioritize them. From those, choose a use case that is high value with low effort for a first-time implementation, then build upon that success to implement more high-value use cases.

In our next chapter, we'll focus on implementation basics and first-time provisioning. Afterward, we'll quickly touch on Data Cloud menu options in Chapter 5 to provide you with an overall navigational understanding. Beyond that, we'll take deep dives in subsequent chapters into the foundational steps and constituent components that will create the necessary conditions to extract Data Cloud value.

CHAPTER 4

Admin Basics and First-Time Provisioning

In Chapter 3, we considered 12 Data Cloud key value activities that contribute to data and AI democratization for the entire organization. We also learned how completing the foundational steps and building constituent components are critical to success and that change management is a necessary ingredient for a successful transition. Importantly, we realized the value of Data Cloud goes beyond traditional marketing use cases.

In addition, prior chapters informed us of how the pricing model for the Data Cloud platform changed to consumption based. We also discovered the importance of planning for an upcoming Data Cloud implementation as we evaluated options to deploy a Data Cloud platform within an existing core platform org or use a separate Data Cloud home org. We also reviewed topologies between Data Cloud and Salesforce CRM, Commerce Cloud, Marketing Cloud, and Marketing Cloud Personalization.

Planning for, architecting, and designing the roadmap for a Salesforce Data Cloud implementation are necessary activities for a successful implementation. Often, a Salesforce partner is enlisted to assist, especially for first-time Data Cloud implementations. Once the Data Cloud roadmap has been developed and validated, implementation can begin.

This chapter focuses on the first step of implementation: getting set up on the Salesforce Data Cloud platform. We'll first learn about the different Data Cloud user personas because we'll eventually need to configure user accounts for each of these different user types. Understanding the responsibilities of each of the personas will help us when we are ready to grant access to the platform.

Next, we'll start our Data Cloud implementation by configuring the Admin user and provisioning the platform. We'll also explore how to create profiles and configure additional Salesforce Data Cloud users. Importantly, we'll learn about connecting our

Data Cloud platform to relevant Salesforce Clouds, and we'll follow the steps to establish the connection to our Salesforce core platform. We'll gain an understanding of the important administrator responsibilities of managing Data Cloud feature access, and we'll learn how to create custom permission sets and leverage sharing rules in our new Salesforce Data Cloud platform.

Getting Started

This section contains the required prework and some important things you should know before you get started in this chapter.

Prework

These requirements must be completed before you can get hands-on with Data Cloud:

- Set up your Salesforce core platform instance. As part of the setup, you'll need a user account created for you with a Salesforce license and an Administrator profile associated with that user account. If you're working with a Salesforce-provided developer org created for Data Cloud training purposes, this will already be done. Otherwise, if you're working in a production environment, you'll need to have an administrator create the user account for you.

- Your organization must have obtained the necessary SKUs for access to the Salesforce Data Cloud platform. As a reminder, there is one Data Cloud SKU, and there are several options for add-ons such as for Marketing Cloud licenses, Loyalty Management Cloud licenses, and Tableau licenses.

- If your Salesforce org does not have the Data Cloud Admin permission set, you'll need to first add Data Cloud to your Salesforce account by clicking Setup → Your Account → Browse & Buy. Scroll through until you find the product labeled Data Cloud Provisioning. Add it to your cart and then check out. If you are not able to successfully provision your Data Cloud org, you'll need to email *myaccount@Salesforce.com* to express your interest in Data Cloud. Make sure you include your org ID in the communication.

What You Should Know

This chapter will explore some of the permission sets associated with Salesforce Data Cloud, and instructions for the examples will be detailed enough that you can complete the process; however, you'd benefit greatly from having at least a basic understanding of how object access works in the Salesforce core platform. Salesforce Data Cloud platform access works similarly in many respects, so it is recommended that you complete some learning modules on Salesforce Trailhead to fill any gaps in your knowledge of org-wide defaults (OWDs) and object-level access, profiles, and permission sets.

Salesforce Data Security for Data Cloud Administrators

You can configure access to data in the Salesforce core platform at four main levels: organization (company-wide), objects, fields, and records. Within Salesforce Data Cloud, the main focus will be on establishing the appropriate object-level security for the various users who will be accessing Data Cloud. To accomplish this, it is important that you possess the requisite knowledge about Salesforce profiles and permission sets. As a Salesforce Data Cloud administrator, it is your responsibility to limit user access to no more than what users need to do their job.

Data Cloud User Administration Is Managed in the Core Platform

User administration for Salesforce Data Cloud is managed within the Salesforce core platform. Thus, it is important that you have administrator privileges in the core platform so you can set up and/or perform certain administrative duties for Salesforce Data Cloud.

As you'll learn later in the chapter, sharing rules for Salesforce Data Cloud operate differently from the sharing rules within the Salesforce core platform. Therefore, it's not an absolute necessity that you have an understanding of how sharing rules work on the core platform. Having a thorough understanding of Salesforce object access through the use of profiles and permission sets is, however, strongly recommended for working as an administrator in Salesforce Data Cloud. It is also helpful if you have experience setting up new Salesforce users.

Data Cloud User Personas

Whether a user is performing hands-on work within Salesforce Data Cloud or just viewing Data Cloud data in the Salesforce platform, they'll need an appropriate permission set associated with their Salesforce user account. Depending on their responsibilities, they'll be assigned one or more permission sets.

The standard Data Cloud permission sets are persona based. A *persona* represents a group of users clustered on shared behavior and goals. Personas are similar to categories of people. Within Salesforce, personas are based on the general tasks users perform in their roles, rather than just focusing only on what they do in the Salesforce platform. The reason personas are created this way is because the Salesforce platform is highly flexible and customizable to support people at different organizations who may carry out the same task using different Salesforce features or products, or perhaps even other systems.

The two main user personas for all Data Cloud instances are Data Cloud Admin and Data Cloud User. Every Data Cloud org comes with standard permission sets to support these two main user personas. It's also possible to create custom permission sets. That's an advanced topic we'll discuss later in the chapter.

Salesforce Data Cloud Integration User

The Salesforce Data Cloud Integration User will be used automatically by the system once you establish that connection to Salesforce core later in the chapter. The Integration User is not a license that can be assigned to a person user who logs in to Data Cloud.

Many, but not all, Data Cloud orgs will have segmentation and activation add-on licenses. For those orgs, there will exist four additional permission sets to support the additional personas. Those four personas are Marketing Admin, Marketing Manager, Marketing Specialist, and Marketing Data Aware Specialist.

So, in total, there are six standard Data Cloud permission sets when segmentation and activation licenses have been purchased (Figure 4-1). Custom permission sets can also be created, and once you set up the connector to your Salesforce core instance, the Salesforce Data Cloud Integration User will be used automatically.

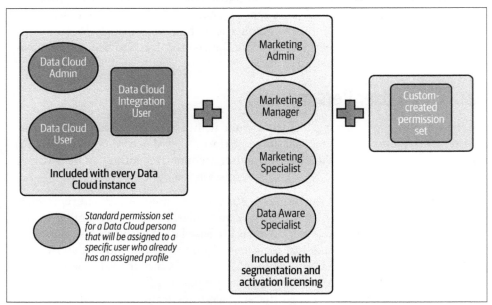

Figure 4-1. Persona-based permission sets included with Data Cloud

Let's take a look at the responsibilities of each of the six different standard Data Cloud personas.

Data Cloud Admin and Data Cloud User

Data Cloud Admins can access all functionality within Data Cloud and are responsible for executing the day-to-day configuration, support, maintenance, and improvement of the Salesforce Data Cloud system. As such, they are also responsible for the first-time setup of the Data Cloud application. In addition, the Data Cloud Admin is responsible for user provisioning and assigning permission sets beyond the initial setup.

Tasks associated with the first-time Data Cloud platform setup and access management are specific to the administrator persona, so the upcoming chapter sections will be most relevant for the administrator persona.

Assign Admin Privileges to a Small Number of Users

Noticee that the Salesforce Data Cloud Admin is given extensive permissions. The Read, Create, Edit, Delete, View All, and Modify All object permissions are granted to almost all of the Salesforce Data Cloud objects. It's therefore recommended that you assign this permission set only to a few users. Data Cloud Admin access given to a user can be revoked at any time, but if you remove the Data Cloud Admin privilege from any user, they will no longer be able to access Data Cloud unless you assign them another Data Cloud permission set.

You can view the complete object settings for this permission set by accessing Permission Sets from the Setup option of the gear icon and clicking on the Data Cloud Admin permission set. Be sure to click on Object Settings within the Apps section.

The Data Cloud User permission set can be assigned to any user who doesn't fit within one of the other Data Cloud personas. The User permission set gives users the ability to Read, Create, Edit, Delete, View All, and Modify All for the data lake source key qualifiers object. For all other objects, the ability to Read and View is granted.

Data Cloud Marketing Admins

Data Cloud Marketing Admins have the same privileges and permissions as Data Cloud Admins. These admins are granted full access to all navigation components in Data Cloud, which means they can manage day-to-day configuration needs like support, maintenance, and enhancements tasks. The Marketing Admin permission set is one of four standard permission sets that come with the Data Cloud for Marketing license.

Data Cloud Marketing Managers

Data Cloud Marketing Managers are responsible for the overall segmentation strategy and identifying target campaigns. This permission set grants full access to segments, activations, and activation targets. However, no access is granted to Data Explorer and Profile Explorer. View-only access is available for all other navigation components.

Data Cloud Marketing Specialists

Data Cloud Marketing Specialists are responsible for creating, managing, and publishing segments of the messaging campaigns identified by the Marketing Manager. This permission set grants full access to segments, but no access is allowed to Data Explorer and Profile Explorer. View-only access is available for all other navigation components.

Data Cloud Marketing Data Aware Specialists

The Data Cloud Marketing Data Aware Specialist persona is specific to Salesforce Data Cloud. Data Aware Specialists are responsible for creating and managing data streams, mapping data, and building the CIs that can be used in segmentation within Data Cloud for Marketing. The Data Aware Specialist manages the logical, marketer-friendly data model defined by the Marketing Manager and Marketing Specialist.

The Data Aware Specialist also works with other team members; for example, the Data Aware Specialist works with the website developer when there is a requirement for activities like setting up the Salesforce Interactions SDK in Data Cloud.

To summarize, there are two permission sets that always exist: Data Cloud Admin and Data Cloud User. There are four more permission sets that exist when you have the Data Cloud for Marketing license (Table 4-1). All of these are standard permission sets that come ready to go OOTB. You just need to assign them to users.

Table 4-1. Data Cloud standard permission sets

Permission Set	Description	License
Data Cloud Admin	Allows access to all Data Cloud features and administration	Data Cloud
Data Cloud User	Allows access to view Data Cloud features	Data Cloud
Data Cloud Marketing Admin	Allows access to all Data Cloud features and administration	Data Cloud for Marketing
Data Cloud Marketing Manager	Allows access to Data Cloud, management of the overall segmentation process, and creation of reports and dashboards	Data Cloud for Marketing
Data Cloud Marketing Data Aware Specialist	Allows access to Data Cloud, creation and management of data sources, registration of activation channels, and creation of reports and dashboards	Data Cloud for Marketing
Data Cloud Marketing Specialist	Allows access to Data Cloud and creation, management, and publishing of segments	Data Cloud for Marketing

You can view the complete object settings for each of the permission sets by accessing Permission Sets from the Setup option of the gear icon and clicking on the specific permission set you want to view. Be sure to click on Object Settings within the Apps section.

Data Cloud for Marketing is an add-on license for the Data Cloud platform that gives users the ability to create segments and send them to activation targets. The Ad Audiences portion of the Data Cloud for Marketing license is what gives users the ability to activate segments to advertising platforms like Google Ads and Meta Ads.

As we later explore the Data Cloud menu options, you'll learn what is possible within the Data Cloud platform and start to see how the standard persona-based permission sets allow you to accomplish specific tasks within the platform. Then, we'll discuss in more detail permission sets and sharing rules. We'll also discuss options for creating new custom permission sets when the standard persona-based permission sets don't meet your organization's needs.

First-Time Data Cloud Platform Setup

Before introducing the Data Cloud platform capabilities and menu options, let's go through what's needed to set up the platform for the first time so that you can access those menu options. Only a user with Salesforce Administrator privileges can perform the first-time Data Cloud platform setup. As a Salesforce Administrator, you'll be able to set yourself up as a Data Cloud Admin. Afterward, you'll be able to add other users to Data Cloud and then connect the platform to Salesforce Marketing Cloud and Salesforce CRM. As discussed in Chapter 2, you'll likely be working with a subset of people for user testing activities before allowing everyone access to Data Cloud.

A basic first-time Data Cloud platform setup involves configuring users and connecting Data Cloud to other Salesforce Clouds by following these steps:

1. Configure the Data Cloud Admin user.
2. Provision the Data Cloud org.
3. Create profiles for new Salesforce users (optional).
4. Add new Salesforce users (optional).
5. Assign permission sets to all users needing Data Cloud access.
6. Connect Data Cloud to other Salesforce Clouds like Salesforce CRM and Marketing Cloud.

Note that you'll only need to create new Salesforce user accounts for anyone who does not already have access to Salesforce CRM core. You may also want to delay assigning permission sets to end users until the Data Cloud instance is built out and ready for testing or ready to go live.

Configuring the Admin User

A new Data Cloud platform can be provisioned for either an existing or a new Salesforce org. In either case, a new or existing Salesforce Administrator internal to your organization will need to assign themselves the Data Cloud Administrator permission set as a first step in setting up the platform. If you are the Salesforce Administrator designated to also be the Data Cloud Admin, you can assign yourself the Data Cloud Admin permission set by following these steps:

1. Click on the gear icon at the top right of the screen and then click on Setup. Search for Users in the Quick Find window.

2. Select your username from the list.

3. Click the Edit Assignments button under the Permission Set Assignments section on the user page (Figure 4-2).

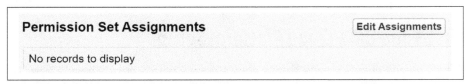

Figure 4-2. Edit assignments to add a new permission set to a Salesforce user account

4. Select the Data Cloud Admin permission set, then click the Add arrow icon. You should now see the Data Cloud Admin permission set in the Enabled Permission Sets box (Figure 4-3).

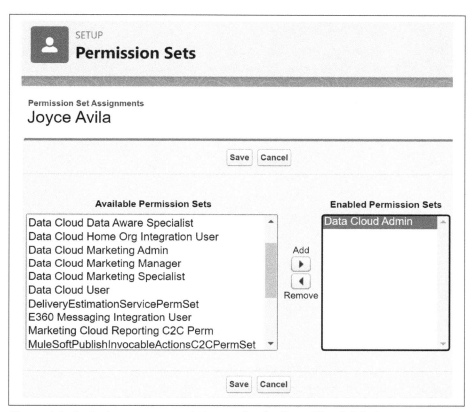

Figure 4-3. Assigning a new permission set for the Data Cloud Admin

5. Be sure to click the Save button.

Data Cloud Setup Success

You'll know that you've been successful in assigning yourself the Data Cloud Admin permission set if you click on the gear icon in the top right corner of the screen and one of your available options is Data Cloud Setup (Figure 4-4). You may need to refresh your screen if you don't see the Data Cloud Setup option.

Figure 4-4. Data Cloud Setup accessed from the gear icon

Contact Your Salesforce Account Executive If Needed

Situations may arise throughout the setup process where you'll need help from your Salesforce.com account executive or the Salesforce.com support team. For example, if you are setting up a new Salesforce org at the same time as your Data Cloud platform and you don't receive your email with a log-link, or if you need your Data Cloud platform moved to a different Salesforce org, you'll need to reach out directly to Salesforce.com for assistance.

Provisioning the Data Cloud Platform

The configuration setup of the Data Cloud platform will need to be done by a Data Cloud Administrator.

If you've successfully assigned yourself the Data Cloud Platform Admin permission set as described in "Configuring the Admin User" on page 94, you're now ready to provision the new Data Cloud platform.

1. Click on the gear icon at the top right of the screen and select Data Cloud Setup. A welcome screen will appear.

2. Click the Get Started button on the bottom right of the screen (Figure 4-5). If you don't see the button, try refreshing the page or logging out and back in again.

Figure 4-5. Welcome screen for Data Cloud initial setup

Success!

Once you've clicked the Get Started button, it may take a few minutes for the provisioning to complete. You'll know that the Data Cloud platform was successfully set up when the message provides you with the location of your Data Cloud instance and your tenant-specific endpoint (Figure 4-6). The location of your Data Cloud instance informs you where your Data Cloud tenant is located, and you can use this information to connect trust site and maintenance notifications with your instance. The instance details will also be important to know if you implement the BYOL capabilities later. The endpoint is your unique, system-generated subdomain assigned to your tenant.

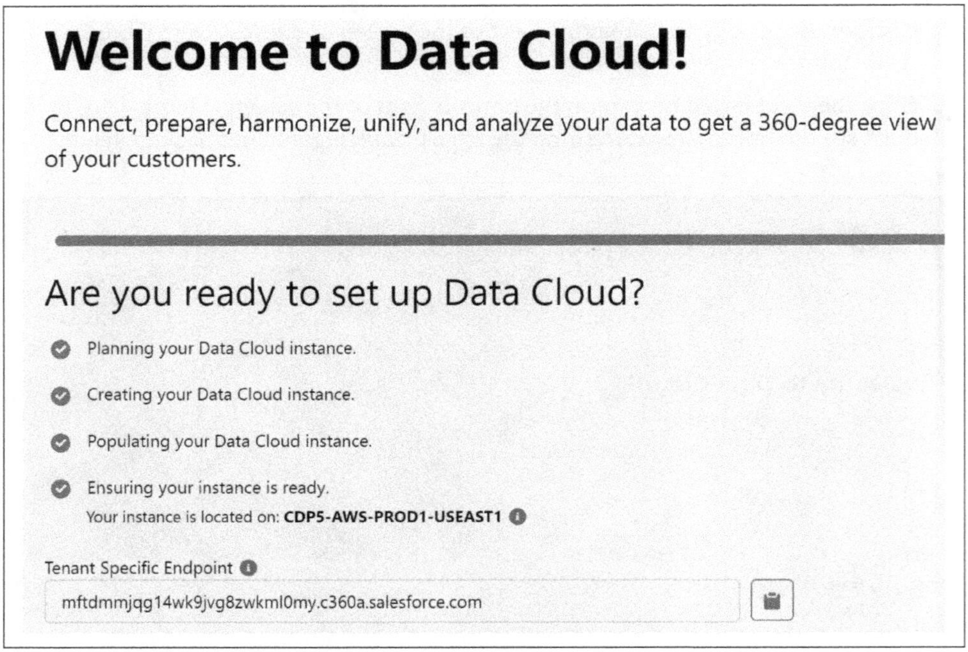

Welcome to Data Cloud!

Connect, prepare, harmonize, unify, and analyze your data to get a 360-degree view of your customers.

Are you ready to set up Data Cloud?

- ✓ Planning your Data Cloud instance.
- ✓ Creating your Data Cloud instance.
- ✓ Populating your Data Cloud instance.
- ✓ Ensuring your instance is ready.
  Your instance is located on: **CDP5-AWS-PROD1-USEAST1** ⓘ

Tenant Specific Endpoint ⓘ

mftdmmjqg14wk9jvg8zwkml0my.c360a.salesforce.com

Figure 4-6. Completed Data Cloud setup screen

At this point in the process, you're the only Data Cloud user able to access the platform. If you want others to access your Data Cloud instance, you'll need to assign standard permission sets to existing Salesforce users. In addition, you'll likely need to create some profiles and configure additional users next. We'll discover how to create new profiles in the next session, but first, let's install the standard starter data bundles we plan to use.

Navigate to Data Cloud Setup → Salesforce CRM, where you can confirm that your Salesforce CRM connection was established and has an active status. You can rename the connection, if desired, by clicking on the pencil icon. You'll need to install each of the starter data bundles by clicking on the arrow to the right of each bundle and clicking the Install button. When prompted, choose the Install for Admin Only option and then click the Install button. Repeat the process for each data bundle you want to install.

Creating Profiles and Configuring Additional Users

As we learned previously, there are standard permission sets that come with each Salesforce Data Cloud account. These permission sets are meant for each of the Data Cloud personas described earlier in the chapter. We'll want to assign permission sets to users, but before we do, we need to think about adding new users who don't already access the Salesforce platform but who will need access to only Data Cloud. In these cases, we should consider creating new profiles for users who will only need access to the Salesforce Data Cloud instance.

As the Salesforce CRM Administrator, you'll have been assigned the Admin profile. If you followed the instructions in the prior section, you added the Data Cloud platform Admin permission set to your user account. This allows you to now perform the admin duties within the Salesforce Data Cloud org.

As part of your admin duties, it's very likely that you'll need to add more Data Cloud users so that the platform functionality can be built out and used by others. Any new Data Cloud user, if already a Salesforce CRM user, will need to be assigned a default or custom permission set to access and use the Data Cloud platform.

If a new Data Cloud user does not already have an existing Salesforce CRM account, then you'll need to configure a new Salesforce user account for them. If that is the case, you'll need to assign them a profile as you are creating their new user account.

Let's explore how to create new Data Cloud platform user profiles that you can assign to new Salesforce Data Cloud users.

Cloning Data Cloud profiles

As the Data Cloud Admin, you'll want to create new profiles for each of the other four personas because these profiles must be created before you attempt to create new user accounts. You can follow these steps to create a custom profile by cloning an existing profile:

1. Click on the gear icon on the top right of the screen and then select Setup. Type **profiles** in the Quick Find box.
2. Click on Profiles to see a list of all existing user profiles (Figure 4-7).

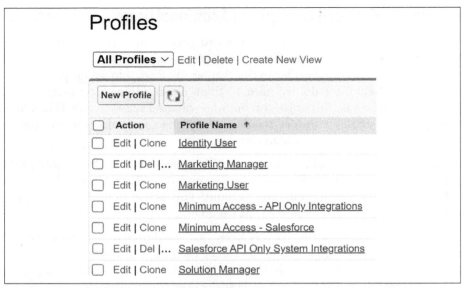

Figure 4-7. Existing Salesforce profiles in the Salesforce core platform

3. Locate the Identity User profile and click on it. Next, click Clone (Figure 4-8).

Figure 4-8. Identity User profile to be cloned

4. Enter the name of the custom profile you want to create in the Profile Name field. For our example, let's create the Marketing Manager profile (Figure 4-9). Be sure to click the Save button when you're done.

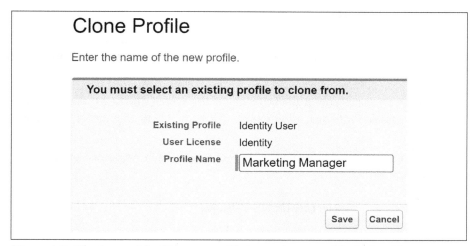

Figure 4-9. Cloning an identity user profile to create a new Marketing Manager profile

5. Repeat the previous steps to create new profiles for any groups of users who need to access Data Cloud but do not already have Salesforce access.

Easy Ways to Limit the Number of New Custom Profiles Created

Every Salesforce user must be assigned a profile, and it's best to use standard profiles when possible and limit the number of new custom profiles created. An alternative to creating more profiles is to consider use permission sets instead. For example, you may not need four different profiles for your marketing team. Depending on your company's requirements, you could create one Marketing User profile, assign that one Marketing User profile to all users, and then assign one of the four standard permission sets to the user.

Creating new Data Cloud users

You can create new user accounts after you create the profiles needed for your new users. This can be done as part of the first-time setup now, or you can complete these steps anytime in the future. Follow these steps:

1. Click on the gear icon at the top right of the screen and select the Setup option. In the Quick Find box, type **users**. Click on Users and select the New User button.

2. Fill in the required information for your user, such as name, alias, email, and username.

Alert for First-Time User Creation

If this is your first time setting up new Salesforce users or it has been a while since you've set up new users, there are a few important things you don't want to overlook. Be sure to review the Salesforce documentation for setting up new users and complete a Trailhead module, if needed. Also, check your company's policies and procedures for creating new Salesforce users. Some organizations have a standard way in which they want to set up an alias or username for new Salesforce users, so ask in advance and be sure you're following those internal naming convention policies.

Make updates to the locale settings and approver settings. Additionally, you'll want to select the following:

- Role: None Specified (the default)
- User License: Identity
- Profile: Select one of the persona-based profiles you previously created

Click the Save button.

Email Notification

When you save a new Salesforce user account, the person receives an email notification with login instructions. However, if you are creating user accounts in advance of training for your users, then you may not want them to receive login instructions just yet. In that case, uncheck the box to send users an email notification. You can always generate that email at a later date, when you're ready for your users to log in to the Data Cloud platform.

3. Assign permission sets just as you did before by clicking the Edit Assignments button under the Permission Set Assignments section. Select the desired permission set(s), click the Add button, and then click the Save button (Figure 4-10).

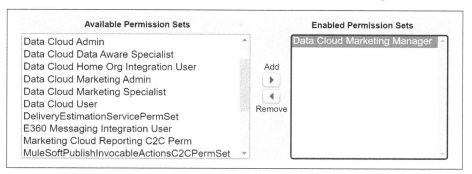

Figure 4-10. Assigning the Data Cloud Marketing Manager permission set

You can also create other Data Cloud administrators to help you with connecting to relevant Salesforce Clouds, as described in the next section.

Use Custom Permission Sets Sparingly

Data Cloud standard permission sets are automatically updated with each release as new features become available. Therefore, using a custom permission set could result in users not having access to new features or functionality in the future unless you manually adjust the custom permission set.

Connecting to Relevant Salesforce Clouds

Chapter 2 discussed the topology of the various Salesforce Clouds that can be connected to the CDP. Now, we'll take an in-depth look how to use Data Cloud connectors to enable the connections between Data Cloud and the various Salesforce Clouds to which a connection can be made. Our discussion will include information about refresh schedules for these Salesforce Cloud connectors. Salesforce is continually improving refresh times, so you should review the Salesforce documentation for the data stream schedule (*https://oreil.ly/x04YJ*) for the most up-to-date information.

Currently, there are six native Salesforce Cloud connectors: CRM, Marketing Cloud, B2C Commerce, Marketing Cloud Account Engagement (formerly Pardot), Marketing Cloud Personalization (formerly Interaction Studio), and Omnichannel Inventory. The Salesforce CRM Connector is needed to access the data within your Salesforce core platform. It's also the connector you'd use for ingesting Loyalty Management Cloud data using starter data bundles.

Salesforce customer relationship management connections

You'll want to connect your Salesforce CRM orgs so that you can ingest data from those orgs. If you have any problems connecting any of your Salesforce CRM orgs to your Data Cloud platform, make sure you have the proper access to the Salesforce org(s) to which you're trying to connect. Also, ensure that your CRM orgs have met the necessary criteria and that you've not exceeded the number of allowable CRM org connections.

Salesforce CRM Connection Limitations

There are some limitations on Salesforce CRM connections. You'll need to use the Salesforce Lighting Experience, rather than the Salesforce Classic console, to enable Data Cloud. A Salesforce org must also have API access if it is to be connected. Some Salesforce editions, such as the Professional Edition, do not come with API access, but that access can be purchased as an add-on. In addition, you can connect no more than five CRM orgs to the Data Cloud platform. The five CRM orgs limit includes both the Salesforce CRM to which you have your Data Cloud provisioned and any external Salesforce orgs. Neither the Salesforce Marketing Cloud connection nor the Salesforce Commerce Cloud connection counts toward the limit.

The Salesforce CRM Connector enables access to one of three types of orgs: home orgs, external orgs, and sandbox orgs. A *home org* is the production org where the Data Cloud platform is installed, and it may include Salesforce CRM data such as Sales, Service, Commerce, Loyalty, and CRM custom objects. *External orgs* are Salesforce CRM production orgs external to the org where the Data Cloud platform is installed. A *sandbox org* is a copy of your organization, completely isolated from your Salesforce production environment, that you can use for a variety of purposes, such as testing and training.

It's possible for a Salesforce Data Cloud org to connect to a Salesforce external production org where another Data Cloud org is installed. A Salesforce Data Cloud platform can also connect to any Salesforce CRM sandbox org, whether associated with the home org or an external org.

Domain Recommendations

If you have My Domain activated on your external Salesforce org and Data Cloud, it is recommended that you select "Don't redirect" from the domain settings. Additionally, you'll want to ensure that "Allow access" is granted for the Salesforce IP range for all external Salesforce orgs you want to connect to the Data Cloud platform. If you need more information about Salesforce IP addresses and domains to allow, you can check the Salesforce Help developer documentation.

During Data Cloud setup, your Data Cloud instance was automatically connected to the existing Salesforce org. If you need to connect to a different Salesforce org, you can follow these steps:

1. Click on the gear icon at the top right of the screen and select Setup. In the Quick Find box, type **configuration**.

2. Click on Salesforce CRM and then the New button if you need to create additional connections. You'll then be able to connect to another Salesforce production org or a sandbox org (Figure 4-11).

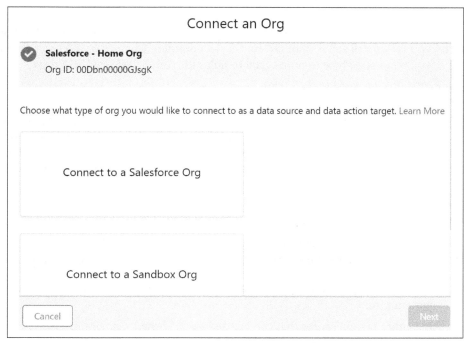

Figure 4-11. Connecting a new Salesforce CRM org to Data Cloud

3. Complete the connection by entering your user credentials to establish the connection with the Data Cloud platform.

At this time, the CRM Connector supports Insert, Upsert, and Delete statements. Also, the sync scheduling options available are every 10 minutes (for Upserts) or biweekly (for a full refresh). However, the updates are ingested into Data Cloud during the next scheduled full refresh whenever you update a formula field created in the Data Cloud data stream using the Salesforce CRM Connector.

Make Sure to Plan for Unlimited Ingestion Lookback for CRM Connector

When creating Salesforce CRM data streams, the lookback is unlimited and this setting cannot be modified. All historical data for the selected objects and fields will be ingested. Thus, you'll want to make sure you estimate in advance the data volume for ingestion of historical data as well as for ongoing data updates and additions. It's possible to reduce processing of the ingested data by adjusting your lookback period in segmentation or queries. Alternatively, if you need precise control over what data gets ingested by Data Cloud and when, it's possible to create a Salesforce Flow in the source system to "push" data to Data Cloud via Apex.

Once you've established your Salesforce CRM org connection to your Data Cloud platform, you can install some standard starter data bundles. Chapter 6 walks you through the steps that explain how to utilize data bundles for your Salesforce CRM orgs.

Marketing Cloud connection

Connecting your Data Cloud platform to Salesforce Marketing Cloud requires that you have admin access to Marketing Cloud. Data Cloud supports only Marketing Cloud Enterprise 2.0 account connections. Another requirement is that your Marketing Cloud account should default to the Enterprise ID (EID), the topmost parent business unit, so that each of the child business units to be used in activation can be accessed. It's also important to note that you're limited to connecting only one Salesforce Marketing Cloud to your Salesforce Data Cloud.

The Marketing Cloud Connector can help enrich customer profile data in many ways. Here are some examples of use cases achievable with the Marketing Cloud Connector:

- Ingesting email open and click data that can be used to identify top engagers for segmentation
- Ingesting Einstein scores that can be used for AI-based segmentation
- Surfacing Salesforce Marketing Insights data to CRM objects

Ingestion Lookback Limited to 90 Days for Marketing Cloud Connector

When creating Marketing Cloud data streams, only 90 days worth of data is ingested into Salesforce Data Cloud.

When you're ready to connect your Salesforce Marketing Cloud account to the Data Cloud platform, you can follow the same steps you used before to set up the Salesforce CRM Connector. This time, you'll just select Marketing Cloud under the Configuration option, instead of Salesforce CRM. You'll then be prompted to enter your credentials (Figure 4-12).

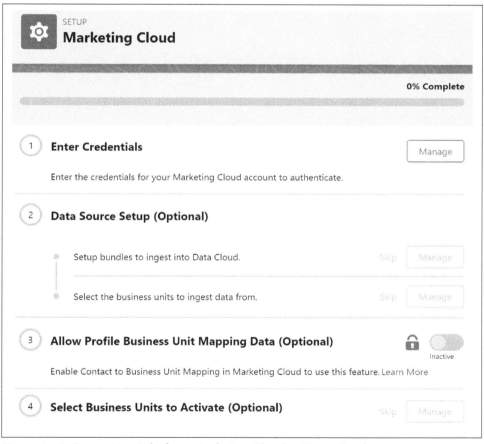

Figure 4-12. Connecting Salesforce Marketing Cloud to Data Cloud

It's best practice to use a dedicated Marketing Cloud API user account for integration with Data Cloud to prevent disruptions resulting from expired passwords. A Marketing Cloud API user's password doesn't expire.

At this time, the Marketing Cloud Connector has a latency of hourly to 24 hours, and the data can be refreshed with an Upsert or a full refresh.

When setting up ingestion, it's possible to use data bundles for Marketing Cloud, including the Email Studio, MobileConnect, MobilePush, and WhatsApp bundles. When it's time for mapping in Chapter 9, there will be certain required mappings for the Affiliation DMO that will need to be completed for Marketing Cloud ingested data.

Salesforce B2C Commerce Cloud connection

You'll need access to the B2C Commerce Business Manager in order to create the B2C Commerce Cloud connection to Data Cloud. Additionally, there is a requirement that Commerce Cloud Einstein must be activated before the B2C Commerce Cloud Connector can access the customer profile and transaction data from the B2C Commerce Cloud.

Importantly, Data Cloud can connect only to a B2C Commerce Cloud production instance. No B2C Commerce sandboxes can be connected to your Data Cloud platform.

Case Insensitivity

Within Salesforce Commerce Cloud, it's possible to create different custom attributes with the same name but different case sensitivities. Salesforce Data Cloud converts all field labels to lowercase, so to avoid any data conflicts, you may need to first modify the field names in your B2C Commerce platform.

You can follow the same steps as before, but this time, select the B2C Commerce configuration. You'll then be prompted to sync with your Commerce Cloud instance by providing the B2C Commerce Business Manager URL (Figure 4-13).

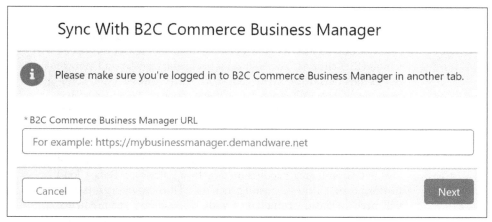

Figure 4-13. Connecting the Salesforce B2C Commerce Cloud to Data Cloud

Using the B2C Commerce Cloud Connectors allows you to ingest Commerce Cloud order data and related customer and catalog data. Sales order and sales order customer data have an hourly latency; all others have a daily latency. Sales order data can be refreshed with an Upsert; all others require a full refresh.

The B2C Commerce Order Bundle deploys mapping to Contact Point-type DMOs that are used in identity resolution. When it's time to perform data mapping, you'll need to ensure that these specific DMO fields are mapped to the individual DMO fields (Table 4-2).

Table 4-2. B2C DMO Mappings

DSO entity	DSO field	DMO entity	CustomerId
Sales order customer	customerId	Individual	CustomerId
Sales order customer	customerListId	Individual	CustomerListId
Sales order customer	customerNo	Individual	CustomerNo
Sales order customer	usId	Individual	UsId

The ingestion lookback period for the B2C Commerce Connector is 30 days, as of the date the connection is established. Going forward, the B2C Commerce Connector will continue to ingest all the data.

Data Residency Requirements

The General Data Protection Regulation (GDPR) has strict residency requirements for the personal data storage of European Union (EU) citizens. The GDPR disallows the transfer and storage of this data outside of the EU, but there are exceptions when countries can receive and store data if the European Commission has determined that such countries have adequate data and privacy protections. The other exception occurs when a person gives consent for their data to be transferred outside of the European Union.

There are no technical restrictions preventing the connection of any B2C Commerce production org to a Salesforce Data Cloud platform, regardless of hosting location. Thus, your organization will need to ensure compliance with all residency requirements, including GDPR restrictions, before connecting your B2C Commerce org to Data Cloud. Salesforce can assist with providing technical information about the platform that will inform data residency decisions, but it is the data owner's responsibility to ensure data residency requirements are met.

Marketing Cloud Account Engagement connection

Marketing Cloud Account Engagement (previously referred to as Pardot) is Salesforce's business-to-business (B2B) marketing automation tool. The Marketing Cloud Account Engagement Connector provides Salesforce Data Cloud information about email activity. Email engagement data from the Email Activity object can be ingested using the Marketing Cloud Account Engagement bundle for Email Activity.

When establishing the Marketing Cloud Account Engagement Connector to Data Cloud, you'll add the Account Engagement business units you want to connect. One caveat is that you can only connect Account Engagement business units that are associated with your Data Cloud Salesforce org.

Marketing Cloud Personalization connection

The Marketing Cloud Personalization (previously referred to as Interaction Studio) connector provides Salesforce Data Cloud with access to the profile-related and behavioral data from the Marketing Cloud Personalization platform. You'll need to have the Admin permission in Marketing Cloud Personalization in order to create the connection to the Data Cloud platform. Additionally, Data Cloud Gear must be enabled, and all user attributes should be defined in the Marketing Cloud Personalization dataset.

Using the Marketing Cloud Personalization Connector allows you to ingest both anonymous and known data. This is really powerful because your Data Cloud stores anonymous, or unknown, data until it can be matched with known data. Refer to Chapter 1 for a more detailed discussion of known and unknown data.

Ingestion Lookback Not Available for Marketing Cloud Personalization Connector

When creating Marketing Cloud Personalization data streams, no historical data is ingested in Salesforce Data Cloud.

The latency for the Marketing Cloud Personalization connection is 15 minutes for Profile data and 2 minutes for Events/Engagement data.

Omnichannel Inventory connection

Salesforce Omnichannel Inventory provides near real-time inventory availability across all fulfillment channels, at the location level. The Omnichannel Inventory Connector creates new data streams for the following:

- Location group product exclusion change
- Location product inventory change
- Location group product inventory change

Do Not Remove Omnichannel Inventory Data Streams

Removing the data streams automatically created by the Omnichannel Inventory Connector will break the Omnichannel Inventory connection to Data Cloud.

Access to this Omnichannel Inventory Connector within Data Cloud is only available if your company has purchased Omnichannel Inventory licenses. The same is true for all other Salesforce Cloud connectors, which are only accessible in your Data Cloud org when they're needed to connect to Salesforce CRM or Salesforce industry clouds.

Beyond the Basics: Managing Feature Access

Earlier in the chapter, you created new profiles for use with the other four default permission sets that come with segmentation and activation. The users given those profiles and permission sets will have the View All/Modify All privileges for the objects to which they have been granted access. However, there may be other users who need access to the Data Cloud platform who should not have those privileges. In those cases, you can manage Data Cloud feature access by creating custom permission sets and leveraging sharing rules.

Creating Data Cloud Custom Permission Sets

Sometimes, you may find yourself needing to give certain accesses to a person who doesn't align with any of the default Data Cloud persona-based permission sets. The six default Salesforce Data Cloud permission sets are not editable, so if you want to make changes by increasing or decreasing what can be done with a specific permission set, you'll need to create a new custom permission set. The easiest way to create a new permission set is to start by cloning an existing permission set.

Best Practice for Managing Data Cloud Feature Access

It's possible for an administrator to create a new profile to assign an individual who doesn't align with any of the default Data Cloud persona-based permission sets. However, creating a new profile is rarely the best approach for assigning access to the Data Cloud platform. Instead, use custom permission sets with an existing profile.

Let's take a look at the recommended steps to create a new Data Cloud custom permission set:

1. Click on the gear icon at the top right of the screen and select Setup. In the Quick Find box, type **users** and then **permission sets**.

2. Select the permission set you want to clone.

Selection of the Default Permission Set

If this is the first custom permission set you are creating, it is recommended that you select whichever default permission set is most like the custom permission set you want to create. That way, you'll have to make the fewest changes.

3. Click the Clone button, give the new custom permission set a relevant name, and click the Save button (Figure 4-14).

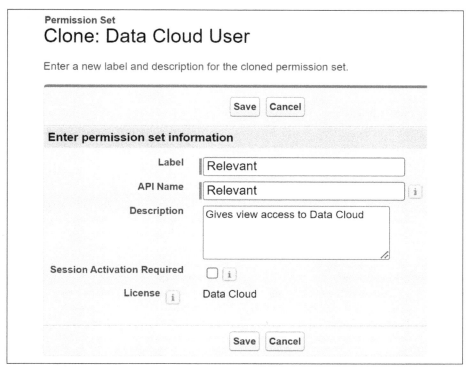

Figure 4-14. Creating a new permission set by cloning an existing permission set

4. Click on the link for the new permission set you just created. Click on the Object Settings link, scroll through the object settings for each object, and review the associated object permissions (Figure 4-15). Click on the name of any object for which you want to change the object settings.

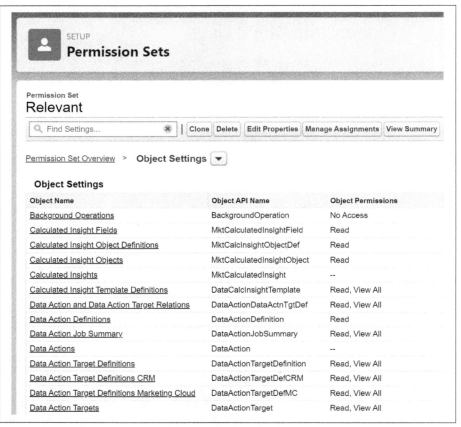

Figure 4-15. Object settings permissions to be edited

5. Check or uncheck the box beside the specific permission name you want to change on the permission set (Figure 4-16). When the box is checked, the permission is enabled for the particular object.

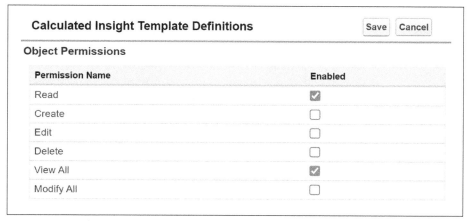

Calculated Insight Template Definitions   Save Cancel

Object Permissions

Permission Name	Enabled
Read	☑
Create	☐
Edit	☐
Delete	☐
View All	☑
Modify All	☐

Figure 4-16. Object permissions to be enabled or disabled

View All and Modify All Special Considerations

For objects such as Segments and Activation Targets, you'll likely want to deselect the View All and Modify All object permissions for your customer permission sets (Figure 4-16), especially if you intend to take advantage of sharing rules. It is important to note that removing the View All and Modify All permissions from a permission set assigned to a user does not take away that permission from the user if the user has been assigned a profile where View All and Modified All privileges are granted.

6. Click the Save button when you've made all the changes to the permission set that you need.

7. Assign the new custom permission set to a user. The steps to accomplish this are described in "Configuring the Admin User" on page 94.

Leveraging Data Cloud Sharing Rules

As we've seen thus far, permission sets give users the ability to access features and undertake certain activities within the Data Cloud platform. Permission sets, profiles, and sharing rules work much the same in Salesforce Data Cloud as they do in the Salesforce core platform. Within Salesforce, the OWD settings determine the overall most restrictive access, and permission sets are not the only way to open up access beyond the OWD settings. Based on defined criteria, sharing rules can also allow particular users greater access to records than is otherwise granted through OWDs.

Sharing Is No Longer Supported on Data Space–Aware Feature Objects

As of May 2024, data security within Data Cloud spaces was aligned with CRM access control, enforcing security for data spaces across all access methods. The upgrade included changes that integrated data space access control into permission sets. As a result, admins can now directly associate multiple data spaces with a permission set.

There are many reasons you might consider using sharing rules for your Data Cloud org. For example, you may want to restrict marketers from being able to see segments created by others outside of their team or regional area. In that case, you'd restrict visibility into segments by removing the View All/Modify All privileges in profiles and permission sets. After that, you'd open up the segments in each region to all those on the same team or in the same region by using sharing rules.

Another use case for sharing rules often occurs when one organization has multiple brands that should be marketed to distinct audiences. Managing activation targets through sharing rules can reduce the risk of activating to a brand audience in error.

Data Cloud Sharing Rules Do Not Apply to the Data

Unlike the sharing rules in the Salesforce core platform, Data Cloud sharing rules do not apply to actual data in the Salesforce data lake. Data Cloud sharing rules apply to Data Cloud objects, rather than data, and can only be based on the membership of a group or role.

Before setting up sharing rules, you'll need to have first created in the org any groups and roles that you'll be needing. Also, make sure that you've created all the profiles and permission sets that you need to enable sharing. Most likely, your profiles and permission sets will have the View All/Modify All privileges removed for all objects for which you want to create sharing rules. When you've prepared your groups, roles, profiles, and permission sets, you're ready to update your sharing settings with the following steps:

1. Click on the gear icon at the top right of the screen and select Setup. In the Quick Find box, type `sharing settings`.

2. Search for the object for which you want to manage the sharing settings using the drop-down menu beside the "Manage sharing settings for:" option. In our example, we'll select the Data Share Target object (Figure 4-17).

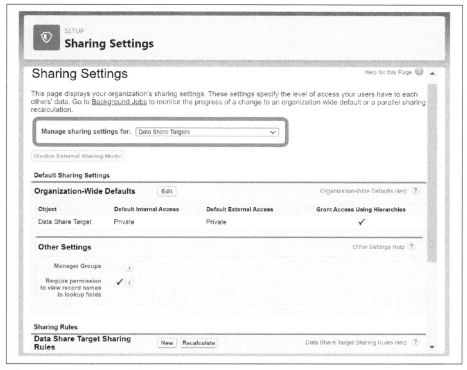

Figure 4-17. Sharing settings for an object

3. Under the Sharing Rules section, click the New button.

4. Define the rule name, select the records to be shared and with whom to share them, and identify the access level (Figure 4-18).

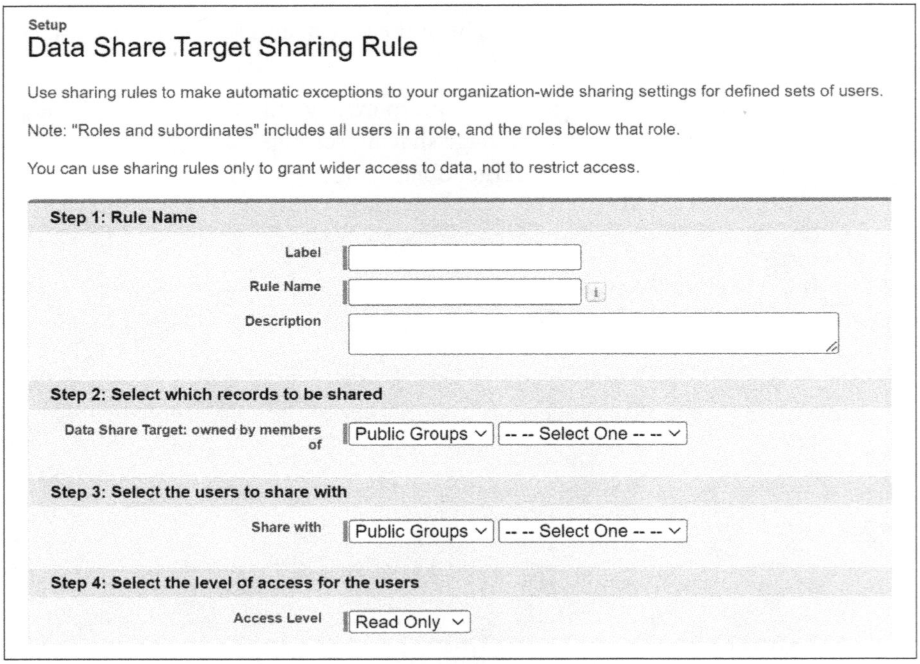

Setup

Data Share Target Sharing Rule

Use sharing rules to make automatic exceptions to your organization-wide sharing settings for defined sets of users.

Note: "Roles and subordinates" includes all users in a role, and the roles below that role.

You can use sharing rules only to grant wider access to data, not to restrict access.

Step 1: Rule Name

Label [_____]

Rule Name [_____] [i]

Description [_____]

Step 2: Select which records to be shared

Data Share Target: owned by members of [Public Groups ∨] [-- -- Select One -- -- ∨]

Step 3: Select the users to share with

Share with [Public Groups ∨] [-- -- Select One -- -- ∨]

Step 4: Select the level of access for the users

Access Level [Read Only ∨]

Figure 4-18. Salesforce Data Cloud sharing rule for an object

5. Click the Save button.

6. Repeat these steps to create any new sharing rules for other Data Cloud objects.

Objects Available for Data Cloud Sharing Rules

Data Cloud sharing rules are supported by the Activation Audience, Activation Targets, Calculated Insights, Data Stream, and Segment configuration objects.

Now that you've taken care of the platform first-time setup, you and the other Data Cloud users will be able to access the Data Cloud application within Salesforce. The next chapter will focus on briefly exploring each of the menu options within Salesforce Data Cloud.

Summary

In this chapter, we explored Salesforce Data Cloud from the perspective of an Admin persona. As such, we performed the first-time platform setup and learned how to manage Data Cloud feature access. In summary, there are five basic Data Cloud initial configuration steps:

1. *Configure the admin user*

    Assign a Data Cloud Admin or Data Cloud Marketing Admin permission system to the Salesforce System Admin who will be completing the initial configuration steps.

2. *Provision the Data Cloud platform*

    Navigate to the Setup gear icon and then click on Data Cloud Setup to get started.

3. *Add new users to the Salesforce platform (optional)*

    If new users need to be added to the Salesforce platform, consider creating new profiles and custom permission sets to assign users who'll be working only in Data Cloud.

4. *Assign permission sets*

    Assign one of the standard permission sets to Salesforce users.

5. *Set up sharing rules (optional)*

    After setting up the necessary groups and roles, set up sharing rules.

6. *Connect to relevant Salesforce Clouds*

    Establish connections to the relevant Salesforce Clouds where OOTB connectors exist. Currently, those OOTB cloud connectors include CRM, Marketing Cloud, B2C Commerce, Marketing Cloud Account Engagement, and Marketing Cloud Personalization.

Now that you've provisioned the Data Cloud platform, you're ready to take a look inside and see what's available. In the next chapter, we'll review each of the Data Cloud menu options as we navigate the platform.

CHAPTER 5

Data Cloud Menu Options

In this chapter, we'll review each of the Salesforce Data Cloud menu options at a high level. In later chapters, we'll explore each of these menu options in detail. The purpose of this chapter is to introduce you to the Salesforce Data Cloud menu options that we'll be using in our learning journey. The menu tabs are presented in alphabetical order.

Core Capabilities

The Salesforce Data Cloud platform empowers users to create a unified customer database that is accessible to other systems and platforms. Within the Data Cloud platform, I've identified five core capabilities whereby we'll divide up the menu tabs:

- Data ingestion and storage
- Data modeling and processing
- Identity
- Segmentation and activation
- Actions and insights

One core capability, segmentation and activation, is specific to Salesforce Data Cloud for Marketing, and those menu options will require additional licensing. Of the four remaining capabilities, the Data Cloud data ingestion and storage capability is the underlying capability that makes all others possible. Once data ingestion and mapping is complete, the unification process of identity resolution is what provides the basis for creating the constituent components described in Chapter 3.

There are more than 20 main menu options available in the Salesforce Data Cloud platform. To provide some context for each option, I've created Figure 5-1, which classifies each menu option based on one of the five Data Cloud core capabilities I've identified.

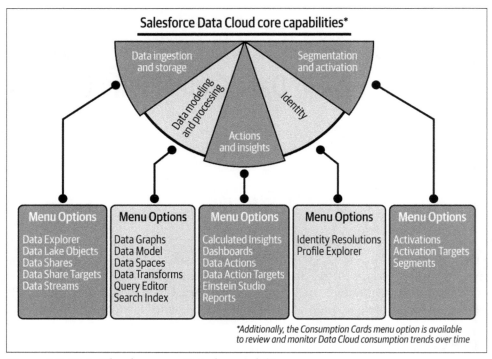

Figure 5-1. Data Cloud menu options by capability

You'll notice that there are several menu options relating to the Data Cloud platform's data ingestion and data storage capabilities, and Chapter 6 is devoted to diving deep into each of these functionalities. Similarly, Chapter 11 is devoted to explaining how to consume and act upon Data Cloud data using calculated insights, streaming insights, data action targets, data actions, and more.

Not all Data Cloud functionality is accessible directly from the Data Cloud user interface. For example, Chapter 11 will also cover important topics for which there are no specific Data Cloud menu options. Examples include Data Cloud–triggered flow, related list enrichments, and copy field enrichments.

Here, we'll introduce the menu options (Figure 5-2) in alphabetical order for all of the related Data Cloud capabilities and provide a brief explanation for each menu option.

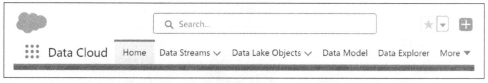

Figure 5-2. Selected menu options for Salesforce Data Cloud within the Salesforce Data Cloud app

If you'd like to change the order in which the menu options appear, you can click on the pencil icon near the top right corner of your screen. You'll then have the option to move your existing navigation items and add more items (Figure 5-3). Note that making the change this way only affects the order of the tabs that you see. Your specific access to each of these tabs and what you can do within each menu option are determined by your profile and permissions. You'll need to contact your internal Salesforce Administrator or work with Salesforce directly if there are Data Cloud menu options you don't see on your list of navigation items.

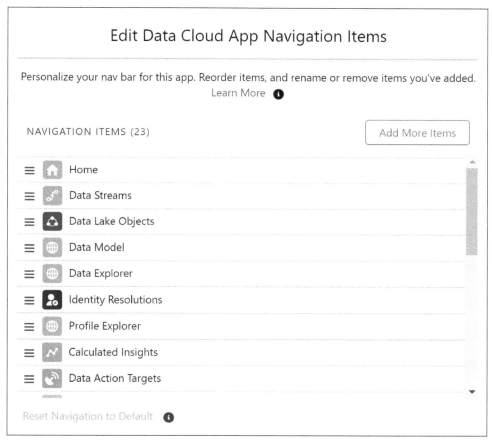

Figure 5-3. Users can rearrange the navigation order of their menu option tabs

An Admin has the ability to change which tabs appear, and in what order, for the entire organization. That can be done by editing the Data Cloud app via the App Manager in the Salesforce core platform.

In Chapter 4, we looked at how to set up the Data Cloud platform to establish account access and privileges for individual Data Cloud users. Once you've established connections to the Data Cloud application for your users, they'll be able to access it via the Salesforce App Launcher (Figure 5-4).

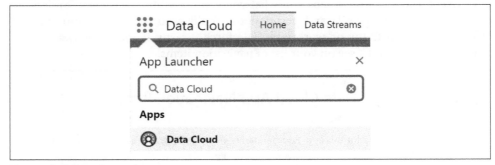

Figure 5-4. App Launcher

In the remainder of this section, we'll be discussing the functionality of each of the menu tab options. If there is some functionality described in this chapter that you aren't able to access in your Data Cloud instance, you'll first want to reach out to your Administrator to determine if you have the necessary profile and permissions to access that particular functionality.

Activation Targets

The user permissions needed to create activation targets in Data Cloud are Marketing Admin, Marketing Manager, or Marketing Data Aware Specialist.

Currently, access to the Salesforce Activation Targets functionality requires additional licensing, so you may need to contact your Salesforce account executive if you don't see this menu option.

The Salesforce Data Cloud *activation target* is the location where a segment's data is sent during activation (Figure 5-5). The activation target, sometimes referred to as the *activation platform*, is the place where you want to use your segment, and it includes the authentication and authorization information. An example of a Data Cloud activation target is Salesforce Marketing Cloud

Activation targets include a file format section so that you can export in either a CSV- or JSON-formatted file to a public cloud, if you want. Activation targets can be used directly in Adtech and Martech platforms like Google, LiveRamp, and Meta.

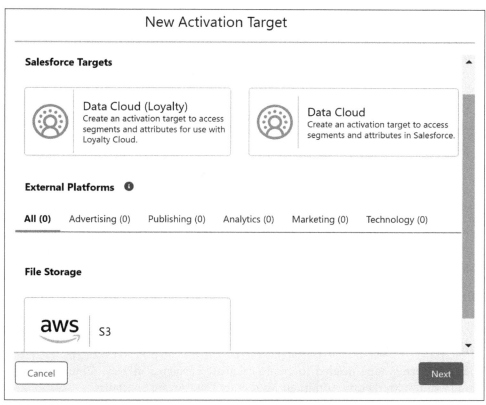

Figure 5-5. Configuring a new activation target

Activation targets are supported by sharing rules. Additionally, activation targets give you the flexibility to publish your segments to specific destinations on an ad hoc manual basis or on a schedule.

Activations

The user permissions needed to create activations in Data Cloud are Marketing Admin, Marketing Manager, or Marketing Data Aware Specialist.

Currently, access to the Salesforce Activations functionality requires additional licensing, so you may need to contact your Salesforce account executive if you don't see this menu option.

A Salesforce Data Cloud activation is the process that materializes and publishes a segment to an activation target. Activations require information about a segment, an activation target, and an activation membership (Figure 5-6).

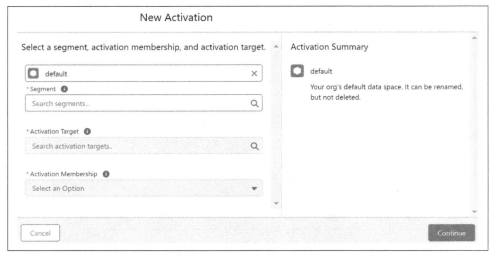

Figure 5-6. Creating a new activation

Remember that you'll need to configure an activation target before attempting to set up an activation.

Calculated Insights

The user permissions needed to create calculated insights in Data Cloud are Data Cloud Admin, Marketing Admin, or Marketing Data Aware Specialist.

The Salesforce Data Cloud Calculated Insights (CIs) tool queries, transforms, and creates complex calculations based on historical transactional data and is natively available for profile-level insights. CIs make it possible to use metrics, dimensions, and filters to define segment criteria and personalization attributes for activations. One reason for using CIs in segmentation is that, unlike segments, CIs create reusable content and perform complex queries on multiple objects.

Within the Calculated Insights tab, you can also access the Streaming Insights feature (Figure 5-7), which computes streaming metrics on near real-time data and performs operations on data contained within temporal windows.

Salesforce Data Cloud Calculated Insights can be expressed in a visual insights builder or in a SQL interface, for more technical users.

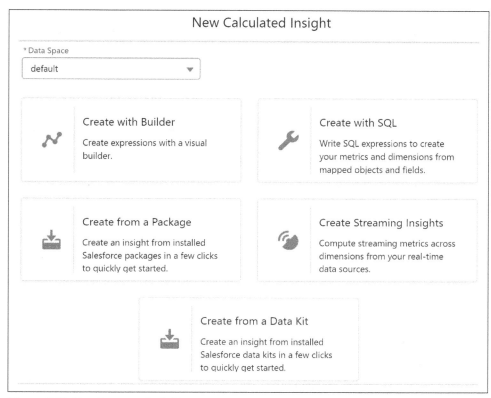

Figure 5-7. Creating new insights

Consumption Cards

The user permissions needed to access consumption cards in Data Cloud are Data Cloud Admin or Marketing Admin. Users who have access to the Your Account app can also access Digital Wallet.

As part of the summer 2024 new release, Data Cloud introduced Digital Wallet for Data Cloud, which is accessible using the Consumption Cards menu tab (Figure 5-8).

In addition to monitoring Data Cloud consumption in near real time, you can use the consumption cards functionality to understand shared capacity and monitor consumption trends over time.

Figure 5-8. Monitoring Data Cloud consumption

Dashboards

The user permissions needed to create dashboards in Data Cloud are Data Cloud Admin or Marketing Admin.

Creating a new dashboard in Data Cloud follows the same process as in Salesforce core. You provide a name for the dashboard and select the folder where you'd like to store your new dashboard (Figure 5-9).

It is very important to remember that using reports and dashboards in Data Cloud could impact the consumption credits used for billing because your data is stored and processed in Data Cloud. Just as in Salesforce core, there is a separate Reports tab, described later in this chapter.

Figure 5-9. Creating a new dashboard

Data Action Targets

The user permissions needed to create data action targets in Data Cloud are Data Cloud Admin, Marketing Admin, Marketing Data Aware Specialist, or Data Cloud Home Org Integration User. The data action targets created by the Home Org Integration User for enrichments or for use in flows are read-only access to users in the Data Cloud UI.

A *data action target* stores authentication and authorization information for a particular platform. OOTB data action targets include webhooks and Salesforce platform events (Figure 5-10).

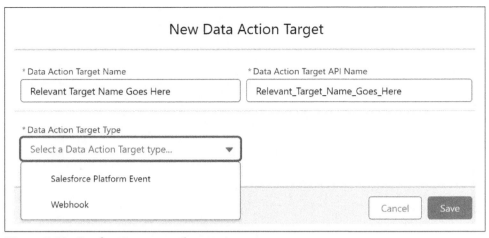

Figure 5-10. Configuring a new data action target

Data Cloud also supports the creation of other data action targets like Salesforce Marketing Cloud. Add-on licenses are required to configure Salesforce Marketing Cloud as a data action target.

Data Action Targets versus Activation Targets

A *data action target* stores the configuration details needed to send an alert or event trigger from Data Cloud. Example data action targets include webhooks, Salesforce platform events, and Salesforce Marketing Cloud.

An *activation target* stores the configuration details needed to send a segment to a destination for the purpose of creating highly personalized interactions. Examples include Salesforce Marketing Cloud and Salesforce Data Cloud, which can be used to publish to other Salesforce apps such as Salesforce Loyalty Management Cloud. Other examples of activation targets include external file storage locations and external platforms like Amazon Ads, Google Ads, and Meta.

Data Actions

The user permissions needed to create data actions in Data Cloud are Data Cloud Admin, Marketing Admin, Marketing Data Aware Specialist, or Data Cloud Home Org Integration User. The data actions created by the Home Org Integration User for enrichments or for use in flows are read-only access to users in the Data Cloud UI.

A *data action* is a process that triggers an action based on data received from a calculated or streaming insight. Actions are data-space aware so you'll need to select the applicable data space when you create a new action (Figure 5-11). Calculated and streaming insights are created in the Calculated Insights tab. Data actions can also be augmented with data graphs created in Data Cloud.

You'll need to configure a data action target before creating a new data action.

Figure 5-11. Creating a new data action

Data Explorer

The user permissions needed to explore data in Data Cloud are Data Cloud Admin, Marketing Admin, Marketing Data Aware Specialist, or Data Cloud User.

The Salesforce Data Cloud Data Explorer tool allows users to access and filter record-level data across any DMO, DLO, or CI object (Figure 5-12). The Data Explorer tool makes it possible to validate and edit your data and formulas to ensure your data streams are working properly and your data is ingested correctly. An additional icon will appear if you select a CI object, allowing you to view your CI visually in a chart.

Figure 5-12. Using the Data Explorer to access and filter record-level data

Data Graphs

The user permissions needed to create data graphs in Data Cloud are Data Cloud Admin, Marketing Admin, or Marketing Data Aware Specialist.

A data graph in Data Cloud combines DMO data you select and transforms it from normalized table data into new, materialized views of your data. In the first step of creating a new data graph, you'll select the primary DMO (Figure 5-13). Data Cloud data graphs are useful when near real-time processing of large amounts of data is needed, such as when using data to augment a prompt when seeking responses from Einstein Copilot.

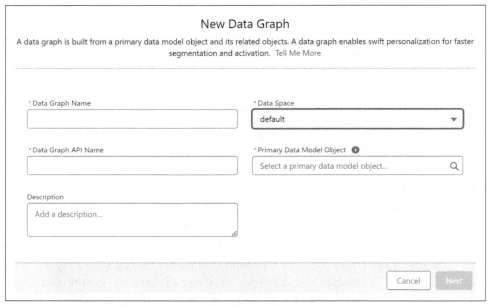

Figure 5-13. First step of creating a new data graph

Care should be taken when creating data graphs because you can't edit or update the data space, data graph API name, or primary DMO after you move beyond the first step in the builder. Once you select the primary DMO and related objects, the primary key field, related key qualifier field, and applicable foreign key fields are selected by default and added to the data graph.

Data Lake Objects

The user permissions needed to create DLOs in Data Cloud are Data Cloud Admin, Marketing Admin, or Marketing Data Aware Specialist.

DLOs are storage containers within the data lake for the data ingested into all data streams within Data Cloud. The *data lake* is a repository of all enterprise data. Although a DLO is automatically created from a DSO, you can also manually create a DLO.

Updates to Data Lake Objects Are Not Possible

It is not possible to add new fields to an existing DLO directly through the UI. Instead, you'll want to update the data streams to incorporate any new fields that will be needed in the DLO. This supports keeping the integrity of the source data and ensures Data Cloud remains a system of reference and is not used as a system of record.

You'll have three choices when creating a new DLO from within the UI (Figure 5-14): from scratch, from an existing object, or from external files.

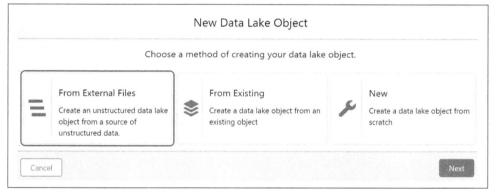

Figure 5-14. Creating a new DLO

Data Model

The user permissions needed to create DMOs in Data Cloud are Data Cloud Admin, Marketing Admin, Marketing Manager, or Marketing Data Aware Specialist.

The Data Model tab within the Data Cloud platform is where a user can create custom DMOs as well as display the existing DMOs. DMOs can be created from scratch as well as from an existing DMO or from a file (Figure 5-15). A DMO can also be downloaded from a Tableau data source.

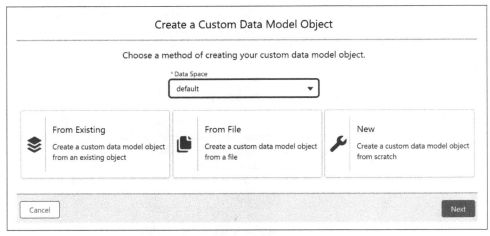

Figure 5-15. Creating a new custom DMO

Physical DMOs are groupings of data created from data streams, insights, and other sources. *Standard DMOs* exist natively, while *custom DMOs* can be created. Examples of standard physical DMOs include Account, Party Identification, Email Engagement, and Sales Orders. Additionally, DMOs can be virtual, like a view into a DLO.

Data Share Targets

The user permissions needed to create data share targets in Data Cloud are Data Cloud Admin, Marketing Admin, or Marketing Data Aware Specialist.

In addition to Snowflake and Google BigQuery (Figure 5-16), another possible data share target is Amazon Redshift.

Figure 5-16. Configuring a new data share target

A Salesforce *Data Cloud share target* is the location, including authentication and authorization information, of the external data platform of the zero copy technology partner like Snowflake or Google BigQuery (Figure 5-17).

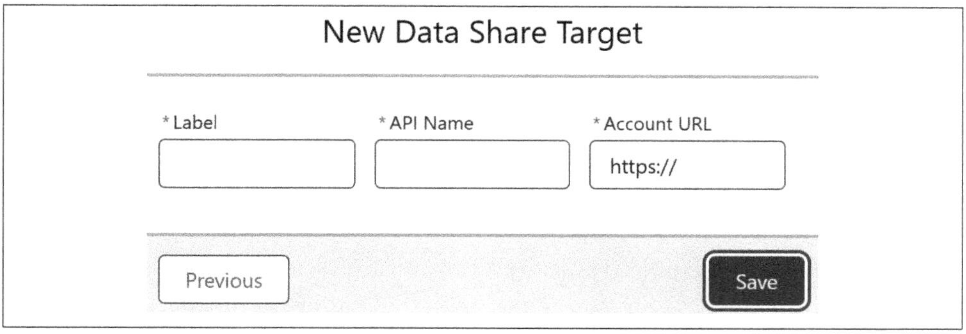

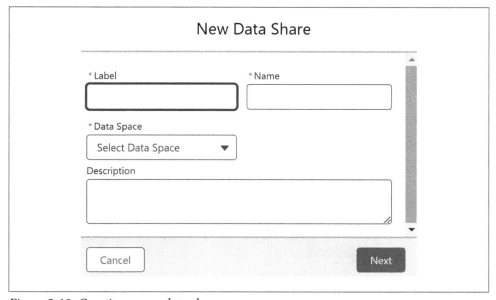

New Data Share Target

* Label   * API Name   * Account URL

https://

Previous   Save

Figure 5-17. Required data share target details

Data Shares

The user permissions needed to create data shares in Data Cloud are Data Cloud Admin, Marketing Admin, or Marketing Data Aware Specialist.

Creating a new data share begins with inputting the name of the new data share (Figure 5-18).

New Data Share

* Label   * Name

* Data Space

Select Data Space ▼

Description

Cancel   Next

Figure 5-18. Creating a new data share

You'll then need to select which objects to include in your data share (Figure 5-19).

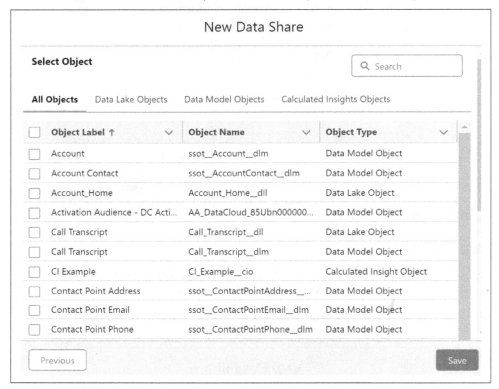

Figure 5-19. Selecting data share objects

Remember to configure data share targets before attempting to create data shares.

Data Spaces

The user permission you'll need to create data spaces is Data Cloud Admin or Marketing Cloud Admin.

Every Data Cloud is created with a default space, but additional data spaces can be used to segregate your brand, region, or department data and services. Add-on licenses must be purchased if you intend to create additional data spaces. Within the Data Spaces tab, you'll be able to see all data spaces that exist (Figure 5-20). However, you'll need to access Data Spaces under Data Cloud Setup if you want to configure a new data space.

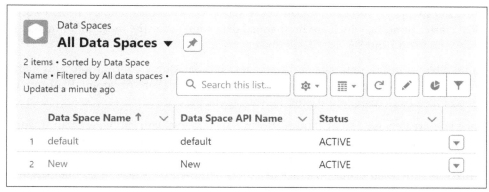

Figure 5-20. Viewing the existing data spaces

Data Streams

The user permissions needed to create data streams in Data Cloud are Data Cloud Admin, Marketing Admin, or Marketing Data Aware Specialist.

Data streams are pipelines that allow you to ingest data directly into Salesforce Data Cloud from a variety of data sources. Data streams can be based on batched data or near real-time data streams and can ingest data sources with many data types. Some of these data types include Boolean, text, number, percent, email, phone, URL, date, and datetime.

In the Salesforce menu for data streams, there are options to create new streams for connected sources and other sources (Figure 5-21). Once you select the source, you can select what objects you want to map to your Data Cloud platform.

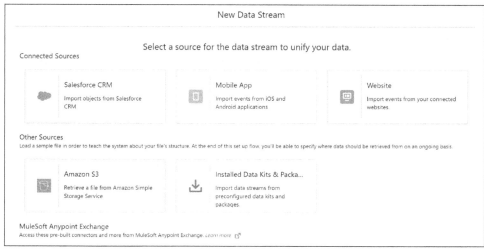

Figure 5-21. Creating new data streams

For easier mapping, you can use Salesforce starter data bundles such as the Salesforce CRM starter bundles, which are premapped data sources for the most common Salesforce Sales Cloud and Service Cloud objects.

It's possible to install data kits and packages, and Salesforce continues to add many new native connectors. You can also leverage the MuleSoft Anypoint Platform to bring in data from many more external data applications.

Once you create your Data Cloud platform data streams, you can view them in your Salesforce list views. You'll also be able to see your last 50 refresh operations and any errors that occurred. All data ingested by Salesforce Data Cloud data streams are written to your Data Cloud instance as DLOs that then will need to be mapped to a data model.

Scenarios Where Data Stream Deletion Is Not Possible

While it is possible to delete a data stream, there are three scenarios where deletion is not possible: if a data stream attribute is mapped to a DMO, if a DSO is used in calculating insights, and if a data stream is associated with a data kit.

Data streams ingest data in raw form, without transforming any fields or data types. Therefore, most of the time you'll need to prepare and/or transform your data after it has been ingested into your Data Cloud via data streams.

Data Transforms

The user permissions needed to create data transforms in Data Cloud are Data Cloud Admin, Marketing Admin, or Marketing Data Aware Specialist.

With Data Cloud's data transformation feature, you can combine, shape, clean, and prepare your data directly within the Data Cloud platform. You'll notice that you can create both batch data transforms and streaming data transforms from within this tab (Figure 5-22).

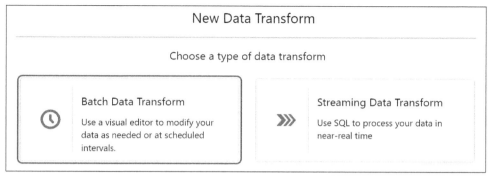

Figure 5-22. Creating a new data transform

Einstein Studio (aka Model Builder)

The user permissions needed to access Einstein Studio capabilities in Data Cloud are Data Cloud Admin, Marketing Admin, or Marketing Data Aware Specialist.

Einstein Studio enables businesses to create and use different kinds of AI models in Salesforce. Use Einstein Studio's Model Builder to access Predictive AI and GenAI capabilities. Select the Predictive tab, then click the Add Predictive Model button where you'll choose the type of predictive model you'd like to build or connect (Figure 5-23).

Figure 5-23. Creating a new predictive model

Creating, training, and deploying ML models can be achieved external to Salesforce with platforms such as Amazon SageMaker, Google Vertex AI, and Databricks. Then, those models can be connected to Data Cloud, where the ML models can be operationalized.

Selecting the Generative option in Einstein Studio gives you access to Salesforce-enabled LLM models you can use to create Einstein prompt templates. Click on the drop-down arrow to the right to create a new prompt template (Figure 5-24).

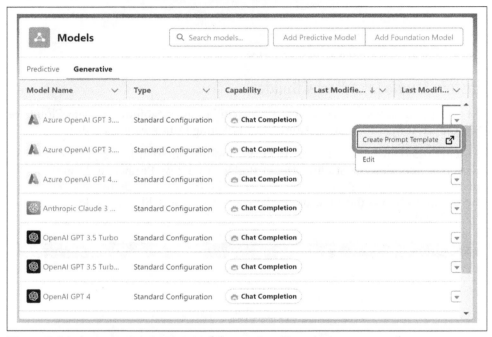

Figure 5-24. Accessing generative models to create Einstein prompt templates

You can also add a new foundation model by clicking the Add Foundation Model button. Next, select the foundational model you want to add (Figure 5-25). You can connect to LLMs like Azure OpenAI, OpenAI, Google Cloud Vertex AI, and Amazon Bedrock.

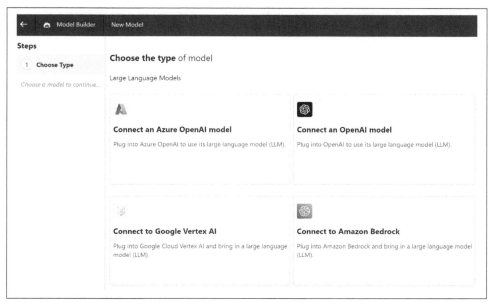

Figure 5-25. Choosing a new generative model

Identity Resolutions

The user permissions needed to create identity resolutions in Data Cloud are Data Cloud Admin, Marketing Admin, or Marketing Data Aware Specialist.

The identity resolution process matches and reconciles data about individuals into a comprehensive view called *unified profiles*. *Identity resolution*, which creates unified and link objects, is a Salesforce native capability powered by rulesets (Figure 5-26). *Rulesets* contain matching and reconciliation rules that inform Data Cloud how to link multiple sources of data into a unified profile.

You'll find all the summary statistics for each ruleset in one place, within the Identity Resolutions tab. Before you enable identity resolutions, you'll need to complete your data services mappings to the required DMO fields.

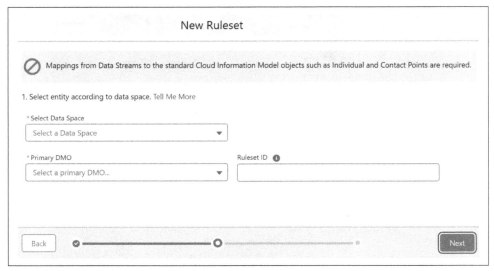

Figure 5-26. Creating a new identity resolution ruleset

Profile Explorer

The user permissions needed to explore profiles in Data Cloud are Data Cloud Admin, Marketing Admin, Marketing Data Aware Specialist, or Data Cloud User.

All Data Cloud users can access the Unified Individual profile and the Unified Account profile via the Profile Explorer menu tab (Figure 5-27). Users can search for individuals by first name, last name, email address, phone number, or individual ID. Note that Profile Explorer only works with Unified Individuals and Accounts so you'll need to make sure the DMOs for Individuals and Accounts are mapped to the appropriate data streams so the Profile Explorer can work as intended.

Figure 5-27. Accessing Profile Explorer

The Salesforce Data Cloud Profile Explorer dashboard allows you to see a complete view of your unified customer, including behavioral and historical data. Customer dashboard components can be added or removed by Data Cloud Admins by using Salesforce Lightning App Builder. These components include Data Cloud Profile Insights, Data Cloud Profile Engagements, and Data Cloud Profile Related Records.

Query Editor

The user permissions needed to explore workspaces via Query Editor in Data Cloud are Data Cloud Admin, Marketing Admin, Marketing Data Aware Specialist, or Data Cloud User.

The Query Editor can be used to write and execute SQL queries built on DLOs, DMOs, CI objects, and data graphs. From within the Query Editor tab, you can create multiple query workspaces, and after a workspace has been created, it can be accessed from the Query Editor tab. Query workspaces (Figure 5-28) also allow you to share queries with other users and collaborate using Salesforce Chatter.

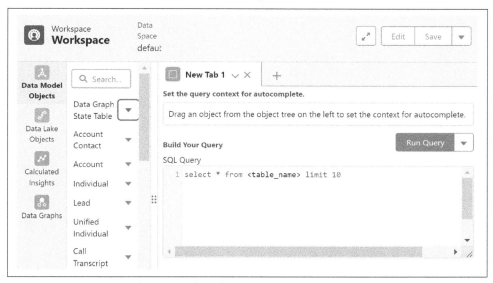

Figure 5-28. Query Workspace within the Query Editor

Reports

The user permissions needed to create reports in Data Cloud are Data Cloud Admin or Marketing Admin.

You can create a Data Cloud report on one or more DMOs. You can group, filter, and summarize records in the report, and you can build a report from scratch or use some of the reports that come OOTB (Figure 5-29).

Create Report

Category	Select a Report Type	
Recently Used	🔍 Search Report Types...	
All		
	Report Type Name	**Category**
Data Cloud	Unified Link Individual	Standard Data Cloud
Accounts & Contacts	Unified Link Individual with Individual	Standard Data Cloud
Opportunities	Unified Indv Contact Point Email	Standard Data Cloud
	Unified Indv Contact Point Email with Unified Link Contact Point Email	Standard Data Cloud
Customer Support Reports	Unified Individual	Standard Data Cloud
Leads	Unified Individual with Unified Link Individual	Standard Data Cloud
	Unified Individual with Unified Indv Contact Point Email	Standard Data Cloud
Activities	Unified Individual with Unified Indv Contact Point Address	Standard Data Cloud
Contracts and Orders	Unified Link Contact Point Address	Standard Data Cloud
Price Books, Products and Assets	Unified Link Contact Point Address with Contact Point Address	Standard Data Cloud

Figure 5-29. Creating a new report

There are some Data Cloud report limits. For example, each Data Cloud report displays a maximum of two thousand rows in run mode, and each report supports at most five row-level formulas.

Additionally, some features and functions are not available. At this time, it is not possible to create custom report types on CIs. Also, keep in mind that Data Cloud reports show totals and subtotals based on all report data, not just the records displayed. It is recommended that you first review the Salesforce documentation pages for "Data Cloud Reports and Dashboards: Limits and Limitations" (*https://oreil.ly/4QL4o*).

Billing for Data Cloud Reports and Dashboards

It's important to remember that processing goes on in the background to retrieve the records to be displayed whenever you run reports and dashboards in Data Cloud. That type of processing consumes credits, thus incurring usage charges. This is different from Salesforce core, which does not incur separate charges when you run reports and dashboards.

Data Cloud reports and dashboards are constructed in the same way as in Salesforce core. For a comprehensive review of Salesforce reports and dashboards, you can review *Mastering Salesforce Reports and Dashboards* by David Carnes (O'Reilly, 2023). For specific details on Data Cloud reports and dashboards, you should visit the Salesforce help documents (*https://oreil.ly/6Z5Yn*).

Search Index

The user permissions needed to create search indexes in Data Cloud are Data Cloud Admin or Marketing Admin.

Use Search Index to create index configurations for objects with text blob fields. These include objects containing data such as Salesforce Knowledge Articles or text documents stored in an external blob store, like Amazon S3. You can create a search index using one of three options: Easy Setup, Advanced Setup, or From a Data Kit (Figure 5-30).

Figure 5-30. Creating a new search index

Segments

The user permissions needed to create segments in Data Cloud are Marketing Admin, Marketing Manager, Marketing Data Aware Specialist, or Marketing Specialist.

Access to the Salesforce Data Cloud Segment Builder requires additional licensing. The Segment Builder gives you the ability to define specific segments of users based on any distinct object or target entity such as a Unified Individual or Account DMO. Standard and waterfall segments can be created using the Visual Builder (Figure 5-31). In addition to selecting your audiences' attributes and related attributes, you can include existing CIs.

Audience members who opted into restriction of processing are removed from the population when segmenting on Unified Individual or Individual. Data protection and privacy compliance controls for personal data are not enforced when segmenting on other objects.

Data Cloud segments can be displayed in a list view under the Segments tab. Within each segment record, you'll see details like total segment population and the segment publishing status. The Salesforce Data Cloud platform automatically creates a DMO once you publish a segment.

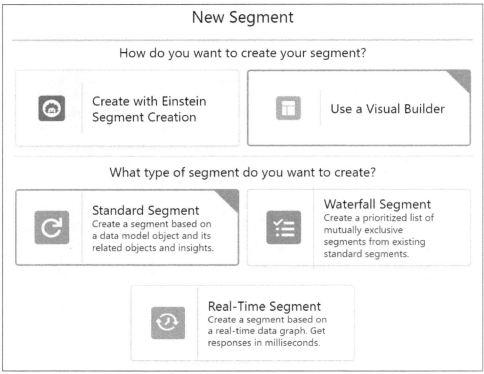

Figure 5-31. Creating a new segment

Summary

In this chapter, we took a look at the Data Cloud menu options to prepare us for the chapters ahead, where we'll dive into each of those menu tabs. There are some Data Cloud activities you'll be undertaking, however, that won't have an associated menu option. For example, access to data mapping is undertaken through the Data Streams tab. Also, building flows for data actions will require you to access Flow Builder through the Salesforce Setup.

In the next chapter, we'll explore the five menu options for data ingestion and storage, where we'll explore creating new data streams by ingesting data from different connector types. We'll also be introduced to the powerful data sharing capabilities available with Salesforce's Zero Copy Partner Network.

CHAPTER 6

Data Ingestion and Storage

In the previous chapter, we were introduced to 23 different Data Cloud menu options that we categorized into five core capabilities. This chapter is a deep dive into the first one, the data ingestion and storage capabilities of Salesforce Data Cloud. We'll be exploring each of the three menu options associated with the following data ingestion and storage capabilities:

- Data Explorer
- Data Streams
- Data Lake Objects

We'll first learn about the Data Explorer tool since it will be referenced throughout the chapter, and we'll then learn about creating data streams. As part of building out data streams, you'll observe some Data Cloud object types. In Data Cloud, object types include DSOs, DLOs, DMOs, unstructured data lake objects (UDLOs), unstructured data model objects (UDMOs), and external data lake objects. Chapter 2 provides a detailed explanation of these Data Cloud object types. Most of the discussion in this chapter focuses on data ingestion and storage of structured data. We will cover how to handle unstructured data in Chapter 13.

Creation of Data Lake Objects

When using the Salesforce CRM Connector, the necessary DLOs can be created automatically. When using the other connectors for structured data, like the Amazon S3 Storage Connector, you'll need to manually create a new DLO. UDLOs need to be manually created to access unstructured data, and they are always automatically mapped to a UDMO.

Once data is ingested and stored in DLOs, it is mapped to DMOs. After they are created, DLOs and DMOs can be viewed using the Data Explorer tool; the DLOs also have their own menu tab where you can explore them in more detail.

After learning about the Data Explorer tool and discovering how to set up connectors to ingest data, we'll discuss another way to access data that doesn't require connectors. The last section of the chapter is devoted to the data share capabilities of Salesforce Data Cloud. This chapter will also provide detailed explanations of the near real-time and batch ingest connectors as well as a high-level overview of accessing data sources via data shares. More detail on the latter will be forthcoming in Chapter 13.

Getting Started

This section contains the required prework and important things you should know before you get started in this chapter.

Prework

Make sure to complete these requirements before attempting data ingestion:

- Complete the steps in "Connecting to Relevant Salesforce Clouds" on page 103 for any Salesforce Clouds from which you'll be ingesting data.
- Obtain programmatic credentials for any cloud storage, external platforms, and connector services you'll be using.

For an actual implementation, you'll want to have completed the following data discovery activities and prepared the necessary items so that you have important details ahead of time:

- A data source asset inventory list, which includes the data locations such as Salesforce CRM, Marketing Cloud, spreadsheets, cloud storage, and more.
- An assessment of the data quality in each source. For example, are words frequently misspelled, or is there important missing data in some fields?
- A description of how individuals in each of the data sources are identified. For example, do you use email or a name, or do you use a unique system identifier such as contact keys, lead IDs, or subscriber keys?
- A list of common data, such as email address and first name, that is consistently shared across systems.
- An understanding of the customer journey, including interaction points.

It's important to capture a holistic picture of all the data, even if you only plan to ingest a subset of the data initially. Doing so allows you to confirm that you've identified all important data and also sets you up for success for future Data Cloud use case implementations.

What You Should Know

For Salesforce core and near-core platform sources, creating data streams can only be done after establishing the data connections to the relevant Salesforce Clouds. That's why you need to have completed the first-time Data Cloud platform setup in Chapter 4. For third-party data sources, you'll need to configure native connectors or use another connector like MuleSoft.

Single Connector Framework

This chapter provides details for connectors and integrations currently available as of the time of publication. However, Salesforce is in the midst of building out a robust single connector framework for Data Cloud, and it continues to add new connectors and integrations at a rapid pace.

When creating data streams using Salesforce CRM Connector, you'll want to use starter data bundles for data ingestion whenever possible, as it is the easiest way to get started. Alternatively, you can use direct object ingestion and/or data kits. More details about starter data bundles and data kits can be found in Chapter 2.

When creating data streams using the Amazon S3 Storage Connector or other native connectors, you'll have to make decisions about which ingestion data category to choose. An *ingestion data category* is a data type grouping that plays an important part in how the data will be used in the data model within Salesforce Data Cloud. In Chapter 7, we'll dive into the Salesforce Customer 360 Data Model, which can help you understand how to attempt direct object ingestion of Salesforce objects.

Noneditable After Ingestion

It is important to select the right ingestion data category at the time of ingestion because data categories cannot be edited after ingestion. The alternative is to disconnect the source and create a new connection with the desired data category. However, this is difficult, especially if mappings have already been completed and constituent components have been built using the ingested data. Not only is it time consuming to rework ingestion, but it's also expensive. You'll consume credits each time you reingest the data.

There are three ingestion data category choices: Profile, Engagement, and Other. *Profile* data provides information about individuals and includes identifiers, demographic and profile-related attributes, and contact points like email and phone number. In Salesforce Data Cloud, Profile data is indexed by ID only. It is important to note that Profile category data can be segmented upon, and that it is the only one of the three categories that can be used in segmentation to segment upon. The Profile category data is also used for calculating unified profile counts for those customers who are using the Salesforce CDP SKU.

The *Engagement* data category is used for time series data points like customer transactions and web browsing histories. In Salesforce Data Cloud, Engagement data is indexed by event date, and to be included in this category, the engagement-related data must have immutable date values. This category is special due to the way the Engagement category requires a date to apply the indexing. As we'll learn later, only Engagement data DLOs can be mapped to DMOs with an inherited Engagement category. In doing so, this could make it possible in the future to create different indexing to support query optimization. For example, it would be fairly easy to index based on binary data to make it possible to immediately discard anonymous data to conserve on the number of rows processed in a query.

The *Other* data category is a miscellaneous category. Examples of Other data include store locations, product information, and loyalty program details. In Salesforce Data Cloud, Other data is indexed by ID only. Importantly, data stored in a DMO with an inherited data category of Other cannot be used to define a unified profile and cannot be used in segmentation to segment upon.

Mutable Date Fields

The Other ingestion data category can include engagement-related data with mutable date fields.

Data is accessible in Data Cloud through either data ingestion or federated access. Data ingestion can be achieved using batch, streaming, and real-time ingestion patterns, while federated access does not result in data being physically ingested and stored in Salesforce Data Cloud. Data sharing, also known as *zero copy*, is discussed in Chapter 13.

For all data ingestion, Salesforce Data Cloud is a *system of reference*, which is different from a system of record in the sense that it's collecting and organizing data from all the different sources within its view. On the other hand, a *system of record* is a location where you enter new data or edit existing data.

There are special considerations when connecting to external services like Amazon S3, GCS, Azure Blob Storage, Snowflake, or SFTP. For these types of connections, you'll need to include the IP addresses used by Data Cloud Services (*https://oreil.ly/ gpk2i*) in your allowlists if your security policy requires a strict network access control list.

Now, we're ready to get started!

Viewing Data Cloud Objects via Data Explorer

The Data Explorer tool gives you the ability to drill down into various DMOs within Salesforce Data Cloud. With this functionality, you can personalize your view of Data Cloud objects to make it easier to validate the accuracy of the data and formulas that are relevant for you at any given time.

Once you click the Data Explorer menu option, you'll need to select an object from the Data Explorer dashboard (Figure 6-1). Initially, there are no objects to select after you choose an object type because you haven't ingested data yet. However, as you progress with data ingestion, you'll see how to select an object after choosing the object type.

Figure 6-1. Salesforce Data Cloud Data Explorer dashboard

It's possible to select the columns using the Edit Columns button and filter the list using the Filter List icon (Figure 6-2) to personalize our Data Explorer view. Once we have created a personalized view, we can use the Copy SOQL button to generate the SOQL that can be used to export the specified data.

Figure 6-2. Data Explorer options to copy SOQL, edit columns, refresh, and filter

We'll be taking a closer look at the DLOs and DMOs in the Data Explorer tool, once we have those objects created. You can view data graphs, described in Chapter 13, in the Data Explorer. It is also possible to view the CI objects within the Data Explorer tool. The CI object is the only object that can be viewed as a chart in Data Explorer. Select the pie icon that appears to the right of the filter icon, after you choose your CI object. CIs will be covered in Chapter 11.

Data Cannot Be Edited Using Data Cloud UI

You can explore the data within Data Cloud, but it's not possible for users to make changes to the data using the Data Cloud UI.

Salesforce Data Cloud is built to function as a system of reference rather than a system of record, which is why you ingest data from source systems like Salesforce CRM, Salesforce Marketing Cloud, and/or external sources. The ingested data in Data Cloud is not edited or changed by a user within the Data Cloud UI. Instead, when the source system data is modified with the addition of new records or the updating of existing records, those updates flow through to Data Cloud.

Although it's not possible to directly edit the data in Data Cloud, it is possible to delete records in Data Cloud. We'll discuss Data Cloud record deletion later in the chapter.

Ingesting Data Sources via Data Streams

Data can be accessed in Salesforce Data Cloud using four ingestion patterns:

- A batch ingestion pattern for planned transfers
- A streaming ingestion pattern, with latency under five minutes
- A real-time ingestion pattern, with latency under 200 milliseconds
- A zero copy pattern, for virtualizing data without moving it

When reviewing documentation, the terms *batch processing* and *bulk processing* are often used interchangeably. We'll use *batch processing* when describing this ingestion pattern. You'll also find the terms *streaming*, *real time*, and *near real time* frequently used interchangeably. In most cases, we'll use the term *near real time*, but understand there are latency differences between streaming and real-time ingestion patterns.

Previously, we learned about Salesforce Cloud connectors and their associated starter data bundles. We'll include these Salesforce Cloud connectors in our discussions in this chapter, but you'll find more details on them in Chapter 4. Additional information about starter data bundles that are included with these connectors can also be found in Chapter 2.

Starter Data Bundles Can Be Ingested Only Once

You'll need to ingest starter data bundles one at a time, and bundles can only be ingested once. If you decide to exclude certain objects or fields from a starter data bundle when you initially ingest the bundle, you'll have to manually ingest and map that data if you decide to ingest it in the future.

With starter data bundles, you don't need to manually create DLOs or manually map the DLO data to a DMO. That is all done automatically for you. However, DLOs need to be created manually for all data sources that don't have starter data bundles or data kits available. More information about data kits can be found in Chapter 2.

A little later in the chapter, we'll see how to ingest data into Salesforce Data Cloud using Salesforce Cloud connectors and native connectors to external sources. For our examples, we'll explore the Salesforce CRM Connector and the Amazon S3 Storage Connector, both of which are integration connectors with a batch pattern.

In addition to these two integration connectors, there are several other APIs and connectors that can be used with Salesforce Data Cloud (Figure 6-3). Data Cloud access can also be built using connector services like MuleSoft Anypoint. It's also possible to access data within Data Cloud that is stored elsewhere without having to ingest the data into Data Cloud. That access via the zero copy pattern is achieved through data federation as part of the BYOL capabilities in Data Cloud. We'll talk more about BYOL in Chapter 13.

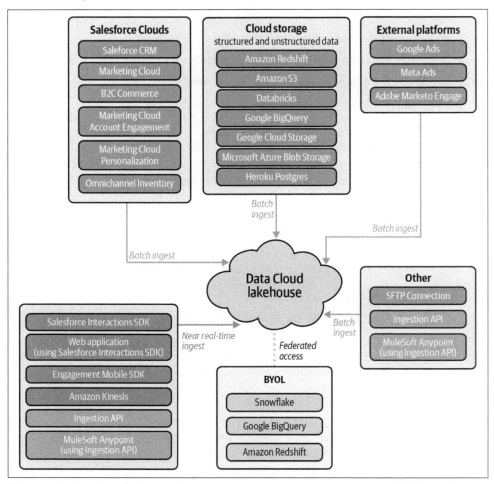

Figure 6-3. Batch and near real-time connectors, connector services, and federated data access

You'll notice that the Ingestion API can be used for both near real-time and batch ingestion. MuleSoft Anypoint, a Salesforce product, leverages the Ingestion API, and there are also native connectors for bulk loading available for major cloud providers' cloud storage systems: Amazon S3, GCS, Microsoft Azure, and Heroku Postgres. These connectors to cloud storage provide support for file ingestion for structured data, but it's also possible to ingest unstructured data stored in blob storage.

The five Salesforce Cloud batch connectors that we've discussed so far are included in Figure 6-3. Each of the five also has starter data bundles included with the connectors. Later in the chapter, we'll explore how to use starter data bundles with Salesforce CRM Connector. It works similarly for the other Salesforce Cloud connectors.

In this chapter, detailed explanations of many of the near real-time and batch ingest connectors and APIs will be provided. When we discuss accessing data sources via federated data access, a high-level overview will be provided.

Cost Considerations

The total cost of leveraging each of these different types of connectors is an important consideration to be evaluated prior to finalizing architectural decisions. Some connectors, such as MuleSoft Anypoint, require additional Salesforce licenses, and there are storage fees and egress fees to consider for data stored in third-party providers such as Amazon S3 and GCS. In addition, there are significantly different Salesforce Data Cloud costs associated with the various types of ingestion methods. At this time, the cost for streaming data into Salesforce Data Cloud is two and a half times the cost of batch ingestion per one million rows processed. Refer to Chapter 2 for more discussion of the consumption charges specific to Data Cloud. When evaluating these data ingestion costs for data outside of the Salesforce core platform, it is recommended that you also consider whether data sharing capabilities are an option; if so, that would allow you access to external data where it resides.

The Data Cloud sources and integrations shown in Figure 6-3 are examples of common connections available as of when this book was written. Salesforce continues to add more connectors and integrations at a rapid pace. You'll want to review the Salesforce documentation (*https://oreil.ly/gmBJ7*) for Data Cloud sources, targets, and integrations for the latest information.

Different data stream types can operate on different refresh schedules, and Salesforce is continually improving refresh schedules. Refer to the data stream schedules for Data Cloud (*https://oreil.ly/wykE9*) for the most current information.

Near Real-Time Ingest Connectors

There are five APIs and connectors that can be selected for ingesting data into Salesforce Data Cloud in near real time:

- Salesforce Interactions SDK
- Salesforce Web and Mobile application SDK
- Amazon Kinesis

- Ingestion API
- MuleSoft Anypoint (using Ingestion API)

Let's review each of these connectors now.

Salesforce Interactions SDK

Salesforce Interactions SDK, an extensible data capture and collection framework, can be used to track different types of customer interactions on your website. These interactions can then be delivered to your Salesforce Data Cloud and used to build behavior profiles. Salesforce Interactions SDK comes with ready-to-use event data models. In addition to tracking customer interactions, the SDK provides details on the following interactions:

- Identity and cookie management for anonymous and named identity tracking
- Consent management integration hooks
- Configuration-driven instrumentation with sitemaps
- Integration hooks for adding custom functionality

An important requirement is that website customers' browsers must be capable of running ECMAScript 6 (ES6)-compatible code for you to take advantage of the Salesforce Interactions SDK.

Salesforce Web and Mobile Application SDK

The Salesforce Web and Mobile application SDK enables you to create Data Cloud data streams in near real time from your mobile applications and websites. It's possible to ingest both engagement-related data and profile-related data using this connector. Engagement data is ingested every 15 minutes, while Profile data is ingested every hour.

If you're interested in what is needed for a Salesforce Data Cloud administrator to set up a near real-time connector, the following explains the steps you would need to take.

First, click on the gear icon at the top right of the screen and go to Data Cloud Setup → Websites & Mobile Apps.

Next, you'll click the New button to Connect a Website or Mobile Source (to connect your online source to import data), fill in the Connector Name, and select either Mobile App or Website as the Connector Type (Figure 6-4). Then, click the Save button.

Figure 6-4. Salesforce Data Cloud setup for website and mobile application sources

You'll notice that a schema is required for a Mobile App connection, so you'll need to provide that. The schema is something you'll get from your developer, and in return, you'll provide the developer with the connector details for the tenant-specific endpoint and the source ID (Figure 6-5). Both of those pieces of information are generated automatically by Salesforce.

Integration Guide

Connect your Source
Use the documentation to connect your online data source to Data Cloud.
https://help.salesforce.com/articleView?id=c360_a_web_mobile_app_connector.htm&type=5

Add the Tenant Specific Endpoint and Source ID to your source code.
Pass this endpoint and your Source ID to your developer for all tenant specific API calls.

Tenant Specific Endpoint 🛈

mftdmmjqg14wk9jvg8zwkml0my.c360a.salesforce.com

Source ID

b2578015-81f3-4ff5-bdc7-84aad14a632a

Figure 6-5. Salesforce Data Cloud mobile application connection details

For a website connection, you'll want to upload a sitemap in addition to the schema. The schema and the prompted sitemap are things you'll get from your developer, and in return, you'll provide the developer with the content delivery network (CDN) script. The CDN is generated automatically by Salesforce (Figure 6-6) once you select the website connector type and click the Save button.

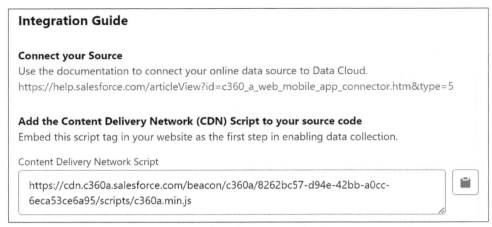

Figure 6-6. Salesforce Data Cloud website connection details

Once you've received the JSON event type schema and the sitemap for a website connection from your developer, you can click Upload Files in the Schema block and Upload Sitemap in the Sitemap block. Be sure to save your work after you've confirmed all events and fields are populated accordingly. You can update your schema by adding new events or fields, but the schema must retain all previous events and fields. Be sure to enter a descriptive name for the website or mobile source you just added to the connector.

Amazon Kinesis

Amazon Kinesis is a fully managed, serverless streaming data service that's built to ingest and process large streams of data in near real time. To use this connector in Data Cloud, you'll need to supply the connection name, connection API name, and authentication and connection details, including the region where your AWS Kinesis exists. Using the Amazon Kinesis Connector, you can ingest profile-related and event-related data.

There are some important limitations with the Amazon Kinesis Connector. It can't read nested JSON data, it can have only a single object in its schema, and it can only contain the type of data that's selected when the data stream is created. Remember that you'll need to identify the primary key when you set up the data stream. If a primary key doesn't exist in the data, you'll need to create one using a formula field.

Ingestion API Connector

The Ingestion API Connector lets you connect an external system to Salesforce Data Cloud with an Ingestion API. The *Ingestion API* is a type of REST API that supports both bulk and streaming patterns for loading data. Interestingly, a single data stream can accept data from both the streaming and the bulk interaction connector.

The process to set up and configure an Ingestion API in Salesforce Data Cloud will require assistance from a Data Cloud developer. A Data Cloud admin is responsible for setting up the Ingestion API Connector and configuring a connected app, so the admin will need to obtain from the developer the open authorization (OAuth) flow details that will be used to connect the API and to provide the developer with the connector endpoint details.

Limits of Ingestion API Connector

There are two limits associated with this streaming Ingestion API Connector. This connector supports only Insert statements, and a single request cannot exceed 200 KB of data.

The Ingestion API Connector streaming pattern accepts incremental updates to a dataset as those changes are captured.

MuleSoft Anypoint Connector for Salesforce Customer Data Platform

The MuleSoft Anypoint Connector can be used to ingest data from any third-party sources into Data Cloud. You're able to automate ingestion from legacy systems into Data Cloud by first setting up the Ingestion API and then MuleSoft Anypoint Connector.

At this time, the connector for Salesforce CDP APIs is the Salesforce CDP Connector 1.1 – Mule 4. This MuleSoft Anypoint Connector for Salesforce CDP uses standard OAuth authorization flows that enable you to automate data ingestions from third parties. The connector supports both bulk and streaming patterns for loading data, and it also supports delete operations. In total, the connector supports query API, streaming ingestion API, bulk ingestion API, profile API, CIs API, and data actions from Salesforce Data Cloud.

The MuleSoft Anypoint Connector for Salesforce CDP also provides the following:

- Read access to DMOs and DLOs
- Read access to retrieve metadata and object records of customer profile information
- Read access to retrieve metadata and object records of CIs
- A webhook listener event source to consume CDP data action events

The Anypoint Exchange prebuilt connectors can be leveraged to connect to some popular SaaS applications, integrate with common cloud infrastructure and services, and connect to many different external databases by using Java Database Connectivity (JDBC) and other open protocols.

Using MuleSoft in conjunction with Data Cloud allows you to access legacy systems and platforms for which native connectors don't exist. Using MuleSoft can help improve efficiency for those use cases because you're able to manage your entire API lifecycle in one place. This makes MuleSoft a great choice to connect legacy systems at scale. Another great benefit of using MuleSoft is its ability to use a powerful scripting language to perform data transformations before data is ingested into Data Cloud.

Batch Data Source Ingest Connectors: Salesforce Clouds

In this section, we're going to explore how to build out data streams using the Salesforce CRM Connector we set up in Chapter 4. The Marketing Cloud Connector, B2C Commerce Connector, Marketing Cloud Engagement Connector, and the Marketing Cloud Personalization and Omnichannel Inventory Connectors all function like the Salesforce CRM Connector. Getting access to any of those four connectors, however, requires additional Salesforce near-core cloud platforms to be licensed.

Let's take a minute to understand a little about the different Salesforce Clouds, how to access them, and where the data for each cloud is stored. In Chapter 2, we learned about the Data Cloud architecture and how data is stored off core in a data lakehouse using a persistent storage known as DLOs. In Chapter 4, when we provisioned Data Cloud, we discovered that access to Data Cloud is accomplished by signing into Salesforce CRM and accessing the Data Cloud app using the Salesforce CRM App Launcher. In that way, it's a seamless experience for the end user, who doesn't need to worry about where the data is actually stored.

Some other Salesforce Clouds, known as Salesforce near-core platforms (Figure 6-7), are not accessible through the Salesforce CRM App Launcher. There is a different log-in URL for those platforms, and the user interfaces look different. However, the Einstein Trust Layer is what gives you peace of mind no matter whether you need to access your Salesforce data that is stored in core, near core, or off core.

The Salesforce core platform includes Sales Cloud, Service Cloud, Loyalty Management Cloud, and more. Each of these clouds is a system of record, where you add new records and update existing records. All of the near-core platforms are also systems of record, and Data Cloud is where you bring together all of the different Salesforce cloud platform data. Also, as we saw in Chapter 2, it's possible to bring CRM data into Data Cloud from more than one Salesforce CRM org. This is incredibly helpful for industries where there is a lot of merger and acquisition activity.

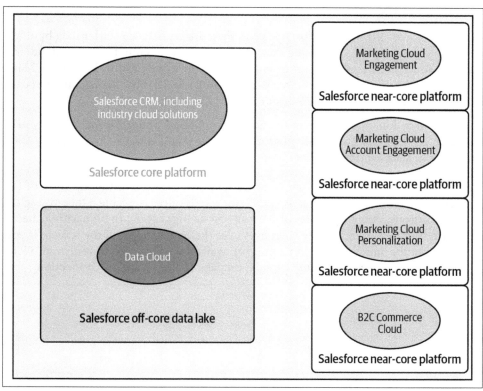

Figure 6-7. Salesforce core, near-core, and off-core data storage

Figure 6-7 also represents the different native Salesforce Cloud connectors that can set up for Data Cloud ingestion. Today, there exist six Salesforce native cloud connectors:

- Salesforce CRM
- Marketing Cloud Engagement (Marketing Cloud)
- B2C Commerce
- Marketing Cloud Account Engagement (formerly Pardot)
- Marketing Cloud Personalization (formerly Interaction Studio)
- Omnichannel Inventory

Each of these six native connectors also includes access to starter data bundles. Refer to the Salesforce "Starter Data Bundles" reference guide (*https://oreil.ly/ZDREr*) for a complete listing of bundles.

Salesforce CRM Connector

Using Salesforce CRM Connector, it is possible to ingest data via starter data bundles, direct object ingestion, or by using data kits. We'll be leveraging the Sales Cloud and Service Cloud data bundles in our example. If you have licenses for the Loyalty Management platform, you can also ingest data using the Loyalty Management starter data bundles available using the Salesforce CRM Connector.

To create new data streams using the Salesforce CRM Connector, make sure you're logged in to your Salesforce core platform. Use the App Launcher to access the Data Cloud application, and then follow these steps:

1. Click on the Data Streams tab, then click the New button at the top right of the screen. You'll see the Salesforce CRM connected source available. Once you select the connector, the top corner of the box will be highlighted in blue with a checkmark (Figure 6-8). Click the Next button at the bottom right of the screen. If you don't see the Salesforce CRM Connector available, you'll need to return to "Connecting to Relevant Salesforce Clouds" on page 103 to set up the connection.

Figure 6-8. Salesforce CRM Connector selected for creating a new data stream

2. You have the option to select a data bundle or a Salesforce object. You'll notice that you have standard data bundles available for the Sales Cloud and Service Cloud (Figure 6-9).

Figure 6-9. Sales Cloud and Service Cloud starter bundles available for creating a new data stream

3. If you click the All Objects button to the right of the Data Bundles button rather than selecting a bundle, you'll see a list of all the Salesforce objects currently available for you to select (Figure 6-10). At this time, we're not going to ingest data for individual objects or fields. We'll revisit this option in "Extending the Data Cloud Standard Data Model" on page 194.

Figure 6-10. All Salesforce objects available for creating a new data stream

4. With the Data Bundles button selected, choose the Sales standard data bundle. You'll notice the top corner of the box will be highlighted in blue with a checkmark (Figure 6-11). On the right, you'll see that the Account, Contact, and Lead objects are included in this Sales bundle. Be sure to click the Next button to proceed.

Figure 6-11. Sales Cloud starter bundle selected to create a new data stream

5. On the left, you'll see the three Sales platform objects included in this bundle: Contact, Lead, and Account. Try selecting a different Sales object to the left to see how the fields change on the right. To the right, you'll see the list of fields for the selected object. The default object for the Sales bundle is the Contact object (Figure 6-12). Remember that this data stream bundle will need to have been previously installed or you'll receive an error message when you click the Next button.

Figure 6-12. Contact object of the Sales Cloud start bundle

On the right, the standard fields are selected. Custom fields are included in the list but are not selected by default. You have the option of selecting and de-selecting most fields, but there are some required fields as indicated by a checkmark in the Required column. You'll not be able to uncheck any of those fields. You'll also notice that you can create a new formula field with the New Formula Field button on the top right. Make any necessary changes on the screen, including creating new formula fields, and then click the Next button on the bottom right. Formula fields are optional, but they're useful for standardizing formatting, adding keys to help join and map data, and to add flags for data that meet certain criteria. We'll learn more about formula fields in Chapter 7.

6. Now you'll see a preview of the three new data streams that will be created. All three streams have been categorized as being Profile data. The default refresh mode is Upsert, and the default refresh schedule is Batch (Figure 6-13). There is also an option to set filters for the data space.

Figure 6-13. Preview of new data streams to be created from the Sales Cloud starter bundle

Click the Deploy button on the bottom right of the screen. It will take just a few minutes for your new data streams to be created.

7. Now we can see the data streams we just created. Within the Data Streams tab, use the drop-down arrow to select the All Data Streams list view (Figure 6-14).

Figure 6-14. All Data Streams list view for all data streams

Make sure you installed the Sales and Service starter data bundles previously when you set up the connectors, as described in Chapter 4. If not, you won't be able to deploy your starter bundles. If you're not sure data bundles have been installed, navigate to Setup → Salesforce CRM and confirm installation has occurred (Figure 6-15).

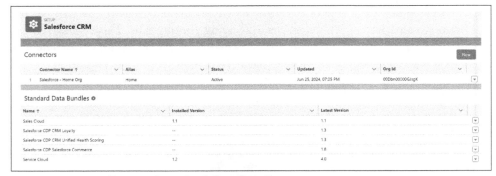

Figure 6-15. Installation of standard data bundles

Additionally, if you experience any errors due to insufficient permissions (Figure 6-16) while setting up data streams, you'll need to take action.

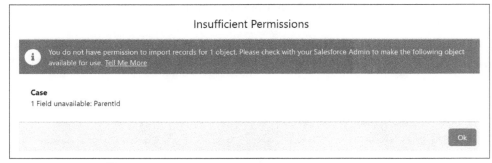

Figure 6-16. Insufficient Permissions error message

Any errors due to insufficient permissions will need to be resolved for the Data Cloud Salesforce Connector permission set. Access permission sets from Setup and then edit the Data Cloud Salesforce Connector permission set by selecting the Object Settings option and granting permission to any object and/or field that you need. The Read and View All object permissions are needed, along with Read Access to specific fields.

Batch Data Sources Ingest Connectors: Cloud Storage

In this section, we're going to see what it looks like to build out data streams using the Amazon S3 Storage Connector. The GCS Connector and the Microsoft Azure Connector both work in ways similar to the Amazon S3 Storage Connector.

Limits

There are two limits associated with cloud connectors like Amazon S3 and GCS Connector: they support a 10 GB maximum per file, and no more than 1,000 files can be scheduled for each run.

It's also possible to build out data streams for batch data sources using the Ingestions API Connector and the MuleSoft Anypoint Connectors. Each will be briefly discussed again as they are also for batch ingestion as well as options for streaming ingestion.

Amazon S3 Storage Connector

To ingest files from Amazon S3, you'll need to set up a connector and then create a new data stream:

1. Use the gear icon on the top right of the screen to select the Setup. In the Quick Find window, search for connectors and click the New button. If you've enabled beta connectors (Figure 6-17) from the Feature Manager, you'll notice many available beta connectors in addition to existing connectors like Amazon S3.

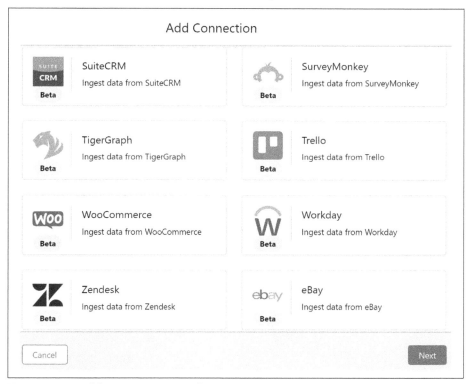

Figure 6-17. Adding a new external connection

There are more than 80 new beta connectors available today. Some of these new Data Cloud native connectors include ActiveCampaign, Asana, Google Contacts, Google Drive, IBM Cloud Object Storage, IBM Db2, Jira, Microsoft Teams, Monday, MongoDB, Oracle Eloqua, Oracle NetSuite, Oracle Service Cloud, PayPal, Redis, SAP HANA, Salesloft, ServiceNow, ShipStation, SurveyMonkey, Trello, WooCommerce, Workday, Zendesk, and eBay.

2. After selecting the Amazon S3 Connector, you'll need to enter authentication and connection details (Figure 6-18). Enter the S3 bucket name, the access key, and the secret key. If relevant, add the directory information. Click the Test Connection button and, once the connection has been confirmed, click the Save button.

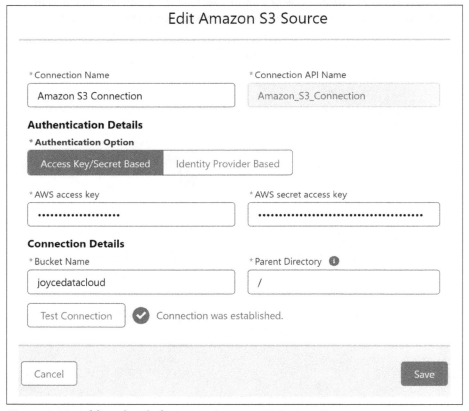

Figure 6-18. Adding details for a new Amazon S3 Source Connector

3. Once your connection has been established, you'll navigate back to the Data Cloud app and click on the Data Streams tab. You'll now see the option to select Amazon S3 for your new data stream (Figure 6-19).

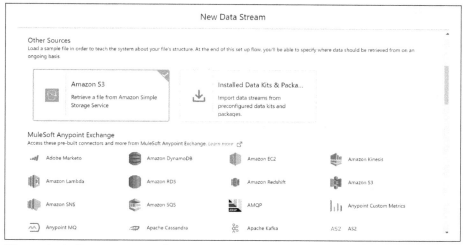

Figure 6-19. Creating a new data stream using an Amazon S3 connected source

4. Select the file type, either CSV or Parquet, and include the details for the file-name (Figure 6-20). Then click the Next button. Note that you'll need to create new data streams for each file you want to ingest from Amazon S3, but you only have to establish the connection once.

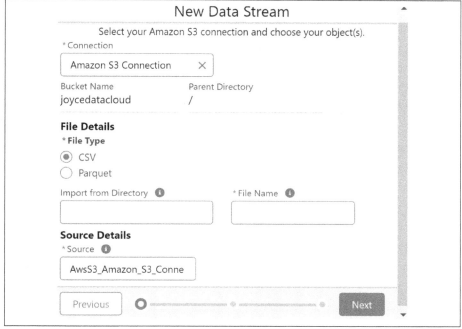

Figure 6-20. Selecting the file type for the new data stream

5. Select the primary key. You'll notice Data Cloud automatically determines the data type for each of the fields in your file. However, these are only suggestions. You can accept all the default selections or you can click on the drop-down menu to the right of any particular field and change the data type (Figure 6-21). When you're done making any changes or adding any new formula fields, be sure to click the Next button.

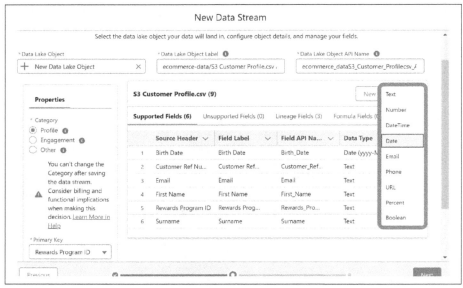

Figure 6-21. Selecting the primary key and reviewing details

6. In this final screen, you'll select the data space and refresh mode. Unless you have a compelling reason for selecting a full refresh, it's best to select the Upsert refresh mode, which will insert new and update existing data. Leave the box checked to refresh the data stream immediately. You'll also have the option to select the schedule frequency (Figure 6-22) before you click the Deploy button.

Figure 6-22. Selecting the data space and refresh mode

7. Success! Now, you can view the fields, details, and refresh history of the new data stream. Unlike our previous example where we used the CRM Connector, we're not quite done with this data stream. When we used starter data bundles with the CRM Connector, the data stream DLO was automatically mapped to the standard DMO. However, when you set up a connector to an external source, none of the fields are automatically mapped. You'll notice that there is a Start button you'll select to get started mapping the DLO (Figure 6-23). We'll learn about data modeling in Chapter 7, so we'll be ready to complete data mapping in Chapter 9.

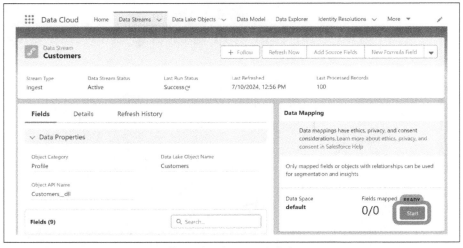

Figure 6-23. Data mapping will need to be completed

Google Cloud Storage Connector

As mentioned before, using the GCS Connector works the same way as using the Amazon S3 Storage Connector. However, to leverage the GCS Connector, you'll first need to set up the new Google connector configuration. Click on the gear icon at the top right of the screen and go to Setup → Connectors. Then, click New. You'll be given the option to add new source connectors, including Google Cloud Storage (Figure 6-24).

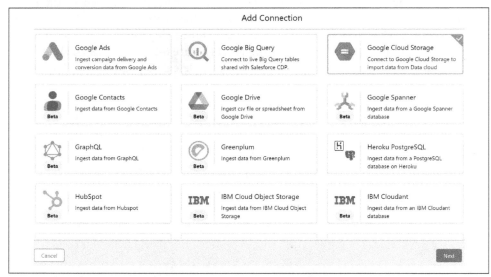

Figure 6-24. Selecting a new Google connector to be used for data streams

Fill in the details for your GCS credentials and click the Save button.

Once you save the Google connector configuration, you can go back to the Data Streams tab to complete the steps to create a new data stream.

Microsoft Azure Connector

The Microsoft Azure Connector works similarly to the Amazon S3 Connector once you set up an Azure Blob Storage connection within Data Cloud Setup. You'll need to make sure your Azure Blob Storage account has a private key setting for public access level, and you'll need to provision at least one account key.

Either a CSV or a Parquet file type can be ingested using the Microsoft Azure Connector. Ingestion of Parquet files is supported for Amazon S3 and GCS, as well as for Microsoft Azure storage. You'll want to make sure you review the Salesforce documentation to understand the conversion of Parquet data types to Data Cloud data types. For example, the STRING, ENUM, and UUID Parquet data types are converted to the Text Data Cloud data type.

Data Cloud supports the GZ and ZIP compression formats for CSV files. The platform supports the following compression formats for Parquet files: GZ, ZIP, NONE, SNAPPY, and ZSTD.

For ingestion of text files, Data Cloud supports the most common content delimiters and automatically evaluates ingested files to determine the delimiter. A best practice is to use double quotes around values in a file to ensure the system detects the correct file delimiter.

Heroku Postgres Connector

Available now is the Heroku Postgres Connector, which can be accessed via Data Cloud Setup. You can also use the AWS RDS for PostgreSQL, Amazon Aurora PostgreSQL, and Azure Database for PostgreSQL, which are currently in beta. You'll just need to enable them in the Feature Manager from within Data Cloud Setup.

External Platform Connectors

Today, a number of native connectors to external platforms exist. Google Ads, Meta Ads, and Adobe Marketo Engage have their own dedicated Data Cloud connectors. In addition, many other native connectors to external platforms are in beta. Examples include Veeva Vault, SuiteCRM, SingleStore, ShipStation, Jira, SAP SuccessFactors, Workday, and many more. Before using connector services to build a custom connection solution, you'll want to review the Salesforce documentation for an updated list of native Data Cloud connectors available to you.

Other Connectors for Batch Ingestion

In this section, we'll briefly review the Ingestion API and MuleSoft Connectors, which can be used for near real-time ingestion as well as batch ingestion. We'll also discuss the SFTP Connector.

Ingestion API Connector

The Ingestion API Connector was discussed in "Ingestion API Connector" on page 158 about near real-time ingest connectors. As previously mentioned, a single Salesforce Data Cloud data stream can accept data from both connector types.

The Ingestion API Connector bulk pattern accepts CSV files in cases where data syncs occur periodically. This batch connector can load large amounts of data on a daily, weekly, or monthly schedule.

Limits

There are two limits associated with a batch ingestion API connector. This connector supports only Insert, Upsert, and Delete statements, and each ingestion file cannot exceed 150 MB of data.

Something really exciting that's available for use with the Ingestion API is *ingestion on demand* capabilities using Salesforce Flow actions. Data flow actions can be autogenerated based on the Salesforce Ingestion API, thus enabling users to include more logic in their data ingestion processes. Some potential use cases for this ingestion on demand capability include the following:

- Processing CRM data, including aggregating certain data, and then conditionally pushing the results to Data Cloud
- Ingesting user consent data from form submits
- Logging engagement-related data based on screen flows

MuleSoft Anypoint Connector for Salesforce Customer Data Platform

The MuleSoft Anypoint Connector for Salesforce Customer Data Platform was discussed in "MuleSoft Anypoint Connector for Salesforce Customer Data Platform" on page 159 about near real-time ingest connectors. In addition to supporting the streaming Ingestion API, the MuleSoft Anypoint Connector supports the bulk Ingestion API.

Secure File Transfer Protocol Connector

Data Cloud allows you to use the new Secure File Transfer Protocol (SFTP) Connector to encrypt and transfer CSV files from your SFTP server into Data Cloud using the Secure Shell (SSH) protocol. You can set up the connection from within Data

Cloud Setup. Under Configuration, select More Connectors and you'll have the option to choose SFTP. Just make sure you've gathered the details in advance that you need: authentication method, username, password, SSH private key, passphrase, hostname, port, and parent directory.

Deleting Ingested Records from Data Cloud

It's possible to delete data ingested in Data Cloud if your data stream has an Upsert refresh model. In addition, the deletion process depends on the type of connector you're using.

Records in the source Salesforce CRM platform will be removed at the next Upsert refresh. Bulk deletions in Salesforce CRM that are in excess of 500,000 are handled at the next scheduled full refresh. All CRM data streams perform scheduled biweekly full refreshes, typically on Friday evenings after business hours.

Cascading Deletions Are Not Supported

When deleting a profile record, its related engagement or other profile records aren't deleted. You'll need to delete these records manually from each table.

Records ingested through Amazon S3, GCS, and SFTP Connectors can also be deleted using the connectors, but row versioning isn't supported for deletions.

Possible to Use a Delete File

It's possible to use a delete file to delete records ingested with the following connectors: Amazon S3, GCS, Microsoft Azure, Ingestion API, and the SFTP Connector. You'll need to create a delete file in either CSV or Parquet file format. A Parquet file format can't be used for Ingestion API or the SFTP Connector, but a CSV file can be used for any of the five connectors listed here.

The Ingestion API supports a delete operation, and after the delete requests are received programmatically, they are processed asynchronously. It's possible to use the Ingestion API to delete records from any source, but it's labor-intensive. Deletion using the Ingestion API should always occur *after* the data is deleted from the source, to prevent reingestion.

It's also possible to disconnect a data source completely. Disconnecting a data source will result in removal of all data in Data Cloud that was provided from that source. That's because Data Cloud is a system of reference that surfaces data from a source system of record. The source data remains intact in the original system of record when the data source is disconnected from Salesforce Data Cloud.

Viewing Data Lake Objects

Once you've created some data streams, you can drill down into the DLOs that were created. We'll also use the Data Explorer tool for a second time in this chapter so that we can view the new Data Cloud objects we created.

When you click on the Data Lake Objects tab, you'll have access to a list view for All Data Lake Objects (Figure 6-25).

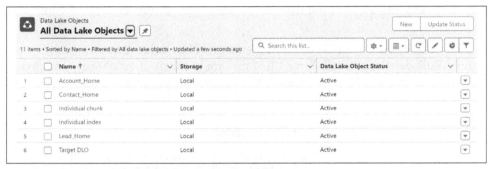

Figure 6-25. Data Lake Objects list view for all DLOs

You can also go back to the Data Explorer tab and use the dashboard to view the DLOs and DMOs.

Accessing Data Sources via Data Federation

The previous section discussed the many ways you can ingest data into Salesforce Data Cloud, and it's also possible to access data that exists outside of Data Cloud and join that data with the data ingested and stored within Data Cloud. We'll take a look at data federation in Chapter 13 when we discuss the BYOL capabilities of Data Cloud.

Summary

As part of our deep dive into the data ingestion and storage capabilities of Salesforce Data Cloud, we explored in detail three different menu options:

- Data Explorer
- Data Streams
- Data Lake Objects

We learned about many types of data ingestion APIs and connectors that can be used within Salesforce Data Cloud. As part of the discussion, several specific limitations were shared about ingestion capabilities, lookback windows, latency times, record deletion, and more. Always refer to Salesforce official documentation for the most up-to-date information because these limitations could change in the future.

In the next chapter, we'll continue our learnings by exploring data modeling topics. Data profiling and source data classification are important first steps because you'll need to understand your data so that you can assign the correct data categorization to the source data. The way a data source is categorized has many downstream implications, such as whether you can segment upon the data.

Next, we'll explore the Data Cloud standard data model and ways to extend the standard model. We'll also discuss the Salesforce Consent Data Model and the various levels of customer consent that are captured and stored within the data model.

CHAPTER 7

Data Modeling

In Chapter 6, we explored the data ingestion and storage capabilities of Salesforce Data Cloud. We also discovered how the Data Streams tab brings data from various sources into DLOs. Using Salesforce starter data bundles allows us to automatically map Salesforce CRM data to some standard DMOs, but any data that wasn't ingested as part of the starter data bundles, including external source data, won't automatically be mapped to a DMO. Thus, you'll need to manually map all DLOs for whichever starter data bundles are not available.

Mapping is a critical step because only mapped fields and objects with relationships can be used for segmentation, activation, and other value activities. Mapping needs to be completed before you can perform next steps like creating calculated and streaming insights or data actions.

There is advance work that needs to be done before you undertake data mapping (Figure 7-1). Someone on your team will need to perform the earlier steps to profile and classify the data before ingesting and mapping it. Therefore, in this chapter, we'll explain the important aspects of these earlier steps. That way, you'll be set up for success when you learn about mapping in Chapter 8.

We'll focus more on data classification because of the importance of determining the correct data category for your source data and laying the groundwork for successful data mapping. We'll also learn about developing a good data model by leveraging the data classification work performed on the source data. Throughout the chapter, we'll discuss the following menu options:

- Data Streams
- Data Model

You will also need to access some of the menu options from Chapter 6, such as Data Explorer and Data Lake objects.

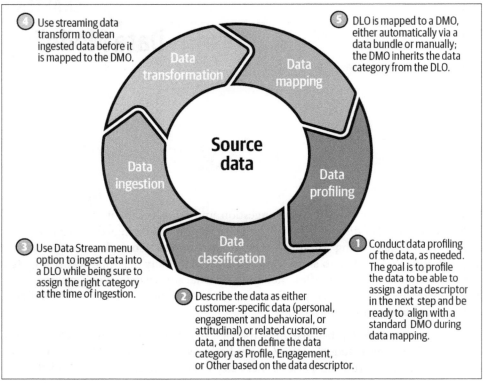

Figure 7-1. Data mapping steps

Furthermore, we'll learn about generating additional fields by creating them as formula fields. We'll also gain an understanding of the use cases for creating formula expressions to help prepare the data for mapping.

As part of the journey, we'll need to familiarize ourselves with the existing standard data model within Salesforce Data Cloud and learn how to customize that model for our purposes. Let's begin by reviewing a few important items in the "Getting Started" section before we dive into the details of data profiling and source data classification.

Getting Started

This section contains the required prework as well as some important things you should know before you get started.

Prework

You'll need to complete setting up the Salesforce CRM Connector and/or any other connectors required for your implementation before attempting the steps in this chapter.

What You Should Know

There are many similarities and some differences between the Salesforce Data Cloud modeling and the Salesforce core platform data models. One very important similarity is that it is always a best practice to start with the standard data model in both the Salesforce core platform and Data Cloud. Both the Salesforce core platform and Data Cloud include many standard objects upon which you can build your desired model. These standard models can be extended easily by adding custom fields to existing standard objects as well as creating new custom objects to fill any gaps.

Let's investigate one important difference by looking at an example. We'll review the standard Salesforce CRM Account object and then compare it to the standard Account DMO in Data Cloud (Table 7-1).

Table 7-1. Standard Account object

Platform	Object label	Object API name	Inherited category
Salesforce core	Account	Account	N/A
Data Cloud	Account	ssot__Account__dlm	Profile

Now, let's compare two standard fields in the standard Account object. The first is the Type standard field (Table 7-2).

Table 7-2. Standard Type field in standard Account object

Platform	Field label	Field API name	Field data type
Salesforce core	Type	Type	Picklist
Data Cloud	Type	ssot__AccountTypeId__c	Text

And next is the Description standard field (Table 7-3).

Table 7-3. Standard Description field in standard Account object

Platform	Field label	Field API name	Field data type
Salesforce core	Description	Description	Long Text Area(32000)
Data Cloud	Description	ssot__Description__c	Text

For standard Salesforce objects, the labels and the API names are the same. Whenever you create a custom Salesforce object or field, however, the API name of the new object or new field is appended with a double underscore and the letter "c." For example, Salesforce would automatically generate an API name of *customobject__c* for a custom object that is given the field label *customobject*. Thus, it is easy to distinguish between standard and custom objects and fields in the Salesforce core platform based on whether the API name includes the __c designation. This is not the same in Salesforce Data Cloud.

You'll notice that all standard Data Cloud objects and fields have the *ssot* prefix and are appended with the __c designation. Thus, having the __c designation in the Salesforce Data Cloud model does not indicate that an object or field is custom created as it does in the Salesforce core platform. An object or field is standard in Data Cloud if you're unable to edit or delete it, and that is an important similarity between the Salesforce core platform and Salesforce Data Cloud. Standard objects and fields cannot be edited or deleted.

Salesforce Record ID

In the Salesforce core platform standard object, there is a unique 18-character Salesforce record ID that exists for each record and should be mapped to the Salesforce Data Cloud ID field.

The ID field is not listed among the Salesforce core platform object fields accessed through the Object Manager. However, you'll be able to see that it was successfully pulled into Data Cloud and mapped correctly if you review the mappings. Remember that the Salesforce record ID is the UID from the Salesforce source system. Data Cloud is a system of reference and, as such, doesn't generate UIDs for source data records that are ingested into Data Cloud.

Also, you'll notice that unlike the Salesforce platform object, the Salesforce Data Cloud ingestion objects include a category. Each Data Cloud ingestion object is categorized as Profile, Engagement, or Other, and this category cannot be changed for Data Cloud objects once the category is inherited from a DLO.

It's worth mentioning again that there are only a limited number of data types (*https://oreil.ly/_Ak1O*) available for Data Cloud objects as compared to data types in Salesforce CRM Clouds: Boolean, text, number, percent, email, phone, URL, date, and datetime.

The *Boolean* data type's values can be `true`, `false`, and blank. The *text* data type stores any kind of text data and is the most commonly used data type in Data Cloud. The *number* data type stores numbers with a fixed scale of 18 and a precision of 38. The *percent* data type holds percentage values and can be used in any formula function that accepts the number data type.

The *email*, *phone*, and *URL* data types are each modeled on the text data type and can be used in formula functions that work with text values. The values for email, phone, and URL data types are not validated for correctness. Each of these data types will accept any text value.

The date and datetime data types are also available in Data Cloud. The *date* data type stores a calendar date for the day, month, and year only. For example, 2025-03-29 is a value that could be stored in a date field. The time portion will be ignored if the source data records include a time part for a field configured as the date data type.

A *datetime* field includes additional information: the time and the time zone. If the time and time zone aren't included, they're inferred as 00:00:00 Coordinated Universal Time (UTC). Data Cloud doesn't consider datetime fields to be constant; they're subject to time zone conversions. Thus, you might want to consider ingesting a datetime source field into Data Cloud as a date field instead.

It's important to know that any value in a record that can't be parsed into a date or datetime would be stored as a null value. Thus, it's important to review in advance the data quality of the source file and whether transformations might be needed before ingestion.

It's also important to get a good understanding of the source data in advance because the attribute data type of the source data field must match the DMO attribute type when mapping a Data Cloud DLO to a DMO. Attempting to map a number data type to a text data type, for example, produces an error. It's also impossible to change between datetime and date field types, and vice versa, once the data type has been selected.

Automatic Suggested Data Types

When you create a new data stream, Data Cloud attempts to detect the data type of each field. You can scroll to the right of the window to review and change, if needed, the auto-suggested data type. This is important because you can't change the field types after the data stream creates the DLO.

One final and important point relates to creating new custom objects. You wouldn't create a custom object in Salesforce core for a standard object that already exists. For example, a standard Account object in Salesforce core exists, so you would not create a custom Account object. Instead, you would add custom fields to the standard object, or you might use record types or enable Person accounts if you really needed to customize the standard Account object in a major way. The same is true in Data Cloud. Use the standard DMOs that exist instead of creating a new custom DMO, and you can always extend the standard DMO by adding custom fields.

The Salesforce Data Cloud model objects are intended to be used for combining similar data from various data sources into a single DMO. Thus, you should avoid creating separate DMOs for each data source ingested into the data lake. You can equate this to what is done for the Salesforce standard Lead object in the core platform. There are often many different data sources where lead information is collected and ingested into the standard Lead object, and when needed, custom fields are added to the standard Lead object to accommodate some of the unique pieces of information from the different data sources. The same is true in Data Cloud. You would want to add new custom fields to the standard DMO, and the Data Cloud standard model would then be able to accommodate multiple data sources that are ingested into the data lake and then mapped to the standard DMO.

Data Profiling

How you approach data modeling, data transformations, and data mapping for Salesforce Data Cloud is largely dependent on your source data. If your source data consists of nothing but Salesforce standard objects with only standard fields, then you won't need to devote a lot of time to profiling your data or designing a Salesforce Data Cloud data model. You'd be able to leverage Salesforce data bundles to automatically create the data streams from Salesforce and map the data to the Data Cloud standard objects. Data profiling and data classification wouldn't be required (Table 7-4).

Table 7-4. Data profiling and data classification requirements

Data source	Data profiling	Data classification
Salesforce standard object – standard fields	Not required	Not required
Salesforce standard object – custom fields	Not needed	Not needed
Salesforce custom object – all fields	Recommended	Required
Non-Salesforce (external)	Required	Required

If, however, you've created some custom fields in your standard Salesforce core objects like most companies do, you might need to add a few custom fields to the Data Cloud standard DMOs and then manually map those custom fields. There is usually a low level of effort associated with handling custom fields that have been added to the Salesforce CRM standard objects. Generally, you won't need to profile or classify the data because the standard fields of the ingested source data will have already been mapped to a DMO. You'll just need to map the few Salesforce CRM custom fields to fields in the DMO.

More planning and work are needed to prepare for Salesforce custom objects to be ingested and mapped to a DMO. Importantly, you'll want to allocate the most time to properly profiling and classifying all non-Salesforce data. Data profiling is a necessary step for all non-Salesforce data (Table 7-4).

There are certainly plenty of data profiling activities you'll likely want to consider undertaking, like identifying key and foreign-key candidates in the data. For data modeling in Salesforce Data Cloud, you need to describe your external source data using the descriptors explained in the next section. From there, you'll use the descriptors to determine which of the three categories is the correct one for any particular data source. This must be determined before the data is ingested into a DLO via a data stream, so the first goal of profiling is to determine the category that will be assigned to the source data at the time of data ingestion. The ultimate goal is to understand your external data in such a way that you can incorporate it into the Salesforce Data Cloud standard model.

After the external data is ingested, you'll manually map the data to an existing Salesforce standard DMO, if an appropriate one exists. If not, you'll create a custom DMO for mapping. Remember, most Salesforce CRM standard fields within standard objects are mapped automatically when you use existing data bundles, so you won't need to give a lot of thought to your data modeling approach (Table 7-5).

Table 7-5. Data modeling approach

Data source	Data bundle	Standard DMO/standard field	Standard DMO/ custom field	Custom DMO/custom field
Salesforce standard object – standard fields	Preferred (when available)	Alternative	Use sparingly	Do not use
Salesforce standard object – custom fields	N/A	Preferred (when available)	Alternative	Use sparingly
Salesforce custom object – all fields	N/A	Preferred (when available)	Alternative	Use sparingly
Non-Salesforce (external)	N/A	Preferred (when available)	Alternative	Use as needed

The process of classifying the data before ingestion and for modeling purposes is most relevant for Salesforce custom objects and external data. Let's now consider with what descriptors and categories we'll want to classify Salesforce custom objects and non-Salesforce data.

Source Data Classification

For classification and modeling purposes, we'll be using the terms *customer* and *individual* interchangeably to describe a person in whom we are interested. A customer could be a client, consumer, buyer, shopper, purchaser, health care patient, patron, donor, or similar. All this information can come from a variety of sources.

First-party data about customers is the data your organization collects from your audience, either through direct interactions or directly from the person. Sometimes, there is a distinction made between *zero-party data* (like an email address or birth date provided to you by the person) and first-party data (which is observed behavior and interactions such as an individual's product purchase history or which pages on your website the person has visited). Throughout this book, we don't make a distinction between zero-party and first-party data. Instead, we've incorporated zero-party data into first-party data whenever we refer to and discuss first-party data.

First-party data is the most reliable data source, as compared to second- and third-party data sources. Second-party data is shared between co-partners, and third-party data comes from external sources.

We design and develop Data Cloud data model objects that aggregate the various first-, second-, and third-party data sources that you've already determined in advance are quality data sources that you want to include in your Data Cloud model. Thus, in our discussions about customer data and data models, we're not going to differentiate between first-, second-, and third-party data sources. We'll focus on learning the ways in which all the data, from various data sources, is described so we can better categorize the data. As part of that discussion, we also need to make note of whether a specific field type is available in the source data for Engagement data.

Data Descriptors

There are several different kinds of data that are useful for describing customers. Personal data, behavioral and engagement-related data, and attitudinal data are the three main data descriptor types when referring to customers. Users of Data Cloud benefit from having all three types of data.

Personal data

Personal data includes information that is personally identifiable and non-personally identifiable. *Personally identifiable information* (PII) encompasses data that can be directly or indirectly linked to an individual's identity. Examples of PII information are:

- Social Security numbers
- Driver's license and passport numbers
- Mailing addresses and telephone numbers
- Email addresses
- Photos
- Biometric data

- Account numbers
- Birthdates
- Admission and discharge dates
- Vehicle identifiers, including license plates
- Payment details
- Login credentials

Personally identifiable details can include medical, educational, financial, and employment data. Protected health information (PHI) is a subset of PII that refers specifically to health information. *PII-linkable data* is information that isn't directly linked to an individual but could be considered PII data when combined with data such as zip code, gender, age group, and job category. *Non-personally identifiable information (non-PII)* includes anonymous data such as IP addresses and device IDs.

Behavioral and engagement data

Behavioral data is information related to a customer's journey. It could include transactional data such as purchase history, subscriptions, cart abandonment, and donations, and it could also include product usage data such as feature usage, frequency, and task completion. *Engagement data*, a subset of behavioral data, consists of information related to how customers engage with your organization via all channels. It could include webpage visits, social media post likes and shares, email open rates and click-through rates, customer service cases, and support ticket requests.

Attitudinal data

Attitudinal data is often qualitative and provides insight into the attitudes and feelings of customers. It includes preferences, satisfaction details, and purchase criteria. This type of information is frequently gathered through surveys, customer reviews, and focus groups.

Related Customer Data

Related customer data includes information related to the customer or the customer journey. Examples include authorization form details, loyalty benefit types, product catalogs, and sales channels. As you would expect, there is a significant number of standard DMOs for related customer data.

Now that we have a good understanding of how to describe the source data, we'll be able to use that knowledge to assign one of three categories to the source data, which is a requirement for all source data ingested into Salesforce Data Cloud. A bit later in the chapter, we'll go through a categorization flowchart, but before we do that, let's review the three Salesforce Data Cloud data categories.

Data Categories

In Chapter 6, we were required to select one of three categories when we created a new data stream. The three available categories were Profile, Engagement, and Other. In addition to these three categories, there are a few others used for DLOs automatically created by Data Cloud processes. Process examples include search index configuration, segmentation, and activation. However, there exist only three categories users can select when creating a new data stream.

The recommended way to approach data category assignment is to first think about how to define your customer data using the three data descriptors previously described. Then, you can decide in which category a particular dataset belongs.

Inheritance of Data Categories

DMOs don't have a first-class concept of category. Instead, a DMO inherits a data category from the first DLO that is mapped to it (Figure 7-2). Subsequent DLOs must be in the same category as the DMO to be mapped to it.

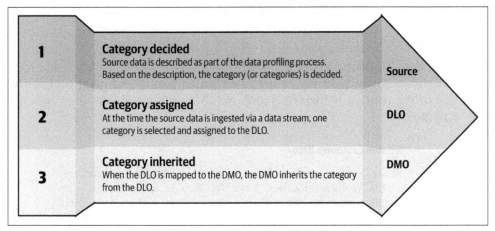

Figure 7-2. Assignment and inheritance of a data category

Each DLO gets assigned to a category as data is ingested via a data stream. The assignment happens automatically when you use a data bundle. Otherwise, you have to select the data category at the time you create the data stream.

Handling Multiple Categories in Source Data

A data source might contain different categories of data. Therefore, you might want to divide a source's data into multiple data streams because only one category can be selected per dataset.

Profile data

Data sets that include PII would most likely be categorized as Profile data in Salesforce Data Cloud. For example, a list of customers that includes customer IDs, email addresses, and phone numbers would be categorized as Profile data. The DMO model will likely have very few DMOs categorized as Profile data, but these are some of the most important DMOs. Examples of Salesforce standard DMOs that belong to the Profile category include the Account, Lead, and Loyalty Program Member objects.

Engagement data

Datasets that include behavioral and engagement-related data would most likely be categorized as Engagement data in Salesforce Data Cloud. Engagement datasets are time-series oriented. When you select Engagement as the category, you'll need to define the event time using a date field from your schema (Figure 7-3).

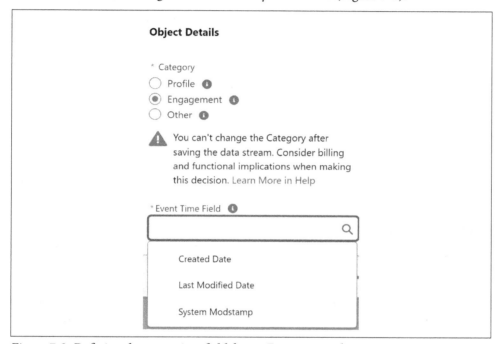

Figure 7-3. Defining the event time field for an Engagement dataset

Event Time with Immutable Value Is Needed

Choose an event time with an immutable value. An *immutable value* is one that can't be modified after it's created. Selecting a date field that could change will cause duplication of records because multiple records with the same primary key will get added to the DLO.

For example, case object data will include the date when the support ticket was created or the date the case was opened. The *created date* won't change, but there could be several status updates to the case over a period of time, so the *last modified date* will probably change. Therefore, you'll want to select the immutable created date as the event time field.

Other data

Datasets that are related to Profile and Engagement data but don't actually contain profile-related or engagement-related data would be categorized as Other data. Examples would be product or store information. Also, you'll choose the Other data category if you have engagement-related data that doesn't have an immutable date field.

Immutable Date and Datetime Fields

As mentioned earlier, Salesforce supports the date and datetime data types in Data Cloud. For data described as behavioral and engagement-related data, it's important to understand more about the date and datetime fields in the source data.

Data described as engagement related will ultimately be categorized as either *engagement* or *Other*, based on the availability of a relevant immutable date or datetime field. Engagement data categorization requires an immutable field value.

An *immutable field value* is one that won't change. For example, the date and time of a sales transaction or when a service was created are examples of values to put in an immutable datetime field. In contrast, the *last modified date* field is a field with mutable values. An example would be a last modified date field for a record that would update accordingly as the status field value of an order changed from "entered" to "shipped" to "delivered."

Data Categorization

We've learned how to describe source data, and we understand each of the three Salesforce Data Cloud categories. We're now ready to walk through a data categorization flowchart. This flowchart assumes you've applied data descriptors to your source data, and for behavioral and engagement-related data, you'll also need to have determined whether an immutable datetime data type exists. One of the main purposes of using the flowchart I've constructed (Figure 7-4) is to help you determine if more than one category of data exists in your source data.

Handling Multiple Data Categories in Source Data

If your data source includes more than one category of data, then you'll likely want to consider splitting the data source before ingesting it, if possible. The reason is because only one category can be assigned to each data stream. Alternatively, if it is not possible to divide the data source, then you should consider creating multiple data streams for the data source. It's possible to accommodate multiple data categories using Data Cloud transformation after the data is ingested. However, that could be an expensive solution because of the number of credits consumed, depending on the volume of data ingested.

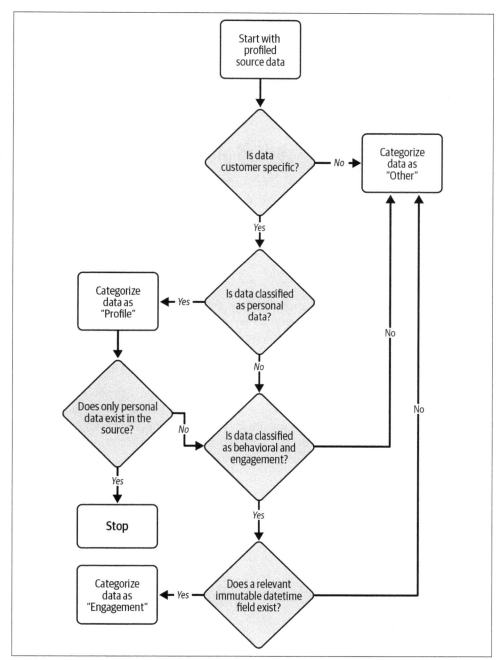

Figure 7-4. Data categorization flowchart

Profiling and classifying your source data are important steps in helping determine the correct category at the time of data ingestion. They are also important steps needed for designing your Salesforce Data Cloud data model, especially for Salesforce CRM custom objects and non-Salesforce source data. Designing your Salesforce Data Cloud data model includes considering how you'd map each data source field to an existing DMO standard field, only creating new DMO custom fields and custom objects if absolutely necessary (Figure 7-4).

Salesforce Data Cloud Standard Model

Deciding which one of the Salesforce standard models to use for your data isn't necessarily something you can do quickly because more than two hundred standard DMOs exist in Salesforce Data Cloud. You'll have a much easier time narrowing down the choices if you follow the process of first determining the primary subject area. From there, you can review the standard DMOs within that primary subject area.

Primary Subject Areas

The many standard DMOs and the relationships among them are complex. I've created a diagram of DMO primary subject areas to simplify some of that complexity (Figure 7-5). As such, the diagram doesn't include all the relationships between the primary subject areas. For that level of detail, you can review the many different Salesforce architectural diagrams in the developer documentation (*https://oreil.ly/zcsRw*).

Generally, data belonging to the Profile category will be located in the Party subject area. There are rare exceptions to that for a few DMOs in the Loyalty and Health Care primary subject area. You'll notice that the Party subject area is heavily darkened. That's to call attention to the fact that certain Party data is required to exist in Salesforce Data Cloud. We'll provide some details about those requirements a bit later in this section.

You'll also notice that the Privacy primary subject area is lightly darkened. Although Privacy data is not a technical requirement for Salesforce Data Cloud, there are important regulatory and legal requirements related to privacy compliance that the Privacy subject area will help you with.

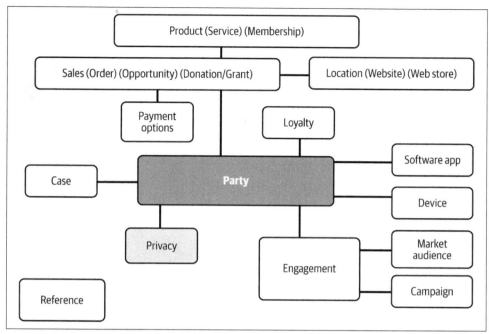

Figure 7-5. DMO primary subject areas

When considering what is included in the Engagement primary subject area, it's important to note that the Engagement category data and the Engagement primary subject area are not synonymous. Both the Engagement category and the Other category exist within the Engagement primary subject area. It's recommended that you stop now and review a list of the Salesforce Data Cloud standard DMOs in the supplemental repository (*https://oreil.ly/SuppRep_HandsOn-Salesforce*) to get an appreciation for how many standard DMOs exist. You certainly have many standard DMOs from which to choose before considering creating a new custom DMO.

Because of its importance, I've provided a diagram with more details on the Party primary subject area (Figure 7-6). One of the things to notice about the Party primary subject area is that the individual DMO information is required. In addition to the Individual standard DMO, at least one other standard DMO is required. Contact Point DMO data or Party Identification DMO data must accompany the Individual DMO in your Salesforce Data Cloud instance.

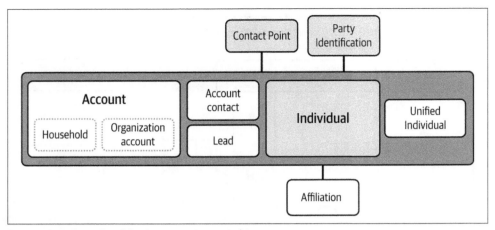

Figure 7-6. Details of the Party primary subject area

Here is a list of some standard Contact Point objects that you can use for primary subject data:

- Contact Point Email
- Contact Point Phone
- Contact Point Address
- Contact Point App
- Contact Point OTT Service
- Contact Point Social

Once you identify the primary subject area that is the most relevant for the data source, you can then consider which standard DMO within that subject area would fit best. You can narrow down the choices in the primary subject area by comparing the category of your data source to the possible DMOs within the primary subject area you've identified. Select a standard DMO with several fields that closely match the fields in your data source, and you can extend the standard DMO in a variety of ways to cover the gaps. It's also possible to create a new custom DMO if you don't find any standard DMO that meets your needs. The next section describes how to extend the standard data model in both scenarios.

Extending the Data Cloud Standard Data Model

The Salesforce Data Cloud standard data model includes prebuilt models based on common use cases. It's a best practice to adhere to the standard model as much as possible, but it will almost certainly be necessary to extend the data model to accommodate your specific data. We'll discuss the four most common ways to extend the Data Cloud data model.

Adding custom fields to standard data model objects

It's a best practice to add new custom fields to standard DMOs rather than create a new custom DMO. New custom fields within a standard Data Cloud model object are created from within the Data Mapping processing.

Adding a New Field to the Data Lake Object First

A new custom field within the standard DMO should only be created after the field has been added to the DLO. Adding the field to the DLO requires you to update the data stream.

To update the data stream with the details about the new custom field, go to the Data Streams tab and locate the data stream you want to edit. Click the Add Source Fields button in the top right corner, and you'll then see a list of source fields that you can add to the data stream (Figure 7-7). For external source data streams, you'll be given the option to add discovered fields automatically or to add fields manually.

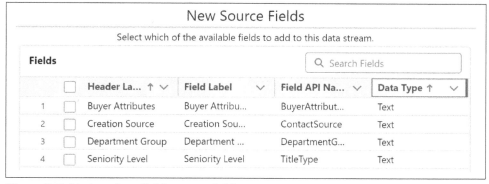

Figure 7-7. Listing of available source fields

Check the box(es) of the field(s) you want to add, then click the Save button. You'll see the confirmation on the screen that new source fields were added to the DLO. Navigate to the DLO tab and confirm that the new field or fields exist in the DLO.

We now need to add the new field to the DMO. Click the Review button in the Data Mapping section on the right (Figure 7-8).

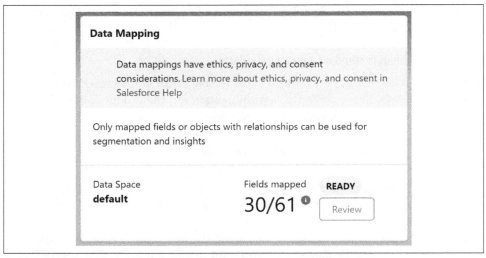

Figure 7-8. Click the Review button to access the mapping canvas

Scroll down on the lefthand side and select the new custom field in the DLO. Once selected, a blue box will appear around the new field. The blue box on your screen indicates you've selected that specific DLO field to be mapped. From the righthand side of the mapping canvas, click on the drop-down arrow beside the Unmapped fields (Figure 7-9). Click on the highlighted link to Add New Field.

Figure 7-9. Click on the Add New Field link to add a new DMO custom field

The Add New Attribute dialog box will then appear (Figure 7-10), and you'll need to enter the field label name and select the data type. The field API name will be generated automatically. Click the Save button to finish adding the new custom field to the DMO, then navigate to the DMO and confirm that the new custom field exists.

Figure 7-10. Add New Attribute dialog box for adding a new DMO custom field

Adding formula fields and formula expressions

We just finished adding a new DMO custom field for handling a new data source field brought into the DLO, but there are other reasons you might need to add a new custom field. You might want to hardcode a supplemental field or create a derived value from existing fields, and you can create a new formula field to address those use cases.

New formula fields are created from the Data Streams tab by clicking the New Formula Field button from within the DLO where the new formula field should reside. When you create a new formula field, you'll still need to provide a field label and select the formula return type (Figure 7-11).

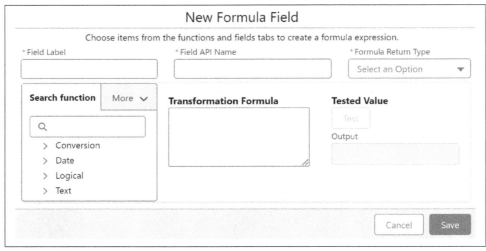

Figure 7-11. Creating a new formula field

Within the syntax editor, you can construct your formula by using free-form text and supported functions and operators. You can also reference existing fields within the data stream. Data Cloud has a robust set of supported library functions (*https:// oreil.ly/s6uPT*), and these functions can be nested.

Let's take a look at a few examples of how to leverage formula fields to enhance or enrich source data in preparation for mapping. You'll notice in our examples that we use all uppercase for Data Cloud formula field functions. That's because they are case-sensitive.

Create a primary key for a source that doesn't include a primary key:

- Consider CONCAT() function
- Example: CONCAT('SFMC_634119895_', sourceField['Email'])

Standardize fields for consistency needed for activation:

- Consider PROPER() or REPLACE() functions
- Example: PROPER(sourceField['First_Name'])

Create bucket values to simplify segmentation:

- Consider `IF()`, `AND()`, or `NOT()` functions
- Example: `IF(sourceField['Spend'] >= 2500, 'Platinum',`
  `IF(sourceField['Spend'] < 2500 && sourceField['Spend'] >= 1000,`
  `'Gold',`
  `IF(sourceField['Spend'] < 1000, 'Silver', 'Unknown')))`

Salesforce also provides detailed formula examples for a variety of scenarios in its online documentation (*https://oreil.ly/VOR2w*). Here are a few of those use cases:

- Create a required party identifier formula field for mobile.
- Create a state-specific primary address flag.
- Set a hardcoded value for the organization unit identifier.
- Convert hours in the day to day parts.
- Add the date and time fields to engagement streams.

You'll notice a section for Tested Value on the right side of the screen where you can validate your transformation formula. Enter the desired test value and click the Test button. You can make changes to your formula logic if the output was not as expected. Click the Save button once you've successfully validated your results.

For Data Cloud formula fields, there are some guardrails put in place by Salesforce. For example, you can use either single quotes or double quotes in free-form text formulas but not both in the same formula. You should refer to the online documentation (*https://oreil.ly/6E6MX*) for a complete list of guardrails for formula fields in Data Cloud.

Configuring a qualifier field to support fully qualified keys

Fully qualified keys (FQKs) are used to prevent conflicts when data from different sources are brought together into a DMO field from different DLOs. FQKs are frequently used for building CIs and creating segments. You have the option to add FQKs when creating CIs and during the segmentation process, but FQKs are automatically created by the system.

An FQK is the combination of a source key and a key qualifier. For profile-related data, a source key would be an identifier (ID) field like a Contact object ID from the CRM source or a subscriber key from the Marketing Cloud source. Two DLOs would exist, one for each source, along with one DMO where the source data would be combined. Each DLO would have an ID field that could hold the same exact values. The key qualifier fields in each DLO, however, would store the values representing the sources, which will not be the same values.

For DLOs, a key qualifier field is automatically added to any DLO containing a primary or foreign key, but the default value of the qualifier field is null. You'll need to create and configure key qualifiers for DLOs, and you can add up to 20 active key qualifiers.

Select the DLO from within the Data Lake Objects tab, then use the drop-down menu located to the right of a field to select the option to Add Key Qualifier (Figure 7-12). From there, click the New Key Qualifier button. Input the label for the key qualifier, and the API name will be automatically generated. Click the Save button.

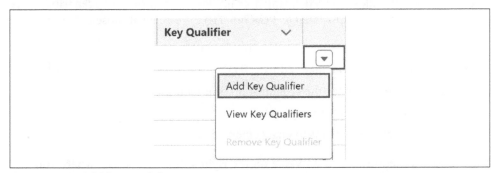

Figure 7-12. Add key qualifier

For DMOs, a key qualifier field is automatically added for each primary key field and for each field that's participating in an object relationship. The key qualifier field of each DLO is then mapped to the DMO key qualifier field. No matter how many relationships a specific DMO field is a part of, that field is associated with only one key qualifier field. Key qualifier fields and their associated DMO fields are listed in the Key Qualifier column on the DMO record home page. Key qualifiers on DMOs are system fields, which means you can't edit them.

Creating custom data model objects

We've considered several ways to extend the Data Cloud standard data model by adding new fields. We can add new custom fields to the DMO when new fields are added to the source data. Additionally, we can create new formula fields to hold supplemental data or a derived value from existing fields. We can also configure new key qualifier fields. Given the many ways to extend the standard DMOs, creating new custom DMOs should be done only after careful consideration.

One way to create a new DMO is from within the Data Model tab. Using the tab, you can create new DMOs from an existing DMO, from a file, or from scratch (Figure 7-13).

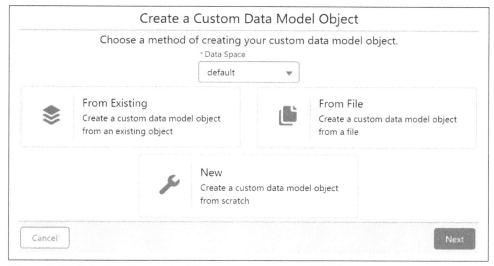

Figure 7-13. Selecting the method for creating a custom DMO

You can also create a new DMO from within the Data Streams tab. This is useful when you need to configure a new DMO that replicates the schema in the original data source.

From the Data Streams tab, select the data stream for which you want to create a new custom DMO. Next, click the Review button on the right side, and on the righthand side of the mapping canvas, click the pencil icon next to Data Model Entities. From within the Select Objects panel, click on the Custom Data Model tab (Figure 7-14), and then select the option to create a new custom object.

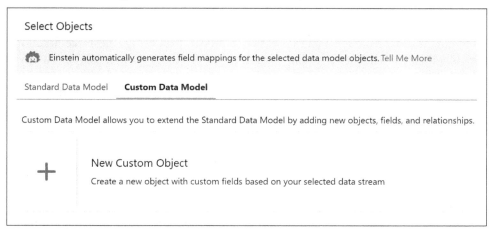

Figure 7-14. Creating a new custom DMO from the Data Streams tab

You can choose which fields from the DLO to include in or exclude from the new custom DMO. You can also update the field labels, but you can't change the primary key settings or add new custom fields. Click the Save button to create the custom DMO along with the completed mappings.

When you navigate back to the Data Model tab, you'll see that the new custom DMO you created is included in the list of mapped DMOs.

Salesforce objects created from processes

Salesforce automatically creates some objects during some Data Cloud processes, like identity resolution. For example, when an identity resolution ruleset is created by the user, Salesforce creates link tables as a bridge between source objects and unified profile objects. Some of the link tables created during the identity resolution process include the following:

- Unified Link Individual or Account tables
- Unified Link Party Identification tables
- Unified Link Contact Point tables for address, app, email, and phone

These DMOs created during the identity resolution process are assigned the Bridge DMO type and the Other DMO category. More examples of Salesforce process-created objects are Data Cloud DMOs created as part of the segmentation and activation process. More details about these objects are discussed in Chapter 12.

Thus far, we've reviewed ways to leverage the Data Cloud standard model and also extend that model as needed. We also learned that some Salesforce Data Cloud objects are created from processes like identity resolution, and we know a Salesforce best practice is to leverage Salesforce standard models whenever possible. This is important for all Salesforce Clouds and platforms like Salesforce Data Cloud because leveraging standard models makes it easier to unlock data using Salesforce functionality like Einstein Predictive AI and GenAI. It's especially important, though, when it comes to managing data requirements for customer consent. Let's discuss consent management and how to leverage the standard Salesforce Consent Data Model.

Salesforce Consent Data Model

In Chapter 1, we highlighted the value of first-party data and discussed consumers' data privacy concerns, which ultimately resulted in legislation like the California Consumer Privacy Act (CCPA) and the European Union's General Data Protection Regulation (GDPR). Therefore, consent management is very important because noncompliance with data privacy laws could result in fines and criminal penalties. Noncompliance could also cause consumers to shop elsewhere if they think your organization doesn't manage their consent fairly and reasonably.

Consent management includes obtaining and managing user consent for the collection, processing, and sharing of users' personal data. Consent management also incorporates the need to document user consent by having a way to effectively log and track consent. In Chapter 3, we discovered that Salesforce Data Cloud is not a consent management system but works in concert with consent management systems.

Most Salesforce users understand the importance of providing customers with the option to opt out of targeted advertising, and many are already familiar with how Marketing Cloud and Salesforce Consent Data Model handle consent. For example, Marketing Cloud Email Studio can capture consent and opt-in confirmation for your marketing messaging activities by using the Marketing Cloud Profile Center and Preference Center functionalities.

The standard Consent Data Model used for consent management in Marketing Cloud can be leveraged in Data Cloud using Salesforce's consent management objects. A list of these objects can be found in the Salesforce documentation (*https://oreil.ly/9S_sg*). The Salesforce consent model is built to offer you the ability to manage consent at multiple levels, from global preferences to more granular controls. Let's review those now.

Global Consent

Global consent documents whether a customer has approved communication or not. It governs all-or-nothing consent settings managed on the Individual DMO and includes several global privacy settings such as the following:

- Block geolocation tracking
- Don't process
- Don't profile
- Don't solicit
- Don't track
- Export individual's data
- Forget this individual
- Individual's age (for determining whether the individual is a minor)
- OK to store PII data elsewhere

The last data privacy setting, whether it's OK to store PII data elsewhere, is particularly important for global organizations. This privacy setting indicates whether you can store PII outside of a customer's location (for example, whether or not you can store an EU citizen's personal data in the United States).

Engagement Channel Consent

Engagement channel consent is used to store consent preferences by a particular contact type, such as email or phone. It is managed on the ContactPointTypeConsent object. Engagement channel consent assumes global consent has been given by the individual.

Contact Point Consent

Contact point consent is a more granular consent. Engagement channel consent may give you consent to contact an individual by email, and contact point consent will specify which email(s) are OK to use. For example, an individual may be OK with communications received at their personal email address but not their work email address. This type of consent is managed on the ContactPointConsent object.

Data Use Purpose Consent

Data use purpose consent is based on the reason for a communication, not the method of communication. The purpose might be for legal, marketing, or support, and examples of these different purposes include recall notices, marketing newsletters, and warranty support service. This consent is managed by the DataUsePurpose object, which can be related to both the Contact Point Type Consent and Contact Point Consent objects.

Consent Management by Brand

Consent management by brand isn't a consent type but rather a way to help keep separate an individual's preferences that vary by brand. The BusinessBrand object helps differentiate between the privacy and consent preferences for different brands within the same Salesforce org. The object has a native relationship with Contact Point Type Consent and Contact Point Consent objects.

Consent API

Differences in preferences among brands is just one example of how an individual may have given different consent. It's possible for differences to exist among different locations, too, and in those scenarios, the Consent API with specific Data Cloud parameters can be used to help aggregate consent preferences among multiple multiple records.

The Consent API brings together consent settings across the Contact, Contact Point Type Consent, Data Use Purpose, Individual, Lead, Person Account, and User objects when the records have a lookup relationship. Importantly, the Consent API can't include records in its aggregation when the email address field is protected by Shield Platform Encryption.

Summary

As part of the deep dive into data modeling, we explored some of the important steps needed prior to data ingestion. Appropriate data profiling and relevant data classification of the source data will result in more precise use of the standard Data Cloud data model. Many organizations find it helpful to construct a data dictionary and other supporting documents, if they don't already have them. More information about documents and information to gather during requirements gathering and implementation planning can be found in Appendix A.

In this chapter, we also laid the groundwork for successful data mapping to occur. As we'll see in a later chapter, faster and better data mapping after data ingestion is achievable with this preferred approach. Before exploring data mapping, we'll focus on data transformations in the next chapter.

CHAPTER 8

Data Transformations

In Chapter 7, we focused our attention on data modeling. As part of our learning, we created the foundations of a successful strategy for data mapping to the Customer 360 standard data model by undertaking the appropriate profiling and relevant classification of the source data. In this chapter, we'll create any necessary streaming *data transformations* (which we call data transforms, for short) to clean and normalize the source data before we map the DLOs to their respective DMOs. We'll also learn how to create batch data transforms for more complex transformations.

Throughout the chapter, we'll discuss the following menu options:

- Data Transforms
- Data Lake Objects
- Data Streams (for mapping)
- Data Explorer (for validation)

Getting Started

This section contains the required prework as well as some important things you should know before you get started.

Prework

Data transformations are the beginning of the hands-on tasks needed to implement your data model, so you'll need to have completed all data modeling and data model planning first. Prior to creating data transforms, connectors must be set up and data streams established for data to be ingested into Data Cloud.

What You Should Know

Most of the DLOs you'll be reviewing and working with were likely automatically created from DSOs when you set up your data streams and leveraged the Salesforce data bundles. It is possible, however, to create a DLO manually, which we will discover as the first step for creating a streaming data transform.

Streaming Data Transforms

The *Data Transforms* menu option (Figure 8-3) can be used to create new streaming data transforms for the purpose of cleaning or standardizing ingested data before mapping to a DMO. A streaming data transform reads one record in a source DLO and reshapes the record data based on the instructions you provide in the data transform. The streaming data transform writes the reshaped data as one or more records to a target DLO. You'll notice there is a source DLO and a target DLO (Figure 8-1). This is because using streaming data transforms requires two DLOs, a source and a target.

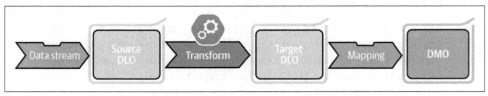

Figure 8-1. Data transform process reads from a source DLO and writes to a target DLO

Once created, a streaming data transform runs continuously, picking up new or changed data in the source DLO in need of transformation. The transformed records are then written to the target DLO, and the target DLO is mapped to a DMO.

First, we'll consider some specific reasons why you'd want to use streaming data transforms, and then, we'll learn more about creating and managing streaming data transforms. Finally, we'll dive deeper into SQL functions and operators that can be used in creating Data Cloud transformation expressions, which is important because SQL is required to create streaming data transformation logic.

Streaming Data Transform Use Cases

There are many reasons you might want to use the Data Cloud streaming data transform capability. We'll focus on the three most common reasons:

- Existence of multiple data categories in a DLO
- Existence of duplicate records
- Mapping exceptions due to denormalization

In "Data Categorization" on page 190, we discussed how to assign the right category to source data. As part of that classification process, we stepped through a data categorization flowchart to confirm that only one category of data exists within the source data before we ingest it. We also identified a few options for addressing source data that has multiple categories. One easy alternative is to create different data streams for the different data categories; if we don't do that, we can still use data transforms to handle source data where multiple data categories exist. To achieve the results, you'll just need to split the data from a single DLO into multiple DLOs.

Multiple Streaming Data Transforms May Be Needed

You'll need to use multiple streaming data transforms to divide data into their different categories within a single DLO. If one DLO includes two different categories, you'll need to create two data transforms. If three different categories exist in the source DLO, then you'll need three data transforms.

When two DLOs mapped to the same DMO contain the same set of primary keys, the mapped data will end up with duplicate records. To prevent the duplications, you'll need to set up one new target DLO where the source data can be merged. Create two streaming data transforms, one for each of the source DLOs, using the one new target DLO for both. In this way, the duplicate data will be merged into the target DLO before being mapped to the DMO.

The Data Cloud data model is normalized, so incoming data must be normalized before it can be mapped to the data model. One way we can quickly normalize data is by using the UNION operator in a streaming data transform. There are a few requirements for using the UNION operator in Data Cloud. Each SELECT statement must reference the same source DLO and map to the same field(s) in the target DLO. The SELECT statement must also generate a unique value for the primary key field.

Setting Up and Managing Streaming Data Transforms

A streaming data transform needs a source DLO as an input and a target DLO as an output. The source DLO is most likely one that was created from the Data Streams tab when you set up the data ingestion. The target DLO will need to be manually created in the user interface before you create your streaming data transform.

A Data Lake Object Must Be Created in the UI

You can only use a DLO created in the UI as a target DLO. It is not possible to use any DLO created by a data stream as a streaming data transform target DLO.

Click on the Data Lake Objects tab and then the New button to create a new DLO. You'll create a new DLO from an existing object or create a new DLO from scratch (Figure 8-2) You can also create an unstructured DLO from Amazon S3, Google Cloud Storage, or Microsoft Azure Storage. Remember, you'll need to use Data Cloud Setup to configure a connection before you can access your unstructured data in one of these three cloud storage locations.

Figure 8-2. Creation of a new DLO

Don't Create a Qualifier Field in Your Target Data Lake Object

You can't use a DLO qualifier field in a data transform as a data source or destination. Although you can create a DLO qualifier field in the destination DLO you are creating, it is better not to include a qualifier field in your new DLO to avoid experiencing a problem later.

It's important to remember that each DLO label must be unique. The API name for the DLO must also be unique, and must be 40 characters or less in length. There are a few other limitations for the DLO API name: it can contain only underscores and alphanumeric characters, can't have two consecutive underscores, can't include any spaces, can only begin with a letter, and can't end with an underscore. Also be sure to follow any naming conventions and standards that your organization uses.

You'll also need to make a category selection of Profile, Engagement, or Other. Unless you have a compelling reason for choosing a different category, it's best to select the category that matches your source DLO.

Once you've created your target DLO, you can proceed to creating your streaming data transform. Click on the Data Transforms tab and then the New button to access the screen where you'll choose the streaming data transform option (Figure 8-3).

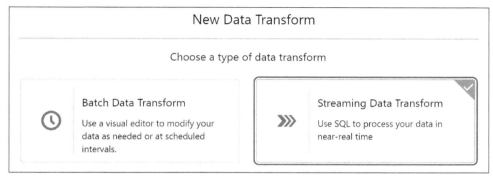

Figure 8-3. Selecting the Streaming Data Transform option

Once you've selected the Streaming Data Transform option, you can create a new data transform (Figure 8-4). You'll be asked to provide a label name; the API name will be automatically created. You'll also be asked to specify the target DLO. Use the drop-down arrow to select the new target DLO you just created in the UI. A warning message will appear if you haven't yet created a target DLO. You'll also need to select the primary key. Click the Next button when you're done.

Data Transform Limitation

If the New button is not visible, it's most likely because you've exceeded the number of data transforms that can be created for your account.

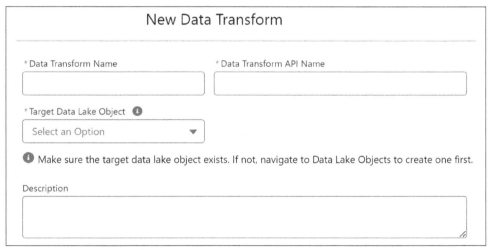

Figure 8-4. Creating a new streaming data transform

Once you've clicked on the Next button, you'll be provided with the area to create your streaming data transformation expressions (Figure 8-5). You can highlight and insert DLO fields shown to the left of the Expression window pane. You can also click on the Examples button to see examples.

There are several data transform functions and operators that can be used in the SQL expression. Those are described in "Streaming Data Transform Functions and Operators" on page 213. Additionally, you can use the WHERE clause to limit which source DLO records the streaming data transformation reads and processes when creating the SQL statement. Streaming data transforms is the only Data Cloud component that requires the user to build it using SQL code. There isn't a low-code/no-code approach available.

Deletion of Records in the Target Data Lake Object

A record will be deleted from the target DLO if the record in the source DLO is updated such that it no longer matches the WHERE filter. However, if there are multiple data transforms that write to the new target DLO, a record isn't deleted in the target DLO until all data in fields other than the primary key field is deleted.

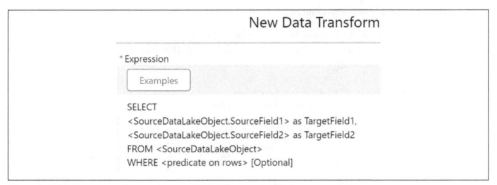

Figure 8-5. Creating the new streaming data transform expressions

When you're done creating your data transform SQL expression, be sure to click on the Check Syntax button at the bottom left of the screen and address any errors shown. When satisfied with what you've created, click the Save button at the bottom right of the screen. The SQL expression can't be changed once you save the data transform.

Slight Lag After Creation of a Streaming Data Transform

It could take up to 30 minutes after creation for the streaming data transform to begin processing records from the source DLO.

The processing metrics of a streaming data transform can be monitored from the Data Transforms tab. Click the name of the streaming data transform and then click Refresh History to view the number of records processed, failed, and removed.

You'll need to delete a streaming data transform if you want to disable or stop it. However, deleting the data transform doesn't affect its source DLO, target DLO, or DMO. Data that was already written to a target DLO as a result of the transform remains in the DLO after a data transform is deleted.

Streaming Data Transform Functions and Operators

There are five different categories of streaming data transforms that can be used in a SQL statement to create the transformation expression:

- Text
- Logic
- Boolean
- Operators
- Date and datetime

At this time, there are seven functions that can be used on the text data type (Table 8-1).

Table 8-1. Available functions for text data type

Function name	Description
COALESCE	Returns the first value from the list that isn't empty.
CONCAT()	Returns a concatenated string of the provided values. Accepts two or more strings or field API names.
LOWER(*<text>*)	Converts all uppercase letters in a text string to lowercase.
RTRIM(*<str>, <trimStr>*)	Removes trailing space characters. trimStr is optional and can be used to remove other characters in addition to spaces.
RTRIM(*<text>*)	Removes all spaces from the end.
TRIM(*<text>*)	Removes all spaces from the text, except for single spaces between words.
UPPER(*<text>*)	Converts all lowercase letters in a string to uppercase.

Logic functions can be applied to the number and datetime data types as well as the text data type. Checking for null values is an important logic function, so it's recommended to include checks for both null values and empty strings for the text data type because both are displayed as NULL in Data Explorer.

It's also possible to perform logical checks for two conditions. A logical AND function checks whether both conditions are true, while a logical OR function checks whether either condition is true. There's also a logical function known as the `CASE WHEN` statement that returns a value when the first condition is met, similar to an if-then-else statement.

The operator functions include a `CAST` function to convert an expression to another data type. This is helpful if you want to use a data type not supported in Data Cloud. For example, you can cast a `VARCHAR` or `STRING` to a text data type, a `TIME` or `TIME STAMP` to a datetime or date data type, and an `INT` or `DECIMAL` to a number data type. This is especially useful because there are only nine data types currently available in Data Cloud.

There are a number of logical operators as well:

- Greater than (>)
- Greater than or equal to (>=)
- Less than (<)
- Less than or equal to (<=)

- Equal to (==)
- Logical AND (&&)
- Logical OR (||)
- Logical NOT (!=, <>)

The Date and Datetime category is the last category of streaming data transformations. The `Current_Date()` function returns the current date as a value of the date data type. It's important to note that the date returned is based on UTC time.

Streaming Transforms versus Batch Transforms

Streaming transforms, which accept one source DLO as an input and create one target DLO as an output, are created via SQL statements and are used when data needs to be updated continuously. The difference between streaming transforms and batch transforms goes well beyond the differences in the transformation frequency (Table 8-2).

Table 8-2. Differences between streaming and batch transforms

	Streaming transforms	Batch transforms
Creation of transforms	Via SQL statements	Via rich drag-and-drop visual editor
General uses	When data needs to be updated continuously	When complex transforms are needed
Input(s)	One source DLO	Either one or more source DLOs or one or more DMOs
Output(s)	One target DLO	Either one or more target DLOs or one or more DMOs
Transformation frequency	Continuously runs and acts on one record at a time	Batch run for a full refresh of all records manually or on a scheduled basis

Among other things, batch transforms are created in the UI and can accept more than one input and create more than one output. In the next section, we'll dive into Salesforce Data Cloud batch transforms.

Batch Data Transforms

The Salesforce batch transformation functionality is composed of repeatable steps of operations that can be run whenever the source data updates. Batch data transforms can be run manually or set up to run at scheduled intervals.

The rich drag-and-drop visual editor used to create batch transformations can also make use of formulas and filters. You can use more than a hundred built-in operations or create your own custom formulas by combining date, string, and numeric data types, window functions, and case statements. The advanced formula builder features multirow operations, typeahead, and syntax highlighting.

Batch Data Transform Use Cases

Batch transforms are better for performing complex transforms where you need to join, aggregate, and append data. This is because they don't rely on SQL statements to create the transforms. Combining multiple data sources in a batch data transform allows for deeper insights.

Setting Up and Managing Batch Data Transforms

Just as with streaming transforms, batch transforms require a target output that will need to be created. Unlike streaming transforms, batch transforms can have multiple DLOs or even multiple DMOs as an output. Batch transforms can also have more than one source DLO; they can alternatively have one or more source DMOs as inputs.

To create a new batch transform, click on the Data Transforms tab, click the New button, and select the Batch Data Transform type (Figure 8-6).

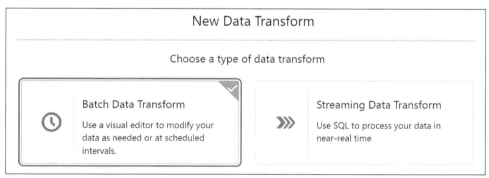

Figure 8-6. Selecting the Batch Data Transform option

Once you select the Batch Data Transform option and hit the Next button, you'll choose whether you want to add DLOs or DMOs (Figure 8-7). If you elect to add DMOs, you'll be prompted to choose the Data Space.

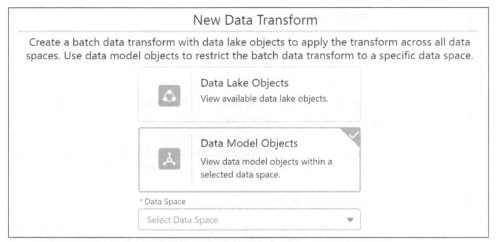

New Data Transform

Create a batch data transform with data lake objects to apply the transform across all data spaces. Use data model objects to restrict the batch data transform to a specific data space.

Data Lake Objects
View available data lake objects.

Data Model Objects
View data model objects within a selected data space.

* Data Space

Select Data Space

Figure 8-7. Adding either new DLOs or new DMOs to a batch transform

The next step is to add your input data. You'll see that there are checkboxes on the left, next to the objects, where you can make selections to add to the canvas (Figure 8-8). Batch data transforms allow you to add more than one object to the Input node.

Add Input Data

Q Search data by name…

Name	API Name	Category	Type
Account	ssot__Account__dlm	Profile	Local
Account Contact	ssot__AccountContact__dlm	Profile	Local
Contact Point Address	ssot__ContactPointAddress__dlm	Other	Local
Contact Point Email	ssot__ContactPointEmail__dlm	Other	Local
Contact Point Phone	ssot__ContactPointPhone__dlm	Other	Local
Individual	ssot__Individual__dlm	Profile	Local
Individual - History	Individual_SMH_172013422971…	Segment Membership	Local
Individual - Latest	Individual_SM_1720134227237…	Segment Membership	Local
Individual chunk	Individual_chunk__dlm	Content	Local
Individual index	Individual_index__dlm	Vector Embedding	Local
IndividualGDPRState	IndividualGDPRState__dlm	Profile	Local
Lead	ssot__Lead__dlm	Profile	Local

Figure 8-8. Adding objects to the batch transform canvas

Now that you've added the objects, you'll use transform nodes to build out your batch data transforms. Afterward, you can return to the Data Transforms tab, where you can view a data transform's status once it's been created. You can also manually run the batch data transform, schedule it, or edit it.

Batch Data Transform Node Types

Data transform nodes (Figure 8-9) represent the source and target data as well as the various operations that you perform on the source data. Different nodes, of different node types, are created in a batch transform to extract the data needed in the next step of the transformation process.

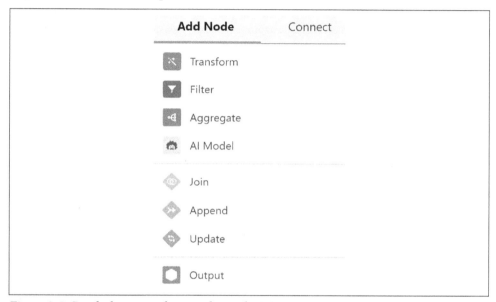

Figure 8-9. Batch data transform nodes in the UI

There are currently eight transformation node types (Table 8-3). You even have the option to add an AI model to your batch transforms.

Table 8-3. Transformation node types

Node type	Description
Aggregate	Rolls up data using one of the following functions: Average, Count, Maximum, Minimum, Stddevp, Stddev, Sum, Uniq, Varp, and Var.
Append	Combines rows from multiple sets of data.
Filter	Removes rows not needed in the target data.
Input	Contains the source data in a DLO.

Node type	Description
Join	Joins two input nodes via a lookup for join. Each input node must have a key field that can be used to join two inputs. Join operations supported: Lookup, Left Join, Right Join, Full Outer Join, Inner Join, and Cross Join.
Output	Contains the transformed data in a (target) DLO that is created in the UI.
Transform	Uses functions to calculate values, modify string values, format dates, edit data attributes, drop columns, and more. One or more transformations can be added to each Transform node.
Update	Swaps column values with data from another data source when key pairs match.

If you've worked in Salesforce CRM Analytics, these Data Cloud batch data transformation node types should be familiar to you. Similar to the CRM Analytics canvas, the Batch Data Transform canvas doesn't display the details of each individual data transform. However, you can select a transformation node to see its transformation details.

On the canvas, there are also shortcuts at the top of the screen (Figure 8-10). The first shortcut is what you'd select to add input data to the canvas. After that, there are options for both undo and redo. The next option can be selected if you want to clean up the nodes so they're presented optimally on the screen. There are also two options for either uploading or downloading a batch transform JSON file. You can also copy, cut, duplicate, or delete nodes.

Figure 8-10. Canvas shortcuts for batch data transforms

As you're building your data transform, you'll find it easier to use search or zoom instead of scrolling to locate a particular node. Also, try using the keyboard shortcuts (*https://oreil.ly/JpiM-*) instead of a mouse to move between elements and add them to the canvas.

Batch Data Transform Limitations and Best Practices

Batch data transforms have a few hard limitations. A data object can only be either an input node or an output node, not both. While a batch transform can have multiple outputs, any particular data object can be used as an output for only one data transform. Upsert, Insert, and Update refresh options are not supported in batch data transforms at this time; output data objects are overwrite only.

There are four general recommendations that will help with the overall efficiency of a batch data transform:

- Think carefully before including more than 150 nodes and definitely avoid including more than 250 nodes. Because it's possible to use the output of a previous data transform as an input into the next batch transform, consider breaking into smaller data transforms any batch data transform that contains a large number of nodes.

- Minimizing overlapping branches and shortening connections will reduce the size of your data transform and also make it easier and faster to navigate the canvas. If you need help organizing the canvas, use the Cleanup button, which will place branches horizontally, with inputs on the left and outputs on the right.

- Specifically for Input nodes, select only the fields (columns) you need for the data transform. It's always possible to add more columns later, as needed.

- Specifically for Join nodes, don't use more than 50 join nodes at a time.

 Critical Warning about Join Operations

A Join node supports both join and lookup operations. A join operation creates separate records for each match when multiple records match, which can result in double counting of measures. When join keys have a many-to-many relationship, using a join operation results in an exploding join. Thus, you should refrain from using the join operation in these situations.

There are a few ways you can address the critical warnings about join operations when creating batch transformations. You can prevent the problem of double counting measures by using a lookup operation rather than a join operation in the Join node. Additionally, one way of lessening the possibility of an exploding join is to try adding more key fields in the join operation to make the keys have more unique values.

Data Transform Jobs

Once you've created a batch data transform, you can manually run the transform job or schedule it to be run later. Click on the Data Transforms tab and select the triangular drop-down arrow to the right of the data transforms job for which you want to manually run, schedule for later, delete, edit, or update the status. If you don't see the data transforms job you want to work with, try changing the list view from Recently Viewed to All.

You can schedule a batch data transform to run as frequently as every hour. You'll notice you can select the day(s) of the week and the start time, in addition to choosing the frequency (Figure 8-11).

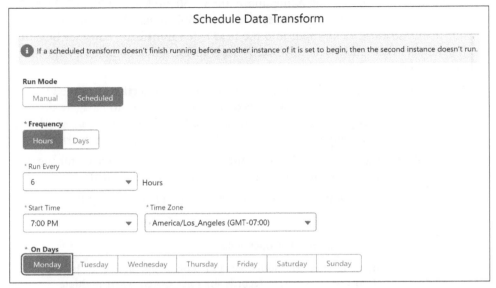

Figure 8-11. Scheduling a batch data transform

In the Data Transforms list view, you can see the current status of the job as well as the status of the last run. There are four different status types for the current transform job: Active, Processing, Deleting, and Error. There are also six different status types for the last run of the transform job: None, Pending, In Progress, Success, Failure, and Canceled.

Status of Streaming Transforms

Streaming data transforms run continuously, so the current status should always be Active and the last run status should be In Progress.

If the data transform job fails or completes with a warning, you can get more details by clicking the job name. The Details screen will display the last run status, the data transform's status, and its definition, created date, and time of last run. The error messages will provide more detail about the date the transform was last run and the status of the last run.

Summary

As part of the deep dive into data transformations, we learned how to create streaming data transforms. These streaming transforms are often used to clean and normalize source data. We also discovered how to create batch data transforms, which are useful when more complex transforms are needed.

In the next chapter, we'll explore the data mapping process. Data mapping, also known as harmonization, can be accomplished in Data Cloud by using a clicks, not code approach. Once data mapping is complete, the next step is to use the harmonized data in ways that will unlock value.

CHAPTER 9

Data Mapping

In Chapters 7 and 8, we looked at data modeling and data transformations. As part of our learning, we created the foundations of a successful strategy for data mapping to the Customer 360 standard data model by undertaking the appropriate data profiling and relevant data classification of the source data. We also created necessary streaming data transforms to clean and normalize the source data. Now, we're ready to map the DLOs to their respective DMOs.

Throughout the chapter, we'll discuss the following menu options:

- Data Lake (for confirming the category)
- Data Streams (for mapping)
- Data Explorer (for validation)

Getting Started

This section contains the required prework as well as some important things you should know before you get started.

Prework

Data mapping activities are hands-on sets of tasks used to implement your data model, so you'll need to have completed all the data modeling exercises and data model planning first. You'll also need to have created any data transforms.

In this chapter, we'll learn how to manually map data from the DLOs to the DMOs. Some data mapping should already have been completed automatically when we installed data bundles. In Chapter 6, we learned how to leverage Data Cloud starter bundles for Sales Cloud, Service Cloud, and Loyalty Management Cloud using the

Salesforce CRM Connector. We also learned about other Salesforce Cloud connectors including B2C Commerce, Omnichannel Inventory, Marketing Cloud, Marketing Cloud Account Engagement, and Marketing Cloud Personalization.

Data Cloud starter bundles automatically map standard fields from selected standard objects like the Account, Contact, Case, and Loyalty objects to the appropriate DMOs. Therefore, all data mapping examples in this chapter assume you've used data bundles wherever possible.

What You Should Know

In Chapter 7, we learned about the Customer 360 standard data model and we extended that standard data model by creating some new custom DMOs. One of the things we observed was that DMOs inherit their category from the first DLO mapped to the DMO.

There is already some data model mapping that comes standard OOTB. For those mapped DMOs, the categories have been inherited. The Individual DMO is one example. Also, when using starter bundles, the associated DLOs get mapped automatically to their respective DMOs. When setting up the data bundle, the DMO also inherits the category from the DLO.

Data categories affect which DLOs can be mapped to a DMO. Data categories can't be changed after they're set, so it's critical to understand the nuances of how data categories are selected, assigned, and inherited (Figure 9-1).

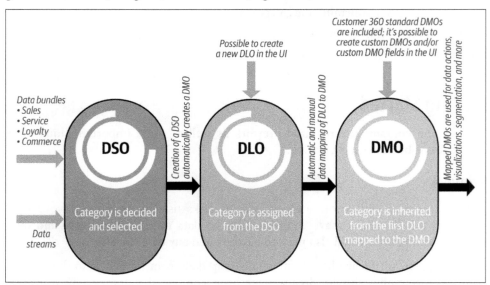

Figure 9-1. Data category is selected, assigned, and inherited for DSO, DLO, and DMO

For our purposes in this chapter, it's important to have selected the right category previously because we can only map DLOs to a DMO that has the same inherited category as the DLO we want to map. If you find that you can't map a DLO to a particular DMO, you should first check to make sure the categories are aligned.

Navigate to the Data Lake Objects tab, click on the name of any DLO, and then review the Fields section (Figure 9-2) to see the category. The category details are also included in the Details section.

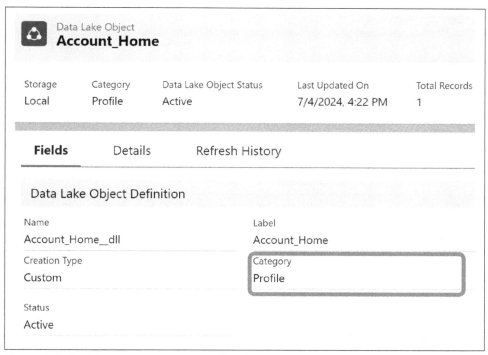

Figure 9-2. Profile category gets assigned to the DLO

Next, navigate to the Data Model tab and click on the name of the DMO to which the DLO is mapped. Review the Details section (Figure 9-3) to see the category.

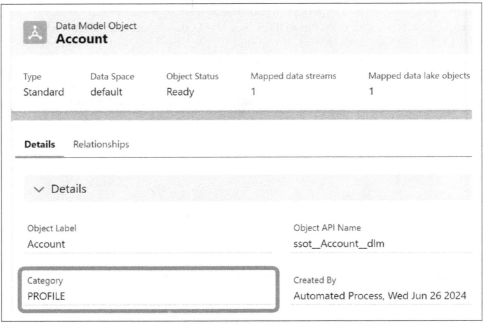

Figure 9-3. Profile category is inherited by the account DMO from the account DLO

If the DMO has not been mapped to any DLO, it has not yet inherited a category. That DMO will inherit the category from the first DLO mapped to it. While it is technically possible to map a Profile category DLO to a DMO with the Other category and vice versa, it's not recommended. DLOs with an Engagement category can only be mapped to a DMO with an inherited Engagement DMO category. Not to worry, though—only DMOs that are compatible with the DLO category are available for selection in the field-mapping canvas.

Changing the Data Model Object Inherited Category

It is possible to change the inherited category for most DMOs. To do so, you'll first need to remove all mappings to the DMO.

Data Mapping

The data mapping process, also known as *harmonization*, is one of the many things that makes Salesforce Data Cloud so special. The power of the Data Cloud is that you can bring in data from different sources with different formats and different naming syntaxes, and then you can use a clicks, not code approach to map all that data to a standard model that can then be used across the entire Customer 360 platform.

As we learned in Chapter 6, you can always extend the Salesforce standard model by adding custom fields or custom objects. Salesforce continually updates existing standard data models and releases new capabilities like Bring Your Own AI, so using the standard Customer 360 Data Model will make it a lot easier for you to adopt those new Salesforce innovations.

The hands-on portion of the data mapping process should only be undertaken after you've aligned your source data with the Customer 360 Data Model. Source data needs to be normalized before it can be mapped because the Data Cloud model is normalized. It could also be really helpful to use a spreadsheet or other tool to map the source data to the Data Cloud DMOs and fields before you actually get hands-on-keyboard.

Salesforce Data Cloud does include some Customer 360 default mappings, known as starter data bundles, for select Salesforce objects. Data bundles are available for Sales Cloud, Service Cloud, Loyalty Management Cloud, and more. Review Chapter 2 about data bundles and Chapter 6 about Salesforce Cloud connectors if you need a refresher.

Something important to emphasize again is that within Data Cloud, data ingestion and data mapping are distinct steps. Data from different sources might have different labels for an individual, and that's OK. Marketers might call an individual a contact or a subscriber, and a nonprofit organization might know its individuals as donors or members.

When you map these different data sources to the Data Cloud standard data model, you'll be bringing all the sources together and really unlocking value. The purpose of data mapping is to make all your data available downstream within Data Cloud so it can be used for identity resolution, unification, and a number of other activities like segmentation and creating insights.

Required Mappings

In Chapter 7, we learned that mapping to the Individual DMO is required for all data sources that have a Profile data category. Beyond that, Profile data must be mapped to either a Party Identification DMO or a Contact Point DMO.

Unified Profile Creation Requires Correct Mapping

Within Data Cloud, the system can't unify profiles unless you achieve the correct data mapping to the Individual DMO and also to a Contact Point object or the Party Identification DMO.

If you plan to activate any segments within Data Cloud, you must map Profile data to a Contact Point DMO. Without a contact point like an email address or phone number, activation is not possible because there won't exist contact details with which to engage with customers.

The Individual ID attribute must be unique across the data streams so that all profile records can be ingested and mapped to the Individual DMO. Within each Contact Point channel object, there is a reference to the Individual ID made via the Party attribute (Figure 9-4).

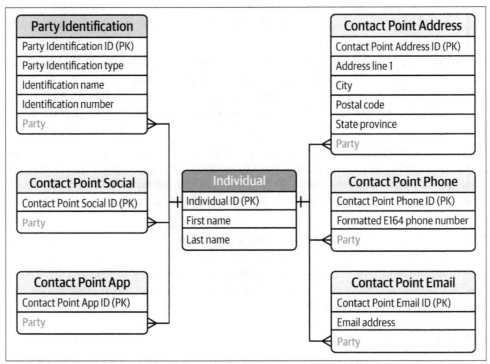

Figure 9-4. Contact Point channel objects related to the individual object via Party ID

Here is a summary of the required mappings in Data Cloud:

- The primary key must be mapped before saving when you're mapping a DMO in the Profile or Other category.
- The primary key and the Event Datetime field must be mapped before saving when you're mapping a DMO in the Engagement category.

- Identity resolution, segmentation, and activation have their own data mapping requirements:
  — Party area data must have the required fields and relationships mapped; refer to the ERD for Party area.
  — The Individual DMO must be mapped.
  — Either a Contact Point object or Party Identification object must be mapped.
- Unification and activation processes have their own data mapping requirement:
  — Map at least one Contact Point <channel> attribute channel.

The hands-on task of mapping in Data Cloud is relatively straightforward. It's the data modeling, creating the data dictionary, and the other planning tasks done in advance that require the most work. If you find yourself struggling with the required mappings as you get hands on in Data Cloud, you might find it helpful to revisit Chapter 7. You may also want to refer to Appendix A, which provides more detailed planning steps.

The Field Mapping Canvas

You'll be using the Data Streams tab to access the data mapping canvas. Within the Data Streams tab, click on the name of the data stream for which you'll be wanting to access the data mapping canvas. For our example, we'll click on the Account data stream created by the Salesforce CRM Connector. Once you're in the Account data stream, you'll notice the Data Mapping section (Figure 9-5) at the top right of the screen on the data stream record page.

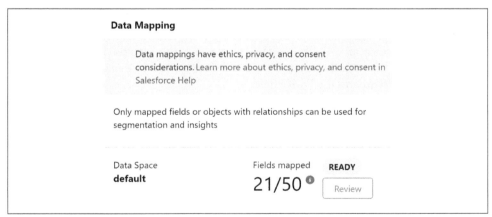

Figure 9-5. Data Mapping section of a data stream record page

Be sure to click the Review button to access the data mapping canvas (Figure 9-6). The Review button is available because the initial mapping for the Account data stream was already completed using the data bundles. If the DLO has not yet been mapped, the Start Data Mapping button will appear. In that case, you'll need to select one or more standard or custom DMOs to use for data mapping. It's important that you consider selecting an existing standard DMO, if applicable, rather than creating a new custom DMO. The supplemental repository (*https://oreil.ly/SuppRep_HandsOn-Salesforce*) lists several hundred standard DMOs from which you can choose. After you select one or more DMOs, Einstein will automatically generate field mappings for the selected DMOs. You'll want to carefully review these mappings and make changes, if needed.

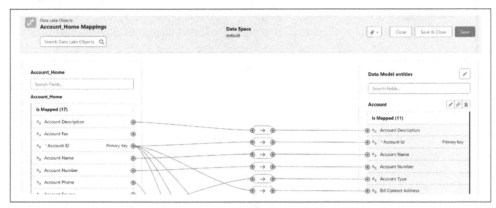

Figure 9-6. Data mapping canvas for the Account DLO

When you used the data bundles earlier, the Account DLO was automatically mapped to three DMOs: Account, Contact Point Address, and Contact Point Phone. If you click on the connector, you'll be able to review the details of the mapping (Figure 9-7). You'll notice that there is also a Delete button to delete the connection between the DLO field and the DMO field.

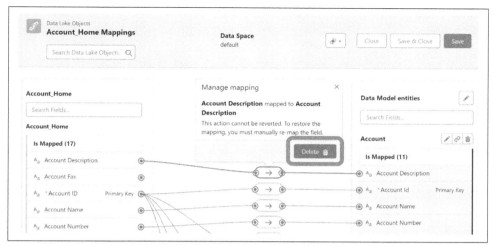

Figure 9-7. Data mapping connector showing details

There are two important things to know about using the Delete button to remove the connection between the fields. The first is that once you click the Delete button, the deletion cannot be reversed. You might be tempted to think that the deletion won't actually happen until you click the Save button in the top right corner, but that isn't the case. The second thing to know is that you'll be unable to delete a connection between the DLO primary key and the DMO primary key.

To add a new connection between two fields, I would first recommend that you locate the DMO field on the right side. The field you are looking for is most likely located in the collapsed Unmapped section. Click on the down arrow to see a listing of all unmapped fields (Figure 9-8).

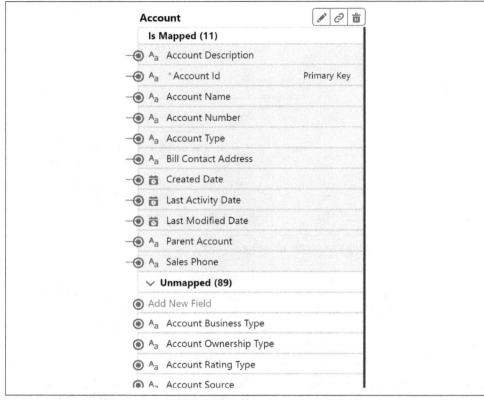

Figure 9-8. Mapped and unmapped fields sections of a DMO in the mapping canvas

Next, click on the DLO field you want to map. Once you start to move your cursor to the right side of the canvas, you'll notice some dashed lines appearing (Figure 9-9). Once you click on the DMO field, the lines will become solid between the newly established connectors. The DMO field will also automatically move from the Unmapped section to the Mapped section.

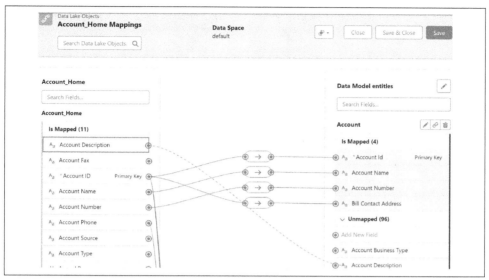

Figure 9-9. Manually establishing a mapping between a DLO field and a DMO field

There are times when you'll need to add a new DMO attribute (for example, when a new formula field is created in a DLO). To do this, navigate to the Add New Field option located directly under the unmapped section of the DMO where you want to add the new field. The Add New Attribute window will appear, allowing you to input the field label and select the data type. For attributes of the text data type, a checkbox appears where you can enable value suggestions. Don't forget to click the Save or Save & Close button to update your mappings when you're done.

Relationships Among Data Model Objects

After configuring the data mapping, you'll want to review the default relationships that have been mapped among objects and make updates as necessary. You'll also want to define additional relationships as needed. Relationships are configured on DMOs rather than DSOs, and you can use the Graph View option to identify *orphan objects*, which are those objects whose relationships haven't been configured yet. The Graph view option, available in the Data Model tab (Figure 9-10), enables you to access the visual representation of the data model.

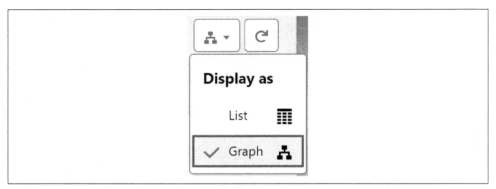

Figure 9-10. Graph view option accessible from within the Data Model tab

Once you toggle from the List view to the Graph view in the Data Model tab, you'll be able to easily see the relationships among the DMOs (Figure 9-11).

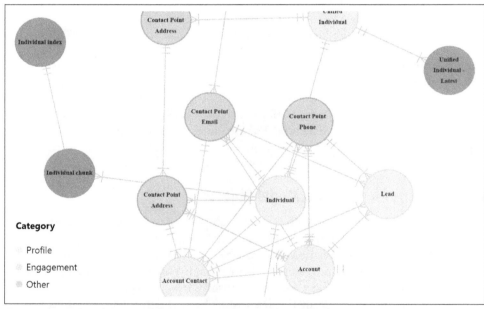

Figure 9-11. Graph view of the DMOs in the Data Model tab

Importance of Establishing Relationships Among Data Model Objects

The importance of establishing the correct relationships among objects should not be overlooked. For example, all objects need to be related either directly or indirectly with an entity that will be used in segmentation.

To edit the current relationship among DMOs or to create a new relationship, you'll want to click the Edit Relationships button within the field mapping canvas (Figure 9-12). As a reminder, you accessed the field mapping canvas by first accessing the DLO to be mapped via the Data Streams tab.

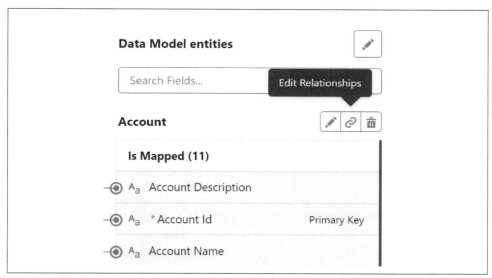

Figure 9-12. Editing and creating relationships within the field mapping canvas

You'll want to set the relationship for Contact Point objects to 1:M to allow a relationship to multiple records. When establishing the relationship, make sure you understand that within the Object relationships summary, the Object refers to the DLO, and the Related Object refers to the DMO (Figure 9-13).

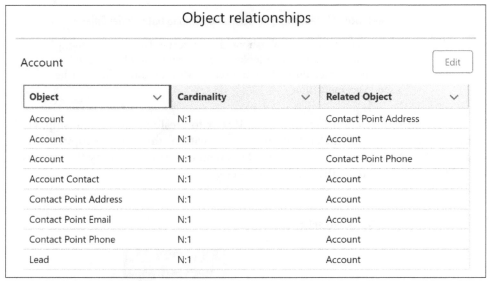

Figure 9-13. Object relationships summary

When you click the Edit button from the "Object relationships" summary, you'll have the option to edit existing relationships or create new relationships (Figure 9-14).

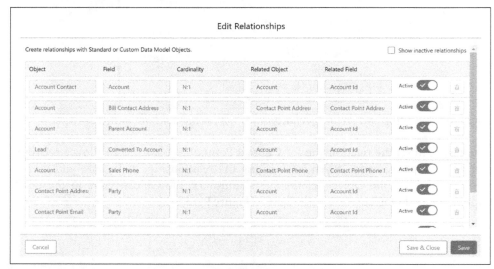

Figure 9-14. Editing existing relationships and creating new relationships

To create a new relationship, click the + New Relationship button at the bottom right of the screen. The DLO object will be automatically populated with the DLO you accessed via the Data Streams tab. You'll need to select the DLO field name, choose the cardinality, and select the related object and the related field (Figure 9-15).

Figure 9-15. Creating a new relationship

Make sure you activate the relationship and save your work.

DMO relationship status

The status of a relationship can be viewed in the Edit Relationships window and can be either Active or Inactive. A deactivated relationship can't be used later in functional areas like segmentation or activation, and an active relationship can't be deactivated if that existing relationship is used in identity resolution, CIs, segmentations, or activations. By default, deactivated relationships aren't visible. You'll need to select the "Show inactive relationships" checkbox if you want to view the deactivated relationships.

Several standard relationships are already established in Data Cloud. Note that a standard relationship is inactive initially. When the related object fields are mapped, the relationship automatically changes to active; the relationship is automatically deactivated when a mapping for at least one field in the relationship is removed. A standard relationship can be deactivated but not deleted.

DMO relationship limits

Data Cloud checks for relationship limits when a data bundle is deployed to an org. There are no limits on the number of standard and inactive relationships. Therefore, starter data bundle installations will not fail due to relationship limits because starter bundles only include standard relationships. Packaged data bundles can include custom relationships, and thus it is possible for a packaged data bundle installation to fail due to DMO relationship limits.

The custom relationship limit applies to direct relationships associated with a DMO, not indirect relationships. At this time, 25 is the maximum number of custom relationships per DMO, but it's a good idea to review the Salesforce limits and guidelines documentation (*https://oreil.ly/h4ZJl*) to get the most up-to-date information about Data Cloud limits.

Using Data Explorer to Validate Results

Configuration of the data objects, including data mapping and establishing relationships among objects, can be validated using the Data Explorer tab, where you can preview and validate actual data results.

From the Data Explorer tab, select the DMO you want to inspect. You'll notice that you can also look at the details of DLOs, CIs, and data graphs (Figure 9-16). For now, you'll want to focus on validating your mapping.

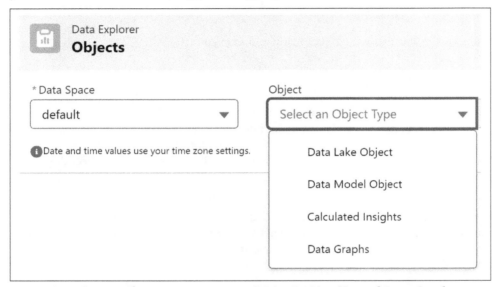

Figure 9-16. Data Explorer option to inspect DLOs, DMOs, CIs, and Data Graphs

Once you select the DMO you want to inspect, you can also change the fields you want to display for that object (Figure 9-17).

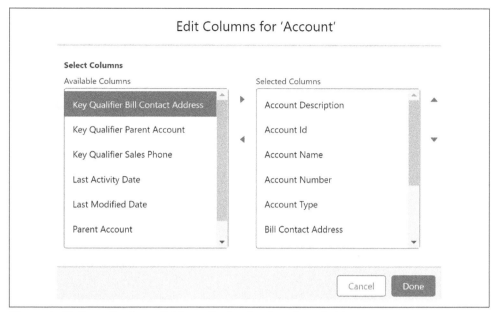

Figure 9-17. Data Explorer fields to display for the selected object

To look at a subset of the records, you can create filters in Data Cloud Data Explorer using the same functionality as you use to create filters in any Salesforce-related list.

Summary

As part of the deep dive into data mapping, we explored the data mapping process. Data mapping, also known as harmonization, can be accomplished in Data Cloud by using a clicks, not code approach. Once data mapping is complete, the next step is to use the harmonized data in ways that will unlock value.

In the next chapter, we'll focus on learning how to unify all the data from various sources so that we can begin unlocking value. We'll accomplish profile unification by using the identity resolution capabilities of Salesforce Data Cloud.

CHAPTER 10

Identity Resolution

In previous chapters, we learned how to ingest data into Data Cloud from multiple sources, add new formula fields and apply transformations, and map the data to the Salesforce Customer 360 Data Model. Our goal now is to learn how to unify all the data from different sources. The most common use of CDPs is to create unified profiles for individuals, and that will be the primary focus of this chapter. Note, however, that it is possible to create unified profiles for accounts using Salesforce Data Cloud. This is especially useful when working with household accounts.

Identity resolution (aka *unification*) is an identity management process whereby the data attributes of people from many different sources are matched and reconciled into comprehensive views called *unified profiles*. In Salesforce, identity resolution is powered by rulesets that include the matching and reconciliation rules needed to stitch together known information about the individual from disparate data sources. Another powerful feature of identity resolution is that unknown audience data stored in Data Cloud can be matched with the right unified profile once some identifying information about the audience becomes known. Within this chapter, you'll discover how to establish identity resolution rulesets and then create match rules and reconciliation rules within each ruleset.

The journey to ultimately getting to the unified profiles begins with a lot of planning and culminates when the Salesforce system runs identity resolution jobs to produce the unified profiles. In between, there are some hands-on-keyboard steps in Data Cloud that need to be undertaken, as shown in Figure 10-1.

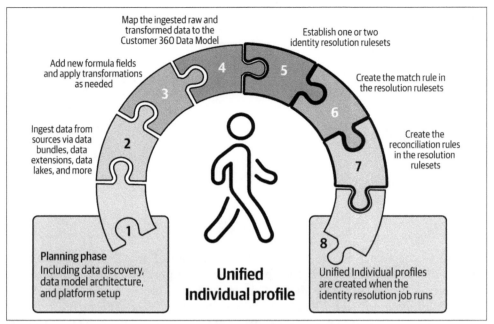

Figure 10-1. Hands-on-keyboard steps to arrive at a Unified Individual profile

When data about individuals exists in multiple places, the many different profiles created from the data streams in Data Cloud can be linked together based on the established match and reconciliation rules. As new profiles are added to Data Cloud and existing profiles are updated, the new Unified Individual information can be viewed within Data Cloud using the Profile Explorer tool.

Getting Started

This section contains the required prework and some important things you should know before you get started in this chapter. As in previous chapters, all data used for demonstration purposes is mock data that was generated for the purpose of providing some realistic sample data.

Prework

Before attempting any hands-on work for identity resolution, you'll need to have ingested and mapped profile data to the Salesforce Customer 360 Data Model as described in previous chapters.

What You Should Know

There are two critical concepts for the Salesforce identity resolution process. First, know that the Salesforce unified profile is not a *golden record*. Even though a unified profile and a golden record are both known to represent the source of truth for a customer, they are very different things. Second, understand the differences among the Data Cloud Party subject area, Party Identification object, and the Party field.

Unified profile versus golden record

Most marketers are familiar with the term *golden record*, which refers to a complete and reliable view of the customer found within an MDM system. A golden record is a single data point intended to provide the most accurate and relevant information about a customer. It is the result of an organization's continual validation of records that have undergone data cleansing and data deduplication processes.

For example, a golden record would likely contain a customer's correct mailing address, phone number, email address, and more. The MDM golden record concept was created out of a need for simplicity and a strong desire to have a single ID for the customer with only the single *best* email and the single *best* phone number.

For most people, this simplistic view doesn't represent reality. For example, it's common for people to have multiple emails: one for work and one or more personal accounts. Sometimes, a person might have a specific email address set up to capture confirmations of tax-deductible donations that can then be given to their accountant, or an email address might be set up for the entire family to use.

There could be any number of reasons why multiple valid email addresses exist for an individual. This makes it difficult to determine which specific email address is the best overall email address, so a single complete view of the customer may not realistically be achievable.

Sometimes, multiple golden records are created based on a single contact point such as email or phone so as not to lose the richness of a person having multiple email addresses, phone numbers, or mailing addresses. In most of those situations, an excessive number of golden records would exist, making it unlikely you'd ever see the complete view of the customer.

Even if a single best email and best phone number could be determined, it isn't easy to combine all the individual records into one record because each record could have different attributes. When the attribute labels are the same, there could be a difference in data type formats that would result in a mismatch between records.

There is one additional consideration. In most MDM systems, it is possible to directly update a golden record, although it is not recommended. Updating a golden record directly in an MDM system, rather than updating the source systems, would result in the creation of yet another source system. You'd end up with the original record in the source system and the updated record in the MDM system, so anyone with access to only the source system would never have the most current information for every individual. Those who have access to both systems would need to first evaluate which system was most recently updated, the source system or the MDM. Giving the user this type of functionality to update a CDP record goes against the very purpose of combining source data to create a single view of the customer.

Salesforce purposely designed Data Cloud to prevent from creating another source system. Data Cloud avoids letting a user create a new source of record by enforcing a *system of reference* approach (Figure 10-2) to the data within the platform. While it is possible to perform data transformations on columns of ingested source data, such as changing the data format type of a particular field, it is not possible to directly edit or delete any individual row of a record within Data Cloud.

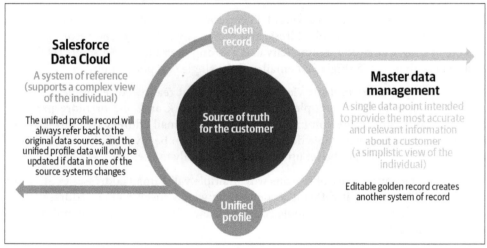

Figure 10-2. Comparison of Data Cloud unified profile with MDM golden record

The many different Salesforce Clouds, external cloud storage locations, and external data platforms where source data is gathered are considered to be *systems of record*. These locations are where a user or automated process would enter new data or edit existing data.

Salesforce Data Cloud is a *system of reference*: the Unified Individual profile record will always refer back to the original data sources. A Data Cloud Unified Individual profile is not a golden record, and the unified profile will only be changed if data in one of the source systems is updated.

Party subject area versus Party Identification DMO versus Party field

In Chapter 7, you were introduced to the Party primary subject area and the Party Identification DMO. In this chapter, you'll see firsthand the importance of the Party Identification DMO, and you'll also discover more about the Data Cloud Party attribute (field) that exists in many DMOs.

Let's quickly review the relationships among fields, DMOs, and subject areas that make up the Data Cloud data model (Figure 10-3). The foundation of the Data Cloud data model is built on source fields that are mapped to DMO standard and DMO custom fields. Data Cloud formula fields can also be created within DMOs. One example of a standard DMO field is the Party field.

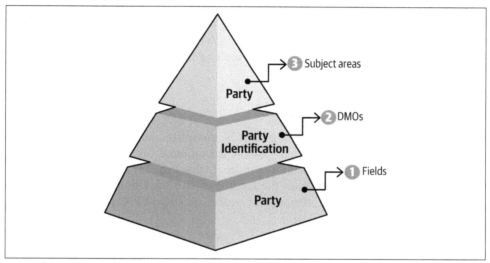

Figure 10-3. Data Cloud data model

The Party field is an attribute in many different DMOs, including the Party Identification DMO. It's a field used in Data Cloud to connect the various DMOs back to the DMO. The Party field is a foreign key to your Individual. Examples of a Party field include the Marketing Cloud contact key and the CRM contact ID. It's important to make sure that your ingested Profile data streams leverage the Party field or some other custom relationship to link back to the Individual.

DMOs in Data Cloud are groupings of data created from data streams, insights, and other sources. DMOs are physical and virtual views of DLOs and are composed of fields and relationships. Standard and custom DMOs can be viewed in either a list view or a graph view. DMOs can also have standard or custom relationships with other DMOs, and those relationships can be structured as one-to-one or many-to-one relationships. There currently exist more than 350 standard Data Cloud DMOs, of which Party Identification is one.

The Identification Number field in the Party Identification object is used in the identity resolution process. As such, it is a required field when using the Party Identification object. An example of an Identification Number field is a driver's license number or external customer ID field. The Party field, a foreign key to an account or individual, is another required field when using the Party Identification DMO.

The Salesforce Customer 360 Data Model organizes similar DMOs together into data model subject areas. Examples of data model subject areas include Case, Engagement, Loyalty, Party, Privacy, Product, and Sales Order.

Ingested data belonging to the Profile category will be located in the Party subject area, which includes several different standard DMOs (see Figure 7-6) and is the only required subject area in Data Cloud. More specifically, within the Party subject area, the Individual standard DMO is required along with either the Party Identification or Contact Point standard DMO. The Individual DMO (*https://oreil.ly/Hrbx_*) is a Data Cloud standard object that includes fields such as first name, last name, birth date, and occupation.

Identity Resolution Rulesets

As previously described, data mapping must be completed before rulesets can be created. We need the profile-related data from all the different data sources to be mapped so we can then use an identity resolution process to link together and consolidate all the data. Identity resolution rulesets are the combination of matching and reconciliation rules that are needed to resolve identity and create unified profiles in Data Cloud.

Creating Identity Rulesets

Identity resolution rulesets are created based on the Individual DMO or the Account DMO. A Salesforce user who desires to create or edit rulesets needs to have one of the following permission sets: Data Cloud Admin, Marketing Admin, or Marketing Data Aware Specialist.

The steps to create a new identity resolution ruleset (Figure 10-4) are as follows:

1. Navigate to the Identity Resolutions tab and click New.
2. Use the default data space or select a different data space, if needed.
3. Select the appropriate primary DMO, either Individual or Account.

Reasons Objects May Be Unavailable to Select

If you don't see any objects available, check to ensure that the data is modeled correctly and that you haven't reached the maximum number of rulesets.

4. Enter a ruleset ID of up to four characters and click Next. This is an optional step if you have only one ruleset for the object. If you have two rulesets for an object, however, this is a required step.

Ruleset IDs Are Not Editable Once Entered

The ruleset ID you enter becomes part of both the DMO and the API name, and it can't be changed later. If you want to reuse the ID of a deleted ruleset, you will encounter an error if Data Cloud has not yet finished deleting the ruleset. If that happens, try again later.

5. Enter a name for your ruleset and, optionally, a description.
6. Keep the "Run jobs automatically" toggle enabled.
7. Click the Save button.

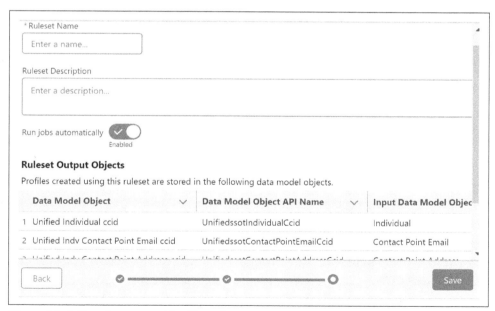

Figure 10-4. Creating a new identity ruleset

It's Possible to Manually Run the Ruleset

Rulesets are scheduled to run at least one time per day after publication. To run the ruleset more frequently during the setup, use the Run Now button.

Deleting Identity Rulesets

You're limited to two identity rulesets. You can edit existing rulesets, and you can also delete a ruleset from the Identity Resolution tab or the ruleset's record home. Deletion takes up to 24 hours to complete and is irreversible. You can't recover previous unification data after deleting a ruleset.

Carefully Consider Whether to Delete a Ruleset

In many cases, it could be better to update the match or reconciliation rules than to delete the ruleset. This is because deleting a ruleset permanently removes all unified customer data, eliminates dependencies on the DMOs, stops all processing of the ruleset, and deletes the history of previous runs.

Ruleset Statuses for the Current Job

Once you've configured one or more match rules and selected any reconciliation rules needed for your ruleset, the ruleset job process will run at least one time per day. If there are changes in your source data or the ruleset configuration is updated, the ruleset job process will run. The ruleset job is skipped if no changes have been made to the ruleset.

A job status for the current job process will be displayed for you. The following are the different statuses for identity resolution rulesets:

New
> The ruleset was created but no match or reconciliation rules have been added. The ruleset job hasn't run yet.

Publishing
> Ruleset publication is in progress. Data from the last publication is available until publishing is complete. Reload the page to see the updated status.

Published
> The ruleset was published. Any changes to the ruleset are used the next time the ruleset job runs.

Deleting
> Ruleset deletion is in progress.

Delete Failed

The ruleset deletion failed. Contact Salesforce Customer Support for help.

Error

The ruleset has a problem. Contact Salesforce Support for help.

Ruleset Statuses for the Last Job

In addition to having access to the current job status, you can see the status of the last ruleset job process. The following are the different job statuses for the last identity resolution ruleset job that was run:

Blank (no status)

The ruleset was created, but no match or reconciliation rules have been added.

Scheduled

The ruleset job is ready and waiting to start running.

In Progress

The ruleset job is running. Unified profiles from the last successful publication are available until the job is complete.

Succeeded

The ruleset job ran successfully.

Skipped

The ruleset job was skipped because there were no changes to data streams, records in the source DMO, or the ruleset's configuration.

Error

There was a problem running the ruleset job. Contact Salesforce Customer Support for help.

Failed

The ruleset job failed. Contact Salesforce Customer Support for help.

You'll need to create at least one match rule when you create a new ruleset. Match rules specify how to compare field values to identity matching records. We'll cover match rules in a subsequent section.

Ruleset Configurations Using Matching Rules

Matching rules (or *match rules*, for short) are a set of default or custom rules created to link multiple source profiles into a Unified Individual. Individual records are matched together into unified profiles based on the match rules you specify. The identity resolution process searches for matching values within a specific field on a DMO using match criteria. Data Cloud comes with a set of default match rules that you can use as is, or you can extend the rules so that you can create a more strict or less strict match definition. You can even create your own customer matching rules from scratch.

Accuracy Can Often Be Improved

Consider adding more criteria to your matching rules when accuracy is your top priority.

Each match rule in a reconciliation ruleset contains one or more criteria, and profiles are matched when all the criteria within a rule are satisfied. It's important to note that match rules can only be created on certain objects. The specific objects depend on whether you're matching individuals or accounts. Of course, the Individual DMO can only be used for individual profile unification, and the Account DMO can only be used for account profile unification.

For either individual or account profile unification, you can match on Contact Point Address, Contact Point Phone, Contact Point Email, and Party Identification. You can also use the Contact Point App and Contact Point Social objects when creating matching rules for individuals.

A Ruleset Must Have at Least One Match Rule

You're unable to delete the last match rule from an existing ruleset because each ruleset must have at least one match rule. To stop a ruleset with only one match rule from running, you'll need to either deactivate it or delete it.

Types of Matching Rules

There are three main types of match rules: Exact, Fuzzy, and Normalized. As you would expect, an *Exact match* means no typos or alternative formats are allowed. An Exact match method is supported for all fields.

A *Fuzzy match* allows for typos and slightly different spellings. There is also a choice given for high, medium, or low precision for Fuzzy matches. At this time, Fuzzy match in Data Cloud is only available for the First Name field.

Normalized matches are based on the exact same information regardless of formatting. Normalized matching is available for Name, Email, Phone, and Address fields. There is currently an address state normalizer supported for 11 countries, including Australia, Canada, France, Germany, Great Britain, Italy, the Netherlands, Spain, Turkey, and the United States. The address country normalizer is supported for all countries.

Configuring Identity Resolution Matching Rules

Steps to create a new identity resolution match rule are as follows:

1. Navigate to the record home page of the identity resolution ruleset.
2. In Match Rules, click Configure. Review the instructions and then click Next.

It's Possible to Edit Match Rules

If you need to update an existing match rule, navigate to the match rule and click Edit.

3. Click Configure to select your first match rule or Add Match Rule for subsequent rules. The default match rules for Individual and Account DMOs are described in the next section.
4. Edit, add, or delete criteria for the match rule.
5. Name your match rule with 80 characters or less and click Save.

Consider Implications Before Matching on a Single Contact Point

Matching on a single contact point isn't recommended because it could lead to overgrouping. Matching on a single data point, such as phone number or email alone, could mix household members with a shared contact point into a single unified profile. An exception is that it's OK to match on a single field as long as it is a unique external identifier like a Party identifier for driver's license number or loyalty member ID.

Default Matching Rules

Salesforce identity resolution provides four default match rules for Individuals to allow you to quickly select one of the more common configurations. You'll notice in Table 10-1 that each of the rules include Fuzzy Name matching for the first name and an exact match for the last name.

Table 10-1. Default matching rules for Individuals

Match criteria	Fuzzy Name and Normalized Email	Fuzzy Name and Normalized Phone	Fuzzy Name and Normalized Phone and Normalized Email	Fuzzy Name and Normalized Address
Individual first name (Fuzzy - medium precision)	X	X	X	X
Individual last name (Exact)	X	X	X	X
Contact Point Email email address (Exact Normalized)	X		X	
Contact Point Phone formatted E164 phone number (Exact Normalized)		X	X	
Contact Point Address address line 1 (Exact Normalized)				X
Contact Point Address city (Exact)				X
Contact Point Address country (Exact Normalized)				X

Similarly, there are two default match rules for Accounts, as shown in Table 10-2. If any of the default matching rules for Individuals or Accounts are inactive, confirm that you've correctly mapped the necessary fields, as described in Chapter 9.

Table 10-2. Default matching rules for Accounts

Match criteria	Exact Name and Normalized Address	Exact Name and Normalized Address and Normalized Phone
Account business name (Exact)	X	X
Contact Point Address address (Exact Normalized)	X	X
Contact Point Phone formatted E164 phone number (Exact Normalized)		X

Using Party Identifiers in Matching Rules

Earlier in the chapter, we learned about the importance of the Party Identification object, which is required if the Contact Point DMO is not used. The Party Identification ID is the primary unique identifier for the object, and the Party field is the foreign key to the Individual or Account DMO. The identification number in the Party Identification DMO is what will be used in the identity resolution process. Table 10-3 shows an example of the entries in the Party Identification DMO representing one individual, assuming there are three different sources ingested that each include a California driver's license.

Table 10-3. Party Identification DMO mock example records

Identification number	Identification name	Party Identification type	Party	Party Identification ID
D1469256	CA license number	CA driver's license	10016-00001	100
D1469256	CA license number	CA driver's license	10017-00001	101
D1469256	CA license number	CA driver's license	10018-00001	102

External identifiers like driver's license numbers or loyalty rewards numbers can be used effectively as a match method for Individuals. There are also excellent external identifiers for Accounts like a data universal numbering system (DUNS) number, which is a unique nine-digit identification number provided to businesses by Dun and Bradstreet (D&B). The DUNS number is site specific, which means each distinct physical location of an entity may be assigned its own DUNS number.

Another great example where it is useful to use a Party identifier in identity resolution match rules is the Salesforce Marketing Cloud. Marketing Cloud bundles represent subscriber data across Email Studio, MobileConnect, and MobilePush. It is recommended that you make a Match Method selection of Exact, a Party Identification Name selection of MC Subscriber Key, and a Party Identification Type selection of Person Identifier. You can also create more custom matching rules (Figure 10-5) and choose an exact match on blank values if required.

Figure 10-5. Creating a custom match rule

It's possible for Marketing Cloud to include both known and unknown records with different subscriber keys for the same individual. In orgs using Salesforce Mobile SDK to track app usage, you'll need to use a custom match rule with an exact match method based on the Mobile SDK shared identifier as the party identification number, and the app identifier as the party identification type.

Ruleset Configurations Using Reconciliation Rules

Profile reconciliation rules are created to help you let the system know how you want it to reconcile the matched records when attribute conflict exists. For fields in a unified profile that can't have multiple values, such as an individual's name, you'll need to use reconciliation rules to tell the system how to select the best value for the field among the different choices. You'll want to select the rule based on what you know about the type of data and your organization's preferences.

Reconciliation Rules Don't Apply to Contact Point DMOs

Reconciliation rules don't apply to contact points such as emails or phone numbers. All contact points remain as part of a unified profile. Thus, all contact points are available when creating segment activations, and you'll want to use the source priority order in activations to make sure you deliver a contact point from the desired source to your activation target.

Default Reconciliation Rules

There are three default reconciliation rules: Last Updated, Most Frequent, and Source Priority (Table 10-4).

Table 10-4. Default Reconciliation Rules

Reconciliation rule	Definition	Additional details
Last Updated	The value from the most recently updated record will be selected.	This rule is available only when the Last Modified Date field is mapped from the data stream.
Most Frequent	The most frequently occurring value will be selected.	If Ignore Empty Values is selected, the process doesn't select null values, even if null is the most frequently occurring value.
Source Priority	This sorts DLOs in order of most to least preferred.	If Ignore Empty Values is selected, the process selects the highest-priority non-null value. If multiple values are in the same source, the process will use the last updated date. This is the recommended solution for ID fields to help stabilize values.

Before selecting one of the default rules, make sure you think through the downstream effects. For example, in order to get the value from the Last Updated reconciliation rule for all sources, each of the data sources will need to have an existing field that can be mapped to the Last Modified Date field.

You'll want to select a default reconciliation rule for the object, of course, but don't forget to think more granularly. There are some fields within an object that might need to have a different reconciliation rule applied. It's also possible to override an object's default reconciliation behavior, and we'll explain how to do that in "Applying a Different Reconciliation Rule to a Specific Field" on page 256.

Setting a Default Reconciliation Rule

At this time, it's only possible to select a default reconciliation rule. Custom reconciliation rules cannot be created, although it is possible to select a different reconciliation rule for a specific field within an object.

When you set the default reconciliation rule for a DMO, all the custom fields as well as standard fields in the DMO will inherit the rule. You'll select one of the three default reconciliation rules and then provide the relevant details to support that rule choice. To edit the default reconciliation rule, click on the pencil icon to change your default rule choice. In this example, we've selected the Source Priority as the default rule, and we've chosen to ignore empty values (Figure 10-6).

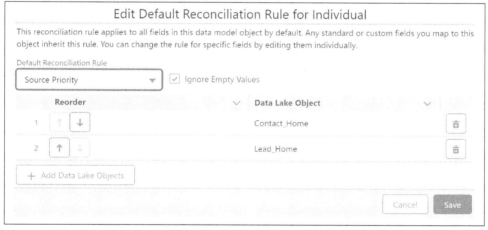

Figure 10-6. Default reconciliation rule example for Source Priority rule

Here are the steps involved in setting a default reconciliation rule:

1. Navigate to the record home page of your identity resolution ruleset.
2. Select a DMO.

3. A default reconciliation rule will already be selected. You can continue with that default rule or click the pencil icon to edit the default rule.

4. Select or unselect the Ignore Empty Values checkbox (your choice).

5. If Source Priority is the default rule selected, you'll need to order or reorder the data sources so that the highest-priority source is at the top of the list.

6. When you're finished making your selections and choices, click the Save button.

Applying a Different Reconciliation Rule to a Specific Field

It's possible to override an object's default reconciliation behavior by applying a reconciliation rule to a specific field. Here are the steps:

1. Navigate to the record home page of your identity resolution ruleset.

2. Select a field or multiple fields and then click the Assign button.

3. Disable the default reconciliation rule and select a different rule.

4. Click Save.

Reconciliation Rule Warnings

Reconciliation rule warnings help you know which fields to review or change. However, the resolution process will still run if you ignore an identity resolution warning.

Do Not Ignore Warnings About ID Fields

There is one particularly important reconciliation rule warning that you should not ignore. A warning notifying you to "Select a supported reconciliation rule for ID fields" will yield better reconciliation results if you first select the Source Priority reconciliation rule and then order source DLOs by priority. Making the change will reduce the frequency of value changes in ID fields.

Anonymous and Known Profiles in Identity Resolution

There are many reasons to understand the difference between known and unknown (i.e., anonymous) profiles in Data Cloud. For one thing, there are limits relating to the number of anonymous profiles that can exist in your Data Cloud instance, relative to the number of known profiles. Currently, you can have up to five times as many anonymous profiles as known profiles.

Let's use a simple example to illustrate how anonymous profile and event data is matched with known profiles to give us a more complete view of the customer. For this example, we'll focus on data ingested into Data Cloud from two different sources. Salesforce Marketing Cloud will be our first data source. When we ingest Marketing

Cloud profile-related data into Data Cloud, we'll include the subscriber ID, first and last name, and email address. As an example, Table 10-5 shows some selected fields from the Marketing Cloud source data stream.

Table 10-5. Profile data mock records example from Marketing Cloud source data stream

Subscriber ID	Data source	Is anonymous	First name	Last name	Email	Registration ID
SUB-6014	SFMC_14787860	0	Howard	Davis	hdavis@gmail.com	9091-7065
SUB-4161	SFMC_14787860	0	Lisa	Jones	ljones@yahoo.com	5751-8369

Individuals become known when they share their information with us, like when they give us their name and email address at the time they sign up for our newsletters. Profile data ingested from your Salesforce CRM, B2C Commerce Cloud, and Marketing Cloud would be considered known profiles because we can clearly identify these individuals. Thus, the value of 0 in the "Is anonymous" column indicates that the individual is not anonymous.

The Registration ID field value is automatically generated when a mobile app is installed. When we receive data from Marketing Cloud, there are values in the Registration ID field when our customers have installed our mobile app on their phones and have shared with us their profile details in the app. When the Registration ID field is null in the Marketing Cloud source data stream, the individual has not installed the mobile app or has installed the mobile app but not shared their details with us in the app.

We can use shared ID fields, like Registration ID, to stitch together information about an individual. Let's see how that works. Assume we receive profile-related data from our second source, our mobile app (Table 10-6). The last record ingested is for Lisa Jones, a known individual. The Individual ID for Lisa Jones can be used to identify the third profile record in Table 10-6 as also belonging to Lisa. Next, we can match the second ingested record, with a Registration ID of 9091-7065, to the first record from Table 10-5. Thus, we know that Individual ID 18123-1002 from Table 10-6 belongs to Howard Davis.

Table 10-6. Profile data mock records example from Mobile App source data stream

Individual ID	Data source	Is anonymous	First name	Last name	Email	Registration ID	Timestamp
18123-1001	My_Mobile_App	1				6571-8001	Time
18123-1002	My_Mobile_App	1				9091-7065	Time
18123-1005	My_Mobile_App	1				5751-8359	Time
18123-1005	My_Mobile_App	0	Lisa	Jones	ljones@yahoo.com	5751-8359	Time

With the data streams shown, we'll be able to use the Registration ID field to help fill in the gaps of the anonymous data. Once the identity process job runs in the Data Cloud, our Unified Individual ID table will have three entries (Table 10-7).

Table 10-7. Unified Individual ID table after identity process job completes

Unified Individual ID	Is anonymous	First name	Last name	Email	Registration ID	Unified profile category
UUID-1 (18123-1001)	1				6571-8001	Anonymous
UUID-2 (18123-1002, SUB-6014)	0	Howard	Davis	hdavis@gmail.com	9091-7065	Known
UUID-3 (18123-1005, SUB-4161)	0	Lisa	Jones	ljones@yahoo.com	5751-8359	Known

Data coming from web and mobile applications like the mobile engagement clicks data stream is not profile-related data. It consists of Engagement data records with a device ID that will, hopefully, be matched up with a known profile to provide more engagement details about these known individuals. In our example (Table 10-8), we are able to match up most of the Engagement data to known profiles.

Table 10-8. Engagement data from mobile engagement clicks data stream that will be matched to known profiles

Event ID	Data source	Device ID	URL	Timestamp
88111-3001	My_Mobile_App	18123-1001	xyz.com/page1	Time
88111-4001	My_Mobile_App	18123-1002	xyz.com/page1	Time
88111-5001	My_Mobile_App	18123-1005	xyz.com/page1	Time
88111-5002	My_Mobile_App	18123-1005	xyz.com/page2	Time
88111-5003	My_Mobile_App	18123-1005	xyz.com/page3	Time
88111-5004	My_Mobile_App	18123-1005	xyz.com/page4	Time
88111-5005	My_Mobile_App	18123-1005	xyz.com/page5	Time
88111-5006	My_Mobile_App	18123-1005	xyz.com/page6	Time

Identity Resolution Summary

Once the processing of the identity resolution rule starts, it could take up to 30 minutes to finish. When the process is complete, you'll have access to a resolution summary that provides ruleset details (Figure 10-7).

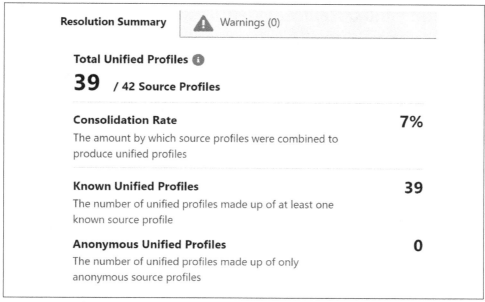

Resolution Summary ⚠ Warnings (0)

Total Unified Profiles ⓘ

39 / 42 Source Profiles

Consolidation Rate   **7%**
The amount by which source profiles were combined to
produce unified profiles

Known Unified Profiles   **39**
The number of unified profiles made up of at least one
known source profile

Anonymous Unified Profiles   **0**
The number of unified profiles made up of only
anonymous source profiles

Figure 10-7. Identity resolution summary

The consolidation rate is the amount by which the source profiles were combined to produce unified profiles, and it is calculated as follows: 1 – (number of unified individuals/number of source individuals). In our example, we would calculate the consolidation rate as 1 – (39/42). The consolidation rate that is realistically achievable will depend on the quantity and quality of your profile source data.

Resolution Rates Can Be Increased

Try adding more match rules to increase the consolidation rate if the resolution rates are lower than desired.

The consolidation rate on the ruleset's identity resolution summary details the results of the last successfully completed run. If you create two different rulesets, you can compare the consolidation rates of the two different rulesets to determine which better meets your needs.

Save Money by Deactivating Unneeded Rulesets

After comparing the consolidation rates and deciding on the one that best meets your needs, it is recommended that you deactivate the other ruleset to reduce usage cost.

Validating and Optimizing Identity Resolution

Once you've unified your profiles and you're satisfied with the consolidation rate you've achieved based on the rules you've created, you'll want to validate the results and make sure you're optimizing your unification approach. As an example, you can use CIs, explained in the next chapter, to find any contact point data points that might be mapped incorrectly. You can also use the Identity Resolution Tableau Dashboard or the Profile Explorer in Data Cloud to review select unified profiles to uncover any discrepancies or unintended results.

You can also use the Data Explorer to review the DLOs and DMOs for accurate values on key fields if things are not as you expect with the results. Taking time to validate and optimize your identity resolution process is critical because you'll be creating segments, insights, and data actions on these unified profiles. The value you'll get from visualizing and taking action on the unified profile data is directly proportional to the quality of the unified profiles you create.

Summary

As part of the deep dive into identity resolution capabilities of the Salesforce Data Cloud, we first clarified the difference between an MDM's golden record and the Data Cloud's unified profile. If the two are used together in the same organization, the golden record provides a one-dimensional foundation upon which the unified profile adds dimensional layers that include the many behavioral and interaction data points being added and updated in near real time.

We then explored identity resolution rulesets while learning how to configure rulesets using matching rules and reconciliation rules. We discovered that it's possible to extend default matching rules and use party identifiers in matching rules, and we also learned more about the default reconciliation rules as well as how to apply a different reconciliation rule to a specific field. Importantly, we also explored the differences between anonymous and known profiles.

In the next chapter, we'll begin to discover some ways to understand and take action with your Data Cloud data. As part of our exploration, we'll learn about calculated and streaming insights, enrichments, data actions, and Data Cloud–triggered flows.

CHAPTER 11

Consuming and Taking Action with Data Cloud Data

We're at an exciting point because all the hard work we've done up until now has been to lay the foundation for extracting value from Data Cloud (Figure 11-1). Data Cloud is deeply integrated with everything in the Salesforce platform, which means all your Salesforce applications can leverage the harmonized and unified data that exists within Data Cloud.

You're therefore able to surface Data Cloud insights back into Sales Cloud and Service Cloud applications for your end users. Your marketers can use Data Cloud unified profiles to build meaningful segments and create more relevant and personalized interactions with your customers, and Data Cloud also offers a secure entry into GenAI. Of course, accelerating the time to value with Data Cloud requires building a solid foundation upon which to extract value.

We first saw the diagram in Figure 11-1 in Chapter 3, and as we've progressed in our efforts to build a solid foundation, we've accomplished each of these necessary steps. We set up our data connectors and created data streams to ingest data into Data Cloud, we modeled our data and created necessary data transformations, and after mapping the data, we completed the identity resolution process. As a result, we now have a 360-degree view of our individuals and accounts from a variety of internal and external data sources.

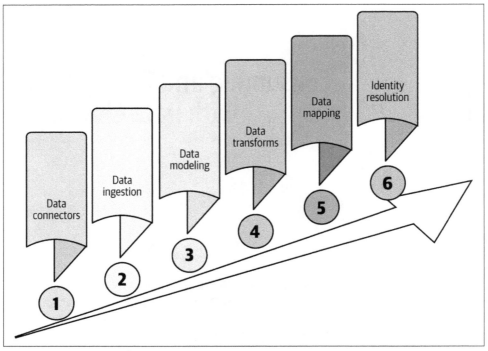

Figure 11-1. Steps needed to lay the foundation for extracting value from Data Cloud

There is certainly some value in just having that unified profile and complete 360-degree view, but we can do so much more, as we'll see in this chapter and subsequent chapters. For one thing, we can take action with our Data Cloud data directly within the UI, where we can create calculated, streaming, and real-time insights. We can also create enrichments, data actions, reports, and dashboards. As we learn about these various OOTB functionalities that are included with all Data Cloud licenses, we'll discuss the following menu option tabs:

- Calculated Insights (for calculated, streaming, and real-time insights)
- Setup → Object Manager → Account/Contact/Lead (for enrichments)
- Data Action Targets
- Data Actions

A major portion of this chapter is devoted to learning about CIs, which are powerful ways to take action with your Data Cloud data. Additionally, they are frequently used downstream in other ways such as Data Cloud enrichments, data actions, Data Cloud–triggered flows, and segmentation and activation. We'll learn about Data Cloud enrichments and data actions in this chapter, and in Chapter 12, we'll cover segmentation and activation. It's important to note that segmentation and activation require additional licensing beyond the basic Data Cloud license.

Let's begin by reviewing a few important items in the "Getting Started" section before we dive into the details of how to consume and take action with Data Cloud data.

Getting Started

This section contains the required prework and some important things you should know before you get started in this chapter. As in previous chapters, all data used for demonstration purposes is mock data that was generated for the purpose of providing some realistic sample data.

Prework

Before attempting any hands-on work for consuming and taking action with Data Cloud data, you'll need to have ingested and mapped Profile data to the Salesforce Customer 360 Data Model, as described in previous chapters. You'll also need to have completed the identity resolution steps.

What You Should Know

CIs are frequently used for segmentation and activation purposes, which we'll cover in detail in Chapter 12. For one thing, using CIs can help reduce the number of rows processed for segmentation, which, in turn, results in fewer credits consumed. However, if you're considering creating CIs for segmentation and activation, you'll want to plan ahead now. There are some important considerations for creating CIs that will be used for segmentation and activation.

Calculated Insights Requirements for Segmentation and Activation

Any CIs you create for segmentation purposes must include the object on which you plan to segment, and the primary key of that object must be a dimension. *Dimensions* are qualitative values used to categorize data, and email address, name, country, and customer ID are examples of dimension fields.

Also, Data Cloud only allows activation of CI measures and not dimensions. *Measures* are numeric or quantitative values that can be aggregated. It's possible to transform dimensions into measures by using FIRST, MAX, or LAST functions, but you'll want to ensure that the dimension you are turning into a measure is what actually aligns with your aggregation.

In addition to segmentation and activation, CIs are frequently thought of as the building blocks that can be used for many other things like data actions, visualizations, and enrichments. CIs are one of the three available insights that can be created within Data Cloud, and the other two are streaming and real-time insights. Let's first take a look at Data Cloud insight capabilities because of their importance in consuming and taking action with Data Cloud data.

Data Cloud Insights

Data Cloud insights are multidimensional metrics created from the data stored within Salesforce Data Cloud. There are three main types of insights: calculated, streaming, and real-time insights. *Streaming insights* are a variant of CIs for near real-time data streams. They're often used for analyzing and acting on time series data, and this is because streaming insights receive a continuous stream of data. Streaming insights are limited to only a few aggregation and internal functions. They are also limited to Individual, Unified, and Streaming DMOs. Real-time insights are built on real-time data graphs.

CIs define and calculate multidimensional metrics at many different levels of granularity, including the individual profile level, segment group level, and complete population levels. We previously compared some features of CIs with formulas, and we can widen that comparison to include streaming insights, real-time insights, and segment operators. Let's look at how these five metrics differ in terms of latency (Figure 11-2). In this case, *latency* is the time between updates of the metrics.

As we get ready to dive into the details of how to create insights, there are a few things we should keep in mind. Streaming insights can be processed in near real time, with the aggregation time window ranging from 1 minute to 24 hours. Streaming insights are frequently used in data actions, but, as you'd probably expect, they are not available for use in segmentation and activation. For segmentation and activation needs, you'll want to use CIs instead.

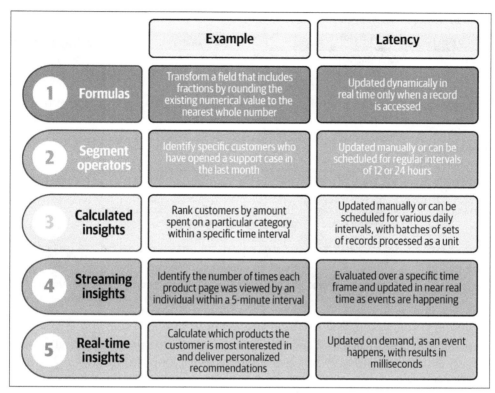

		Example	Latency
1	**Formulas**	Transform a field that includes fractions by rounding the existing numerical value to the nearest whole number	Updated dynamically in real time only when a record is accessed
2	**Segment operators**	Identify specific customers who have opened a support case in the last month	Updated manually or can be scheduled for regular intervals of 12 or 24 hours
3	**Calculated insights**	Rank customers by amount spent on a particular category within a specific time interval	Updated manually or can be scheduled for various daily intervals, with batches of sets of records processed as a unit
4	**Streaming insights**	Identify the number of times each product page was viewed by an individual within a 5-minute interval	Evaluated over a specific time frame and updated in near real time as events are happening
5	**Real-time insights**	Calculate which products the customer is most interested in and deliver personalized recommendations	Updated on demand, as an event happens, with results in milliseconds

Figure 11-2. Latency levels of each Data Cloud metric

CIs are robust and powerful metrics. You can use CIs for complex purposes by creating logical steps and stitching them together for improved reuse and consistency. Data Cloud allows you to combine up to three CIs. Next, let's learn more about CIs, followed by some more details about streaming insights.

Creating Insights

We've already touched on a few of the considerations when deciding whether to create a calculated, streaming, or real-time insight. A more complete list of comparisons (Table 11-1) also includes considering the data source from which you'll be creating an insight.

Streaming insights are limited to engagement data only from near real-time sources like Salesforce Web and Mobile SDK and Marketing Cloud Personalization (previously known as Interaction Studio), as well as the Individual and Unified DMOs. Real-time insights are powered by real-time data graphs. In contrast, CIs can leverage all DMOs and all data sources, including Profile and Engagement event data.

Table 11-1. Comparison of calculated, streaming, and real-time insights

	Calculated insights	Streaming insights	Real-time insights
Volume	Batch handling of complex calculations over large historical data	Handles micro batches of a few records	Processes individual records, with results in milliseconds
Processing frequency	Recalculated at intervals selected by the user	Calculated near real time, and calculated for a specific time window	Calculated on demand for every event that is updated in the real-time data graph
Creation method: programmatic (SQL)	Yes	Yes	No
Creation method: Insight Builder	Yes	Yes	Yes
Data sources	All sources (Profile and Engagement events)	Engagement data only from real-time sources like Web and Mobile SDK or ingestion API	Real-time data graph
Complexity supported	High	Low (inner JOINS, SUM, and COUNT aggregations only)	Low (SUM and COUNT aggregations only)
Example use case	Customer rank by spend	Click-stream analysis	Personalized ecommerce experience with recommendations based on which products the user is viewing

It's possible to create calculated and streaming insights either programmatically using SQL or declaratively using *Insight Builder*, a Salesforce tool used to build SQL statements using clicks, not code. Real-time insights can only be built using Insight Builder, which is very similar to *Flow Builder*, another Salesforce drag-and-drop tool. Using Insight Builder is the easiest way to build an insight, but writing a SQL statement gives you more flexibility in terms of writing subqueries and using operators.

Calculated insights

It's possible to use up to 50 measures per CI to support using CIs to build metrics on large-scale data. There are several different ways to create a CI within the Data Cloud UI once you click on the Calculated Insights tab in Data Cloud (Figure 11-3). You can create with the Insight Builder, with SQL, from a package, or from a data kit.

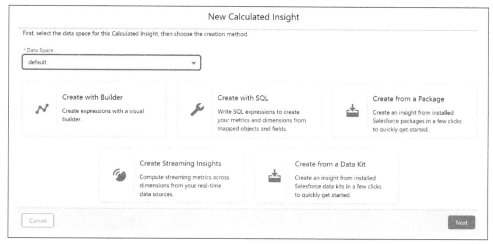

Figure 11-3. Creating a new CI

Keep in mind you must complete the required foundational steps before you can create a CI.

Wait Time Before Configuring a Calculated Insight

It's important to note that you'll need to wait about 30–60 minutes after creating a data stream and setting up the DMO before you can configure a CI on that DMO.

You'll want to first install any packages or data kits that are needed to create new CIs. You can click on the "Create with SQL" option if you prefer to build the CI yourself using SQL. Selecting the "Create with Builder" option will provide you with the options to create all insights, including CIs.

When using Insight Builder, you'll be prompted to select an object (Figure 11-4). This object is the primary object you'll use to create the CIs. You can select only one primary object, and you'll notice the object fields of the selected object appear on the right.

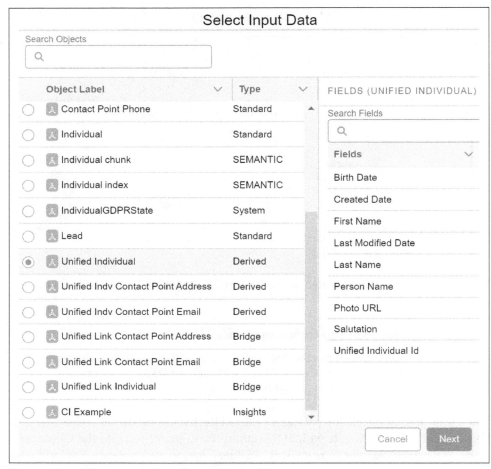

Figure 11-4. Selecting an object for creating a CI

After selecting the object, you'll be able to either join that primary object with another object or perform an operation to aggregate, create case conditions, add filters, create a transformation, or build an arithmetic expression (Figure 11-5). Remember, your CI must contain at least one measure in an Aggregate node or you'll not be allowed to save and run the CI.

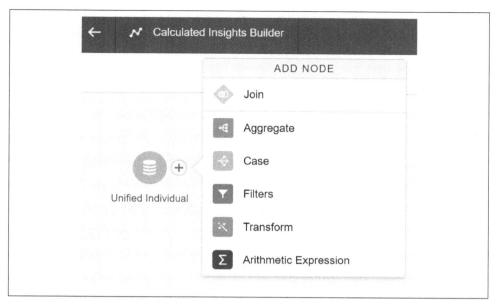

Figure 11-5. Adding nodes in the Insight Builder for calculated insights

The Join node is frequently used to add a secondary object for the purpose of ultimately connecting to the Individual ID. If you add a Join node, you'll need to decide on a few things. First, you'll need to select the Join type: Left, Right, Inner, or Full. You'll also need to identify any additional Join keys you want to add by selecting the appropriate foreign key in each data object. A *foreign key* is used to establish a link between two objects by referencing the primary key of another object.

Once you've joined objects to obtain all the desired data, you will probably want additional nodes for other purposes like aggregating the data, creating case conditions, or filtering the data. For data aggregation, you'll need to create measures and dimensions within the node. *Measures* are aggregated values of attributes, while *dimensions* are values that categorize a measure. Dimensions are frequently used to group the data.

After creating a CI, you may want to consider setting up a schedule to have the CIs recalculated every 1, 6, 12, or 24 hours (Figure 11-6). As part of setting up the schedule, you'll input the start date and time and the end date. Keep in mind that the schedule you select should consider the latency of the data upon which you've built your CI. Thus, you wouldn't want to have a CI recalculated every 6 hours if the underlying source data is only updated once a day. This will help avoid unnecessary processing of data, which results in lower consumption costs.

You'll want to align your choice of scheduling recalculation times every 1, 6, 12, or 24 hours for your CIs if they will be used downstream for flows, data actions, or segmentation. For example, you'd likely set your CI to be updated every 12 hours if that CI is included in a segment that is published every 12 hours. Setting the CI update schedule for every 24 hours would result in suboptimal segments half the time, and setting the schedule for every 6 hours would consume Data Cloud credits unnecessarily.

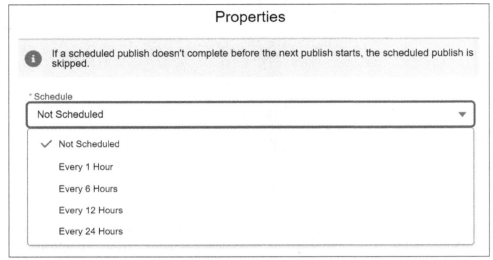

Figure 11-6. Setting a CI recalculation schedule

Alternatively, you can select the Not Scheduled picklist value option in the Schedule field and manually publish the CI from the drop-down menu (Figure 11-7) to the right of the desired CI entry. You can also use the Publish Now option even if you have an established schedule but just want to immediately publish.

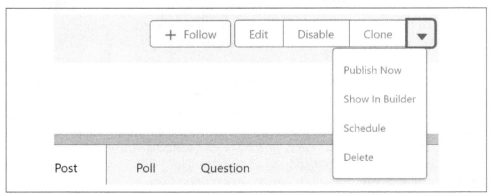

Figure 11-7. Publish options for CIs

Once you click into the newly created CIs, you'll see the CI details. In the Details tab, there are fields showing the CI label and the CI API name, among other things. The CI record includes these name fields because each CI is stored as a record in the Calculated Insights object (CI object). Each CI record in the CI object is a metric that is calculated when the CI runs.

You'll also have the option to click the Expression tab, where you'll see the SQL statement that was automatically created based on what was configured in the builder (Figure 11-8).

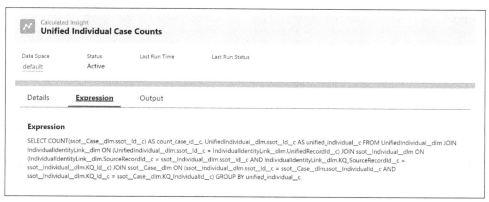

Figure 11-8. Details and Expression tabs on the CI page

Once the CI status shows Success, you can navigate to the Data Explorer tab to check the results. If a time interval isn't defined in the CIs, the CI value will refresh at least once a day. The CIs will automatically display the most current value based on the last refresh.

So that Data Cloud remains performant, there is a record retention limit for the following five metrics: COUNT, AVG, SUM, MAX, and MIN. For each metric time granularity, there is an associated retention period:

- Hourly: 48 hours retention
- Daily: 365 days retention
- Monthly: 5 years retention
- Quarterly: 5 years retention
- Yearly: 20 years retention

For the five metrics, each time granularity automatically rolls up to the next-tier time dimension when using date/time functions. For example, hourly data wouldn't exist for data that's 3 days old, but the daily data (24-hour time period) for 3 days ago would exist.

Planning in Advance to Avoid CI Editing Constraints

Plan your CI logic in advance to avoid running into editing constraints. For example, you can't remove existing measures or dimensions from a saved CI. It is recommended to review the "Guidelines and Limits for Editing a Calculated Insight" document (*https://oreil.ly/endTx*) in advance. The best way to make major changes to a CI is to clone the insight and create a new one.

It's possible to combine CIs by creating a CI from another CI. This gives you the flexibility to organize complex CI SQL data into logical steps and improve reuse.

As you're planning out the CIs you'll create, keep in mind some of the hard limits:

- Maximum of 200 CIs per tenant
- Maximum of 5 measures per CI
- Maximum of 10 dimensions per CI

Calculated Insights Use Spark SQL

If you're using SQL tools like DBeaver and the legacy Query Workspaces tool to model your insight logic and test your Joins, you'll want to note that CIs use Spark SQL rather than Trino SQL, so you'll need to make the appropriate adjustments. DBeaver is a SQL client that is good for developing CIs, and the legacy Query Workspaces tool is a browser-based tool for accessing Data Cloud data. If you're using either of these external SQL querying tools, you may want to consider migrating to the new collaborative Query Editor within Data Cloud. Query Editor gives you the ability to create multiple workspaces directly in the application to query your Data Cloud data.

We explored the Data Cloud architecture in detail in Chapter 2, where we learned how Salesforce built the new architecture from the ground up to be a modern technology solution. Insights are a great example of how Data Cloud capabilities leverage the new architecture, so let's look at the five steps that happen under the hood when you create a CI in Data Cloud:

1. Validation

The CI query is validated by the system.

2. Creation

The CI entity is inserted into the database with the corresponding metadata information.

3. Scheduling

CI processing runs every 30 minutes. The CIs are sent to a message queue at Amazon Simple Queue Service (SQS), where new CIs are picked immediately. Old CIs are picked if they haven't been processed for six hours.

4. Orchestration and translation

CIs are picked from the message queue, and the CI queries are translated to Spark SQL. The Spark batch job to process CIs is then submitted.

5. Execution

Spark jobs running on Amazon EMR clusters compute CI results and persist the results in the Data Cloud lakehouse tables.

We've taken a look at creating CIs using Insight Builder. We could've created the CIs in the UI using SQL instead. Calculated, streaming, and real-time insights can all be created using Insight Builder, and calculated and streaming insights can optionally be created using SQL code.

Streaming insights

Streaming insights can be created using Insight Builder or SQL. You can create a streaming insight using the Visual Insight Builder tool by clicking on the "Create with Builder" option.

To create a streaming insight using SQL, click on the Create Streaming Insights option (Figure 11-3). Do not click on the "Create with SQL" option; that option is only for using SQL to create CIs. If you select "Create with SQL," you'll see a screen from which to select the fields, insights, and functions to create a new CI. Since you want to create a streaming insight instead of a calculated insight, you'll need to click the Previous button at the bottom left of the screen to return to the previous menu.

After clicking the Create Streaming Insights option, you'll be presented with a dialog box asking you to provide the streaming insight's name. On the left side of the panel, there is a list of fields and functions you can use in your query. You'll also see some example code on the right side of the panel (Figure 11-9).

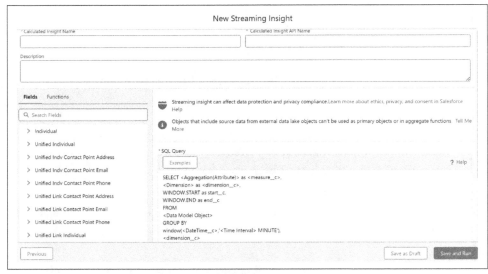

Figure 11-9. Streaming insights created using SQL

You'll notice a WINDOW function and a GROUP BY clause in the sample code, both of which are required. The WINDOW.start and WINDOW.end commands define the time window for aggregation. The time window interval can be anything from 1 minute to 24 hours. You must also specify which datetime field is to be used for the window calculation.

You can save the streaming insight as a draft, or you can click the "Save and Run" button. Once the streaming insights status shows Success, you can navigate back to the Data Explorer tab to check the results.

Real-time insights

Real-time insights, created exclusively in the Insight Builder, are built from real-time data graphs. All dimensions and measures used in the real-time data graph must be added to the real-time data graph first, before using the data graph in a real-time insight.

Real-time insights automatically include as a dimension the primary key from the real-time graph, and that primary key can't be removed. Real-time insights require aggregations that work on fields with a real-time source. Otherwise, the real-time insight value will be blank if the fields don't have a real-time source.

Using Insights

Streaming insights are useful for triggering time-sensitive, rule-based actions. Examples include anomaly detection, process orchestration, and alerting. Streaming insights are frequently used for data actions, but insight results can also be surfaced via a JDBC driver, including Tableau, to support real-time analytics. The use of insights for data actions isn't just limited to streaming insights; both calculated insights and streaming insights can be used in data actions.

CIs are useful for many other things, too, including refining segments and improving personalization efforts. CIs can be used in segmentation and activation, and CI results can be surfaced in enrichments, analytics, and APIs. Let's take a look at a few specific ways we can extract value from CIs.

Calculated insights benefits

CIs are useful for aggregations, especially those needed to support more complex use cases. Additionally, one of the benefits of CIs is that they promote reusability and consistency. It's important to realize that CIs are created within Data Cloud but can be used in many ways outside of the Data Cloud application, both within and outside of Salesforce.

For example, data enrichments can surface CI values in Sales Cloud. CIs can be used in segmentation and activations that are published to the Salesforce Marketing Cloud, and CRM Analytics can also make use of CIs.

CI values can also be used in other CI calculations called *metrics on metrics* functionality. In addition, CIs can be used externally. They can be shared externally via APIs, they can be used to create data actions, and they can be included in Data Cloud–triggered flows that take action with data both within Salesforce and with targets outside of Salesforce.

Much of the time, you'll be creating aggregate CI metrics like lifetime value (LTV) or nonaggregate CI metrics like customer rank. However, it is possible to also create datetime measures, dimensions, and text measures for CIs. One example would be a customer's last purchase date, which could be useful as an activation attribute.

Let's take a look at some of the more common aggregatable and nonaggregatable types of CIs (Figure 11-10).

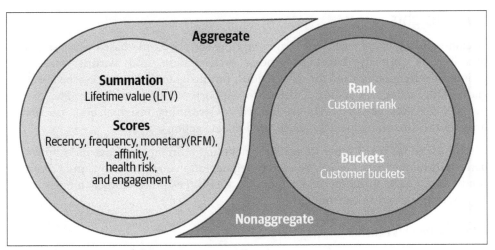

Figure 11-10. Aggregate and nonaggregate CI values

An LTV calculation aggregates a customer's total spending amount from the first interaction until now. LTV is a commonly used CI because it can be used to make decisions that increase the value of existing customers, which is less costly than acquiring new ones. LTV can be used in segmentation to identify and target for re-engagement those customers whose LTV has not increased recently. It's also possible to use LTV in analytics to compare LTV with product dimensions like product category and product brand. In addition, individual customer LTVs can be used to create a customer rank, a type of nonaggregate CI. Using a customer rank can help you identify your top customers.

Scores are another type of aggregate CI value. Recency, frequency, and monetary (RFM) scores are an advanced type of CI. A holistic RFM score is determined from individual CI scores that are calculated separately for the R, F, and M values. Often, the RFM score is then used in a `CASE` statement to help bucket customers into specific groups such as top customers. The cutoff RFM score where a customer qualifies as a top customer is subjective and not based on any particular industry standard.

Affinity scores are common CIs used by marketers. *Social channel affinity* is a CI metric that aggregates the number of times a Unified Individual interacts with your organization via each social media channel (such as your company website or your mobile app), and also the dimension for that channel, whether it's Facebook, Google, Pinterest, Instagram, or the X app. There are other types of calculated affinity scores where guest behavioral data can be used to create personalized product rankings for each customer. With this information, personalized messaging can be created easily.

Marketers also use another type of score known as an *engagement score*. Website engagement scores and email engagement scores are some examples. A website engagement score CI could have a value of 0 to 100 for each individual, with 100 representing the maximum number of engagements. The higher the score, the more interactions with your website and thus the higher the engagement. You could create a segment to email individuals who have a low website engagement score, and engagement scores can also be used to categorize customers within certain customer buckets. For example, you could use engagement scores in a CASE statement to identify individuals by high, medium or low engagement.

Thus far, we've looked at very specific examples of CIs. Once calculated, these insights are important not only for the immediate value they provide but also in the many ways they can be used downstream. Two of the most common uses for CIs are in segmentation and activation. CIs can be used in segment criteria to define segments, to narrow an existing segment, and in activation to personalize the messaging to an individual. Segmentation and activation is a topic of great interest to marketers, and we'll discuss it in detail in Chapter 12.

CIs are useful to marketers and an important part of understanding customers throughout their lifecycle journey (Figure 11-11).

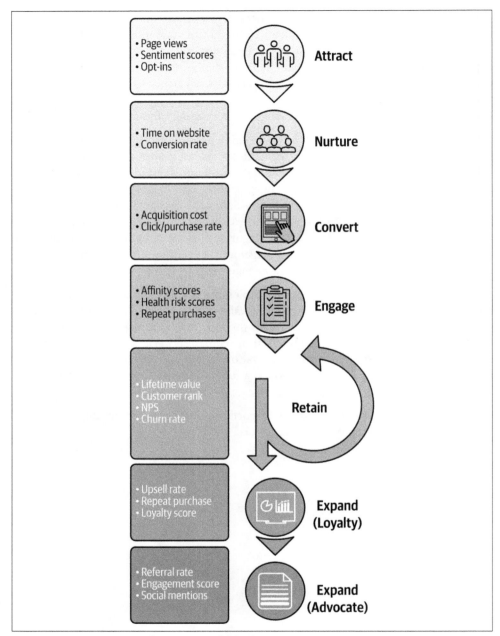

Figure 11-11. CIs across the customer lifecycle journey

It's also possible to use CIs to check data quality and troubleshoot identity resolution results. In Chapter 11, we discussed the identity resolution process, which is used to build a 360-degree view of an individual. There are several examples of identity resolution insights and data quality insights in the Salesforce developer documents (*https://oreil.ly/zrmNn*).

Another great use of CIs is for surfacing insights within Salesforce core. A great way to accomplish this is with the use of a copy field enrichment. In a later section, we'll dive into enrichments, including how to create a copy field. Following the discussion of Salesforce enrichments, we'll look at data actions and Data Cloud–triggered flows, which often use CIs to automatically make things happen both within and outside of Salesforce. While using CIs for data actions is fairly new, data actions were originally created to take advantage of streaming insights.

Calculated Insights versus Formula Fields

It's important to understand the similarities and differences between Salesforce formulas and CIs. Both can result in highly reusable content, and neither is intended for end-user self-service capabilities. Formulas and CIs can solve for quite complex use cases, and to create either of these requires someone with the requisite knowledge and appropriate Salesforce access.

Beyond those similarities, there are two very important differences between formula fields and CIs. First, formulas are created with simpler logic—partly because formulas are row-based operations typically used at ingestion time and applied to individual records. In contrast, CIs work well in multiple records and multiple objects.

Secondly, formula fields are not updated on a regular basis. Instead, they are updated dynamically in near real time whenever a record is accessed. On the other hand, CIs can be updated daily, on a regular basis, to provide a stored value in the CI field. Having a stored value, rather than a dynamic value, makes it possible for a CI to be used for downstream purposes, like segmentation or triggering a flow or data action.

Streaming insights benefits

There are plenty of examples of how streaming insights can be used in general for real-time analytics, anomaly detection, process orchestration, alerting, and more. Anytime you have time series or fast-moving data, you can use streaming insights to find useful patterns upon which you can take action quickly. Therefore, there are certain industries that can take great advantage of streaming insights because the nature of their business depends on taking action in near real time.

These specific industry types benefit greatly from streaming insights' ability to trigger time-sensitive actions. For example, financial services enterprises can use streaming insights to detect fraudulent transactions in near real time. Rule-based actions for time-sensitive events mean that notifications can be sent immediately whenever critical measurements of any kind reach dangerous levels. This is important for any industry or organization that monitors these types of life-threatening metrics.

Some other impactful examples of a more general nature include sales and customer service use cases. Lead scores can be quickly updated when individuals request information while on your website, in one of your forums, or on social media. Proactive, personalized customer service is possible because streaming insights can automatically log a case anytime a customer visits multiple troubleshooting FAQ pages.

Whenever sales representatives or customer service agents are alerted quickly to a situation, it's of great benefit for them to have the most complete information possible at their fingertips. Because these two personas frequently work in Sales Cloud and Service Cloud, it's very helpful to have some of the rich Data Cloud insights surfaced directly in Salesforce core. Using Data Cloud enrichments is one powerful way this can be achieved.

Data Cloud Enrichments

Data Cloud enrichments allow you to access harmonized and unified data from Data Cloud within your standard Salesforce Account, Contact, or Lead object individual records by using Object Manager to add the enrichment. In addition, it's possible to enrich most Salesforce objects in your org using the Enrichment option within Setup.

Improved Data Cloud Enrichments Available Summer 2024

Beginning Summer 2024, it will be possible to enrich most Salesforce objects in your org from within Setup → Integrations → Enrichments and then selecting either the Related List Enrichment or the Copy Field Enrichment option.

It's possible to query Data Cloud data in a related list enrichment or to copy Data Cloud data into your org using the copy field enrichment. You'll create your Data Cloud enrichments from within the Object Manager for the Contact (Figure 11-12) or Lead object. More recently, Salesforce also added the ability to place enrichments on the Account object.

The enrichments appear as a field on the record page or as a related list. For an end user to access the data in the field or related list, they'll need to have a Data Cloud user permission set assigned to them. More information about permission sets is available in Chapter 4.

SETUP > OBJECT MANAGER
Contact

Details

Data Cloud Related List

Data Cloud Copy Field

Figure 11-12. Object Manager for the Contact standard object

Let's review each of these Data Cloud enrichments.

Related List Enrichments

Salesforce related lists display a list of related records from different objects so that you don't have to exit the current record to view those related list records. It's a quick way to query engagement data to easily view all the cases or email engagements for an individual, for example. What's really great is that if your Data Cloud instance is ingesting data from multiple other systems, you'll see related records from all the systems.

Data Latency

Data in a Data Cloud related list is displayed in near real time. When you click to see more information in a related list, the list queries Data Cloud and returns seven days' worth of data, by default. Alternatively, you can create a dynamic related list using Data Cloud data where you'll have the option to use a filter to return more or less than seven days' worth of data. If you increase the default range, it's possible the related list could experience significant latency, depending on the amount of data retrieved.

To create a Data Cloud related list, navigate to the Setup → Object Manager → Account, Contact, or Lead object and then click on the Data Cloud Related List link on the left side of the screen.

You'll need to select the checkbox to "Enable Controlled by Parent permissions" (Figure 11-13). Enabling this option provides a better way to control who can see the Data Cloud related lists.

Figure 11-13. Contact object Data Cloud enrichment controlled by parent permissions

After clicking the Next button, you'll be prompted to select the Data Cloud object for your related list (Figure 11-14).

Figure 11-14. Select a Data Cloud object for the related list

Check the box for any page layouts or record pages you want updated with the related list (Figure 11-15).

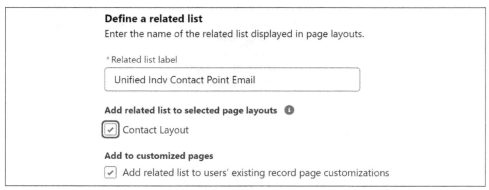

Figure 11-15. Add a related list to page layouts and record pages

If you forget to check the box or if you change your mind later, you can always edit the page layout within the Object Manager settings.

In addition, you can edit the Data Cloud related list in the same way as any other list. Navigate to Setup → Object Manager → Account, Contact, or Lead Object → Page Layouts → <Data Cloud Related List> → and then click on the wrench icon to Edit Properties (Figure 11-16).

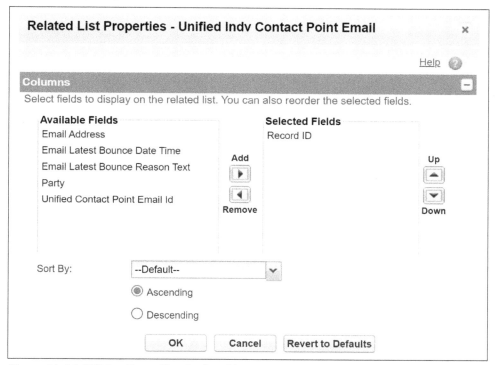

Figure 11-16. Editing Data Cloud related list properties

To the left of the wrench icon is the icon to remove the related list from the page layout. If you click on that icon, the related list will no longer appear on the record page, but the related list will still exist.

If you want to delete the Data Cloud related list or change the label name of the related list, you'll need to navigate to Setup → Object Manager → Account, Contact, or Lead object and then click on Data Cloud Related List. Next, click on the link of the related list you want to delete or make changes to, and you'll see the two buttons on the right of the screen (Figure 11-17).

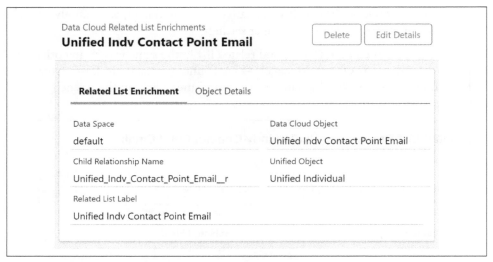

Figure 11-17. Delete related list or edit details

If you click on the Edit Object Details button, you can change the label name of the related list. However, the API name is not editable and will not change. Deleting the related list cannot be reversed, but you can always re-create the same related list if you end up needing it again in the future.

Copy Field Enrichments

Copy field enrichments allow you to copy a Data Cloud field value and include that value in an individual Contact or Lead record in your Salesforce org. For example, you can copy a Data Cloud CI with a single dimension. Alternatively, you can copy any field that is ingested from any Data Cloud source system and made available in a DMO.

Copy field enrichments include a sync history tab for the copy fields, so it's possible to track full sync progress and access log information. You can also obtain information about incremental sync errors and the number of records updated.

One other nice feature about copy field enrichments is that you can use a key qualifier to identify the data source, including non-CRM data stream data.

You'll create a copy field enrichment by navigating to either the Contact or Lead object in the Object Manager. Click on the Data Cloud Copy Field link and then click the New button. Choose the desired Data Cloud object (Figure 11-18) and then click the Next button.

Figure 11-18. Creating a Data Cloud copy field enrichment

Select the Data Cloud object you want to use and click the Next button. You'll then select the specific fields to be included (Figure 11-19). Not all objects may appear on the list. Copy fields support one-dimensional CI objects, and they support the following DMOs: Unified Individual, Unified Account, and Mapped DMOs. Only records that match the primary key of the source object are displayed when the target DMO doesn't have a 1:1 relationship with a unified object. Copy fields for multidimensional CI objects, like LTV, aren't supported.

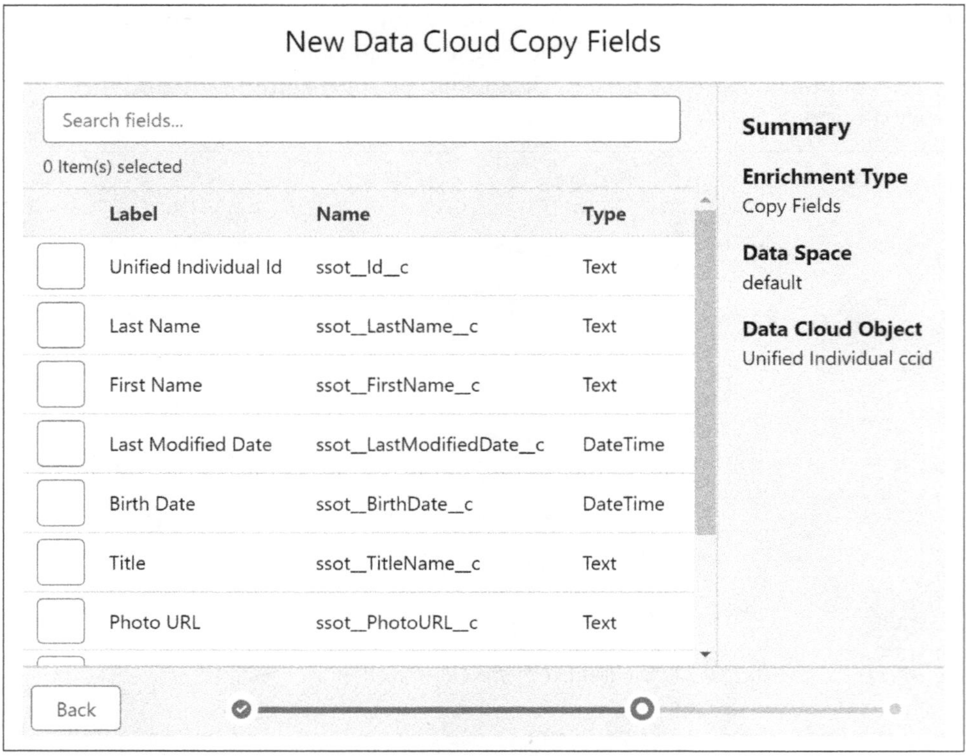

Figure 11-19. Select the fields for the copy field enrichment

Click the Next button and then the Save button. You'll need to map the Data Cloud field(s) to the Contact or Lead field(s). It's possible to use an existing Contact or Lead field to hold the copy field enrichment value, but it's more likely that you'll need to create a new field to hold the value, depending on your use case.

From the mapping screen, you can always add another field to the copy field enrichment by clicking the Add Field button. Just remember, you'll need to click the Save and Start Sync button for the copy field enrichment to be active (Figure 11-20).

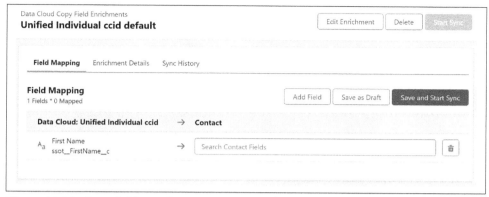

Figure 11-20. Copy field enrichment mapping and activation

When you save and activate your copy field enrichment, you'll be reminded that the Data Cloud copy field values will overwrite any existing Salesforce field values. The notice also informs you that it could take several hours the first time you populate your copy field enrichment fields; subsequent updates are incremental and will take less time (Figure 11-21). It's not uncommon to experience permission-related errors. When that happens, make sure the Data Cloud Integration User permission set has the necessary permissions on the object field where you want to store the Copy Field data.

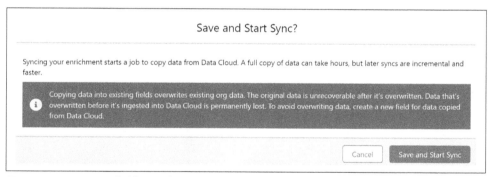

Figure 11-21. Copy field enrichment alerts when saving and activating

Remember that Salesforce makes it possible only to create a Data Cloud copy field enrichment natively for Contact and Lead objects. It's important to note that while you can create multiple related list enrichments per object, there is a limit on the number of copy field enrichments you can create because these enrichments count toward your overall limit for data actions and data action targets. Each copy field enrichment uses one data action and one data action target available for your Data Cloud license. One other important limitation mentioned earlier is that only CI objects with a single dimension are supported by copy field enrichments. You can find more information about enrichment considerations (*https://oreil.ly/m1-8H*) in the Salesforce online help documents.

Impact on Total Number of Data Actions and Data Targets Available

Interestingly, a data action target and corresponding data action is created for any copy field enrichment that you create. You can verify this by clicking on the Data Action Target tab and the Data Action tab and reviewing the information. Copy field enrichments impact the total number of data actions and data targets available. At this time, there is a limit of 100 data actions and 50 data action targets per account.

Look at the drop-down menu beside a data action created by a user in the Data Cloud UI. You'll notice you can Delete, Disable, or Edit the data action (Figure 11-22). Now, look at the drop-down menu beside any data action created from the copy field and you'll notice that there are no actions available to select. You're not able to edit or delete the data action or data action target. Once you delete the copy field, though, the corresponding data action and data action target will automatically be removed from Data Cloud by the system.

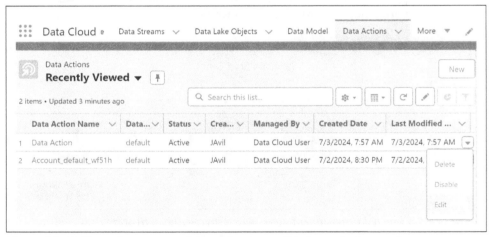

Figure 11-22. Drop-down menu shows what is possible for each data action

So, what exactly are data actions and data action targets? Let's dive into that topic now.

Data Actions and Data Cloud–Triggered Flow

Data actions are events sent by Data Cloud to predefined targets whenever certain conditions are met. The targets then use the events to trigger their own downstream business processes.

We first saw the Figure 11-23 graphic in Chapter 3 when we briefly discussed Data Cloud value activities. You'll notice from the diagram that both calculated insights and streaming insights, discussed earlier in this chapter, can be used as inputs to a data action.

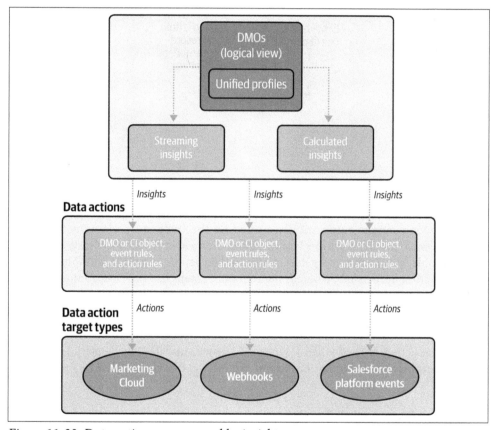

Figure 11-23. Data actions are powered by insights

In this chapter, let's focus on more of the details for data actions. Creating a data action requires four steps (Figure 11-24).

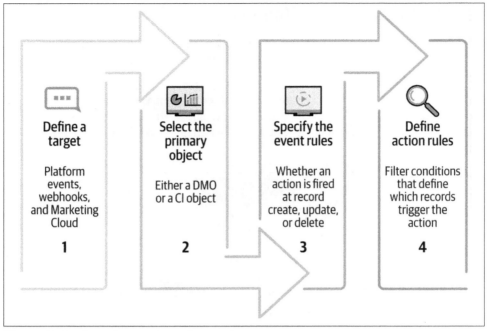

Figure 11-24. Steps for creating a data action

First, a data action target is needed to define where an action will be sent. Note that any data action targets automatically created by the Integration User, such as for a Salesforce enrichment or within Flow Builder, are read-only, so you'll not be able to delete, disable, or edit these targets. Creating a data action target is accomplished with the Data Action Targets tab, whereas the remaining steps use the Data Actions tab.

After setting up the data action target, you'll select which primary object triggers the action. The primary object will be either a DMO or a CI object. Next, you'll specify *event rules* that define when the action is fired. Specifically, you'll need to state whether the action is fired when a record is created, updated, or deleted. Lastly, you need to define *action rules* that have filter conditions to define which records trigger the action.

Defining a Data Action Target

There are currently three supported targets available for data actions: platform event, webhook, and Marketing Cloud. You'll need to set up one or more of these targets before creating a data action. Navigate to the Data Action Targets tab and click the New button to access the dialog box where you can enter the details (Figure 11-25).

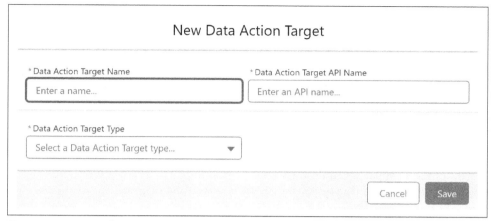

Figure 11-25. Configuring a new data action target

You can select one of the three data action target types, so let's discuss all three.

Platform Event data action target

When you select a Salesforce Platform Event as the data action target type, you'll be prompted to select the associated Salesforce org. The default selection is the Salesforce Home Org. There are a number of different standard platform event objects (*https:// oreil.ly/aVX7O*)that Salesforce publishes. Of those, a Data Cloud platform event target always publishes an event called `DataObjectDataChgEvent` that notifies subscribers of an action resulting from within Data Cloud. The receiver of the platform event in the target Salesforce org has to subscribe to the `DataObjectDataChgEvent`. You can accomplish this using any number of options, including creating a Salesforce flow, using Apex code, or employing other technology options like Pub/Sub API or MuleSoft API.

The `DataObjectDataChgEvent` has many properties, of which the most important are the `ActionDeveloperName` and the `PayloadCurrentValue`. The `ActionDeveloperName` contains the name of the data action that fired this platform event. Different data actions created for different purposes fire the same type of platform event, so this field helps you identify which data action fired the event so that you can branch your business logic accordingly. The `PayloadCurrentValue` contains a JSON representation of the fields in the record that triggered the data actions.

If you subscribe to the platform event using a custom-created Salesforce flow, you can add a decision element to filter events. However, to parse the JSON payload, you'll have to include an Apex action that will extract the values from the JSON and return them as output properties so that you can map them to your flow variables.

Another option is to write your own invocable Apex action. If you subscribe to the platform event via Apex alone, you can filter the events based on the developer data action name field and easily parse the JSON payload using built-in Apex methods.

Data Actions for Platform Events versus Data Cloud–Triggered Flow

It's possible to use the Data Cloud–triggered flow rather than creating a data action for a platform event that uses a custom Salesforce flow or Apex code. Once set up, the Data Cloud–triggered flow starts when conditions are met in a DMO or CI object. You'll just need to select the Data Cloud object and the conditions in the Start element of your autolaunched flow. It's important to note that any DMO selected must be a part of a mapped data stream or else the flow won't be triggered.

Not sure whether to use a Data Action or a Data Cloud–triggered flow for your platform event? You can use a Data Cloud–triggered flow if the flow will run in the same Salesforce org as Data Cloud, but you'll need to use Data Actions if the flow needs to run in a different Salesforce org from where your Data Cloud is provisioned.

One other important consideration is that data actions can send events to the two other targets, webhooks and Marketing Cloud, in addition to firing platform events.

Webhook data action target

A *webhook* is an API endpoint that will be triggered by a Data Cloud event. A webhook is event driven, rather than request driven. Once invoked, the webhook transports an HTTP payload to a destination system.

When you create a webhook as a data action target, you'll want to generate a secret key within the UI by clicking on the Generate Key button in the Secret Keys section of the Details section of the page.

Generating a Secret Key Is Required

Data Cloud will not send events to the webhook unless you generate the secret key. It's recommended to regenerate the secret key at least every 12 months. Note that it takes up to 15 minutes to be effective after you regenerate a secret key, during which time validations at the webhook target will fail.

The secret key consists of a signing key and a signing algorithm. Data Cloud uses this key to sign the requests it sends to the webhook, and the webhook then validates the signature.

Marketing Cloud data action target

Using Salesforce Marketing Cloud as a data action target allows you to automate simple operational tasks and personalize transactions by having Data Cloud events trigger emails and journeys in Marketing Cloud. Access to Marketing Cloud requires the purchase of add-on licenses.

Before you can set up Marketing Cloud as a data action target, you'll need to ensure that you've previously connected Marketing Cloud to Data Cloud. You'll also need to have set up your business units and created email templates and subscriber lists. Access to Marketing Cloud requires the purchase of add-on licenses, and Marketing Cloud will only appear as a data action target for you to select if your organization has obtained the required licenses.

If you want to trigger a journey, your journey's entry source must be an API event (*https://oreil.ly/aVOiZ*), which will send a single individual into a journey at just the right time, rather than sending a batch of people.

Data action errors occur more frequently for a Marketing Cloud data action target than for the other two target types. You'll need to make sure any required fields are present in the event payload, and the selected subscriber key value can't be null. The field data types configured in Marketing Cloud and Data Cloud must match, and the length of the Data Cloud attribute can't exceed the value that you've defined in the data extension in Marketing Cloud Journey Builder. You can visit the Salesforce help documents (*https://oreil.ly/klB8B*) for more information on troubleshooting data action errors.

Selecting the Data Action Primary Object

After setting up one or more data action targets, proceed to the Data Actions tab. Click the New button, select the data action target where you want the data action to be sent, and then click the Next button. You'll enter the object type, either Data Model Object or Calculated Insight, and then select the primary object (Figure 11-26).

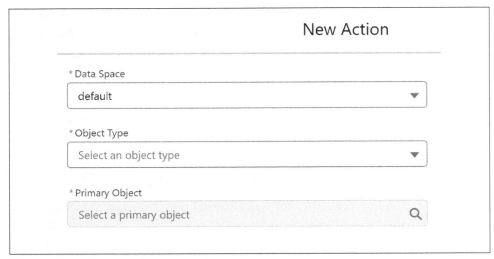

Figure 11-26. Create a new data action

Optionally, you can also select a related object and then up to 10 related attributes from the related object.

Enriching Data Actions with Data Graphs

It's possible to use data graph attributes to enrich data actions. Simply include the data graph as a related object and then select the desired attributes. More information about data graphs can be found in Chapter 13.

If you plan to create a data action based on a CI, select the Calculated Insights object type. If you plan to create a data action based on a streaming insight, select the appropriate primary streaming object DMO.

Specifying the Data Action Event Rules

After selecting the object(s), you'll next need to establish the data action event rules, which tell Salesforce when to trigger the action. In our example, it's possible to trigger a data action whenever a record is created, updated, or deleted (Figure 11-27).

Figure 11-27. Event rules to be selected

Note that you're required to select one or more data action event rules.

Defining the Action Rules for the Data Action

Action rules are defined (Figure 11-28) in the same UI dialog box as the event rules.

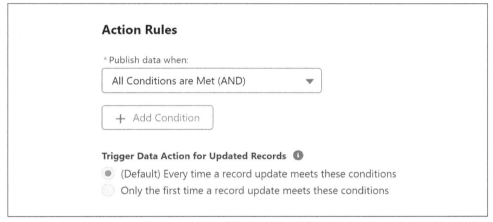

Figure 11-28. Action rules created

You can choose the AND operator to publish data when all conditions are met. Alternatively, you can select the OR operator to publish data when any condition is met. You'll then create one or more conditions by clicking the Add Condition button. The data action will be triggered every time a record action meets the conditions unless you select the option to trigger the action only the first time a record update meets conditions. Then, click the Next button.

The final screen to create a data action is where you'll enter the action name. The action API name will then automatically be created. Click the Save and Publish button, and you'll then be taken to the Data Action record page, which shows an active status and indicates that the data action is managed by a Data Cloud user. It's possible to disable or delete the data action you've just created, and it's also possible to edit the event and action rules but not the data space and objects information. You also can't edit the data action API name.

Data Actions versus Change Data Capture

Data actions are triggered by custom logic or code that you create. In contrast, *change data capture* (CDC) automatically captures and records all changes for newly added data or modified data.

Enriching Data Actions with Data Graphs

Data actions can be enriched with data graphs by including the data graph as a related object. The data graph can contain the specific attributes you determine are needed to provide personalized communications.

Remember that a data graph is stored in JSON format, so if you're using a Marketing Cloud data action target to enrich a data action, you'll need to configure a data extension in such a way that it can store the data action payload. To do so, follow these steps:

1. Create a data extension in Marketing Cloud with one attribute.
2. Set the data type as text and the length as −1 (unlimited).
3. Make sure the data extension attribute name matches the data graph's API name in Data Cloud.
4. In Marketing Cloud, parse the data graph data from the attribute using the supported scripting language in Journey Builder. At this time, the maximum number of data graph records you can use to enrich the primary object is set at 10 million.

Extracting Data Programmatically

Salesforce users consume and take action with Data Cloud data mostly within CRM core, Data Cloud, Marketing Cloud, and other Salesforce Clouds. There are situations, however, when your team may get the most value from consuming and taking action with data outside of these Salesforce locations. Data Cloud is an open and extensible platform that allows your team to take advantage of Data Cloud capabilities and data within its own flow of work. In this section, we'll briefly discuss how to extract data programmatically from Data Cloud. There are other possibilities for extending the Data Cloud platform, and Appendix B provides a more complete summary of the ways you can accomplish sharing Data Cloud data externally with other tools and platforms. Some use cases require you to extract data programmatically from Data Cloud using APIs and connectors. Previously, we discussed using a webhook data action target to programmatically extract data from Data Cloud, but there are other ways, as follows:

Profile APIs
These API calls can be included in external web or mobile applications to look up customer profile information.

Calculated Insights APIs
These API calls support data collection from the CI object.

Query API V1 and V2
These API calls support a variety of use cases for data stream, profile, and engagement DMOs. They also support large-volume data reads, external application integration, and interactive on-demand querying on the data lake.

CDP Python Connector
This connector uses the query API and extracts data from Data Cloud into Python. Using this connector, it's possible to fetch data in Pandas DataFrames.

Data graph APIs
These API calls query metadata and data from data graphs.

Universal ID lookup APIs
These API calls retrieve all individual records associated with a unified record. It's possible to query an individual ID from one source and get all the individual IDs for that individual from other data sources.

Newer Data Cloud instances don't have limits for profile, calculated insights, and query APIs. If your Data Cloud instance is an older SKU, however, you'll want to review the API Limits for Data Cloud documentation (*https://oreil.ly/rPEgc*) to ensure that your use cases won't be impacted by those limits.

Summary

As part of our deep dive into consuming and taking action with Data Cloud data natively in this chapter, we first learned how to create calculated, streaming, and real-time insights. We discussed how CIs are frequently used downstream in flows, in data actions, and for segmentation. In contrast, streaming insights provide near real-time information and, thus, are often used for near real-time analytics, anomaly detection, process orchestration, and alerting.

In addition, we learned about two different types of Data Cloud enrichments, the copy field and related lists. We then discovered how to create a data action target and reviewed different uses for data actions. We considered a Data Cloud–triggered flow as an alternative to a data action platform event.

The functionality described in this chapter is automatically included OOTB with your standard Data Cloud license. Additional licensing is required to utilize the segmentation and activation features within Data Cloud that will be described in the next chapter. You'll want to reach out to your Salesforce account executive to discuss licensing if the segmentation and activation tabs are not currently available in your Data Cloud instance and you want to explore the functionality.

CHAPTER 12

Segmentation and Activation

In Chapter 11, we looked into ways you can take action with your data through CIs, data actions, data enrichments, and more. Features demonstrated there were OOTB standard functionalities that are included with Data Cloud licensing.

Here, we're going to explore segmentation and activation. Given the history of the Data Cloud platform, it's not surprising that segmentation and activation are currently the most common use cases for Data Cloud.

We were introduced to segmentation and activation in Chapter 3 when we discussed Figure 3-7 (appearing here again in Figure 12-1). In this chapter, we'll dive deep into the topic.

Some of the segmentation functionality described in this chapter might be familiar to you if you have Salesforce Marketing Cloud experience. For example, it's possible to create nested segments in both Data Cloud and Marketing Cloud.

It's important to note that access to all Data Cloud segmentation and activation functionality requires an add-on license. If you don't see in your Data Cloud org the menu options and functionality described, you'll want to reach out to your Salesforce account executive to obtain the necessary licensing.

We'll discuss the following menu option tabs:

- Activation Targets
- Segments
- Activations
- Data Explorer (to review segment-specific DMOs)

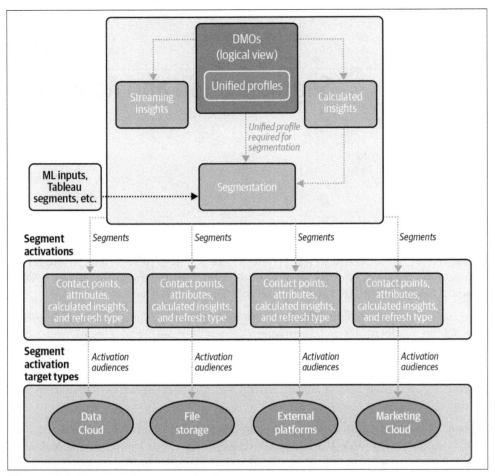

Figure 12-1. Segmentation and activation

Segments are most often created in the Data Cloud user interface, although they can be created via APIs. We'll focus on learning how to create segments and activations in the UI. The segmentation and activation functionality in Data Cloud is powerful, with many decision points. You can use the flowchart (Figure 12-2) as a general guide to help you keep track of where you are in the process, and you can also use it to confirm in advance that you have obtained the necessary information and decisions to complete the segmentation and activation process.

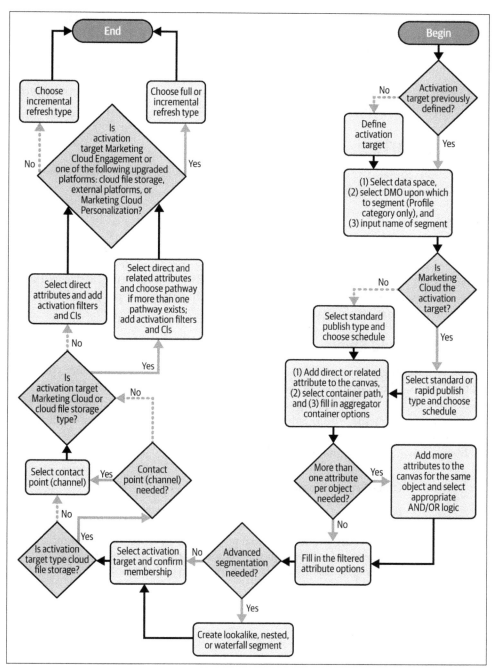

Figure 12-2. Detailed steps for building segmentations and activations in the Data Cloud UI

As part of the segmentation and activation process, some additional Data Cloud DMOs are created. We'll look at Segment Membership DMOs that result from published segments and Activation Audience DMOs that result from activated segments. In addition, we'll briefly discuss ways you can query and report on the segments.

Let's begin by reviewing a few important items in the "Getting Started" section before we dive into the details of segmentation and activation.

Getting Started

This section contains the required prework as well as some important things you should know before you get started.

Prework

You'll need to have completed all the steps leading up to and including identity resolutions, like establishing the connections, ingesting the data, and harmonizing and unifying the data. If you plan to incorporate any CIs into your segments, you'll need those insights created in advance. Refer to "Creating Insights" on page 265 if you need more information about creating CIs.

What You Should Know

As you're planning your segmentation strategy, it's important to remember that only profile DMOs, like Individual or Loyalty Member, can be segmented. In Chapter 9, we discovered that some mappings are required, and we also learned that if you plan to activate any segments within Salesforce or activate segments to external platforms, you must map Profile data to a Contact Point DMO. Without this mapping, you'll be unable to activate your segment to these locations.

Critical Segment Considerations

Segmentation referencing Engagement category data is restricted to a two-year lookback window for standard publication or a seven-day lookback window for rapid publication. Never select a different category to circumvent this limitation. Instead, consider using CIs to aggregate historical data for periods beyond the lookback window limit.

Another important consideration is that running segments consumes credits. Be sure to develop a segmentation plan that includes expected outcomes against which you can compare your results. This will help you avoid consuming large amounts of credits that will tweak your segment unnecessarily. Make use of features like the Approximate Segment Population field (described in more detail later) to help you determine if your segment population count is what you're expecting. Also, consider carefully your needs for a published schedule. The more frequent your publishing, the greater the number of credits needed to publish your segments on an ongoing basis.

Segmentation and Activation Explained

The purpose of segmentation and activation is to turn insights into outcomes by supporting the right engagement with the right audience at the right time. *Segmentation* is the process of dividing a broad population of existing and/or potential customers into subgroups of consumers who share a common identity or interest or have similar behavioral factors. Data Cloud uses attribute filtering to narrow the population to a segment.

The segment is then *activated* and sent to a platform like Marketing Cloud, where attributes are used to send a personalized message to segment members. The message could be personalized with some of the same attributes used in segmentation, but oftentimes, the attributes included in the activation are different.

For example, a segment could be filtered using the Opportunity object with Stage, Close Date, and Amount fields, but the personalization might only use the Amount field of the Opportunity object. Other attribute fields could be included in the activation that were not part of the segmentation process. Specifically, you might want to create a segment of existing consumers who had a total amount of at least $5,000 (using the Total Amount field) of closed won opportunities (using the Stage field) within the last year (using the Close Date field). The message you send to each member of the segment could be personalized with their first name (from the Contact object) and the amount of their most recent opportunity.

Let's look at the four distinct phases or steps in the segmentation and activation process (Figure 12-3). We'll consider activation targets before getting into the details of how to create a segment in Data Cloud. We'll then consider the options available to manually publish a segment or set up a publishing schedule, and we'll finally take a look at segment activation, the last phase in the data orchestration process.

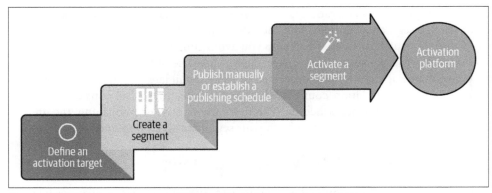

Figure 12-3. High-level steps in the segmentation and activation process

These high-level steps, combined with the flowchart in the introduction, should provide a roadmap for us to follow in this chapter. So, let's begin the segmentation and activation process by learning about activation targets.

Defining Activation Targets

Activation targets are the locations where you want to use your segment (Figure 12-4). You'll need to define one or more activation targets before you can publish a segment. The activation target definition includes the authentication and authorization information when the target is located outside of Salesforce.

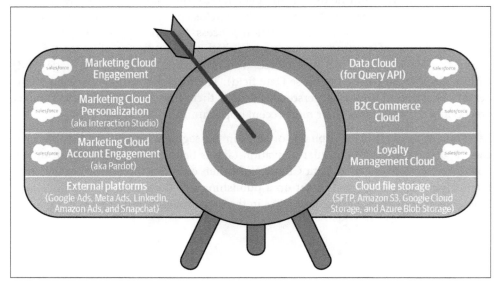

Figure 12-4. Activation platform targets

There are many Salesforce locations you can select as an activation target: Marketing Cloud Engagement, Marketing Cloud Personalization, Marketing Cloud Account Engagement, Loyalty Management Cloud, B2C Commerce Cloud, and Data Cloud.

It's possible to activate your segments directly to external platforms like Google Ads, Meta Ads, Amazon Ads, LinkedIn, Snapchat, and Google Display & Video 360. Additionally, you can activate Data Cloud segments to cloud file storage locations such as Amazon S3, Google Cloud Storage, and Microsoft Azure Blob Storage.

An activation target is automatically created when a B2C Commerce Connector or Marketing Cloud Personalization Connector to the Data Cloud is created. All other activation targets can be created, edited, and deleted in the Data Cloud user interface.

Activation targets created need to be enabled before they can be used. Disabling a previously enabled activation target temporarily removes access to selecting that activation target in the activation process. Deleting an activation target is irreversible, although you can create a new activation target in the previously deleted location.

There are important notes for some of the activation targets:

All external activation platforms
    In Data Cloud setup, you must select the privacy type applicable to your organization. These privacy types are specific to the California Privacy Rights Act (CPRA), and you'll check the box to indicate your organization is either a CPRA Third Party or a CPRA Service Provider. Alternatively, you can select the Not Applicable checkbox if your customers aren't impacted by the CPRA.

Amazon S3
    You'll need your S3 access key and secret key to set up an Amazon S3 Connector. Note that the S3 credentials must have the following permissions: `PutObject`, `GetObject`, `ListBucket`, `DeleteObject`, and `GetBucketLocation`.

SFTP, Google Cloud Storage, and Microsoft Azure Blob Storage
    The child directory name is case-sensitive, and the child directory must have Write permissions. Selecting the "Create a folder within child directory" checkbox results in the files being added to a separate folder rather than the child directory. Pretty Good Privacy (PGP) encryption is supported for CSV and JSON file formats, but not Parquet. The maximum file size for each file exported to the file storage system is 500 MB, but that can be increased by the Salesforce support team. Note that the payload will be split into multiple files before being exported if the activation payload is larger than the specified file size.

Marketing Cloud activation target

When an activation target has multiple business units (BUs), the activation filters contacts by BU. You'll need to modify the activation target configuration to include only one BU if an activation target has multiple BUs configured. Also, it's important to note that the segment activates as a shared data extension (SDE) and not as a data extension (DE) to Marketing Cloud.

Google Ads

It's possible that you'll be able to obtain Google Audience insights when Google Ads is your activation platform. A Google Audience report can give you insights into your customers' unique characteristics, interests, and behaviors. Three categories are considered: demographics, in-market, and affinity. *Demographics* categorize members based on age and gender, the *in-market* category displays customers who are actively researching your products, and *affinity* categorizes customers who exhibit specific characteristics. Affinity groups are based on lifestyle, long-term buying habits, and interests.

Segment Population Requirements and Privacy Considerations

The activated segment population must be greater than one thousand users to qualify for Audience insights reporting. Google also implements privacy safeguards, like category reduction and differential privacy, to better ensure insights remain anonymous and can't be linked to individuals. Category reduction excludes categories if the resulting population is too small, while differential privacy adds randomized noise to reports to protect individual membership records without significantly impacting reporting results.

The Audience report generates up to 20 scores that represent the likelihood of members of the Google Customer Match audience, which is your activated segment membership population, being part of a specific demographic or behavioral category. Report scores are generated by comparing the Customer Match audience with the average Google user population in a particular country.

A Google Audience report is generated about five to seven days after you activate a segment to Google, and the report is updated when there's a major change to the segment membership.

Activation targets are created in the Data Cloud user interface by accessing the Activation Targets tab. From within the tab, click New Activation Target, then select your target platform. For activation targets outside of Salesforce, you'll need to enter authentication and authorization information required to set up the activation target.

You'll only need to define a particular activation target once. Once created, an activation target can receive many different segments.

Creating a Segment

Segments can be created via the Segment Builder in the UI, or they can be created via the API. You can even send Data Cloud your segments created in Tableau. Creating advanced segments such as lookalike segments, nested segments, and waterfall segments is also possible in the UI, but as mentioned previously, only Profile category DMOs can be selected for segmentation.

When building a segment, it's possible to get a quick estimate of the segment population count by using the Approximate Segment Population field. This allows you to confirm that the segment count meets your expectations and that if not, you can adjust the segment rules. Knowing the approximate segment count at the time of creation can also help prevent problems later during the activation phase that arise due to segment size limitations.

Once created, most of your segments will have an Active status. There are five different status values possible:

- Active
- Error
- Inactive
- Processing
- Recounting

You can select the Update Status option from the drop-down menu to view the current status. A segment with an Error status is one that is active but can't be manually published. It's only possible to delete an Inactive segment.

Consent Management for Data Cloud

Consider carefully the implications of building segments based on Data Cloud objects other than Individual and Unified Individual DMOs. This is because there are native ways within Salesforce to assist you in complying with the data protection and privacy regulations applicable to your organization, but they only work if you incorporate the best practice of building segments on the Individual and Unified Individual DMOs.

Specifically, you can submit Restriction of Processing requests in Data Cloud to manage consumer rights and expectations. However, those requests must be submitted using the Consent API, which leverages the Individual and Unified Individual DMOs. If you build segments on any other object, you'll be responsible for implementing an alternative process for managing consent restrictions.

Review the Consent Management for Data Cloud documentation (*https://oreil.ly/mE2tr*) for more information about Restriction of Processing requests. You can also review more details about the Salesforce Consent Data Model in Chapter 7.

Now, let's learn how to build segments in Data Cloud using the Segment Builder UI. We'll need to create the segment, select a publishing type and schedule, and then filter the segment to arrive at the targeted audience. Creating and filtering the segment is covered first, followed by an explanation of publishing types and schedule options.

Segment Builder User Interface

From the Segment tab, click the New button in the top right corner to begin the process of creating a new segment in the Data Cloud UI. You'll choose between the Visual Builder and Create with Einstein segment creation options. Using the Visual Builder, you can create a standard, waterfall, or real-time segment (Figure 12-5).

If you're using something other than the default data space, choose the data space. For the Segment On selection, choose from the drop-down list the DMO upon which you want to create a segment. Remember, you can only choose from the DMOs with a Profile category, such as the following objects: Account, Account Contact, Lead, Loyalty Program Member, Party Identification, Unified Individual, and Unified Party Identification.

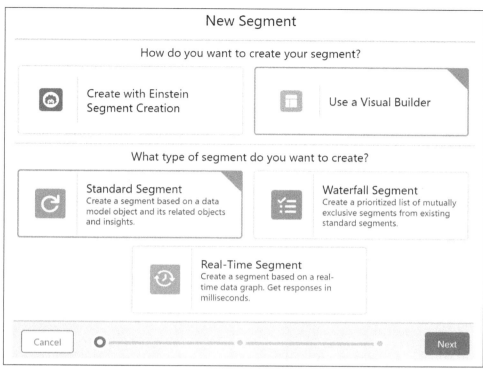

New Segment

How do you want to create your segment?

Create with Einstein
Segment Creation

Use a Visual Builder

What type of segment do you want to create?

Standard Segment
Create a segment based on a data
model object and its related objects
and insights.

Waterfall Segment
Create a prioritized list of mutually
exclusive segments from existing
standard segments.

Real-Time Segment
Create a segment based on a real-
time data graph. Get responses in
milliseconds.

Cancel

Next

Figure 12-5. Creating a new segment from the segment tab in the Data Cloud app

After you select the data space and the target upon which you want to create your segment, you'll provide a name for the segment and click the Next button. You'll see a dialog box for selecting the publishing type and schedule (Figure 12-6). More information about publishing a segment is described in the next section.

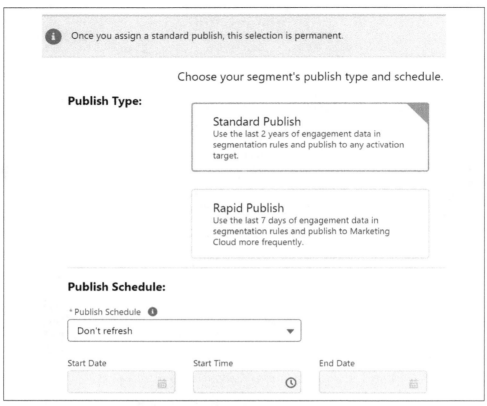

Figure 12-6. Decide on the publishing type and schedule

Once you've selected the publishing type and schedule and clicked the Save button, you'll have access to the Segment Builder canvas (Figure 12-7).

Figure 12-7. Segment Builder canvas

It may take a few minutes before you get access to the attributes. Try refreshing your screen if more than a few minutes pass without access.

You'll notice that the current segment population is included on the canvas once your audience has been created through segmentation. You'll see a list of direct attributes and related attributes on the lefthand side, and you can use these to build your segment using the canvas. Together, the two attribute types form your attribute library.

Notice in the center of the canvas there is a place for you to add attributes from the attribute library. You'll add each of the attributes in their own container and use some AND/OR logic to combine those attribute containers in the segment. Let's use the attribute library to add attributes to the canvas so we can use those attributes to filter our segment.

Using the attribute library

Attributes are used to create target audiences from the population. Narrowing the population to arrive at the target audience is achieved through segmentation filtering using filter operators and logic on the attributes.

There are two types of attributes: direct attributes and related attributes. Both types are listed in the attribute library on the left side of the segmentation canvas. Included in the attribute library list are those attributes available for segmentation purposes. They are the attributes associated with the selected segment target that have been mapped in your data model. If there is an attribute you expected but don't see in the attribute library, be sure to check the data mapping.

Direct attributes such as first name have a one-to-one relationship with the target segment. Thus, there is only one data point for a profile attribute for each segmented entity. In contrast, *related attributes* can have multiple data points for each segmented entity. For example, one person can have multiple purchases. Remember that we want to select attributes that we'll use to narrow our population. Later in the activation process, we'll select attributes that we want to include in our messaging.

Each attribute belongs to an object, and in our case, we'll segment on the Unified Individual DMO and use a related attribute from the Lead object. You'll want to select one or more attributes to place in the container by holding down your cursor on the attribute and dragging it to the center of the canvas (Figure 12-8). Now, you'll see the container path, the container aggregator, and the container filtered attributes sections for the Is US Based attribute.

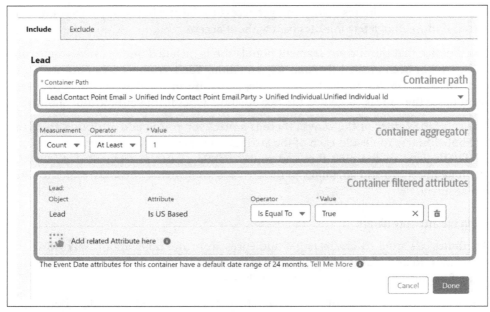

Figure 12-8. Segment canvas container

The container path includes a default path, but additional options exist in the drop-down menu whenever there are multiple data source options. Only one container path can be selected for the attribute, and that path should align with the marketing campaign goals. For example, select the path with the retail sales source if the purpose of the campaign is to market to individuals who have made certain types of purchases.

Once you fill out the information in the container aggregator and container filtered attributes sections and save your work, you'll no longer be able to edit the container path for that segment. You can delete the container and create a different one.

There is a section on the canvas for you to add another related attribute. Afterward, click Save and you should notice that the number of records matching your filter criteria (the segment population) will be automatically refreshed (Figure 12-9).

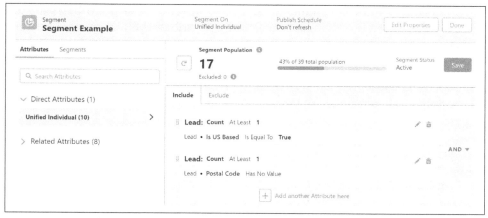

Figure 12-9. Lead object–related attributes added to the canvas

Now that we've used the attribute library to pull two attributes from the Lead object into the Segment Builder canvas, let's proceed with creating the desired audience by filtering the segment within the containers.

Creating filtered segments in containers

You can keep the container logic of AND so that the two containers will be evaluated such that an individual must meet both criteria to be included in the filtered segment. If instead we had changed the logic to OR, then an individual would only need to meet one or the other requirement (Figure 12-10).

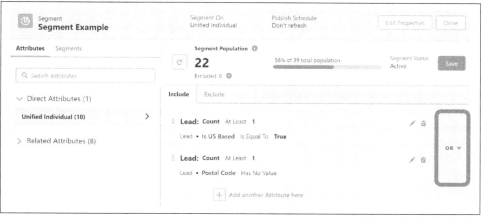

Figure 12-10. Using the OR logic in the container

You'll notice that you can continue to add more direct or related attributes for the same object, and you can also edit or delete object attributes you just created. Be sure to click the Done button in the bottom right corner when you've entered the required values and operators.

Within the aggregator container section, there are three of four pieces of required information when selecting DMO fields:

Measurement
Average, Count, Min, Max, Sum

Attribute
Options available are based on both the object and the measurement selected (but are not needed for the Count measurement)

Operator
Depends on the measurement

Value(s)
Numerical value(s)

The Count measurement is based on the number of records and doesn't require an attribute. For all measurements other than Count, you'll be asked to select an attribute. The attribute options available are limited to fields with numerical data types within the object selected. For example, you'll have the option of the Discount Percent or Face Value Amount attribute for the Voucher object; you'll have the option of Probability or Total Amount for the Opportunity object.

The operator options depend on the selected measurement. For the Count measurement, you can choose At Least, At Most, or Exactly. For all other measurements, you can select from Has Value, Has No Value, Is Equal To, Is Not Equal To, Is Less Than, Is Less Than or Equal To, Is Greater Than, Is Greater Than or Equal To, Is Between, and Is Not Between.

The last piece of information you'll enter is one or more values. If you select an operator of Is Between or Is Not Between, you'll need to enter two values. For all other operator selections, you'll enter one value. All values must be a numerical data type, and although rarely needed, negative values are supported.

It's possible to use CIs as segmentation criteria in the filtered segments section (Figure 12-11).

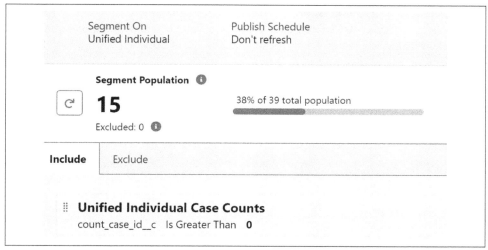

Figure 12-11. Using CI in a filtered segment within the container aggregator section of the Segment Builder canvas

There is only one aggregator container section for each object selected, but there will be one or more filtered attribute containers for each selected object. If there is more than one filtered attribute container, you'll ultimately select one AND/OR logic to stitch together those containers.

Within each container filtered attribute section, the object and attribute values are not editable. They are based on the specific attribute you dragged to the middle of the canvas. Two pieces of required information for each attribute are needed to accomplish the filtering:

Operator (sometimes referred to as the Expression)
  Depends on the attribute data type

Value
  Depends on the attribute data type and the selected operator

The available operators depend on the attribute data type. Currently, Data Cloud supports date, numeric, and text data types. More data types are coming soon:

DATE data type operators
  Is/Is Not Anniversary Of, Is Today, Is Yesterday, Is Tomorrow, Is Between, Is This Month, Is Next Month, Is Last Month, Last Year, This Year, Next Year, Last Number of Days, Greater Than Last Number of Days, Next Number of Days, Last Number of Days, Next Number of Months, Last Number of Months, Day/Not Day of Week, Day of Month, Before/After Day of Month, Has/Has No Value

NUMERIC data type operators
Has/Has No Value, Is/Is Not Equal To, Is Less Thank, Is Less Than or Equal To, Is Greater Than, Is Greater Than or Equal To, Is/Is Not Between

TEXT data type operators
Has/Has No Value, Is/Is Not Equal To, Contains, Does Not Contain, Matches, Doesn't Match, Begins With, Exists As A Whole Word, Is/Is Not In

EMAIL data type operators
Available in a future release

URL data type operators
Available in a future release

PHONE data type operators
Available in a future release

PERCENT data type operators
Available in a future release

BOOLEAN data type operators
Has/Has No Value, Is True/False

After selecting the operator, you'll enter one or more values. The value(s) used for filtering can be numerical, date, or text values and depend on the attribute data type and selected operator.

Once you've selected all required operators and values, click the Done button. The AND logic will appear on the far right if there exist multiple containers for an object. The AND logic is the default value, but it can be changed to OR by clicking on the down arrow.

When you've finished adding all the attributes and filters, click the Save button and the segment status will temporarily change to Counting. Once the segmentation counting is complete, the new segment population will be displayed and the segment status will return to Active.

Considering the Implications of Clicking the Save Button

Wait to click the Save button until you've added all the filters and you're sure you're ready for the recount to get underway. Credits are consumed by recounting because the population undergoes segmentation again.

We've focused our attention on building segments within the Data Cloud user interface. However, it's possible for segments to be built through APIs and also by using GenAI capabilities. Let's explore both.

Einstein Segment Creation

It's possible to use GenAI to build targeted audience segments in Data Cloud with Einstein segment creation. To access the functionality, you'll need to turn on Einstein GenAI. Navigate to Setup → Einstein Setup → Enable to start the process, then type **Feature Manager** in the Quick Find box and enable Einstein segment creation. You'll notice that you can enable additional features, including the approximate segment population feature and the Data Cloud in Sandbox feature (Figure 12-12).

When using Einstein segment creation, just describe the target audience in the Einstein Segment Creation chat and let Einstein do the rest. Be sure to use at least two words to describe the segment and also be sure to use simple phrases. Your words will then be translated into attributes and values based on the data that exists in your Data Cloud org.

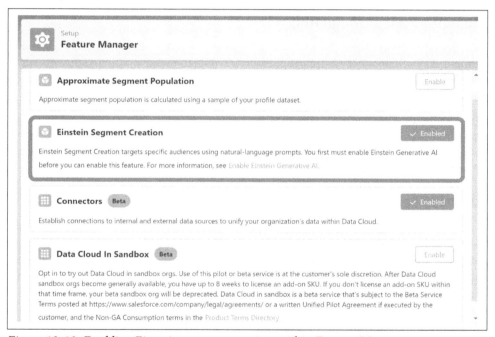

Figure 12-12. Enabling Einstein segment creation within Feature Manager

You can, of course, edit the description or start over by clicking the Refine Segment button. You can also click the Count Population button for an accurate population number. To manually change any of the attributes or values, click the Edit Segment Rules button, and when you're satisfied, click the Create Segment button. You can then publish this segment just as you would any other segment.

When Einstein goes through the process of generating a segment using GenAI, Salesforce doesn't send any PII data to third-party sources. Instead, Salesforce sends sample data for each field so the GenAI can understand the context.

Another important feature of Einstein segmentation in Data Cloud is that unethical or biased language isn't allowed when creating an Einstein segment. If a description includes unethical or biased language, you'll be asked to change your description. And all demographic attributes that can create bias are deselected by default to help reduce the possibility of creating bias in segments using Einstein GenAI capabilities.

It's important to know that before you can use Einstein segment creation in Data Cloud, you'll need to enable GenAI and then turn on Einstein segments. You'll enable Einstein segment creation using the Feature Manager option from within Data Cloud Setup.

Segments Built Through APIs

Most end users will utilize Data Cloud to build and manage segments. However, with segment API, it's possible to use programmatic tools to create and manage segmentation from external systems and platforms. This is especially useful for managing integrations between Salesforce Data Cloud and other Salesforce products like Tableau.

APIs can be used to create, update, read, and delete segments, and the same API access capabilities can be used to manage rule definitions, publishing schedules, and more. Functionality has also been improved with the new MarketSegmentDefinition metadata type, which provides an easier way to define segment filters programmatically.

Advanced Segmentation

After one or more segments have been created, you'll have the option to take advantage of some advanced segment functionality. You can use one existing segment to create an Einstein lookalike segment, or you can use two segments to create nested segments. Furthermore, you can use multiple segments to create a waterfall segment. Let's briefly review each of these three advanced segment types.

Einstein lookalike segments

Einstein lookalike segments are based on insights from your existing segments, so you'll need to have already created segments to use as a seed segment. Using the existing seed segment, you'll use Einstein to find a similar audience. Once created, the Einstein lookalike model runs every seven days.

Within the Segments tab, open the segment you want to use as a seed segment, click the Create Einstein Lookalike Segment button, and then click the Run button to run the Einstein lookalike model. Processing should complete in less than 24 hours, after which time you can click Create Einstein Lookalike Segment again to specify the audience size, segment name, and description. You'll also need to select the publishing schedule and activation target.

You can make edits to the lookalike segment or stop running the Einstein lookalike segment altogether. Just select Stop Running Einstein Lookalike Segment from the drop-down menu. It's best practice to stop running an Einstein lookalike segment if you're not actively publishing it because running one every 7 days consumes credits.

It's possible, but not necessary, to delete a lookalike segment if you're no longer using it on an activation platform. However, you are required to delete lookalike segments and stop running a lookalike segment before you can delete a seed segment. It's possible to use one seed segment to create several Einstein lookalike segments, so you'll need to stop running all models and delete all lookalike segments that use that seed segment before deleting the seed segment.

Nested segments

A *nested segment* combines an outer segment (known as the *target segment*) with an inner segment (known as the *base segment*), which allows for reusability of filters and componentization of segments. Nested segments simplify segment creation for common elements and make it possible to reuse segments for efficiency and organizational consistency.

Nested segments can reduce the number of records processed, especially for situations when target segments can be built on a base segment that doesn't need to be refreshed as frequently as the target segments. Reducing the number of records that need to be processed for segmentation, without negatively impacting the results, results in fewer overall credits consumed.

Nested Segment Limitations

It's not possible to create a nested segment using rapid segments or segments in an inactive or error state. It's also not possible to use an outer nested segment as an inner segment. Inner and outer segments must be in the same Segment On entity, and there is also a limitation of 50 filters in each nested segment tab.

From the Segments tab, click the segment you want to reuse and then click Edit Rules. Drag the desired segment to the canvas, and on the Include or Exclude tab, select the publishing behavior. Just make sure that the segment has been published at least one time if you select Use Last Published Membership for access to the segment's population from the most recent publication. Choosing this publishing behavior results in the inner segment, rather than the outer segment, determining the publishing schedule. If instead you want to refresh the segment when the outer segment publishes, select the option to Use Segment Criteria.

Waterfall segments

Traditional segments are based on attributes like identity, interest, and behavioral factors. Therefore, it's possible that an individual customer can exist in more than one segment. When running a campaign with multiple offers, you can use a *waterfall segment* to create a hierarchical structure and prioritize your campaigns for more precision and control against oversaturation of key audiences.

For example, you can have four different discounted offers where you don't want a customer to receive more than one offer. In the absence of using waterfall segments, it would be possible for one customer to receive multiple offers as long as they meet the segment criteria for each of the segments. You can solve this problem with waterfall segmentation, which is easily accomplished by using the Salesforce drag-and-drop user interface.

To have a waterfall segment, you'll need to start by creating the individual segments that will be included in your waterfall segment. Next, from the Segments tab, create a waterfall segment and then drag in those individual segments to define the priority. Be sure to activate the individual segments after saving your waterfall segment.

Publishing a Segment

Data Cloud segments can be published manually or on a schedule. When you created your segments, you had the option of scheduling either a standard 12-hour schedule or a 24-hour schedule to send activation data. You can always change the publishing options between a manual or scheduled publication as well as change between a 12-hour and a 24-hour schedule.

In some situations, a regularly scheduled publish based on a time interval may not be the best choice. If you instead need a segment published based on an event, it's recommended that you use a flow to refresh the segment. This will help prevent unnecessary processing of records that would occur at regularly scheduled intervals. Depending on the use case, you could also consider using a data action to send an individual into a marketing journey.

Another best practice is to periodically review the segmentation results for segments with a scheduled publish to ensure results are still as expected. Published segments that yield empty segment results still incur consumption costs for processing records. Thus, you should stop the scheduled publish and deactivate the segment if it's no longer needed.

For Salesforce Marketing Cloud activations, there is another possibility. Rapid segment publishing can be used to increase the frequency of segment refreshment and shorten publishing time for activations from Data Cloud to Marketing Cloud. When you create the segment, you can choose either a 1-hour or a 4-hour schedule to send activation data to Marketing Cloud.

Filter Limit

Each rapid segment publish can only filter the last seven days of engagement data to be used for your output values.

For segments on a publishing schedule of 12 or 24 hours or a rapid segment publish schedule of 1 or 4 hours, there will be a Next Publish Date Time listed. That information is only an estimate and can change depending on concurrency limits and how many segments are in progress for publishing. You'll define the start and end date along with the start time when you set up a publishing schedule.

Preset Publishing Schedule Requirements

Segments with a preset publishing schedule need to have a valid enabled activation created first.

You can manually publish segments by navigating to the Segments tab, selecting the segment from your list, and then selecting the Publish Now option via the drop-down menu on the segment details page (Figure 12-13). You can check the Publish History page to see when the segment was actually published. Publishing isn't necessarily instantaneous; the amount of time it takes to manually publish the segment depends on your data volume and the activation target.

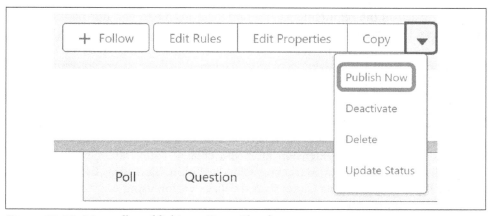

Figure 12-13. Manually publishing a Data Cloud segment

Segment details include a Publish Status field that provides information about the most recent publishing status of the segment to the activation target. The various publishing statuses are as follows:

- Success
- Error
- Skipped
- Deferred
- Publishing
- Blank (No Status)

A blank status indicates that a segment was created but not published. When a publishing status indicates *Skipped*, the publication is temporarily delayed for 30 minutes due to the maximum number of segments publishing simultaneously. When a publishing status indicates *Deferred*, the publishing time is pushed out due to exceeding the maximum number of simultaneous publications.

Once a segment has been created, the publishing type and schedule has been chosen, and the filter attributes have been selected and filled out, it's time to activate the segment to get value from it.

Activating a Segment

We began this chapter by creating activation targets, and in doing so, we observed that there are a lot of different activation platforms available to receive our Data Cloud segments. The activation platform you choose for any particular segment will have an impact on the requirements and options available to you during the activation process. For example, contact points are required for all platforms other than the cloud file storage targets. The choice between activation refresh types, full or incremental, depends on the activation platform selected. All platforms have the incremental refresh type available, and Marketing Cloud Engagement and some platforms with upgrades can be sent full refreshes.

Many Data Cloud users have Salesforce Marketing Cloud as one of their activation platforms. When this is the case, the related attributes are stored in a field of Marketing Cloud's activated data extension after you created your Data Cloud activation and publish the segment to Marketing Cloud. Within Marketing Cloud, you can parse the JSON from the Data Cloud shared data extension using AMPscript, GTL, or server-side scripting language (SSJS) to use the attributes and values in email personalization.

Salesforce Marketing Cloud is one of the many activation platforms that require you to select a contact point. You're not required to provide a contact point for cloud file storage activation target types, but you can elect to provide a phone number or email address, if you'd like. Let's take a look at the contact points available for the various activation platforms.

Contact Points

Phone number and email address contact points can be included in activations for any platform. It's also possible to select mobile app contact points for Salesforce Marketing Cloud. You can choose a mobile advertiser ID (MAID) or an over-the-top (OTT) ID when using external activation platforms (Table 12-1).

Table 12-1. Activation platform contact point options

Activation contact point	Salesforce Marketing Cloud	External platforms	Salesforce Marketing Cloud Personalization	Cloud file storage	Salesforce B2C Commerce Cloud
Phone number	Yes	Yes	Yes	Yes	Yes
Email address	Yes	Yes	Yes	Yes	Yes
Mobile app (mobile push)	Yes				
Mobile advertiser ID (MAID)		Yes			
Over-the-top (OTT) ID		Yes			

There are contact point mapping requirements, depending on the contact point(s) selected in the activation process (Table 12-2).

Table 12-2. Contact point requirements

Activation contact point	Required mapping (from)	Required mapping (to)	Object	Required fields
Phone number	Contact Point Phone.Party	Individual.Individual ID	Contact Point Phone	Contact Point Phone ID, Formatted E164 Phone Number, Country
Email address	Contact Point Email.Party	Individual.Individual ID	Contact Point Email	Contact Point Email, Email Address
Mobile app (mobile push)	Contact Point App.Party	Individual.Individual ID	Contact Point App	Contact Point App ID
Mobile advertiser ID (MAID)	1. Contact Point App.Party	1. Individual.Individual ID	1. Contact Point App	1. Contact Point App ID, Device
	2. Contact Point App.Device	2. Device.Device ID	2. Device	2. Device ID, Advertiser ID, OS Name
Over-the-top (OTT) ID	1. Contact Point App.Party	1. Individual.Individual ID	1. Contact Point App	1. Contact Point App ID, Device
	2. Contact Point App.Device	2. Device.Device ID	2. Device	2. Device ID, Advertiser ID, OS Name

Notice that all activation contact points have a mapping requirement of the Party field to the Individual ID. MAID and OTT contact points are specifically for external platforms and thus also require mapping to a Device ID field.

Some additional details:

Phone number
For Marketing Cloud, the country code must be in ISO 3166 (*https://oreil.ly/caAlz*) two-letter format.

MAID
The OS name field value must be iOS or Android.

OTT
The OS name field value must be RokuOS, AndroidTV, tvOS, FireOS, Tizen, SmartCast, or WebOS.

You'll need to select the contact point within the Data Cloud Segment tab, after you choose the activation target and confirm activation membership. Email Address is a frequently selected contact point.

Activating Direct and Related Attributes

In addition to a contact point, you'll most likely want to add one or more direct attributes such as an individual's first name. *Direct attributes* are attributes of the Activation Membership object.

Additionally, you may want to add one or more activation-related attributes like policy number, starting date, and product type. Be sure to click the Add Attributes button (Figure 12-14) to include these direct and related attributes.

Figure 12-14. Adding attributes to an activation

Related attributes are only available to choose when the activation platform is Marketing Cloud or a cloud file storage type. Related attributes are selected from DMOs with a path to that object from the Activated On object. There are some important considerations and guidelines when selecting related attributes.

Activation Related Attribute Limitations

You can use up to 30 activations with related attributes, and each of those activations can have no more than 20 total related attributes per activation. Note that it is 20 attributes in total, not per each DMO included in the activation.

DMOs are related to the Individual DMO via pathways. If multiple paths exist, you'll need to select the path with the relevant DMOs you want to activate because you can only select one pathway for activating related attributes. In the example provided (Figure 12-15), if you need related attributes from DMOs 7 and 8, then you'll want to select Path #3 for your activation. As a result, related attributes from DMOs 2, 3, 5, and 6 will not be available in the current activation, which includes DMOs 7 and 8.

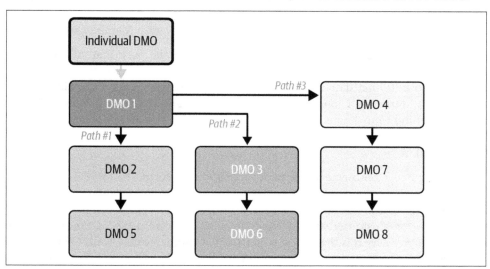

Figure 12-15. DMO pathway possibilities for activating related attributes

It's important to note that unlike with segmentation filters, which display the entire DMO hierarchy, only the DMOs one hop away from the object are displayed. Thus, when creating activation filters, you'll need to click through the hierarchy to get to the other DMOs. In our example, getting to the related attributes in DMO 8 requires a total of four hops.

Pathway Limitations

You can traverse no more than four hops from the related objects.

Earlier, we mentioned using the Approximate Segment Population field to get faster segment counts. There are many reasons why knowing the segment size is important. For one thing, there are limitations enforced in the activation phase that are dependent on the segment size.

Segment Size Limitations When Related Attributes Are Included

Segment size is checked at the time of activation. If the segment contains more than 10 million records and includes related attributes when you publish, the segment won't activate.

Another consideration is that we previously stated that selecting contact points is optional for file storage target activations such as Amazon S3, SFTP, Google Cloud Storage, and Microsoft Azure activations. Thus, you can elect to remove the default attribute that is included automatically based on the Activation Membership object.

For Marketing Cloud target activations specifically, make sure that Allow Profile Business Unit Mapping Data is enabled and that segments are filtered by BU. It's important to note that datetime values always convert from your Data Cloud org's time zone to Marketing Cloud server time, which is Central Standard Time (CST) or six hours behind Coordinated Universal Time (UTC-6). Also, the population must be one or greater for some Marketing Cloud activation targets such as Marketing Cloud Personalization.

When using B2C Commerce as the target activation platform, the DMO is chosen by default in the activation membership. Therefore, it is very important that you make sure field mappings are done correctly for all data sources because you'll need to have valid values for CustomerNo and CustomerListID for non-B2C Commerce data sources. Another caveat is that if you select a B2C Commerce data source for filtering activation data, there can be no blank or null values for all the activated attributes.

All segments must have an active publishing schedule, and the privacy type must be set if you're using an external target activation platform.

Activation Filters

Activation filters are used to find the right attributes for message personalization, and activation filters can only be applied on the DMO fields in the chosen activation pathway. Activated segments don't automatically acquire segmentation filters, and activation filtering is supported by the following subset of the segmentation operators:

DATE operator type values
> Has No Value, Is On, Is Before, Is Between, Is/Is Not Anniversary Of, Greater Than Last Number of Days, Last Number of Days, Next Number of Days, Last Number of Months, Next Number of Months

NUMERIC operator type values
> Is/Is Not Equal To, Is Less Than, Is Less Than or Equal To, Is Greater Than

TEXT operator type values
> Has No Value, Is/Is Not Equal To, Contains, Does Not Contain, Begins With, Exists As A Whole Word, Is/Is Not In

EMAIL operator type values
> Available in a future release

URL operator type values
> Available in a future release

PHONE operator type values
> Available in a future release

PERCENT operator type values
> Available in a future release

BOOLEAN operator type values
> Available in a future release

Calculated Insights in Activation

Activation journey decisions and content personalization can be enhanced with the use of Data Cloud CIs, as discussed in Chapter 11. Simply drag your CI metric onto a new or existing activation (Figure 12-16). You can also add dimension filters to your CI metric for more granular insights on an activation.

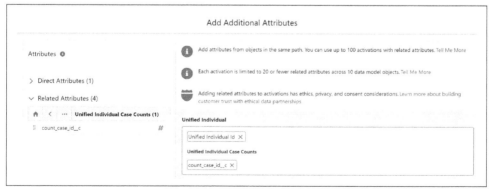

Figure 12-16. Adding CI metrics to an activation

Datetime metrics are a type of aggregatable metric, whereas text is a nonaggregatable metric. Numeric metrics can be either aggregatable or nonaggregatable. Aggregatable metrics include Sum totals for Numeric metrics. Datetime aggregatable metrics can include Min and Max values (for example, the first date an event occurred and the most recent date the same event occurred).

There are different filter requirements for aggregatable and nonaggregatable metrics, which are the two CI categories available for activation metrics. Filters are optional for aggregatable metrics but required for nonaggregatable metrics because nonaggregatable metric filtering is needed to narrow down the attribute to one specific value. Dimensional filters for nonaggregatable metrics can include date or datetime filters, but the nonaggregatable datetime metric used will be hidden unless the same datetime metric is also used as an aggregatable metric.

Activation Refresh Types

There are two possible activation refresh types: full and incremental. During activation, a *full refresh* updates all records in the segment, whereas an *incremental refresh* updates only the records that changed since the last refresh. Your choice of refresh type depends on your use case and what is possible for the activation target. Choose incremental, when appropriate, to limit the number of records processed, which, in turn, decreases your consumption costs.

Marketing Cloud Engagement, Amazon S3, SFTP, Google Cloud Storage, and Microsoft Azure Storage activation targets allow for either a full or an incremental refresh. The incremental refresh is the default selection.

For Marketing Cloud Personalization, as well as external platforms and cloud file storage activation targets, you'll need to request an upgrade to have access to a full refresh. OOTB, incremental refresh is the only option for Marketing Cloud Personalization and strategic partners, with the exception of the first publication.

For either refresh type chosen, the first publication for all activation targets is always a full refresh, which results in the entire segment being transferred to the activation target. Also, if an activation fails, the next refresh is automatically incremental from the last successful segment published.

Limitations for Changing Between Refresh Types

It's possible to change a full refresh to an incremental refresh when editing an activation for a standard segment. However, you can't change an incremental refresh to a full refresh.

There are some additional considerations for activation refresh types specific to activation targets:

Marketing Cloud Engagement and Marketing Cloud Personalization

Every 24 hours, you can trigger a full refresh manually for either of these activation targets.

Marketing Cloud Engagement

Switching between refresh types results in the activation payload being written to a new DE. If you change from full to incremental refresh, a full update occurs to move the entire segment to the new DE.

Incremental refresh for Marketing Cloud Engagement versus Amazon S3

A Marketing Cloud API uses the subscriber ID as the key to write any updates to Marketing Cloud Engagement. Alternatively, Amazon S3 consumes and processes the incremental payload, which contains the adds, deletes, and updates in the audience.

After an activation has been created, you'll see it in your Activation related lists on the Activations tab. One option available to you is copying an existing activation, which allows you to reuse filters or other selections among different segments. Note that it's not possible to edit the activation target and activation membership of a copied activation, but you can select one or more contact points and add attributes to your copied activation, after which the new activation will be added to the selected segment.

Troubleshooting Activation Errors

Occasionally, things go wrong during activation. Some of the common errors involve invalid data formats or data extension problems when using Marketing Cloud data extensions (Table 12-3).

Table 12-3. Tips for solving common activation errors

Error	Troubleshooting suggestion
Required fields don't have a value	Complete the required fields.
Invalid email address	Use an email address with proper characters (@ and .) and make sure the length is less than 254 characters.
Invalid date	Use MM/DD/YYYY or DD/MM/YYYY.
Invalid locale	Use a locale (such as en-US) to define the country of the subscriber.
Invalid phone	Use ###-###-#### and make sure the country code number is correct.
Field not found	Determine if the field still exists in the data extension. Be sure to modify the field mapping if the data extension schema changes.
Invalid field count	Make sure the number of fields is correct when you import a data extension.
Invalid decimal	Use a value that is within the length range. For example, a value of XXXX or XXX.X or XX.XX would satisfy a length value of 4.

In addition to actual activation errors, you probably want to compare the number of activation records to the number of segment records. Most of the time, you'll find the numbers are the same. If you notice that there are different numbers of records between your segment and activation counts, you can begin investigating with the following questions:

- Did you activate on a different object on which you created a segment?
- Is Individual data coming from more than one data stream?
- Did you activate on a Unified DMO and select a direct attribute with an N:1 attribute relationship?

The most obvious thing to check first is whether segmentation and activation were performed on different DMOs, which could easily result in different record counts. You may have a valid reason for choosing different DMOs, so just be sure to understand that doing so could lead to fewer activated records than your segment population.

Next, look upstream to see if Individual data originates from more than one data stream. If so, next check to see if the attributes from those multiple data streams are mapped to the same or different fields in the DMO. If they are mapped to different fields, then duplicate records could exist in the segment. Segmentation does a distinct count on Individual IDs, whereas activation only deduplicates these records if the attribute values of the distinct Individual IDs are the same. Thus, you could end up with a larger activation record count.

Lastly, duplicate activation records could exist if you activate on a Unified DMO and select a direct attribute with an N:1 attribute relationship. To avoid duplicate activation records in this scenario, it's recommend that you either activate on a non-Unified DMO or that you select a direct attribute with a 1:1 relationship.

Segment-Specific Data Model Objects

We mentioned early on in the chapter that some additional Data Cloud DMOs are created as part of the segmentation and activation process. In a previous chapter, we learned about standard and custom DMOs, but we didn't discuss segment-specific DMOs. These object types are only created during the segmentation and activation process.

In addition to the standard and custom model objects, there exist two additional DMO types: Segment Membership DMOs and Activation Audience DMOs. We'll review first the Segment Membership DMOs, which are of the SEGMENT_MEMBERSHIP category.

Segment Membership Data Model Objects from Published Segments

A Segment Membership DMO is created to store information about segment members whenever you publish a segment. You can access segment DMOs to determine to which segments a profile belongs.

It's possible to verify and investigate segmentation results using the Segment Membership DMOs in Data Cloud via the Data Explorer tab in the user interface. Segment insights can also be visualized using CRM Analytics, Tableau, or another third-party BI tool or platform. It's also possible to query the Segment Membership DMO using SOQL in the Developer Console, Query APIs, or the segmentation REST API.

Segment Membership DMOs are based on the object on which you are building a segment. Each object has two associated Segment Membership DMOs, if a segment has been built on it. The objects and their Segment Membership DMOs are as follows:

- Latest Segment Membership DMO
  Object label name: *Objectname* - `Latest`
  Object API name: *Objectname*`_SM_(timestamp)__dlm`
- Historical Segment Membership DMO
  Object label name: *Objectname* - `History`
  Object API name: *Objectname*`_SMH_(timestamp)__dlm`

As the label names imply, the latest Segment Membership DMO includes the profile IDs from the most recent segment publication, and the historical Segment Membership DMO includes the profile IDs from the previous segment publication.

Activation Audience Data Model Objects from Activated Segments

The Data Cloud Activation Audience DMOs are useful for understanding and analyzing your activated audiences over time. When an activation is created for the first time for any activation target, an Activation Audience DMO is created for that activation target. Thus, each of your activation targets will have its own Activation Audience DMO once a segment has been activated to each of the targets.

The Activation Audience DMO naming convention is *Activation Audience - <Activation Target name>*. Among others, the attributes include a unique ID for each segment and the delta type. There are four distinct delta types included in an Activation Audience DMO:

Added (A)
    The profile was added but wasn't found in the previous activation.

Deleted (D)
    The profile was dropped but was found in the previous run.

Updated (U)
> The profile was updated after the previous activation run.

Existing (E)
> The profile continues to be part of the activation with no change.

It's possible to view activated profile details in different activations for any given target via the Data Explorer tab. The results are available for up to the past 30 days only.

An Activation Audience DMO can't be deleted if an activation is using it, and it's automatically deleted if you delete either the connected activation target or the DMO.

Querying and Reporting for Segments

The details contained within the Segment Membership and Activation Audience DMOs can be reviewed using the Data Explorer (Figure 12-17). Click on the Data Explorer tab and then use the search box to find the DMO you'd like to review. Remember from the previous section that Segment Membership DMOs incorporate the base DMO in the naming convention. It also includes a snapshot type as one of the DMO fields.

Figure 12-17. Segment Membership DMOs are accessible in Data Explorer

In addition to using the Data Explorer menu option, it's possible to query segment data using a Connect REST API. You can use a GET request to query a segment member's latest and historical data, and results can be refined using filters, limits, and sort order. It's important to note that a Connect REST API can query segments within a specific data space or all data spaces.

One specialized Data Cloud segmentation reporting capability is *Segment Intelligence*, which includes OOTB data connectors as well as prebuilt visualizations. Segment Intelligence helps optimize segments and activations in common channels, including Marketing Cloud Engagement, Google Ads, Meta Ads, and Commerce Cloud.

To enable Segment Intelligence, you'll need to search for "Segment Intel Setup" in the Quick Find field. There are several prerequisites required for Segment Intelligence, and the setup tasks must be completed sequentially (Figure 12-18).

Figure 12-18. Segment Intelligence setup screen

Data Cloud Segment Intelligence capabilities are very similar to Marketing Cloud Intelligence capabilities but can provide detail at a more granular level. Data Cloud Segment Intelligence is part of the Data Cloud for Advertising Studio offering, which will require additional licensing beyond the segmentation and activation add-on license. You'll need to speak to your Salesforce account executive for additional information.

Best Practices for Segmentation and Activation

As we wrap up the chapter, it's important to remember that segmentation and activation are two different processes in Data Cloud. As such, they use different filters for different purposes. Filters applied in the segmentation process help narrow your audience so that you can send the right message to the right person at the right time. In contrast, activation filters narrow down relevant values with related attributes that personalize messages.

There are also a few best practices for segmentation and activation in the Data Cloud platform that we should review. It's always recommended to have clean, valid data, and it's also crucial to either have a good understanding of the Data Cloud data model or collaborate with a data modeler or data architect. Here are eleven best-practice recommendations for Data Cloud segmentation and activation:

- Plan ahead before getting hands-on to build your segments to *ensure the data you need will be available*. As part of planning ahead, you'll need to have a good understanding of the Data Cloud data model or work with a data modeler to design the segments.

- As part of your plan, make sure to evaluate the data quality of the source fields to determine if you need to *create formula fields*. In Chapter 7, we looked at two examples of formula fields often used for segmentation and activation. One example explained how to create a formula field to bucket values to simplify segmentation, and the other example showed how to standardize fields for consistency needed for activation by applying the PROPER() function to the First_Name field.

- Further considerations for data quality may necessitate refining Identity Resolution rulesets to help *mitigate duplicate records* in the data.

- Follow that well-thought-out plan you created to *avoid unnecessary consumption* of Data Cloud credits. Avoid a "building the segments as you go" approach by just adding one filter at a time and checking the results. Every time you click the Save button after adding another filter, credits will be consumed as the segment will be processed every time.

- *Validate the results* of your Data Cloud segmentation using Data Explorer to check the results and to compare the expected count to the actual count.

- *Use CIs if your segment is complex.* CIs will allow you to define and calculate multidimensional metrics and aggregate historical events. Be sure to review the CI requirements for segmentation and activation in Chapter 11.

- *Review system limits* for segmentation and activation as well as refresh timings for your segments because they could vary.

- Evaluate the *best time to publish* any particular segment, especially in relation to other segment publications.

- Use the Unified Individual DMO for activation membership. If you instead use the Individual DMO, duplicate entries could result. Data Cloud is not designed to deduplicate or merge segmentation records.

- Don't rely on Data Cloud to dictate the correct contact point such as an email address. It's the marketers' job to know the data and *select which contact point is the most relevant* for the use case. This is especially important when considering consent. Data Cloud can aggregate all consent preferences from different source systems, but it's up to the marketers to make the correct selections. Again, this goes back to having a good understanding of the data model and collaborating with a data architect or data modeler when in doubt.

- *Stagger publishing times* when you have a large number of Data Cloud activation audiences.

Summary

In this chapter, we devoted significant time to exploring Data Cloud segmentation and activation capabilities because these are the most common Data Cloud use case scenarios today. Specifically, we learned how to create Einstein lookalike segments, nested segments, and waterfall segments in addition to individual segments. We then explored how to publish and activate segments.

In the next chapter, we'll explore other ways to extract value from Data Cloud. We'll learn about the Einstein 1 platform, which includes Model Builder, Prompt Builder, and Einstein Copilot. As part of that discussion, we'll learn about the BYOM and BYOLLM capabilities that can be accessed within Model Builder to manage and deploy models more efficiently and cost effectively. We'll also focus our attention on the downstream AI capabilities that come from using data graphs and vector databases created within Data Cloud.

CHAPTER 13

The Einstein 1 Platform and the Zero Copy Partner Network

In Chapter 3, we discussed how Data Cloud works its magic and the key value activities that can be leveraged by Data Cloud users (see Figure 13-1). We've previously explored several key value activities listed in that chapter. In Chapter 7, we reviewed how to build a unified consent repository using the standard Salesforce Consent Data Model. Enrichments, data actions, Data Cloud–triggered flows, and ways to programmatically extract data were explored in Chapter 11. More recently, we discussed segment activation in detail in Chapter 12.

In this chapter, we'll be exploring the six remaining Data Cloud key value business activities. The most important thing we'll learn in this chapter is that the Salesforce Data Cloud platform has an important place in an organization's Predictive AI and GenAI strategy. We won't be covering AI strategy or LLMs in detail, but there are plenty of resources available to help inform you about those topics. *Prompt Engineering for LLMs*, by John Berryman and Albert Ziegler (O'Reilly, forthcoming), and *Prompt Engineering for Generative AI*, by James Phoenix and Mike Taylor (O'Reilly, 2024), are two technical books focused on important GenAI topics. Martin Kihn's new book, *Customer 360: How Data, AI, and Trust Change Everything*, is also an excellent resource if you want to understand how to connect AI technology, people, processes, and strategy.

GenAI brings to organizations the possibility of automating human work and improving both the customer experience and the employee experience. Implementing GenAI isn't easy, though. It takes a great deal of time, money, and specialized expertise, and GenAI requires a massive amount of data. It's no secret that AI tools perform better with more accurate, comprehensive, and diverse datasets like those that exist in a well-architected Salesforce Data Cloud platform.

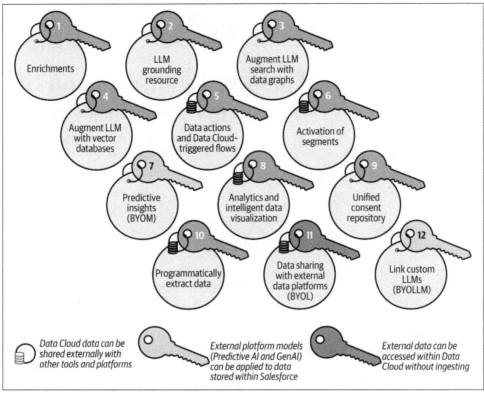

Figure 13-1. Data Cloud key value activities

Large language models (LLMs) are forms of GenAI that generate responses by processing natural language inputs in the form of a prompt. It's possible for LLMs to reason, make logical inferences, and draw conclusions, especially when they've been trained on massive datasets and are grounded with proprietary data. There are four GenAI key value activities directly supported by Data Cloud:

- Grounding the LLM resource with structured data
- Augmenting LLM search with data graphs for near real-time searches
- Augmenting LLM search with vector databases for unstructured data
- Linking and using custom LLMs

Using linked LLMs within the Salesforce Einstein Trust Layer is often referred to as a BYOLLM approach. The Einstein Trust Layer is Salesforce's secure AI architecture, which is built into the Salesforce platform to keep your organization's data safe while you explore GenAI solutions.

There's an important distinction to be made about this BYOLLM business value activity. Leveraging a custom LLM through BYOLLM can be applied to Salesforce CRM data as well as Data Cloud data, but the Data Cloud application is where you access the Einstein Studio menu tab to establish the link to the external LLM (Figure 13-2). This is different from the other 11 key value activities we described in Chapter 3, which all provide value by leveraging Data Cloud data. We'll cover this again later in the chapter when we discuss the Einstein 1 platform.

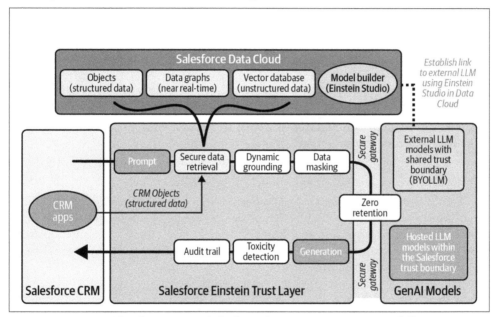

Figure 13-2. Data Cloud supports a Salesforce GenAI strategy in many different ways

We'll focus on learning more about the Einstein 1 platform in this chapter so that we can better understand each of the four GenAI key value activities we've mentioned. We'll revisit Figure 13-2 as we learn how Data Cloud data is an important input for the LLM models we can use to generate responses to our questions.

In addition to being a hub for GenAI features, the Einstein 1 platform supports Predictive AI capabilities that can be built directly within Data Cloud using Einstein Model Builder features. Importantly, an organization's Predictive AI strategy can be extended with powerful external ML tools like Amazon SageMaker, Google Vertex AI, and Databricks. This is achieved using Salesforce's Zero Copy Partner Network, which allows access to data where it lives, among a trusted network of partners. We'll explore two very exciting value activities that can be leveraged through the Zero Copy Partner Network:

- Predictive AI ML insights
- External platform data sharing

Extending ML capabilities with access to zero copy technology partners is frequently known as BYOM capabilities. Taking advantage of external platform data sharing with zero copy technology partners like Snowflake, Google BigQuery, and Amazon Redshift is frequently referred to as a BYOL approach.

Getting Started

This section contains the required prework as well as some important things you should know before you get started.

Prework

As we know from earlier chapters, it's important that you've planned in advance how you'll implement your key value activities before actually getting hands-on in Data Cloud. As part of preparation to take advantage of the features and functionalities described in this chapter, you'll need to have completed the six foundational steps first shown way back in Figure 2-5.

What You Should Know

There are special considerations when connecting to external services like Azure Blob Storage or Snowflake. For these types of connections, you'll need to include the IP addresses used by Data Cloud Services (*https://oreil.ly/bInlL*) in your allowlists if your security policy requires a strict network access control list.

Decide in advance what credentials you'll want to use for any connections with external services or external platforms. Most external platforms support using key pair authentication for enhanced authentication security as an alternative to basic authentication like username and password.

Don't Use Encrypted Private Keys for Connections

Make sure you don't use an encrypted private key for your connection. Reach out to your internal team responsible for security if you have any questions or concerns.

This chapter isn't meant to be a complete guide to all the Salesforce GenAI and Predictive AI capabilities available within the Salesforce platform. It's intended to provide you with information sufficient for you to understand and appreciate the key value activities of Data Cloud that can support your AI strategies. We'll focus our AI discussions in this chapter mostly on the Einstein 1 platform, but before we get there, let's briefly touch on Salesforce Einstein in general.

Salesforce Einstein

Salesforce Einstein is often touted as the first comprehensive AI for CRM. It's described as comprehensive because it's modeling ready across various clouds, and production ready so that no DevOps are needed to take advantage of Salesforce AI capabilities. It's also available to Salesforce users everywhere, in their normal flow of work. You'll find several options for Einstein within the Setup → Quick Find menu, assuming you have the necessary permissions and access. Here's a list of several Einstein options you may see in your Salesforce environment:

Einstein Assessors
- Einstein Bots Assessor
- Einstein Conversation Insights Assessor
- Sales Cloud Einstein Assessor
- Service Cloud Einstein Assessor

Einstein Generative AI
- Einstein Copilot
- Einstein Prompt Builder
- Einstein Setup

Einstein Platform
- Einstein.ai

Einstein Search

- Prompted Search Terms
- Search Layouts
- Search Manager
- Settings
- Synonyms

Einstein Readiness Assessor is a tool that analyzes your existing Salesforce implementation and provides a personalized report telling you whether your environment meets the necessary requirements for specific Einstein features. The Einstein Assessor works in either a production or sandbox environment.

Einstein Generative AI is turned on by accessing the Einstein Setup menu option and clicking the "Turn on Einstein" toggle. You'll have access to Einstein Copilot Studio and Prompt Builder once you turn on Einstein Generative AI capabilities, assuming your Salesforce org is licensed for these features.

Prompt templates can be used to generate countless versions of personalized content in your workflow by helping you create relevant prompts that safely connect your data with LLMs. Prompt templates allow you to access merge fields in your CRM that reference record fields, flows, related lists, and Apex code. These prompts can be invoked in a variety of ways, including with Einstein Copilot actions.

Einstein Copilot is Salesforce's AI-powered conversational assistant integrated with your Salesforce CRM. Copilot allows you to use standard prebuilt actions OOTB to explore your data conversationally. Einstein Copilot can also be extended with custom actions you build using Flow, Apex, and prompts created in Prompt Builder.

Einstein Search brings the power of AI to Salesforce Search. Einstein Search boosts productivity by making searches faster, easier, and more accurate, and it does this by using personalization, natural language search, and actionable instant results. It's important to remember that security is built into Einstein Search; org and user permissions could limit the search results.

Einstein Search

The Einstein Search capabilities mentioned here describe how Einstein Search works within the Salesforce core platform to locate certain records, for example. This is different from semantic search that's part of retrieval-augmented generation (RAG) in Einstein Copilot Search, which we'll discuss in a later section. Review Salesforce content (*https://oreil.ly/K_O5P*) for more information about getting better answers using RAG.

You'll notice Einstein Copilot and Einstein Prompt Builder are included under the listing for Generative AI on the Salesforce platform. Both of these GenAI capabilities are part of the Einstein 1 platform, which also includes Predictive AI capabilities available within Einstein Model Builder. Let's dive a little deeper into the Einstein 1 platform.

Einstein 1 Platform

Salesforce invests a lot in its Einstein 1 platform, previously known as Einstein 1 Studio, so you don't have to build your own Predictive AI and GenAI capabilities from scratch. Salesforce provides democratized AI to users in the form of their Einstein 1 platform's low-code/no-code AI tools, making it possible for many different people in an organization to use AI functionality without needing to possess advanced technical skill sets.

The Salesforce Einstein 1 platform includes three main products: Einstein Model Builder, Einstein Prompt Builder, and Einstein Copilot. Each of these products is accessed from within the Salesforce trusted platform. Model Builder Einstein Studio is unique in that it is accessed only from within the Salesforce Data Cloud application.

Model Builder lets you create your own custom Einstein predictive models faster. You can also use Model Builder to take advantage of prebuilt ML models with external platforms that are part of the Salesforce Zero Copy Partner Network, like Amazon SageMaker, Databricks, and Google Vertex AI.

Additionally, Model Builder allows organizations to leverage their own LLMs for use with data that exists within Salesforce. We'll discuss Model Builder capabilities in two different sections in this chapter: "Einstein Model Builder" on page 345 and "Bring Your Own Model" on page 369.

Einstein Prompt Builder and Einstein Copilot Builder support GenAI capabilities known as LLMs, which are deep learning models trained on really big datasets to better achieve language processing tasks. Using LLM functionality requires you to submit a prompt to a model, frequently in the form of a question. An important goal is to curate effective reusable prompts, which consistently achieves the desired results. It's much easier to accomplish this with Einstein Prompt Builder, which operates within a single consolidated framework. In effect, Prompt Builder is a prompt-engineering playground.

Within Prompt Builder, users access a point-and-click interface to build prompts that often rely on relevant data fields from Data Cloud and Salesforce CRM objects. In this way, specific data points from Data Cloud's structured data can be used as grounding resources as part of the secure data retrieval process (Figure 13-2) to provide the LLM a way to better understand the context and generate more accurate responses.

Invoking prompts created in Prompt Builder can be achieved in a variety of different ways. One way is by using Einstein Copilot, Salesforce's conversational AI assistant that is embedded directly in every application within the Salesforce core platform. Einstein Copilot provides a conversational experience to deliver trusted, generative responses grounded in your Salesforce CRM and Data Cloud data. For example, it can help the sales team better know which deals are likely to close soon and which opportunities require immediate attention.

Einstein Copilot comes OOTB with certain standard actions that will perform a variety of different tasks, and these standard actions provide a foundation upon which a framework can be built. What's really exciting, though, is the ability to enhance Einstein Copilot standard actions and add new custom actions that can use refined prompts, including those built into Einstein Prompt Builder.

The Einstein 1 platform is fueled by data and needs lots of it, but data quality is as important, if not more important, than data quantity. The more high-quality data provided to GenAI models, the better the performance and outcome. That's why Data Cloud is so important. Harmonized and unified customer data ensures more accurate customer profiles and more complete information about customer interactions, including sales interactions. Combining AI capabilities with harmonized and unified customer data improves accuracy and reliability.

It was previously mentioned that individual Data Cloud fields can serve as a grounding resource for a prompt, but using structured data as a grounding resource isn't something that requires Data Cloud data. Specific data points from a Salesforce CRM org can be used instead of or in addition to Data Cloud data, and Figure 13-2 demonstrates this. For structured data, you'll notice that the secure data retrieval process can use CRM app data as an input along with objects and data graphs from Data Cloud.

We also discussed this back in Chapter 2, when we looked at the technical details of how Data Cloud works under the hood. As a reminder of what was discussed in Chapter 2, the Salesforce CRM transactional database can power some of your Einstein AI activities, but you'd benefit greatly from the near real-time hyperscale capabilities of the Salesforce Data Cloud platform for your AI strategy (Figure 13-3).

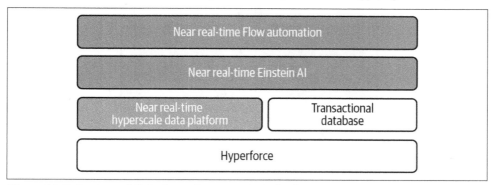

Figure 13-3. Integrated Salesforce Customer 360 platform

There are two types of searches, however, solely dependent on Data Cloud data available from the near real-time hyperscale data platform. The first is a search of unstructured data stored in a Data Cloud vector database, and the second relies on *data graphs*, which are materialized views of precalculated data. Data graphs, which exist in Data Cloud, allow Einstein to make fewer calls to the data and also make it possible to receive near real-time responses to data queries. Both of these are shown in Figure 13-2 as secure data retrieval inputs from Data Cloud, where they are stored. We'll discuss vector databases and data graphs in more detail later, when we review how to augment LLM searches. First, let's explore each of the three Einstein 1 platform products, starting with Einstein Model Builder.

Einstein Model Builder

Model Builder gives you access to both Predictive AI and GenAI (Figure 13-4) capabilities. You'll need to access Model Builder within Data Cloud using the Einstein Studio tab.

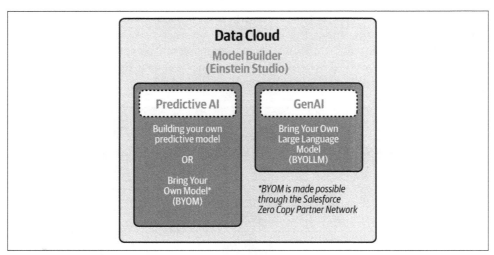

Figure 13-4. Predictive AI and GenAI capabilities available in Model Builder

Once inside Einstein Studio, you can choose either the *Predictive* tab or the *Generative* tab on the left side. Options within the Predictive tab let you build your own predictive model, or you can bring in your own predictive model output results from a trusted partner (Figure 13-5). It's important to note that Data Cloud data is necessary to power the predictive capabilities of Model Builder.

Before bringing the predictive results from an external platform like Amazon Sage-Maker or Google Vertex AI, there are some steps you'll need to take so that your Data Cloud data can be used in one of those external models. The BYOM approach will be discussed in more detail in "Zero Copy Technology Partners" on page 362.

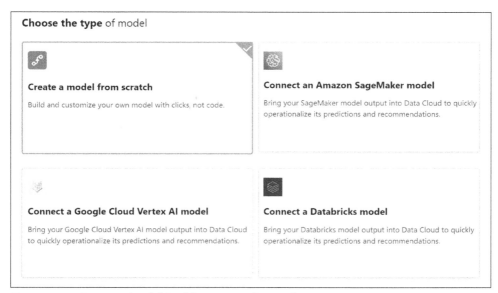

Figure 13-5. Einstein Model Builder options for Predictive AI

Within the Generative tab inside Einstein Studio, you can link to a custom LLM. You can connect to external platforms like Azure OpenAI, OpenAI, Google Gemini, or Amazon Bedrock (Figure 13-6). You can select the "Connect to your LLM" option to link to a custom LLM. This is what's referred to as the Bring Your Own LLM (BYOLLM) approach.

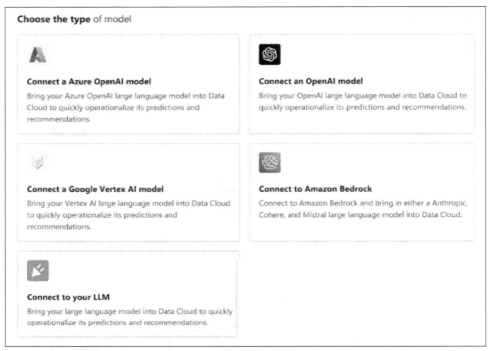

Figure 13-6. Einstein Model Builder options for GenAI

You're not required to link to a custom LLM to use GenAI functionality in Salesforce. Salesforce already provides hosted LLM models from Amazon, Anthropic, Cohere, and others, all within the Salesforce trust boundary. The Salesforce AI Research division even makes an LLM benchmark for CRM information (*https://oreil.ly/1s9pz*) publicly available to aid you in deciding which LLM model to choose. Whether you use a hosted LLM or link to your own external LLM, you'll need to start with a prompt (Figure 13-2). Fortunately, Salesforce makes it easy to get started right away with its Einstein Prompt Builder templates, which can include one or more objects used to help provide context to generate summaries or content.

Einstein Prompt Builder

Einstein Prompt Builder is a Salesforce low-code tool used to build and manage trusted AI prompts grounded in Salesforce data. It's an excellent example of AI democratization because it allows admins to build prompts quickly and easily, without needing to invest enormous amounts of time or money and without needing to learn specialized skill sets.

Prompt Builder templates can help to embed GenAI experiences in the flow of work for use by all team members working within the Salesforce platform. For example, Prompt Builder templates can be used by service teams to provide an improved customer experience even more quickly in response to customers' inquiries or issues.

It's also possible to reuse the templates created in Einstein Prompt Builder and invoke them in many different ways, including in sales emails, record pages, flow, Apex, and Einstein Copilot. When it's important, a human in the loop can test and preview the resolution and response when creating templates, and even version them.

Of course, Einstein prompts can be enriched with your business data, creating more relevant prompts grounded in your customer data from multiple clouds and sources, including Salesforce Sales Cloud, Salesforce Service Cloud, Salesforce Data Cloud, external sources, and more.

Prompt template types

There are four different prompt template types within Einstein Prompt Builder:

- Record Summary template
- Sales Email template
- Field Generation template
- Flex template

The *Record Summary* prompt template is specifically limited to customizing the standard Copilot action that summarizes records. In this way, the Record Summary prompt template is different from the other template types because the only way it can be invoked is when using Einstein Copilot. We'll learn later about the different methods by which the other prompt template types can be invoked.

Data Cloud Record Summaries Not Supported

At this time, only Salesforce CRM records that are searchable and UI API enabled can be summarized using the Summarize Record standard Copilot action. Thus, Data Cloud data isn't supported for that prompt type.

The *Sales Email* prompt template enables users to generate personalized, targeted emails at scale that leverage each customer's relationship history. Using a Sales Email prompt templates makes it easy for an LLM to write emails for you, especially because you can reuse the same template for different products and customers.

The *Field Generation* prompt template creates content for record fields where Salesforce users can click a button to run the prompt and then populate the field with the output once the user is satisfied with the LLM's response. One of the great things about using the Field Generation prompt is that the user can get dynamic summaries or descriptions without ever needing to leave the record page. For example, an Open Case Summary field can be populated right on the Account record page without needing to switch over to the Salesforce Case object.

The *Flex* prompt template allows users to generate content for any business purposes not handled by the other templates. For example, you can use a Flex prompt template to generate a newsletter using many different Product, Campaign, and Event records. You can also create a prompt that generates a text message as a follow-up to a customer case. Determining the method by which you'll invoke a Flex prompt will depend on the purpose of the prompt template you've created. Prompt segments and prompt chaining are two reasons you'd consider passing text into a Flex template. Passing in end-user input is also a great use case for Flex Prompt templates. The Flex template provides greater flexibility, letting you define your own resources, but there are a few limitations (*https://oreil.ly/dClmr*) for Flex templates. For one thing, you can't import or export metadata from Flex templates.

Use the Quick Find menu in Setup to access Einstein Prompt Builder, and then you'll click the New Prompt Template button at the top right of the screen. If Prompt Builder isn't accessible in your org, try toggling on the Einstein capabilities. If you don't see that option, you'll need to reach out to your Salesforce account executive to confirm that your Salesforce environment has Einstein Prompt Builder enabled.

Another way to access Prompt Builder is directly within Data Cloud. Click on the Einstein Studio tab and then select the Generative tab, to the right of the Predictive tab. You'll see a list of generative models available to you. Click on the drop-down arrow to the right of the model you'd like to use and then select the option to create a new prompt template.

Here are the steps involved in creating a new prompt template:

1. Create the prompt template (Figure 13-7). Once you select the template type, the input screen will vary slightly. Select the relevant Salesforce object type, and if you're creating a Field Generation template type, you'll need to also select the field. This is because the Einstein prompt will be associated with a field in the record where you can click the Einstein button, review the prompt, and generate a response all right there in the individual record.

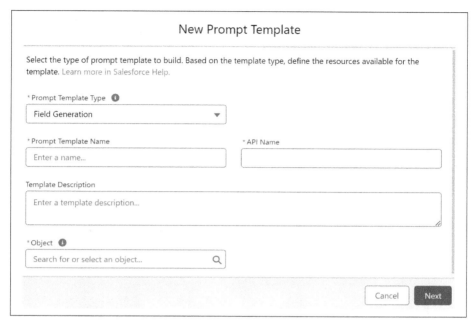

New Prompt Template

Select the type of prompt template to build. Based on the template type, define the resources available for the template. Learn more in Salesforce Help.

* Prompt Template Type ⓘ

Field Generation ▾

* Prompt Template Name

Enter a name...

* API Name

Template Description

Enter a template description...

* Object ⓘ

Search for or select an object... 🔍

Cancel   Next

Figure 13-7. New prompt template

2. Include ways to dynamically ground the prompt using your Salesforce CRM data, Data Cloud data, user input, and external data sources.

For example, you can insert Data Cloud graph data in Einstein Prompt Builder just as you would any other merge field object.

You can also create a template-triggered prompt flow (Figure 13-8) to include external data sources in your prompt. Navigate to Flow Builder and choose to create a new flow from scratch. Select the Template-Triggered Prompt Flow type and click the Create button. Build a flow that you want to use later when configuring a prompt template.

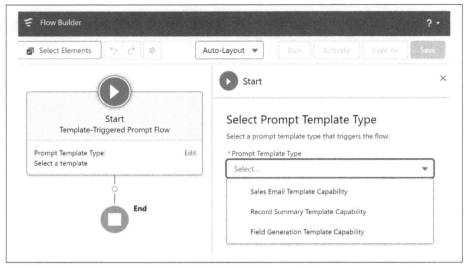

Figure 13-8. Template-triggered prompt flow

3. Preview your prompt and make changes, as necessary. As discussed previously, it's possible to change the LLM configuration. When you're satisfied with your prompt, click the Activate button at the top right of the Prompt Builder area to activate your prompt. Only activated prompts can be invoked.

4. Invoke your prompt using one of the methods described in the next section.

Ways to invoke Einstein prompts

There are various ways to invoke prompt templates (Table 13-1). For example, the Sales Email prompt can be invoked using the *Draft Email* feature to create a sales email to a customer or prospect based on the user's request and available email types. Email drafts include a recipient, subject, and email body and can be sent through the Salesforce email composer or copied to another email client.

Table 13-1. Ways to invoke Einstein prompts

	Sales Email prompt	Field Generation prompt	Record Summary prompt	Flex Template prompt
Copilot action	X	X	X	X
Flow	X	X		X
REST API	X	X		X
Apex	X	X		X
Draft email feature	X			
Record page		X		

You'll notice that most prompts can be invoked using Flow, REST API, and Apex, but all prompts can be invoked using an Einstein Copilot action. We'll learn about Einstein Copilot in the next section.

Consider When a Human-in-the-Loop Is Needed

It's important to think about the implications of choosing how to invoke an Einstein prompt. When using Einstein Copilot actions, a human is given the option to review and edit the generated content. In contrast, a prompt invoked by a flow automatically populates a response as instructed by the flow without human review of the output.

Einstein Copilot Builder

Einstein Copilot, one of the many tools Salesforce users can use to invoke prompts in the flow of their work (Table 13-1), offers the promise to be a productivity multiplier. Einstein Copilot is Salesforce's new and exciting capability that embeds AI functionality directly into Salesforce applications such as Sales Cloud, Service Cloud, Marketing Cloud, Commerce Cloud, and others. Einstein Copilot is accessible through an entirely new user interface within Einstein Copilot Builder.

Einstein Copilot Builder includes a library of actions classified as either standard or custom actions. Standard actions are the ones that come OOTB with your Einstein Copilot, and custom actions are ones that you create yourself.

This library of actions represents a set of tasks Copilot can complete. For example, Copilot launches an action to draft and revise emails if a user asks it for help writing an email. Furthermore, Copilot grounds the action in Salesforce data to provide a more relevant and meaningful response.

When to use Einstein Copilot

Einstein Copilot capabilities are based on technology that continues to rapidly evolve, so we'll continue to experience new and exciting ways to use Copilot. Today, some of the most common use cases for Copilot include the following:

- Information retrieval that provides concise summaries of Salesforce records
- Text mining and sentiment analysis
- Content creation, including drafting professional emails

Einstein Copilot holds great promise for Salesforce users, but there are some situations where caution should be exercised. Organizations that store highly sensitive or regulated data need to evaluate the impact of AI on data privacy and security to remain in compliance with relevant laws and regulations.

Don't use Copilot actions when a simpler or less costly solution will suffice. The cost associated with any particular Copilot action depends on the number and size of LLM calls, which vary by action and use case. It's important to select the right tool for the right use case for reasons other than cost. For example, it might make more sense to use specialized analytics platforms like Tableau when tasks involve complex data analytics.

For use cases where Einstein Copilot is the right choice, Salesforce provides standard Copilot actions OOTB so you can get started right away.

Standard Copilot actions

Standard actions are included by default. Some standard Copilot actions are critical for the basic functionality of Copilot to work. These are referred to as *system actions*, and they include actions that retrieve certain information (like the ID of a record) or execute another action. System actions can't be removed from Einstein Copilot.

Here's a list of some standard Einstein Copilot actions:

- Answer questions with knowledge
- Draft or revise sales email
- Explore conversation
- Find similar opportunities
- Get forecast guidance
- Identify object by name
- Identify record by name
- Query records
- Query records with aggregate
- Summarize record
- Create close plan
- Send meeting request

It's important to note that many standard actions are available to all users who have permission to access Einstein Copilot. However, some standard actions are built to work specifically with certain Salesforce Clouds or products, which means they'll only be available when you're assigned additional permissions. Some permissions are only available when additional licenses have been purchased, so be sure to contact your Salesforce account executive with any questions about licenses.

Custom Copilot actions

Custom Copilot actions can be created to assist with specific tasks relevant to your organization. Before creating a new custom action, review the list of all standard and custom Copilot actions to ensure that what you want doesn't already exist.

If you determine that a custom action is needed, be sure to collaborate with others in your organization to make sure you've incorporated into your custom action everything needed to achieve the expected results. Also, consider whether it's appropriate to incorporate prompt templates into your solution. You'll need a prompt template if your action makes calls directly to the LLM gateway. If so, you can leverage Einstein Prompt Builder to create your template.

Access to each custom Copilot action depends on how the action was built. Be sure to refer to the Salesforce documentation when building out a new custom action.

Copilot action assignments

Einstein Copilot uses actions that are assigned to it, and you can assign actions to your copilot from the Copilot Actions page, the record page for an action, or the Copilot Action Library tab of the actions panel in the Einstein Copilot Builder. It's recommended that no more than 15 actions be assigned to a copilot.

The Actions tab of your copilot's record page provides you a view of all the actions assigned to your copilot. You can also access the information on the This Copilot's Actions tab of the actions panel in the Copilot Builder.

Copilot actions are frequently used in situations where near real-time LLM responses are required. LLM responses are also greatly enhanced whenever unstructured data is used to augment the search, and Data Cloud offers some innovative ways to augment an LLM search to support near real-time responses and access to unstructured data.

Augmenting Large Language Model Search

Earlier, we discussed how Salesforce securely retrieves structured data from Salesforce CRM and Data Cloud to use as grounding resources for prompts. It's also possible to augment LLM search capabilities further with data graphs, to support near real-time searches, and vector databases, which make it possible to extract meaning from unstructured data. Data graphs and vector databases are both created within the Data Cloud platform.

Using Data Graphs for Near Real-Time Searches

Data graphs are materialized views that precalculate a subset of the data. This means that Einstein makes fewer calls to the data, which also makes it possible to receive near real-time responses to data queries. Not only can data graphs be used to augment LLM searches, but they are required to run real-time identity resolution, real-time CIs, and real-time segments.

It's important to consider the billing impacts of data graphs because computation is required to join the data for batch processes or responses to on-demand queries. Data graphs leverage batch data transforms and accelerated queries. For batch data transforms, usage is based on the number of rows processed each time the data graph is created or refreshed. All data graph queries are considered accelerated data queries, so you'll need to factor that into your calculations.

Before creating a data graph in the Data Cloud UI, make sure you've decided which DMO you'll use as the primary DMO. The primary DMO must belong to the Profile category and will determine which related objects you can include in the data graph. CIs, described in detail in Chapter 11, can also be added to a data graph. Here are the steps to create a data graph in Data Cloud:

1. Access the Data Graphs tab and click the New button.
2. Provide a value for the data graph name, select the primary DMO upon which you want to build the graph, and click the Save button. It's important that you choose these property values carefully because you can't edit or update the data space, data graph name, or selected primary DMO once you click the Save button in this step.
3. Select the fields from the primary DMO to include in the data graph. The primary key field, the related key qualifier field, and applicable foreign key fields are selected by default and added to the data graph for the primary DMO and its related objects. However, you can make changes. You can also see details about a DMO while creating a data graph by selecting the DMO in the data graph tree editor.
4. To add related objects, click the + sign and select fields for each related object.
5. Click the Preview button to see the structure of the JSON blob (optional).
6. Click the Save and Build button. Depending on the size of the primary DMO and related objects, it could take from 15 minutes to several hours to process the results.

After the data graph is created, you can view, clone, refresh, and delete it. You can also query the metadata and JSON blob data using the Data Cloud metadata and query APIs.

Data graphs help to make near real-time Data Cloud capabilities possible and also are important inputs for augmenting LLM searches. Another way to augment LLM searches is by using vector databases, which provide meaning and context for unstructured data.

Using Vector Databases for Unstructured Data

Enterprises have vast amounts of unstructured data, including some of the following examples:

- Chat messages
- Emails
- Logos
- Notes
- Press releases
- Blog posts
- Sensor data
- Call transcripts
- Knowledge articles

Answers and insights are scattered across this unstructured data, and until now, there hasn't been an easy way to extract answers and insights from the data. With Data Cloud, it's possible to ingest unstructured data and combine it with structured data where it's accessible just like other DMOs in your organization's data graph. There's an important difference, though.

When we search for answers from structured data, we can use a keyword search, similar to what we do in a document when we press Ctrl + F and search for a word. But this same kind of search won't work on unstructured data. Instead, we'll want to perform a semantic search, which returns results based on the intent and contextual meaning behind the search. However, to do that, we'll need to turn our unstructured data into embeddings so that the semantic search will work on the data. *Embeddings* are numeric representations of words and their meaning loaded into a vector database.

Fortunately, it's easy to enable semantic search on a DMO in Data Cloud. Navigate to a DMO, such as the Call Transcript DMO, and then click on the option to Enable Semantic Search in the top right corner of the screen. The option to enable semantic search is available for unstructured data model objects (UDMOs). Unstructured data used in Salesforce is persistently stored in an external blob store like Amazon S3. Metadata stored in a UDMO is used to reference the unstructured data. Both structured and unstructured data can be inputs to configure a vector search index (Figure 13-9). One exception is that you can't select a DMO that has mappings from one or more external DLOs. External DLOs are storage containers with metadata for the data federated from an external data source.

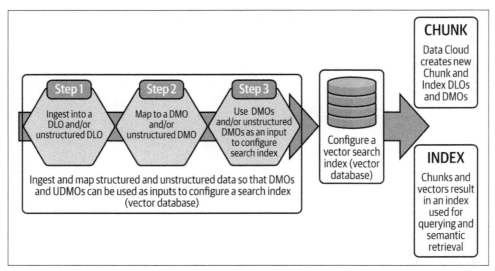

Figure 13-9. Unstructured and structured data are the inputs to configure a vector search index

The process of ingesting and using unstructured data in Data Cloud uses familiar processes within the UI, but there are some differences. UDLOs must be manually created. This is in contrast to DLOs for structured data because most DLOs are automatically created from data streams, although it's possible to manually create DLOs for such things as data transforms. DMOs that are part of a starter data bundle are automatically mapped, but in other cases, you'll need to manually map your DLOs to your DMOs. A UDMO, however, is always automatically mapped from the UDLO.

As part of enabling semantic search on a Data Cloud DMO that stores unstructured data, you'll have the option to set up the new search index configuration using the Easy Setup, Advanced Setup, or Data Kit options (Figure 13-10).

For Easy Setup, you'll only need to select the DMO or UDMO for which you want to build a search index, and Data Cloud will automatically create the necessary Chunk and Vector DMOs for you. It's advisable to create index configurations for objects with text blob fields like Salesforce Knowledge Articles. Once you've created your search index, navigate to Data Explorer and see if the data is loaded for the chunk and vector objects. When the DMOs are accessible in the Data Explorer, your search index is ready.

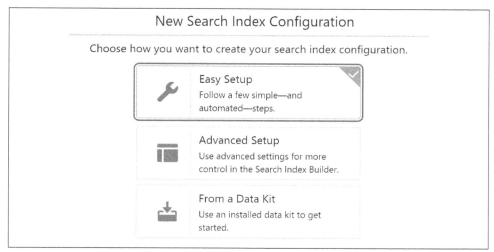

Figure 13-10. Set up search index configuration as the next step for semantic search

The Advanced Builder option lets you configure your search index using a wizard where you'll have the option to select the fields from the DMO you want to index. It's possible to also select a chunking strategy (see Figure 13-11). You can even add fields to be used for filtering later by dragging them onto the canvas.

Figure 13-11. Select fields to chunk and choose a chunking strategy

Behind the scenes in Data Cloud, the vector embeddings are automatically created and loaded into a vector database, making semantic search possible. Your work in Data Cloud is now done; return to your Einstein Prompt Builder to add some resources for Einstein Search to your template. Within Prompt Builder, you can use Einstein search retrievers to connect to Data Cloud vector data. Using search retrievers from Einstein Studio allows you to search for relevant information in unstructured data by grounding the prompt through RAG or with flows. Your GenAI answers will include citations for the unstructured data that was used to dynamically ground the prompt.

Einstein Prompt Builder and Einstein Copilot power the GenAI capabilities within Salesforce, and you can use both of them with your rich Salesforce CRM data only. However, Data Cloud is where you'll need to ingest and prepare any unstructured data used to augment the LLM search, and Data Cloud is also where you'll ingest structured data from external cloud storage and external platforms that can be used in Einstein Prompt Builder and Einstein Copilot.

In this section, we've discussed how to augment LLM searches within the Einstein Trust Layer using data graphs and vector databases. Data graphs support near real-time searches, and vector databases make it possible to leverage unstructured data in searches. Both of these help to ultimately achieve better responses from external LLMs with a shared trust boundary and LLMs hosted within the Salesforce trust boundary (Figure 13-2).

Using external and hosted LLMs is one example of how the Salesforce Data Cloud platform is open and extensible. In addition, there are other ways Salesforce users can leverage external tools and platforms within a trusted network of technology partners to extend the capabilities of Data Cloud. These trusted technology partners are part of Salesforce's Zero Copy Partner Network.

Zero Copy Partner Network

In Chapter 2, we discovered how Salesforce Data Cloud works under the hood. We learned that Data Cloud takes advantage of the enhanced Apache Iceberg ability to support fast and incremental updates, and also adds Salesforce metadata. That powerful combination is what allows Salesforce Data Cloud to open up access to partners, making it possible for end users to connect, perform live queries, and act on any data within the Partner Network without the need to build and maintain data pipelines. There are three ways the Zero Copy Partner Network delivers on the promise of a Customer 360 unified view that scales to the whole organization:

- Rapid deployment of real-time access to all data within the network
- Closing the feedback loop by making insights from one platform available in another platform, bringing actionable insights to users in the flow of their work
- Enrichment of CRM first-party data with third-party external data, including data sourced from the Snowflake marketplace

Data Cloud data can be directly shared and queried in two ways. One way is by using a JDBC connector, which is also zero data copy, for use with tools like Power BI. The other way is to allow access at the file level itself for platforms like Snowflake that read Iceberg. Regardless of whether the access is via JDBC or at the file level, the end user is getting a zero copy way of looking at the Salesforce Data Cloud data all within control of the Salesforce administrator.

It's also possible to experience the zero copy in reverse. Organizations that have existing data warehouses would rather not have to copy all that data and re-create everything on a new platform, so the Salesforce Data Cloud now allows you to mount those data warehouse tables virtually so that they are accessible within the Data Cloud environment.

Zero copy capabilities are a great way to leverage the technology investments your organization has made. Not only does using Zero Copy Partner Network capabilities save you money, it also helps to accelerate your time to value. BYOL and BYOM are two ways to leverage the Zero Copy Partner Network and quickly get value from your Data Cloud implementation. We'll describe both of these a little later in this section. First, let's quickly review traditional methods of sharing data and explain why the Zero Copy Partner Network is such an innovative and collaborative solution.

Traditional Methods of Sharing Data

Companies make choices to use different cloud technology tools and data platforms for a variety of reasons. Perhaps a vendor offers a specialized technology tool that works on a subset of the data to provide an organization with a competitive advantage, or perhaps the vendor supplies outputs that allow the organization to make better business decisions. Often, this may start as a single project created by a line-of-business team that just needs a portion of the data. Whatever the reason, the end result is that the source of truth for various pieces of organizational data ends up being owned by different teams and often is spread among different physical locations. It therefore isn't always easy to share the source data with other tools or platforms.

Traditional data sharing options—such as FTP transfers, API calls, sending and receiving CSV files, and extract, transform, and load (ETL) tools and processes—often require building complex infrastructure. Similarly, traditional sharing approaches, which involve transferring data copies and reconstructing and storing duplicate data, can be expensive and error-prone (Figure 13-12).

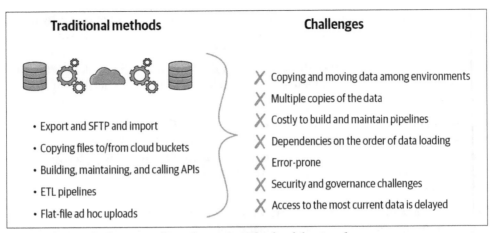

Figure 13-12. Challenges with traditional methods of sharing data

Because of the challenges with traditional methods of sharing data, it's likely that fewer actionable insights are achieved due to delayed access to stale and sometimes incomplete data. Overcoming some of these challenges, however, can be accomplished with Salesforce's Zero Copy Partner Network.

The Salesforce Zero Copy Partner Network consists of a group of technology companies that have entered into an agreement that makes it possible for their shared customers to easily access data across the network. With zero copy integration, an organization's teams can access data right where it lives—either through direct queries or data virtualization.

The Salesforce Zero Copy Partner Network supports both BYOL and BYOM capabilities within the Salesforce Data Cloud platform.

Zero Copy Technology Partners

At this time, there are five technology partners in the Zero Copy Partner Network, along with Salesforce. Let's take a quick look at each partner and how it participates in the Zero Copy Partner Network.

Amazon

Amazon Web Services (AWS) is a subsidiary of Amazon that offers on-demand cloud computing platforms. Amazon currently participates in the Salesforce Zero Copy Partner Network, supporting the BYOL data-in and data-out capabilities with Amazon Redshift. Amazon also supports the BYOM capabilities with Amazon SageMaker.

Databricks

Databricks is a cloud-based platform specializing in GenAI and other ML models. Databricks currently participates in the Salesforce Zero Copy Partner Network supporting BYOM capabilities. BYOM makes it possible to access Salesforce DMOs from within Databricks and combine the Data Cloud data with other data in the Databricks lakehouse for ML purposes.

Google

Google is a technology company specializing in cloud computing and focused on other areas such as online advertising, search engine technology, quantum computing, and AI. Google currently participates in the Salesforce Zero Copy Partner Network supporting BYOL data-in and data-out capabilities with Google BigQuery. Google also supports BYOM capabilities with Google Vertex AI.

Microsoft

Microsoft is a technology company known for software products, cloud computing, video games, and more. Microsoft will be participating in the Salesforce Zero Copy Partner Network in the near future.

Snowflake

Snowflake is a cloud computing–based data cloud company often credited with developing a fifth data platform by separating computing and storage, which made secure data sharing possible. Snowflake currently participates in the Salesforce Zero Copy Partner Network supporting BYOL data-in and data-out capabilities.

Bring Your Own Lake

Now that we have an idea of the trusted partners participating in the Zero Copy Partner Network, let's look at the capabilities that make it possible to connect, perform live queries, and act on data within the Partner Network without duplicating sources. Let's start with the BYOL capabilities.

Using bidirectional data sharing capabilities, you can visualize and take action with joined data within the Salesforce Data Cloud platform or within trusted third-party platforms like Snowflake, Google BigQuery, and Amazon Redshift. These bidirectional data sharing features, also called *data-in* and *data-out* capabilities, are part of the Data Cloud BYOL offering. Sometimes, this feature is referred to as *zero copy integration*.

BYOL and BYOM support making Data Cloud data accessible in a trusted way within an external platform. What makes BYOL different is the data-in part of the data-sharing capabilities. Technology partners in the BYOL category make their external platform data available through federated access within Data Cloud, and the data-in and data-out capabilities are what make bidirectional data sharing possible.

Bring Your Own Lake federated access (data in)

Data-in access is a type of federated access providing an end user the ability to natively query external data from within the Salesforce Data Cloud platform. Let's consider an example of how BYOL federated access works between Salesforce and Snowflake.

Within the Snowflake platform, an administrator creates a Snowflake user account with an assigned role that is granted specific permissions needed to view data stored in tables, external tables, and views within the Snowflake platform. The user is assigned a consumption-based Snowflake virtual warehouse for usage activities like querying Snowflake data. The Snowflake administrator will need to document for you all the details about the Snowflake user, including the authentication details, the user's role, and the virtual warehouse assigned to the user. In addition, you'll need to know the database details of the Snowflake data that you'll want to access within Data Cloud.

Within the Salesforce platform, an administrator completes the necessary steps to configure the Snowflake data-in connection. An external DLO within Data Cloud will need to be created from the Snowflake metadata. These Salesforce Data Cloud objects, sometimes referred to as Snowflake proxy objects, behave as reference points to the data physically stored in an external platform like Snowflake (Figure 13-13). While setting up the objects within Data Cloud, it's possible to enable acceleration in data federation when creating a data stream. Acceleration ensures data is retrieved periodically from the data platform to eliminate the risk of potential timeouts or run-time latencies. Acceleration is enabled by default with the refresh interval set at every 24 hours. You can choose a different refresh schedule or disable acceleration altogether by editing the data stream.

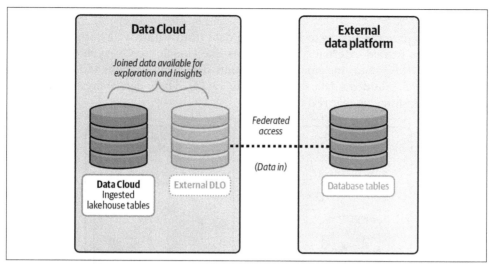

Figure 13-13. Federated access (data in)

After the tables are created, the Snowflake data can be logically combined with Data Cloud ingested data inside of Data Cloud for activities like identity resolution, segmentation, and activation. When a query of the Snowflake data is initiated within Salesforce Data Cloud, the relevant portion of the query is pushed down to the Snowflake account via federated access. The query initiated in Data Cloud is then executed within the Snowflake platform, and the results are returned to Salesforce. Snowflake consumption credits are used when the assigned Snowflake virtual warehouse executes a query on Snowflake data, even though the query was initiated in Salesforce Data Cloud.

It's important to consider the various billing impacts of federated data access. The Data Cloud multiplier assesses usage charges for accelerated data queries as well as data federation or sharing rows accessed. Importantly, you'll also want to review any consumption charges by the data platform provider that are assessed whenever you query the external data within Data Cloud.

Once you've completed the steps to set up federated access and map the fields in the external DLO to the Data Cloud semantic model, you can use the joined data to build constituent components like CIs and segments. However, a limited set of predicates for creating calculated insights and segments using federated data is supported today. In addition, streaming insights are supported only for related objects, and data actions are supported only for secondary objects. You can review the BYOL data federation supportability documentation (*https://oreil.ly/7OBQa*) for more information about what is currently supported and not supported for data-in capabilities.

Bring Your Own Lake data shares (data out)

BYOL data shares give access to Data Cloud data from within an external data platform. Certain trusted external data platforms like Google BigQuery and Snowflake can receive DMO data, insights, segmentation data, data graphs, and more from Salesforce Data Cloud via data shares (Figure 13-14). These data shares can be used outside of Salesforce in near real time.

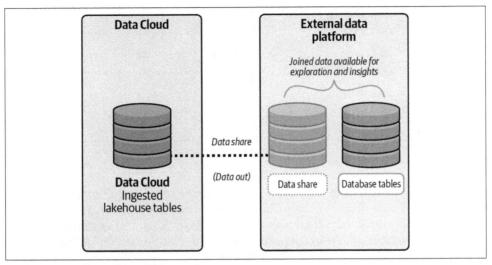

Figure 13-14. Data share (data out)

You'll first need to create a data share target for Snowflake, Google BigQuery, or Amazon Redshift using the Data Share Target tab. The *data share target* is the location, including authentication and authorization information, of the external data platform of the zero copy technology partner.

Once a data share target is established, creating data shares and linking them to the data share target is relatively easy for users to accomplish. Here are the basic steps:

1. Create a new data share by accessing the Data Shares tab and clicking the New button.

2. Enter the name of the data share in the Label field and press the Tab key. The API name will be autopopulated, although you can choose a different API name. Select the data space, if other than the default data space, and add a description.

3. Select the Data Cloud objects you want to include in the data share and click the Save button. A success message will let you know when the data share is created.

4. You'll need to link the data share to the data share target. From within the Data Shares tab, click the data share you want to link.

5. Click Link/Unlink Data Share Target on the data share's record home page. Click the Save button.

It's possible to edit a data share to add or remove DLOs, DMOs, and CIs. When you add a Data Cloud object to a data share, it's accessible right away in the external platform. The same is true in reverse; an object is no longer accessible in the external platform whenever you remove an object from the data share.

It's important to consider the billing impacts of providing data-out capabilities to an external data platform. Data Cloud consumption charges are incurred whenever you query Data Cloud data while logged in to the external data platform. This is in addition to the usage charges assessed by the external data platform provider for querying the joined datasets. Currently, the multiplier for data-out rows processed is on par with other Data Cloud multipliers for real-time usage types.

Important BYOL considerations

BYOL capabilities are powerful and have many benefits. However, there are some important considerations. For one thing, you'll want to make sure you've confirmed the data storage location on the external data platform before you embark on a BYOL journey. This is especially important for BYOL with major cloud providers like Amazon, Google, and Microsoft.

Snowflake is a single unified platform so there are few limitations to accessing data on the Snowflake platform for bidirectional data sharing purposes. For major cloud providers like Amazon and Google, however, you'll need to ascertain the specific external platform storage location. Salesforce BYOL capabilities work with Amazon Redshift and Google Cloud BigQuery, data warehouse solutions that store data in a columnar format. It's possible to ingest data into Data Cloud from other Amazon storage locations, like an S3 bucket, but you can't establish bidirectional data sharing between Amazon S3 and Salesforce Data Cloud.

It's also important to consider integrations between Salesforce and external platforms your organization has already built in the past. You can continue leveraging existing integrations or you might discover some of those data pipelines may no longer be needed if you implement Data Cloud and leverage BYOL capabilities. Also, it's good to be aware that Salesforce CRM core and Marketing Cloud data will only be accessible through BYOL bidirectional data sharing if that data is first ingested in Salesforce Data Cloud. To illustrate, let's consider an example of the data pipelines possible between Salesforce and Snowflake (Figure 13-15).

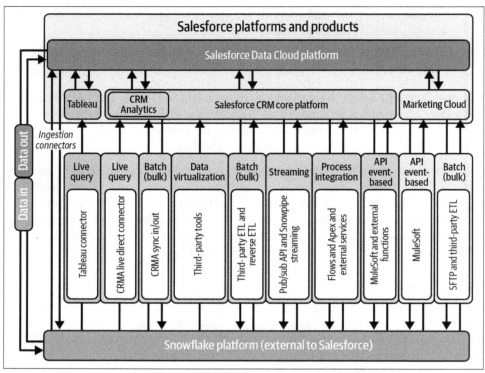

Figure 13-15. Data pipelines between Snowflake and Salesforce platforms and products

You'll notice that data can flow into Data Cloud from Salesforce CRM core platform or Marketing Cloud via the connectors and starter data bundles we described in earlier chapters. Data Cloud data can also flow in the other direction. Related list and copy field enrichments from Data Cloud can be surfaced in the Salesforce CRM core platform. Segments created in Data Cloud can be activated to the Marketing Cloud platform. In addition, Tableau can receive Data Cloud data inputs but can also send data to Data Cloud like new segments created in Tableau. Before Data Cloud, there were many ways to leverage Salesforce data within Snowflake, and Snowflake data within Salesforce, but most of them required data movement.

Data pipelines between Snowflake and the Salesforce CRM core platform or the Marketing Cloud platform can be built using batch, streaming, or API event-based methods. It's also possible to use process integration methods like Salesforce flows, apex, and external services. Interestingly, there exist some data virtualization tools like CData, Denodo, Informatica, and Omnata that can surface your Snowflake data within Salesforce CRM without data movement. This data virtualization works similarly to the data virtualization of the BYOL federated access for the data-in capabilities we described earlier. In the case of Omnata, a custom Apex adapter is used with

Salesforce Connect to give Salesforce users the ability to live-query data from a data platform like Snowflake. With so many available data access options, be sure to consider the use case for the data you plan to share before making decisions about the continued need for existing connectors and integrations.

BYOL bidirectional data sharing is a good option to consider for use cases involving profile or engagement data from an external platform that will be used for identity resolution and segmentation within Data Cloud. However, because of the inherent data access limitations for bidirectional data sharing, BYOL is probably not a good choice if you plan to use the combined data for BYOM features where a different external platform will be used for predictive models. Don't begin your Data Cloud implementation project until you've clearly defined the key value activity or activities you want to achieve. Start with the end in mind.

Bring Your Own Model

Using federated access, organizations can leverage their proprietary customer data from Salesforce Data Cloud to train external Predictive AI models. This is achieved using the Einstein Studio BYOM capabilities, accessed from within Data Cloud (Figure 13-16). Einstein Studio gives you the option to build your own model from scratch, as described earlier, or to leverage a predictive model built on an external platform. Examples of external models available in Einstein Studio include Amazon SageMaker, Databricks, and Google Vertex AI.

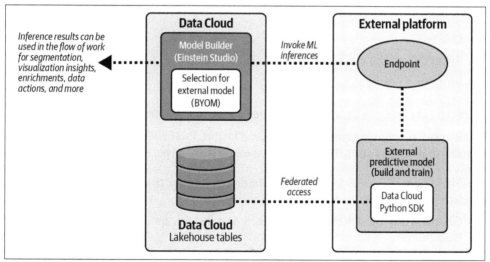

Figure 13-16. BYOM capability within Einstein Studio

Once you've built your external predictive model and completed the foundational Data Cloud steps, you're ready to set up federated access. Setting up federated access requires you to install a Data Cloud Python connector within your AI model. Then you'll need to connect the external model to Salesforce Data Cloud to receive and use predictions from your model. Let's take a look at the details of how to accomplish both.

Installing Python Connector and creating a Salesforce-connected app

You'll need to install the Data Cloud Python Connector within Amazon SageMaker, Databricks, or Google Vertex AI to ingest Salesforce data into the predictive model. The Data Cloud Python Connector uses the Query API and extracts data from Data Cloud into Python, which lets you fetch data in Pandas DataFrames.

You can authenticate the CDP Python Connector either with a username and password or by using an OAuth endpoint. As part of the configuration process, you'll need to create a Salesforce *connected app*, which is a framework that enables external applications like Amazon Sagemaker and Google Vertex AI platforms to integrate with Salesforce using APIs and standard protocols like OAuth. Salesforce connected apps use these protocols to authenticate, authorize, and provide single sign-on (SSO) for the external applications.

Using the Data Cloud Python Connector requires you to create a connection object, create a cursor object to execute queries, and fetch Data Cloud data. Data Cloud data can be fetched in three ways:

- One row at a time
- By getting all the rows
- By getting results in a dataframe

Connecting the model to Data Cloud to get predictions from your model

You'll need to connect your SageMaker, Databricks, or Vertex AI model to Data Cloud to consume your ML predictions. Follow these steps:

1. Navigate to Einstein Studio tab → Predictive (rather than Generative) tab on the left → Add Predictive Model button.

2. Choose your model type (SageMaker, Databricks, or Vertex AI) and click the Next button.

3. Provide the following details needed to access your model inferences and then click the Next button:
   - Endpoint name
   - Endpoint URL

- Authentication: key based or JSON web token (JWT; API gateway required for both)
- Audience: alphanumeric string or combination for JWT authentication
- Authorization header
- Secret key
- Request format: either JSON dense or CSV
- Response format: either JSON or CSV

4. Add a schema by clicking the Add Input and Add Output options, then click the Next button. Also make sure to take into account the following on inputs and outputs:

   - Inputs are variables that can impact your predictions, so it's important that you position inputs in the same order that matches your query. It's also possible to move an input to a different location by dragging it to the preferred position in the Inputs section.

   - Outputs require you to specify a data type and the JSON key in addition to specifying the output label name.

5. Save your work after you've reviewed the model settings. Click the Save button, name your model, and then click "Save and Connect." Afterward, the model can be found in the list view under the Predictive Models tab of the Einstein Studio tab.

6. You'll need to activate the model and then navigate to the Usage tab to create prediction jobs, thus enabling you to consume predictions from the model. Batch prediction jobs can be refreshed by clicking the Run button. For streaming predictions, a change in the input on your DMO will initiate a new inference. Keep in mind that usage charges are assessed for each inference produced by an AI model that has been connected through Einstein Studio.

The predictive models on external platforms use Data Cloud data to solve for a variety of different use cases such as lead conversion, case classification, and sentiment analysis. Whatever the purpose of the predictive model, the output of the model can be used to power any sales, marketing, commerce, or other application within Salesforce.

Summary

In this chapter, we've learned a lot about Salesforce Einstein and the Zero Copy Partner Network. In conjunction with the Data Cloud platform, leveraging Einstein and the Partner Network can help you more quickly extract business value from all of your data, no matter where your source data is located.

It's possible to accelerate your time to value with Data Cloud while also remaining focused on building a scalable and sustainable solution. Doing so requires that you have a good understanding of the Data Cloud consumption model and that you monitor your usage; there are new tools that can help you with this task.

As part of the summer 2024 release, Data Cloud introduced Digital Wallet for Data Cloud. This new feature gives users the ability to monitor their consumption easily in near real time. This functionality is accessible to Data Cloud administrators and is available from the Consumption Cards tab within Data Cloud.

In addition to monitoring consumption in near real time, you can use the Consumption Cards functionality to help you understand shared capacity and monitor consumption trends over time.

Data Cloud's usage-based pricing gives you more control over your costs and rewards you for using resources more efficiently.

The Road Ahead

I think it's exciting to be working in the Salesforce ecosystem at a time when the speed of innovation is astonishingly rapid. The Salesforce team has accomplished much already with its customer data platform—but what does the future hold for Data Cloud and for you?

There are some incredible things we can expect to see as Salesforce continues to improve ingestion and processing latency in its quest to get ever closer to real-time capabilities. Segmentation and activation features are already robust within Data Cloud, so marketers are sure to be delighted as they learn to leverage the powerful features within Data Cloud. And, of course, we're still in the early stages of tapping into the Predictive AI and GenAI capabilities made possible by the openness and extensibility of the Data Cloud platform.

Continuing the Learning Journey

This book covers a great deal of content meant to provide you with a solid foundation for understanding Salesforce's innovative new platform and getting hands-on with Data Cloud. The Salesforce Data Cloud platform continues evolving at a rapid pace, so it's important to continue your learning journey.

Salesforce seasonal releases

Three times a year, Salesforce issues regular releases with many new features for the entire Salesforce platform. The Salesforce Seasonal Release blog (*https://oreil.ly/mCK7S*) keeps you updated every winter, spring, and summer as new features are released. The blog also links to the Salesforce Release Notes (*https://oreil.ly/cyp3V*) available for every new release. You'll notice the Release Notes break down the upcoming new features by category, one of which is Salesforce Data Cloud. Additionally, Salesforce issues a Seasonal Release Strategies Trailhead badge three times a year.

Salesforce in-person events

Attending in-person events is a great way to keep current with Salesforce updates. The largest Salesforce in-person event is Dreamforce, held annually in San Francisco, California. There are other Salesforce in-person events such as TrailblazerDX for Salesforce developers and Salesforce Connections for Salesforce marketers. In addition, Salesforce sponsors global World Tour events in various cities throughout the world.

Salesforce partner resources

Individuals employed by Salesforce partners have access to some additional resources through the Salesforce partner portal (*https://partners.salesforce.com*). A few of those resources are as follows:

- Data Cloud Pocket Guide
- Data Cloud Implementation Toolkit
- Data Cloud Solutions Kits and POVs
- Data Cloud videos (*https://datacloud.hubs.vidyard.com*) from the Partner Product Success Team

You can explore the possibilities and review the requirements on the Salesforce Become-a-Partner page (*https://oreil.ly/K13qC*) if you are not yet a Salesforce consulting partner or ISV partner.

Salesforce Data Cloud Consultant certification

Salesforce offers a Data Cloud Consultant certification meant for those who have a broad understanding of Salesforce technology as well as knowledge of Data Cloud and its capabilities and terminology. You'll want to review the "Salesforce Certified Data Cloud Consultant Exam Guide" (*https://oreil.ly/eWB3k*) if you're interested in becoming Data Cloud certified.

Keep Blazing the Trail

Thank you for going on this Data Cloud journey with me. In our time together, we've learned a brand-new vocabulary to describe many facets of the Data Cloud platform. You'll find many of these new terms listed in the Glossary.

We've also discovered how Data Cloud works its magic and the importance of devoting sufficient time to planning and building a strong data foundation. A successful Data Cloud implementation depends on completing the foundational steps so that the right amount of quality data is available for business value activities.

Predictive AI and GenAI models can't be accurate without enough quality data, but with too much data, the models might be too costly in proportion to the value extracted. Salesforce architects should be a part of data conversations because they know data and understand how to take advantage of Salesforce's expert-created metadata models. Leveraging standard Salesforce data models whenever possible makes it much easier to support AI democratization for all Salesforce users and the time to value for a Data Cloud investment.

Throughout the book, I've shared Data Cloud best practices and called out limitations and warnings. Appendix A includes a summary of some important implementation guidelines for a first-time Data Cloud implementation.

My sincerest hope is that you'll go far beyond the lessons learned in this book to blaze your own trail. Build something amazing as your Data Cloud + AI journey continues!

Guidance for Data Cloud Implementation

The following guide to the phases of a first-time Data Cloud implementation project and the steps outlined in them is intended to provide you with high-level guidance. There isn't necessarily one right way to approach a first-time Data Cloud implementation project, and the process isn't necessarily a linear one. Use the guide as a starting point for your own Data Cloud implementation plan.

General Guidelines

Here are some general guidelines to be aware of throughout all phases of the project:

- Make sure you keep in mind and frequently review Data Cloud limits and guidelines (*https://oreil.ly/oEH0a*) and Data Cloud standard editions and feature licenses (*https://oreil.ly/137aV*). Review, as needed, best practices that are described in various chapters throughout this book.

- Understand factors that affect Data Cloud billable usage types (*https://oreil.ly/ ZLK8l*) and weigh the need for near real-time patterns against the expected costs to ensure you're managing your budget appropriately. It's advisable to also periodically review the billing multipliers (*https://oreil.ly/MLi5E*) for Data Cloud. Make sure any refresh schedules you select are really needed and that you're not refreshing the CIs or segments more frequently than the underlying data is updated. Profile unification consumes considerable service credits, so avoid ingesting inactive profiles.

- Consider ingestion lookback windows for Salesforce Cloud connectors and plan accordingly. *Ingestion lookback windows* determine how much, if any, historical data will be ingested once a connector is established. More information is available in Chapter 4.

- Make sure you review your company's naming convention standards and any other policies and procedures for implementations. This is especially important for Data Cloud implementations because many of the things built out in Data Cloud cannot be undone or relabeled later.

- Be aware that most external platforms like Snowflake support using key pair authentication for enhanced authentication security as an alternative to basic authentication like username and password. Reach out to the team within your organization responsible for security and compliance if you have any questions or concerns about the credentials to be used for establishing connections to Data Cloud.

- Ensure you have a good understanding of all data models and related topics, and use the standard models whenever possible. Leverage the expertise of data architects, data modelers, and data engineers when needed. Here is a list of documentation that would be good to review:
  - "Salesforce Customer 360 Data Model" (*https://oreil.ly/8BGeT*)
  - Data Cloud "Standard Data Model Objects (DMOs)" (*https://oreil.ly/r-DTP*)
  - Data Cloud "Data Model Subject Areas" (*https://oreil.ly/FiKWq*)
  - Data Cloud "Data Model Object Relationships" (*https://oreil.ly/iZqYp*)
  - "Data Modeling Requirements for Identity Resolution" (*https://oreil.ly/vrBPj*)

- If an organization has more than one brand, it'll need to consider multibrand management (*https://oreil.ly/_zkJF*) in Data Cloud.

- Consult with your legal counsel and review your organization's policies for data residency requirements that are applicable to your Salesforce Data Cloud implementation. Your Data Cloud org may be hosted in a different region from your Salesforce Clouds and/or your external source systems. While it's possible for Data Cloud to ingest data from multiple regions, it may be necessary for some organizations to implement separate Data Cloud instances per region.

- Always be thinking of ethics, privacy, and consent (*https://oreil.ly/ZpPbN*). These should never be afterthoughts where customers' data is concerned.

Evaluation Phase

During the evaluation phase, your organization will want to identify whether Salesforce Data Cloud is the right solution. If it is, you'll need to decide whether to provision in a Salesforce home org or a separate Salesforce org. You'll need to make this decision early on because it will be necessary to include this in your Salesforce contract, so here's a quick guide to the steps of the decision-making process:

1. Identify whether a CDP is needed to solve your customer data problem.

2. Decide whether Salesforce Data Cloud is a better solution than building a composable CDP.

3. Decide whether to provision Data Cloud in a Salesforce home org or a separate Salesforce org.

Chapter 1 can help you with the first two steps, and Chapter 2 provides information about the different provisioning options.

Discovery and Design Phases

The discovery and design stages overlap in some ways. As you're going through discovery, you may need to make some preliminary design decisions that will influence discovery sessions. Documents created during discovery will often be expanded during the design phase, so there will be some pieces of information that you won't be able to fill in on documentation initially. However, you can create a placeholder for that information to be filled in later. Here's a list of steps you can follow to make the discovery and design process run smoothly:

1. Outline the roles and responsibilities of all the stakeholders. Decide who will be leading the implementation project, and make sure it's clear who from the organization will be the decision maker if a group consensus cannot be reached for any decision point. Business requirements documentation is essential for defining scope, estimating timelines, and identifying resources needed to complete the project. It's not unusual for there to be two project managers on a project: one on a Salesforce implementation partner's team managing the overall project, and one representing the organization to help coordinate schedules and efforts from different departments and teams.

2. Create a schedule for the Discovery phase so that stakeholders can make arrangements to be available, ensuring Discovery is completed in a timely manner and that everyone involved has had an opportunity to weigh in on things. When creating the schedule, be sure to factor in holidays and any critical organizational endeavors when team members are likely to be unavailable. For example, you wouldn't want to schedule discovery sessions with the marketing team during their most important marketing campaign of the year.

3. During the discovery phase, identify use cases and have the appropriate stakeholder assign a priority ranking to each use case. It's common to use a scale of 1 to 3 for the rankings, with 1 being the highest priority. Chapter 3 includes details about Data Cloud value activities and example user stories that could help the team in deciding on use cases.

4. From the list of use cases, decide which use case(s) would likely make good candidates for a first-time Data Cloud implementation. Remember that it's good practice to choose high-priority use cases that can be implemented quickly. This is where an ultimate decision maker might be needed to prioritize use cases from across the organization to decide which one(s) to focus on first.

5. For the use cases identified, identify end users and members of the implementation team who will need access. Document the type of access needed and determine if new users, new profiles, or custom permission sets need to be created.

6. For the use cases identified as possible first-time implementation use cases, you'll want to gather more details. For example, if a segmentation and activation use case is being considered, you'll want to have the marketing team provide you with the details of each segment and each activation target. How exactly are the segments created? Is the segment one that is used today but is difficult to put together because of disparate data sources, or is it a new segment that the marketing team is hoping to create in the future? What are the segment criteria, and which field(s) from which source(s) are needed to build the segment? Be sure to document whether you'll build a segment on a Unified Individual DMO or a Unified Account DMO, and recognize that there are downstream implications of these choices during the design and implementation phases. For example, the target object chosen for segmentation determines which attributes are available in the attribute library that can be used as segment filters.

7. Review sample data from each of the source fields needed for the first use case(s). You're taking a quick look to determine whether the necessary field values exist, whether they are what is expected for the use case, whether they are of sufficient quality to be usable as is, or whether transformations will likely be needed.

8. Once the use case(s) have been identified, you'll want to review the organization's system architecture, data flow diagrams, data dictionaries, and any other documentation available from the IT department. An *architecture diagram* illustrates systems and how they interact with each other, while a *data flow diagram* is a visual overview of how data flows from one application or transfer point to another. An important piece of information from the data flow diagram is how often data is transferred to or from each touchpoint. It's important to identify existing data sources and integrations, even if you don't think they'll be used in a Data Cloud implementation. The goal is to get an understanding of all system of record data sources, the various connectors and data pipelines, how much data exists, and how frequently the data is updated.

9. For the source systems of record needed for the use case(s) to be implemented, here is a list of some of the information you may want to document:

- Source number: assign a sequential number to track the source.
- System of record data sources, such as the following:
  - Salesforce Cloud: CRM
  - Salesforce Cloud: marketing
  - Cloud storage: Amazon S3
  - External platform: Google Ads
  - External platform: Meta Ads
- Salesforce object name, cloud storage table name, etc.
- Identifying details like the Salesforce org ID, directory, file path, or bucket, if applicable.
- Data owner: name of the team or department in charge of access credentials.
- Ingest update pattern for the source: batch or near real time. If batch, specify the schedule or the refresh rate.
- Data volumes (estimated).
- Anticipated ingest pattern for Data Cloud: batch or near real time. If batch, specify the schedule or the refresh rate.
- Data Cloud Connector to be considered: see Chapter 6 for details.
- Data Cloud DLO: this will likely be filled in later during the design phase.
- Category: Profile, Engagement, or Other. See Chapter 7 for more details.
- Primary key/UID: if no primary key is identified, indicate the formula to be used.
- Engagement event time field (optional): relevant for Engagement category.
- Key qualifier fields: determine which key qualifiers need to be created and configured.

10. For the individual fields from the source systems of record needed for the use case(s) to be implemented, here is some of the information that you may want to document:

- Source #: refers to the source documented in step 9.
- Source field label or field API name.
- Source field data type, such as text, number, or email.
- Source sample field values and/or a list of the range of values expected. In other words, what is the length of the text field, or can the number value be negative?

- Data Cloud DMO to be mapped: this will likely be filled in during the design phase.

- Data Cloud DMO field value to be mapped: this will likely be filled in during the design phase.

11. Determine whether formula fields will be needed, and if so, define the formula. *Formula fields* allow you to cleanse your data in minor ways or derive more fields to be used as a primary field. Chapter 7 includes information about creating new formula fields. For more complex data cleansing needs, you'll want to consider data transformations.

12. Determine what transformations, if any, will be needed. Remember that both streaming and batch transformations are possible and that they are quite different from each other. You'll want to document desired transformations and associated mappings to ensure that the requirements can be implemented using the source data and the planned Data Cloud architecture you've designed. More information about data transforms can be found in Chapter 8. Here are some reasons you might want to use transforms:

- Batch data transform use cases:
  — Complex transformations needed to join, aggregate, or append data
  — No-code approach (SQL not needed)

- Streaming data transform use cases:
  — Existence of multiple data categories in a DLO
  — Existence of duplicate records
  — Mapping exceptions due to denormalization

13. For identity resolution purposes, identify what data is shared across sources. Examples include email, first name, and IDs. To meet the requirements of the party primary subject area, you'll need to map to the Individual object and either the Party Identification object or a Contact Point object. More information about the party primary subject area and a list of standard Contact Point objects can be found in Chapter 7. Here is a list of further actions you need to take in this step:

a. Define the match rules needed for the resolution ruleset. It's possible to use Exact, Fuzzy, and Normalized match rules:

   i. Review default match rules to see which one(s) are needed.

   ii. Review any required match rules like exact party ID match for Marketing Cloud data.

   iii. Design any custom match rules that are needed.

b. Create reconciliation rules to let the system know how to reconcile the matched records when an attribute conflict arises:

- Review the default reconciliation rules and select one:
  - Last updated
  - Most frequent
  - Source priority

14. Confirm which constituent components will be needed to support the use case(s) and outline the requirements for each of those constituent components. For example, CIs might be needed to precalculate metrics for use in segmentation. Be sure to identify whether real-time data sources are needed for streaming insights or data actions, and confirm that the source data is updated with a frequency that supports the use case. For example, you wouldn't want to set up a streaming insight using source data that's updated only once a day.

15. Create a test plan and include as part of the plan who will be responsible for testing and how entries will be made on test result documents.

Implementation and Testing

After planning for your implementation by going through the discovery and design phases, you'll be ready to provision your Data Cloud org, as described in Chapter 4, and get hands-on. After provisioning your org, you'll move on to completing the six foundational steps and creating the necessary constituent components as part of the implementation and testing phases.

Sharing Data Cloud Data Externally with Other Tools and Platforms

Figure 3-4 highlights 12 Data Cloud key value activities in which business value can be realized by leveraging various Data Cloud components, such as calculated and streaming insights, segments, data graphs, and vector databases. Most of the key value activities are designed to extract value by exploring and taking action with data directly within Salesforce, but there are some key value activities in which it's expected that external tools or platforms will be leveraged. Here is a list of those key value activities where Data Cloud data and insights are likely to be shared with external tools and platforms that are part of your existing technology stack:

- Data sharing with external platforms
- Activation of segments
- Data actions and Data Cloud-triggered flows
- Programmatic extraction of data
- Analytics and intelligent data visualization

Data sharing with external platforms can be accomplished bidirectionally using the BYOL capabilities that leverage the Salesforce Zero Copy Partner Network. Data Cloud data shares give access to Data Cloud data while within an external data platform like Snowflake or Google BigQuery. These data shares can be used outside of Salesforce in near real time, and data shares and bidirectional data sharing are discussed in detail in Chapter 13.

Segments created in Data Cloud can be shared within the Salesforce ecosystem to activation targets like Salesforce Marketing Cloud and Salesforce Loyalty Management Cloud. They can be shared with external platforms like LinkedIn and Google

Ads, and they can also be shared with file storage targets like Amazon S3, SFTP, Microsoft Azure Blob, and Google Cloud Storage. Segmentation and activation are described in detail in Chapter 12.

Data Actions are another type of Data Cloud key value activity in which data can be shared externally by leveraging targets such as platform events and webhooks, as well as Salesforce targets like Marketing Cloud. Data Actions trigger actions based on individual record changes within Data Cloud data. Data Actions are very powerful, especially when they're combined with data graphs, which bring with them the possibility of near real-time data actions. Data Actions are described in detail in Chapter 11, and also in Chapter 11 is our discussion of programmatically extracting data from Data Cloud using various APIs and connectors.

For the analytics and intelligent data visualization key value activity, we mentioned several Salesforce tools and platforms that can make use of Data Cloud data to provide insights. These include the Salesforce CRM Analytics platform and Salesforce intelligent apps like Segment Intelligence and Amazon Insights.

In addition, it's possible to connect Data Cloud to external BI tools and platforms like Tableau, which is an interactive data visualization software company that was acquired by Salesforce in 2019. There are several excellent resources for learning more about Tableau, including *Tableau Strategies* by Ann Jackson and Luke Stanke (O'Reilly, 2021), *Statistical Tableau* by Ethan Lang (O'Reilly, 2024), and *Innovative Tableau* by Ryan Sleeper (O'Reilly, 2020).

Tableau can access DMOs, DLOs, and CI objects. Interestingly, Tableau can also be used to perform vector searches on unstructured data using the vector search index database in Data Cloud. Accessing Data Cloud data within Tableau is accomplished using the Salesforce Data Cloud Connector, and the way you'll access Data Cloud from Tableau depends on whether you're using Tableau Server, Tableau Desktop, Tableau Prep, or Tableau Cloud:

- Data Cloud access to Tableau Server, which is designed to help organize and share Tableau dashboards and workbooks, requires version 2023.3 or later. The steps to connect Tableau Server to Data Cloud can be found in the Tableau documentation (*https://oreil.ly/9-OmP*).

- Data Cloud access to Tableau Desktop, which is a visualization tool that produces interactive visual representations like dashboards and workbooks, requires version 2023.2 or later. The steps to connect Tableau Desktop to Data Cloud can be found in the Tableau documentation (*https://oreil.ly/YVdBy*).

- Data Cloud access to Tableau Prep, which is designed to clean and shape customer data to optimize analysis, requires prep web authoring, Conductor version 2023.2, or Prep Builder 2023.2. The steps to connect Tableau Prep to Data Cloud can be found in the Tableau documentation (*https://oreil.ly/S3PTO*).

- Data Cloud can also be connected to Tableau Cloud, which is used for authoring, sharing, distributing, and collaborating on content. The steps to connect Tableau Cloud to Data Cloud can be found in the Tableau documentation (*https://oreil.ly/ fyM8e*).

The Data Cloud Tableau Connector provides both a live method and an extract method to interact with Data Cloud data. Live mode is the default mode. It's important to remember that using the live mode incurs consumption costs every time you run a query or update a dashboard in Tableau. Consumption charges are also incurred for the *extract* method, but once the data is extracted, there are no additional charges each time you query the data in Tableau.

Consider the tradeoffs in latency, freshness, and cost when you're deciding which method is best for your particular use case. Data privacy is another important factor when deciding between a live method and an extract method, and it's the reason why a live connection is recommended as best practice. Consumer rights are supported by the Data Cloud query engine at query execution time. Thus, when dashboards are published, you'll need to ensure changes made to Data Cloud data are reflected in Tableau with the most up-to-date consumer rights requests, such as the right to be forgotten or restriction of processing.

For data shared externally, it's important to understand the nuances of Data Cloud when using the data in those other tools and platforms. For example, you must use key qualifier fields in table joins and ad hoc table joins in Tableau. You should use the IFNULL() function on key qualifier fields to ensure null-safe join if the key qualifiers aren't configured in Data Cloud. You'll also need to use identity link files in your Tableau mappings when building visualizations from Data Cloud unified data.

We've highlighted five ways Data Cloud data can purposefully be shared with external tools and platforms. There are also ways to use external tools on Data Cloud data inside the Salesforce Einstein Trust Layer, and examples include BYOM and BYOLLM available in the Einstein Studio tab within Data Cloud. Both of these are discussed in detail in Chapter 13.

Glossary

activation (of segments)

The process of materializing and publishing a segment to an activation platform (target). The target platform must be established as an activation target in Data Cloud before segments can be activated to the target platform. See *activation target*.

Activation Audience data category

The data category automatically assigned to the Activation Audience DLO and inherited by the Activation Audience DMO when an activation target is created in Data Cloud.

Activation Audience DLO

A type of DLO automatically created by the system when an activation target is configured. Stores activation details. The system-generated data category of Activation Audience is automatically assigned to the Activation Audience DLO when it's created.

Activation Audience DMO

A type of DMO automatically created by the system when an activation target is configured. Inherits the Activation Audience data category from the Activation Audience DLO.

activation platform

See *activation target*.

activation target (for segmentation)

The location, including authentication and authorization information, where a segment's data will be sent during activation of a segment. Example activation targets include Salesforce Clouds like Marketing Cloud, Loyalty Cloud, Marketing Cloud Personalization, B2C Commerce Cloud, as well as Data Cloud. Activation targets also include file storage activation targets like Amazon S3, SFTP, Google Cloud Storage, and Microsoft Azure blob storage where you can export either a CSV or JSON formatted file. Activation targets are created before setting up an activation of segments. An activation target object is supported by sharing rules.

Activation Targets

A menu tab in the Data Cloud app for configuring an activation target.

Activations

A menu tab in the Data Cloud app for setting up published segments to be sent to activation targets.

aggregate functions

Used in creating calculated insights in the Insight Builder or by using SQL. Performs a calculation on a set of values and returns a single value. At least one aggregate function must be used when you define a calculated insight using SQL statements. Only numeric measures can be used with an aggregate function. Aggregation functions include SUM, MIN, MAX, COUNT, AVG, MEAN, and StdDev.

AI Builder Tools

See *Einstein 1 Studio*.

allowlist

A list of trusted IP addresses used for allowed traffic. Includes application layer allowlists and network layer allowlists.

anonymous data

Data not associated with a specific person or account, sometimes referred to as unknown data. Data is stripped of any personally identifiable information. Examples include mobile ad ID, first-party cookies, and hashed email addresses. Data Cloud profiles can be either anonymous or known.

AppExchange

A marketplace offering app solutions, components, and consulting services available from Salesforce partners and Salesforce Labs solutions. Salesforce Labs solutions are free apps built by Salesforce employees to help extend the Salesforce platform.

assigned data category

See *ingestion data category*.

audience

A grouping of customers, individuals, or accounts that share a set of characteristics. Similar to a segment but is specific to an activation target like Marketing Cloud. A person in one segment can belong to multiple audiences, which means they can receive similar marketing messages via different activation targets if that one segment is published to different activation targets.

batch data transform

One of the two types of transformations possible within the Data Cloud app. Batch data transforms are composed of repeatable steps of operations that can be run whenever the source data updates. They're often used for complex transformations.

Bridge data model object

A special type of DMO for link objects automatically created by the system during the identity resolution process.

Bring Your Own Lake (BYOL)

Sometimes referred to as bidirectional data sharing, zero ETL, or zero copy. BYOL is made possible by storage layering that supports metadata at the storage level and collaboration with trusted technology partners. BYOL capabilities make it possible for users to connect, perform live queries, and act on data within the Zero Copy Partner Network without duplicating sources. Sharing includes data in, which uses federated access. Sharing also includes data out, which uses data shares.

Bring Your Own Large Language Model (BYOLLM)

A way to extend the capabilities of the Salesforce platform by connecting to an external LLM. From the Einstein Studio tab in the Data Cloud app, a user can connect to an external generative models like Azure Open AI.

Bring Your Own Model (BYOM)

One of the ways to leverage the capabilities within the Zero Copy Partner Network. From the Einstein Studio tab in the Data Cloud app, a user can connect to an external predictive model like Amazon SageMaker or Google Vertex AI.

Builder tools

Salesforce's drag-and-drop tools that support data and AI democratization. Examples include Copilot Builder, Flow Builder, Insight Builder, Lighting App Builder, Model Builder, and Prompt Builder.

calculated insight (CI)

Used to query, transform, and create complex calculations based on stored data in Data Cloud. This feature is natively available for profile-level insights and, unlike segments, can create reusable content and perform complex queries on multiple objects. Can be used to support many use cases like segmentation to help define segment criteria and personalization attributes for activation using metrics, dimensions, and filters that can enable activity journey decisions and inform message personalizations. Also used for enrichments that can surface insights in Salesforce Sales Cloud and Service Cloud.

calculated insight object

A specific kind of Insights DMO created after a calculated insight is processed. Viewable in Data Explorer and supported by sharing rules.

Calculated Insights

A menu tab in the Data Cloud app where users can create any of the three insights: calculated, streaming, and real-time.

canonical data model

Data model designed to be the standard data model across systems, platforms, and applications. Includes a common set of definitions for data types, data structures, relationships, and rules. Using a canonical data model standardizes the data model, which helps ensure consistency across applications and business processes. The Customer 360 canonical data model standard objects can be found in the supplemental repository (*https://oreil.ly/ SuppRep_HandsOn-Salesforce*).

capacity

Increments of consumption purchased in advance. These increments of usage are entitlement limits that allow an organization to store data or files up to the maximum amount stated in the entitlement.

category

See *data category*.

Chunk data lake object (CDLO)

A special type of DLO automatically created by the system when a search index is configured. Stores chunks of content. The system-generated data category of Content is automatically assigned to the Index DLO when it's created.

Chunk data model object (CDMO)

A special type of DMO automatically created by the system when a search index is configured. Inherits the Content data category from the Chunk DLO.

consent management

Process of capturing and managing consumer consent that ideally adheres to lawful requirements and addresses customer concerns about data accessibility, data usage, and data deletion.

constituent components

Data Cloud items built after the six foundational steps have been completed. Includes calculated, streaming, and real-time insights. Also includes segments, data graphs, search indexes, and vector databases. Constituent components lead to value creation, which can be used to achieve organizational goals.

Consumption Cards

A menu tab in the Data Cloud app for monitoring Data Cloud consumption.

consumption-based products

A type of product category that allows you to purchase in advance increments of usage, such as consumption credits, instead of purchasing access to the product for a set number of users. As resources of the consumption-based product are consumed, the number of available prepurchased credits decrease. Examples of resources include number of SMS messages, file storage space, and number of records processed.

contact point (field)

Field or set of fields representing data points used to contact or engage with an individual. Examples include email address and phone number. Contact points are included when creating a segment activation. Different contact points for an individual can be sent to different activation targets based on the type of contact point the target expects to receive.

Contact Point (objects)

Object storage for specific contact point groups. An example would be the Contact Point Email DMO which stores a party's email address. The party's email address is an example of a contact point field.

Content data category

The data category automatically assigned to the Chunk DLO and inherited by the Chunk DMO when a search index configuration is created in Data Cloud.

Copilot

A conversational AI assistant. One of the many ways Salesforce users can invoke prompts in the flow of their work. See also *Copilot Builder*.

Copilot Builder

An AI Builder tool that is part of the Einstein 1 platform. Accessible in Setup. Includes a library of actions classified as either standard or custom actions.

copy field enrichment

A type of enrichment that copies data from Data Cloud into the Salesforce core org. Can display calculated insights. Also possible to display field data for DMOs like Accounts, Assets, Individuals, Unified Accounts, or Unified Individuals. A data action target and corresponding data action are automatically created by the system for any copy field enrichment a user creates.

CRM enrichment

See *enrichment*.

custom starter bundle

A starter data bundle type that doesn't come with standard Salesforce connectors.

Customer 360

Also known as Salesforce Customer 360. Customer 360 isn't one specific product but rather the name for a collection of Salesforce tools that are used to provide a customer 360-degree view.

Customer 360 Data Model

Data model that defines Salesforce standard subject areas, objects, fields, metadata, and relationships. It's a canonical data model also used for Data Cloud which helps ensure interoperability with other Salesforce Clouds and platforms.

customer data platform (CDP)

Primarily a data store—a repository for persistently storing and managing collections of data that support marketing and customer experience use cases. A CDP gathers all available first-party customer data from an organization's CRM software, websites, automation platforms, email marketing software, and point of sale (POS) systems into a single repository. Second- and third-party data is ingested to augment first-party data. The CDP then aggregates all the information to build single, unified customer profiles.

data action

Events sent by Data Cloud to predefined targets whenever certain conditions are met. One of the key business value activities possible with Data Cloud.

data action targets

Recipients of data actions that can trigger their own business processes based on the information received from the data action. Data action targets include platform events, webhooks, and Salesforce Marketing Cloud. Salesforce Marketing Cloud requires an additional license.

Data Actions

A menu tab in the Data Cloud app where a data action can be configured.

Data Aware Specialist

A persona for a specific type of Salesforce user who will be granted access to Data Cloud. A corresponding permission set for this persona is included with the Data Cloud for Marketing license.

data bundle

See *starter data bundle*.

data category

A way to group, or categorize, data stored within different object containers. DLOs can have an ingestion data category or a system-generated data category. DMOs have an inherited data category. Data ingestion categories can be assigned to a DLO by the user when creating a new data stream. Those ingestion data categories include the following options: Profile, Engagement, and Other. Each object container can be assigned only one data category. All DLO objects must be assigned a category. DMOs inherit a data category as assigned by the system, based on the category of the first DLO that is mapped to that particular DMO. The data category for any DMO is Unassigned until it is assigned an inherited data category. In addition to ingestion data categories, there are system-generated categories that are assigned during certain processes like segmentation and search index configuration. Segment DLOs are assigned the Segment Membership data category by the system. Activation DLOs are assigned an Activation Audience data category by the system. During the search index configuration process, Chunk DLOs are assigned a Content data category and the Index DLOs are assigned a Vector Embedding data category by the system. The associated DMOs then inherit the data category from the relevant DLOs. Thus, an Index DMO would inherit a Vector Embedding data category from its associated Index DLO.

Data Cloud

Salesforce's near real-time CDP, which is at the heart of the Salesforce modern data tech stack. It is a transformative platform built from the ground up to empower users to unlock the value of their structured and unstructured data, especially when combined with the Salesforce Einstein capabilities. Data Cloud has a consumption-based pricing model. Outside of the context of this book, Data Cloud can also refer to the Snowflake Data Cloud platform. Snowflake was the first technology company to refer to their platform as a data cloud.

Data Cloud Admin

A persona for a specific type of Salesforce user who will be granted access to Data Cloud. A corresponding permission set for this persona is included with the Data Cloud license.

Data Cloud Integration User

A type of system user. A corresponding permission set for this persona is included with the Data Cloud license. This permission set cannot be assigned to a person who logs into Data Cloud.

Data Cloud User

A persona for a specific type of Salesforce user who will be granted access to Data Cloud. A corresponding permission set for this persona is included with the Data Cloud license.

data entity

An abstraction of a physical implementation of database tables. Within Data Cloud, there are two main types of data entities: data stream entities and data model entities. Data stream entities include data streams, DSOs, and DLOs. Data model entities include DLOs and DMOs. You'll notice that DLOs are classified as both a data stream entity and a data model entity.

Data Explorer

A menu tab option in the Data Cloud app to access a tool that allows users to drill down into various objects like DLOs, DMOs, calculated insight objects, and data graphs. Can be used to query and explore data at the record level. Initially, no objects are available to be selected when you first provision your Data Cloud org because no data is ingested yet. Objects will appear in the Data Explorer after you ingest and map data and after you've created calculated insights.

data graph

Pre-calculated or materialized views of Data Cloud data, built from DMOs, that make it possible to use Data Cloud data in near real time for many purposes, including to augment an LLM prompt. After you select the desired DMO data, the system creates a new data graph by transforming the normalized table data into new, materialized views of your data. Useful when near real-time processing of large amounts of data is needed, such as when using to augment a prompt when seeking responses from Einstein Copilot.

Data Graphs

A menu tab option in the Data Cloud app where a data graph can be created.

data in

See *data virtualization* and *zero copy*.

data kit

A portable and customizable bundle of independently packageable metadata in the form of templates that allows you to streamline the Data Cloud package creation and installation process. Data Cloud objects, such as metadata, relationships, and other components, can be wrapped together with a clicks, not code approach. Used so that you don't have to re-create data models between Data Cloud environments.

data lake

Centralized repository where all types of structured and unstructured data are stored. Typically includes raw copies of source system data. Frequently includes transformed data used for tasks like reporting, visualization, predictive analytics, and GenAI.

data lake object (DLO)

A data stream entity type and a data model entity type. Persistent (permanent) cloud storage object in Data Cloud where data is stored in Parquet format. Automatically created by the system when data is ingested in data source object (DSO), and

can also be manually created to support data transformations.

Data Lake Objects

A menu tab in the Data Cloud app where a DLO can be created. Can also view the complete list of DLOs that have been created.

data mapping

Used interchangeably with the term *harmonization*. Process of using a clicks, not code approach to map (associate) ingested data from DLOs to DMOs. Data mapping is an important process because only mapped fields and objects with established relationships can be used for components and activities like segmentation and activation.

data model

A way to define and visualize data relationships and constraints that reference how data is stored and accessed. Salesforce provides expert-created standard integrated data models for its various platforms. It's also possible to extend the Salesforce canonical data model with custom fields and custom objects (tables).

Data Model

A menu tab option in the Data Cloud app where users can create custom DMOs as well as display the existing DMOs.

data model category

See *data category*.

data model entities

A type of data entity that is built by mapping data from one or more data streams. Data model entities include DLOs and DMOs.

data model graph view

A type of view that is available after accessing the Data Model menu tab in the Data Cloud app. An alternative to the traditional list view.

data model object (DMO)

Logical (virtual) views of data created from the data mapping process and from special Data Cloud processes like transformation, identity resolution, and segmentation. All DMOs have both a type, which describes the DMO structure, and a category, which describes the data stored in the DMO. Similar to Salesforce core objects, DMOs used for data ingestion can be of two types: standard and custom. DMOs created from these standard and custom types used for data ingestion can be categorized as Profile, Engagement, or Other. DMOs created from processes are of special types, including Activation Audience, ADG (for graphs), Bridge (for link objects), Chunk, Derived (for unification objects), Index, Insights, Semantic, and Segment Membership. These special DMO types can be categorized as Profile and Other but also have special categories such as Activation Audience, Chunk, Content, Index, Segmentation Membership, and Vector Embeddings.

data out

See *data share* and *zero copy*.

data share

Used to achieve the data out bidirectional data sharing of the Bring Your Own Lake (BYOL) feature. See *zero copy*.

Data Share Targets

A menu tab option in the Data Cloud app where a data share target can be configured.

Data Shares

A menu tab option in the Data Cloud app where a data share can be created.

data source category

See *ingestion data category*.

data source object (DSO)

Transient (temporary) staging cloud storage object in Data Cloud. A data stream entity type. Original data source in the original file format, sometimes referred to as a dataset. Includes internal Salesforce system data from Sales Cloud, Service Cloud, Loyalty Cloud, Marketing Cloud, and more. Also includes data from external sources like Amazon S3. Once data is ingested in DSO, a data lake object (DLO) is automatically created by the system.

data space

Logical partitions to organize your Data Cloud data for profile unification, insights, and marketing. Used to segregate data, metadata, and processes within a single Data Cloud instance. Common data space use cases include organization for different brands, regions, and departments.

Data Spaces

A menu tab option in the Data Cloud app where a list of data spaces can be viewed. New data spaces are not created using this menu tab. Instead, you'll need to use the Setup option to configure new data spaces.

data stream entities

A type of data entity that makes it easy to connect to and ingest data from a source object. Data stream entity types include data streams, DSOs, and DLOs.

Data Streams

A menu tab in the Data Cloud app where users can set up an ingestion of data from Salesforce Clouds or external sources.

Data Transforms

A menu tab in the Data Cloud app where users can create a batch or streaming data transform to combine, shape, clean, and prepare data directly from within Data Cloud.

data virtualization

Data management process that creates a logical layer for data that can be accessed by data consumers without consumers needing to know the technical details of how the data is formatted or where it's physically stored. Federated data access is one example. See also *zero copy*.

dataset

See *data source object (DSO)*.

derived data model object

A special type of DMO for unified objects automatically created by the system during the identity resolution process.

Digital Wallet

A free Salesforce account management tool that provides near real-time usage data for Salesforce consumption-based products. Gives you the ability to manage your increments of consumption in multiple ways: pool consumption across contracts, monitor product usage, and detect consumption trends.

Einstein 1 Platform

See *Einstein 1 Studio*.

Einstein 1 Studio

A platform that includes three custom AI Builder tools to create and extend AI capabilities for Salesforce CRM: Model Builder, Prompt Builder, and Copilot Builder. AI Builders leverage low-code/ no-code AI democratization capabilities to bring AI experiences into the flow of work for Salesforce users by providing AI actions, prompts, and models, all grounded on an organization's own data.

Einstein Copilot

Salesforce's AI-powered conversational assistant integrated with the Salesforce CRM core platform.

Einstein Copilot Builder

See *Copilot Builder*.

Einstein Model Builder

See *Model Builder*.

Einstein Prompt Builder

See *Prompt Builder*.

Einstein Studio

A menu tab in the Data Cloud app where users can natively build predictive models or establish access to external predictive and generative models. The

Einstein Studio menu tab is how a user accesses Model Builder.

Einstein Trust Layer

Salesforce's secure AI architecture, built into the Salesforce platform to keep an organization's data safe while you explore GenAI solutions.

Engagement data category

One of the three ingestion data category options available for users to select when creating a new data stream. Used for time-series data points like customer transactions and web browsing histories. An immutable event date value is required when selecting the Engagement data category. The ingestion data category selected by the user for the DLO will be inherited by the DMO once the mapping process occurs. When mapping a DLO to an Engagement data category, it's required to map the primary key and Event datetime field. Not synonymous with Engagement primary subject area.

enrichment

Previously referred to as CRM enrichment. A type of key value activity that allows users to access selected Data Cloud data within their Salesforce CRM org in the normal flow of work. There are two types of enrichments: related list enrichments, which allow you to query related list data, and copy field enrichments, which allow you to copy a specific Data Cloud field into your Salesforce core org.

entitlement

The amount of usage credits, capacity, or other digital currency an organization purchases for Digital Wallet–enabled products.

external data lake object

Persistent (permanent) cloud storage object in Data Cloud to store metadata for the data federated from an external data source. Serves as a reference that points to data physically stored in an external data source.

federated data access

Used to achieve the data in bidirectional data sharing of Bring Your Own Lake (BYOL).

first-party data

Data your organization has collected from your audience either through direct interactions or provided directly by an individual. Sometimes there is a distinction made between zero-party data (provided by the person) and first-party data (observed behavior and interactions). Examples include an individual's product purchase history, which pages on your website the person visited, and a customer providing their birth date or details of the social media followers who entered a contest with your company. First-party data is the most reliable data source, as compared to second- and third-party data sources.

flow

An automated workflow with the structure of a flowchart built in Salesforce Flow Builder. Supports the automation of a business process. Has the ability to affect things in an external system as well as within a Salesforce org. Narrower in scope than the *Salesforce Flow* term.

Flow Builder

Point-and-click process automation tool that provides a declarative user interface for building individual workflows for Salesforce apps. See *flow*.

foreign key

Column or group of columns that establish a link between data in two tables in a relational database. One example is the Salesforce Contact ID used by Salesforce Sales Cloud or Service Cloud as a primary key and as a foreign key in Salesforce Marketing Cloud.

fully qualified key (FQK)

The combination of the key qualifier and source key is known as the fully qualified key. Its purpose is to help accurately interpret data ingested from different sources. Specifically, it's used to identify data sources for harmonized records which is especially important for differentiating between profile-related data and engagement-related data, and for aggregating results from specific data sources.

graph view

See *data model graph view*.

harmonization

See *data mapping*.

identity resolution

Sometimes referred to as unification. An identity management process whereby the data attributes about people from many different sources are matched and reconciled into a comprehensive view called unified profiles which makes it possible to build a single source of truth for a complete 360-degree view of the customer. An important part of identity resolution is stitching together unified profiles by associating pseudonymous, unknown identifiers with known data. The identity resolution process is the last Data Cloud foundational step needed to create a unified profile. Unified profiles, and thus identity resolution, are required for segmentation and related list enrichments. Identity resolution uses rulesets made up of matching and reconciliation rules defined by the user.

Identity Resolutions

A menu tab in the Data Cloud app where users can create new identity resolution rulesets with matching rules and reconciliation rules.

increments of consumption

Also known as increments of usage. A bucket of credits to use throughout a period of time or a set of capacity of data storage your org must stay within.

increments of usage

See *increments of consumption*.

Index data lake object

A special type of DLO automatically created by the system when a search index is configured. Stores generated vector embeddings. The system-generated data category of Vector Embedding is automatically assigned to the Index DLO when it's created.

Index data model object

A special type of DMO automatically created by the system when a search index is configured. Inherits the Vector Embedding data category from the Index DLO.

ingestion data category

One of the available data categories that can be assigned to a DLO at the time it's created from a data stream. Currently, those available categories are Profile, Engagement, and Other. When a new DLO is manually created, a data category will be selected by the user.

inherited data category

The data category assigned to a DMO by the system. A DMO initially has an inherited data category of Unassigned. When a DLO is mapped to a DMO, the mapped DMO inherits the data category from the DLO. For example, an Index DMO would inherit a Vector Embedding data category from its associated Index DLO.

Insight Builder

A Builder tool used to create calculated and streaming insights using drag-and-drop functionality. Easily leveraged by users with limited SQL knowledge.

insights

In Data Cloud, insights specifically refers to the insights created within the Calculated Insights menu tab using the Insight Builder tool or SQL code. The three insights created within the Calculated Insights menu tab include calculated, streaming, and real-time insights.

insights data model object

A special type of DMO for insight objects automatically created by the system during the insight creation process.

key qualifier

Value automatically populated by the system in a field to distinguish data received from different sources. A key qualifier is especially important for DLOs that contain primary or foreign key values shared by multiple data sources (i.e., Contact ID from CRM and Marketing Cloud), because the key qualifier makes it easier to differentiate when all source data is joined in the DMO. Only one key qualifier field is generated per object no matter how many relationships the object has with other objects. The combination of the key qualifier and source key is known as the fully qualified key.

known data

Data that includes personally identifiable information that can be associated with a specific person or account. Examples include postal addresses, mobile phone numbers, and email addresses. Data Cloud profiles can be either known data or anonymous data.

Lightning App Builder

A point-and-click tool for configuring Lightning apps and creating custom pages for the Salesforce mobile app and Lightning Experience.

Marketing Admin

A persona for a specific type of Salesforce user who will be granted access to Data Cloud. A corresponding permission set for this persona is included with the Data Cloud for Marketing license.

Marketing Data Aware Specialist

See *Data Aware Specialist*.

Marketing Manager

A persona for a specific type of Salesforce user who will be granted access to Data Cloud. A corresponding permission set for this persona is included with the Data Cloud for Marketing license.

Marketing Specialist

A persona for a specific type of Salesforce user who will be granted access to Data Cloud. A corresponding permission set for this persona is included with the Data Cloud for Marketing license.

match rules (for identity resolution rulesets)

Set of default or custom rules created to link multiple records into a unified individual within identity resolution rulesets.

matching rules

Term used interchangeably with match rules.

Model Builder

An AI Builder tool that is part of the Einstein 1 platform. Accessible in Data Cloud through the Einstein Studio menu tab. Gives you the option to build your own machine learning model from scratch. Alternatively, you can take advantage of connected models already built by data science teams using Amazon SageMaker, Databricks, or Google Vertex AI. Leveraging these connected models is often referred to as the Data Cloud Bring Your Own Model (BYOM) capabilities. Also includes ways to access external generative models as part of the BYOLLM process.

Other data category

One of the three ingestion data category types available for users to select when creating a new data stream. The Other data category is a miscellaneous data category and includes engagement data without an immutable event date field value.

Party

Can refer to a subject area in Salesforce or a field in Data Cloud. See *Party field* and *Party subject area*.

Party field

An attribute in many different DMOs, including the Party Identification DMO. A field used to connect various DMOs back to the Individual DMO, thus it's a foreign key to an individual. Examples include the Marketing Cloud contact key and the CRM contact ID.

Party Identification object

A standard Data Cloud DMO that includes information for the ways to identify a person, such as a driver's license or a birth certificate. This object is required if a Contact Point object is not used.

Party subject area

Includes several different standard DMOs like Individual, Unified Individual, Account, Account Contact, and Lead. It's the only required subject area in Data Cloud. More specifically, the Individual standard DMO within the Party subject area is required along with either the Party Identification object or one of the Contact Point DMOs.

primary key

Uniquely identifies a record in a relational database table. Cannot include NULL values. An example is Salesforce Contact ID.

Profile data category

One of the three ingestion data category options available for users to select when creating a new data stream. It is the only one of the three data category types that can be segmented upon. Profile data category DMOs are indexed by ID only.

Profile Explorer

A menu tab in the Data Cloud app where a user can access the Unified Individual and Unified Account profile. Users can search for individuals by first name, last name, email address, phone number, or individual ID.

Prompt Builder

An AI Builder tool that is part of the Einstein 1 platform. Accessible in Setup. Also accessible directly within Data Cloud by clicking on the Einstein Studio tab, selecting the Generative tab option, and then clicking on the drop-down arrow to the right of the LLM model for which you want to build a prompt.

Query Editor

A menu tab in the Data Cloud app where a user can create a query workspace. Previously, a legacy Query Editor app was available through the AppExchange. The current Query Editor is now natively available within Data Cloud.

query workspace

Accessed through the Query Editor tab in the Data Cloud app. Used to write and execute SQL queries built on DLOs, DMOs, CI objects, and data graphs.

real-time insights

One of the three types of insights that can be built in the Data Cloud app. Leverages data graphs to achieve real-time processing needed to provide the insights in real time.

reconciliation rules (for identity resolution)

Part of the identity resolution rulesets created by the user to let the system know how to reconcile the matched records during the identity resolution process, when attribute conflict exists.

related list enrichment

A type of enrichment that surfaces data from Data Cloud as a related list in the Salesforce core org. It's required that you complete identity resolution to use related list enrichments. It's possible to create a related list for a DMO with an associated Engagement category. That Engagement DMO will, however, need to have a single many-to-one relationship to the Individual DMO or the Unified Individual DMO. It's also possible to create a related list for a Unified Contact Point DMO.

rulesets (for identity resolution)

Used in the identity resolution process to create unified profiles. Made up of matching and reconciliation rules defined by the user.

Salesforce Flow

A blanket term for everything in Salesforce making it possible to create, manage, and run automation with clicks, not code.

Includes separate products like Flow Orchestration and Flow Integration powered by MuleSoft. Wider in scope than the term *flow*.

Search Index

A menu tab in the Data Cloud app where a user creates an index confirmation for objects with text blob fields. Create a search index using one of three options: Easy Setup, Advanced Setup, or From a Data Kit.

search index configuration

During the search index configuration process, Data Cloud creates chunks and vectors, which results in an index used for querying and semantic retrieval. The process results in Chunk and Index DLOs and DMOs being created.

second-party data

Data that is shared between co-partners. Generally not as reliable as first-party data but more reliable than third-party data.

segment

A grouping of customers, either individuals or accounts that share a set of characteristics. One segment can be published as an audience to multiple activation targets. Thus, a person in one segment can be included in multiple audiences if they have a contact point that can be selected for that activation target.

Segment Membership data category

The data category automatically assigned to a Segment Membership DLO and inherited by a Segment Membership DMO when a new segment is published in Data Cloud.

Segment Membership DLO

A type of DLO automatically created by the system when a segment is published. There are two types of Segment Membership DLOs: Latest Segment Membership DMO and Historical Segment Membership DMO. The system-generated data category of Segment Membership is automatically assigned to the Segment Membership DLO when it's created.

Segment Membership DMO

A type of DMO automatically created by the system when a segment is published. There are two types of Segment Membership DMOs: Latest Segment Membership DMO and Historical Segment Membership DMO. Inherits the Segment Membership data category from the Segment Membership DLO.

Segment On

Defines the target object used to build your segment during the segmentation process.

segmentation

The process of organizing customers, either individuals or accounts, into a segment. See *segment*.

Segments

A menu tab in Data Cloud for creating and publishing segments.

semantic search

Unlike a keyword search, semantic search returns results based on the intent and contextual meaning behind a search. To achieve the best semantic search results, a user needs to unlock the power of unstructured data. Using Data Cloud, unstructured data can be turned into numeric representations of words and their meanings, which are stored in a vector database.

semistructured data

A type of data that is more fluid than structured data but does have some properties like tags or metadata to make it easier to organize. Examples include comma-separated values (CSV), extensible markup language (XML), and JavaScript Object Notation (JSON) format types. See also *structured data* and *unstructured data*.

single source of truth (SSOT)

Not a specific platform, tool, or system but rather an existence, or state of being, of an organization's data that is aggregated to a primary single source of truth location. The SSOT view of the data can include data at a physical and logical level. Data virtualization makes it possible for a SSOT view of the data to exist even when data is physically stored in different systems and platforms.

source key

A primary or foreign key that unique identifies a record. One example is the Salesforce Contact ID used by both Salesforce Sales and Service Clouds and Salesforce Marketing Cloud. A source key is combined with the key qualifier in Data Cloud to form the fully qualified key, which is used to identify the data source in DMO harmonized data.

standard data bundle

A starter data bundle type that comes standard with the Salesforce connectors.

starter data bundle

When enabled, a starter data bundle imports system-defined, standard datasets from related Salesforce Clouds such as Sales Cloud, Service Cloud, Loyalty Cloud, B2C Commerce Cloud, Marketing Cloud, Marketing Cloud Account Engagement, and Marketing Cloud Personalization. The collection of data streams in a starter data bundle are automatically created and mapped to data model objects because the schemas or blueprints are already known in advance and leverage the standard model in Data Cloud. Most starter data bundles are of the standard type, but custom data bundles also exist.

streaming data transform

A type of transformation generally used for cleaning or standardizing ingested data in near real time before mapping to a DMO. A streaming data transform reads one record in a source DLO and reshapes the record data based on the instructions you provide in the data transform. The instructions will need to be provided using SQL code as there is no low-code/

no-code Data Cloud tool available for creating a streaming data transform.

streaming insight

One of the three types of insights that can be built in the Data Cloud app. Often used as an input to a data action.

subject area

Grouping of similar DMOs that help to standardize the data modeling process and provide better understanding of the existing data models. DMO primary subject areas include Party, Privacy, Case, Loyalty, Engagement, and more.

system-generated data category

The group of data category types assigned to a DLO by the system during certain processes like segmentation and search index configuration. Includes Segment Membership, Activation Audience, Content, and Vector Embedding data categories.

third-party data

Data that originates from external sources other than data shared between trusted partners. Generally not as reliable as first-party or second-party data.

Unassigned data category

The initial data category for DMOs. The data category changes from Unassigned once a DLO is mapped to the DMO, at which time the DMO inherits the category from the DLO.

unification

See *identity resolution*.

Unified Individual DMO

A special type of unification object automatically created by the system during the identity resolution process. It is of the Derived type of DMO and in the inherited category of Other.

unified profile

A comprehensive view of a customer achieved from matching and reconciliation data brought in from disparate data sources. Created as part of the last step in the identity resolution process. Unified profiles are required for segmentation and related list enrichments and are also important for creating other constituent components like insights and data actions. Within Data Cloud, unified profiles of customers can be created for Unified Individuals or Unified Accounts.

unstructured data

A type of data that doesn't have an associated data structure or model. Examples include PDFs, text files, social media content, sensor data, photographs, and audio files. The majority of data by volume is unstructured data. See also *structured data* and *semistructured data*.

unstructured data lake object (UDLO)

A special type of DLO. Cloud storage container for unstructured data details. Created manually. Automatically mapped to a new or existing UDMO.

unstructured data model object (UDMO)

A special type of DMO. A logical grouping of unstructured data details.

vector database

In general, a vector database is a collection of data stored as mathematical representations. Salesforce vector database is the storage location where structured and unstructured data is chunked and indexed to provide more robust ways to power automation, analytics, search, and AI.

Vector Embedding data category

The data category automatically assigned to the Index DLO and inherited by the Index DMO when a search index configuration is created in Data Cloud.

Visual Builder

See *Insight Builder*.

visualization insights

Insights resulting from translating complex or large amounts of data into a visualization representation that is easier for users to process. Examples include charts, graphs, maps, and dashboards.

webhook

An API endpoint triggered by a Data Cloud event that can be used to allow web applications to communicate with each other. A webhook is event driven rather than request driven. Once invoked, the webhook transports an HTTP payload to a destination system. One of three supported targets available as a data action target.

zero copy

A Salesforce term that refers to a way users can access data from an external platform within their normal flow of work. For example, data from Snowflake can be joined with data in Data Cloud for a user working in Salesforce, and vice versa. Data Cloud data can be joined with Snowflake data for a user working in Snowflake. Zero copy is possible for ingested Data Cloud data. For Salesforce CRM and Marketing Cloud data to be available for zero copy, the data must first be ingested in Data Cloud. Zero copy is technically achieved in two different ways. One way is to use federated access for data virtualization, referred to as data in from a Salesforce perspective. The other way is to use the Snowflake secure data sharing approach, referred to as data out from a Salesforce perspective. See also *Bring Your Own Lake (BYOL)* and *Bring Your Own Model (BYOM)*.

Zero Copy Partner Network

An affiliation of technology partners that have an agreement to provide a trusted network to share data between data platforms in a zero copy manner. See *zero copy technology partners*.

zero copy technology partners

In addition to Salesforce, there are five partners involved in the Zero Copy Partner Network: Amazon, Databricks, Google, Microsoft, and Snowflake. IBM is expected to be added soon as another technology partner in the Zero Copy Partner Network.

zero ETL

See *zero copy*.

Index

Interaction Studio, 2
ISV (independent software vendor) packaging, 40-41
IT team, 74-75
ITP (Intelligent Tracking Prevention), 13

J

JavaScript Object Notation (JSON), 28
job status, rulesets, 248-249
joins
    cautions, 219
    CIs (calculated insights), 269
JSON (JavaScript Object Notation), 28

K

key qualifier, 396
key value activities, 59, 337
    Data Cloud enrichments, 61
keyword searches, 357
Kihn, Martin, 1
knowledge articles, 357
known customer data, 9-10
known data, 396

L

lake library, 44
Lead object, 164
licensing, 6, 124
    licensed-based platforms, 23
life sciences industry, 82
Lightning App Builder, 396
Lightning Web Components (LWC), 33
LLMs (large language models), 338
    custom, 70
    data graphs and, 62
    Einstein Trust Layer, 339
    searches
        data graphs and, 355-356
        near real-time, 355-356
    structured data and, 62
    unstructured data, 357-360
    vector databases and, 62, 357-360
logos, 357
lookalike segments, 307, 318
low-code no-code platforms, 52
low-code/no-code offerings, 2

Loyalty Management Cloud, ingesting data and, 33
LWCs (Lightning Web Components), 33

M

manufacturing industry, 82
mapping, 179
    (see also data mapping)
Marketing Admin, 396
Marketing Cloud
    connection, 32-36, 106-108
    as data action target, 293
    relationships, 35
Marketing Cloud Account Engagement Connector, 110
Marketing Cloud API user accounts, 108
Marketing Cloud Enterprise ID (EID), 35, 106
Marketing Cloud Intelligence (MCI), 43
Marketing Cloud Personalization
    activation targets and, 305
    dataset, connecting, 32-36
Marketing Cloud Personalization connection, 110
marketing journeys, 66
Marketing Manager, 396
Marketing Specialist, 397
marketing technology stack, 7
Martech stack, 7-8
master data management (MDM), 71
match rules, 249
    configuring, 251
    default, 251-252
    Exact match, 250
    Fuzzy match, 250
    identity resolution rulesets, 397
    Normalized match, 250
    Party Identification object, 252-254
    reconciliation rulesets, 250
MCI (Marketing Cloud Intelligence), 43
MDM (master data management), 71
    golden records, 243-244
menu options
    Activation Targets, 124-125, 299, 307
    Activations, 125-126, 299
    Calculated Insights, 126-127, 262, 264
    Consumption Cards, 127, 372
    Dashboards, 128

Snowflake, 6
    BYOL (Bring Your Own Lake), 367
    data pipelines between Salesforce and, 368
    Zero Copy Partner Network and, 363
SOQL, 33
    Data Explorer and, 152
source data
    attitudinal, 187
    behavioral, 187
    data categories, multiple, 190
    engagement, 187
    personal, 186
    related customer data, 187
    value categories, 54
source key, 399
SQL (Structured Query Language)
    Spark SQL, CIs (calculated insights) and,
        272
    streaming insights, 273
SSOT (single source of truth), 24, 399
    real-time, 27
standalone orgs, 34
standard data bundle, 399
starter data bundles, 49, 399
    data mapping and, 224
    ingestion, 153
    Loyalty Management Cloud, 162
stock-keeping unit (see SKU)
storage
    Azure Blob Storage, 173
    core capabilities, 122
storage layering, 43-44
streaming, 153
streaming data
    ingests, 24
    transforms, 24
streaming data transforms, 208, 400
    functions, 213
        logic functions, 213
        operator functions, 214
    lag, 212
    multiple, 209
    setup, 209-213
    status list, 220
    use cases, 208
streaming insights, 264, 400
    Engagement data, 265

Insight Builder, 273-274
    time-sensitive actions, 279
    uses, 279-280
streaming transforms versus batch transforms,
    214
structured data, 28
    LLMs (large language models) and, 62
Subject area, 400
system generated data category, 400
system of reference, 150, 244

T

Tableau, 2, 67
    external sharing and, 384
tables
    events, 25
    interchangeable, 25
Technical Capability Map, 26-27
Template Gallery, 26
templates, Prompt Builder, 349
    creating, 350-352
    Field Generation, 350
    Flex, 350
    invoking, 352
    Record Summary, 349
    Sales Email, 349
terminology, 55-56
text data type, 182
third-party data, 400
Thunderhead, 2
time travel, 25
topologies
    Commerce Cloud, 35
    evaluating, 36
Trailhead module, 102
transactional data, 25
transforms, 24
    (see also data transforms)
    batch data, use cases, 215
travel, transportation, and hospitality industry,
    79-81
Turtle Bay Resort, 81

U

UDLOs (unstructured DLOs), 48, 400
    creating, 147
UDMO (unstructured DMO), 48, 357, 400

pattern, 45, 153
Zero Copy Partner Network, 49, 54, 340,
  360-371, 383, 401
  accelerate time to value with, 361
  Amazon, 362
  BYOL (Bring Your Own Lake), 363-369
    Amazon Redshift, 363
    bidirectional data sharing, 364, 367, 369
    data shares (data out), 366-367
    external platforms, 362-363, 367
    federated access (data in), 364-365
    Google BigQuery, 363
    Snowflake, 363, 368
  BYOM (Bring Your Own Model), 369-371
    Amazon Sagemaker, 369
    Databricks, 369
    Google Vertex AI, 369
  data sharing, tradition methods, 361-362
  Databricks, 363

Google, 363
Microsoft, 363
Snowflake, 363
value activity of external platform data sharing available from, 340
value activity of Predictive AI ML insights
  available from, 340
zero copy technology partners, 54, 135,
  362-363, 401
  AWS (Amazon Web Services), 362
  data share target of, 135
  Databricks, 363
  Google, 363
  Microsoft, 363
  Snowflake, 363
zero-party data, 185
Zettabyte Era, 23
zettabytes, 23

About the Author

Joyce Kay Avila has more than 25 years of experience as a business and technology leader. She has bachelor's and master's degrees in the fields of computer science and accounting business administration, and she completed her PhD coursework in accounting information systems.

Joyce holds 19 Salesforce certifications and accreditations and is Tableau certified. She is a Salesforce All Star Ranger and a Salesforce Einstein Champion alumna, and she is also certified in Snowflake and is a Snowflake Data Superhero.

For the Salesforce and Snowflake communities, Joyce produces a running series of how-to videos on her YouTube channel. She is also the author of *Snowflake: The Definitive Guide* (O'Reilly, 2022).

Colophon

The animal on the cover of *Hands-On Salesforce Data Cloud* is the white-rumped babbler (*Turdoides leucopygia*), native to the Horn of Africa and parts of South Sudan.

Its name is accurately suggestive of certain characteristics. The white-rumped babbler has a white rump that sets it apart from many other birds (its other coloration varies widely). And its cry is a harsh babbling, typically heard in groups. The white-rumped babbler is a social bird, most often seen in groups of up to ten.

Many of the animals on O'Reilly covers are endangered; all of them are important to the world.

The cover illustration is by Karen Montgomery, based on an antique line engraving from *Lydekker's Royal Natural History*. The series design is by Edie Freedman, Ellie Volckhausen, and Karen Montgomery. The cover fonts are Gilroy Semibold and Guardian Sans. The text font is Adobe Minion Pro; the heading font is Adobe Myriad Condensed; and the code font is Dalton Maag's Ubuntu Mono.

Printed in the USA
CPSIA information can be obtained
at www.ICGtesting.com
JSHW061810090924
69564JS00022B/421